Contact

Customer Services

English Heritage
PO Box 569
Swindon SN2 2YP
England

T: 0870 333 1181

E: customers@english-heritage.org.uk
www.english-heritage.org.uk

Photo: Tony Bartholomew

The Abbey Inn at Byland

Holiday cottage at Rievaulx Abbey

Images: All pictures in this handbook are courtesy of the English Heritage Photo Library unless otherwise stated. Cover image: The monks' common room at Battle Abbey by Peter Richardson.

Transport Information: Barry Doe.

Paper: All paper used in this handbook is made from wood fibre from sustainable forests, and comes from paper mills which hold ISO14001 (environmental management system) accreditations.

Please remember to recycle this handbook when you no longer need it.

recycle

Welcome

SIMON THURLEY Chief Executive of English Heritage

Over the past year we have again been investing to ensure that we provide more interesting and entertaining days out for you.

New investment includes £2.5 million for Kenilworth Castle, to renovate and re-present Leicester's Gatehouse, install a new exhibition and open it to the public for the first time in many years. And if you visit this year you will also see the archaeological work that we are undertaking in order to inform the recreation of the castle's original Elizabethan gardens. A grant from the Wolfson Foundation, together with donations from the public, has supported both the exhibition and garden projects.

We are spending £2.3 million at Battle Abbey to build a new visitor centre including interactive and audio visual displays that dramatically bring to life one of the most significant events in this country's history.

2006 also sees the launch of our new collection of holiday cottages (see page 19), and we have even opened our first pub, at Byland in Yorkshire.

In London, English Heritage has joined forces with the London Borough of Hounslow to create the Chiswick House and Gardens Trust to oversee a major programme of restoration and re-presentation of this elegant Palladian-style villa and the stunning parkland that surrounds it.

This investment, year after year, is a vital part of ensuring that the landmarks of our past are understood, valued, cared for and enjoyed today and in the future. It would not be possible without your support.

On average, a quarter of our funds – that's more than £35 million – come from income we generate through fundraising, membership and other activities.

There are a number of ways you can help. By visiting our properties you are helping to protect them, and as one of our 600,000 members you're making a more significant contribution to our work.

But, if you wish, you can also make an additional donation, perhaps arrange to leave a legacy.

We have been given the same benefits from tax relief as charities, so by Gift Aiding your donation, for every pound that you give, we get an extra 28 pence from the Inland Revenue. For more information on how to help turn to page 12.

However you choose to get involved, I would like to thank you. I hope this handbook helps you to enjoy what you have helped to protect.

SIMON THURLEY

How to use this handbook

Navigate your way around the handbook as easily as possible

This handbook gives details of all English Heritage properties and other properties to which English Heritage members receive discounted entry. Property entries are colour-coded by region (see map opposite for breakdown), and are listed alphabetically within these regions.

Website listings are on all site pages, should you prefer to look electronically for property details. We recommend that you check the website before you visit for the latest events information and last-minute property updates.

A full listing of the properties is provided in the front section of each region, with a regional map showing the counties and key towns/cities.

More detailed maps can be found on pages 264-276.

Essential information such as opening times, admission prices for non-members, contact details and travel directions are included for each property. Where possible, we have included postcodes to assist with digital route-planning.

Symbols show the facilities which are available, from catering and toilet facilities to whether a property is available for corporate or private hire or licensed for civil wedding ceremonies. The key is on the inside front cover.

Details of OS map references are provided for easy location of each property, with specific map numbers and co-ordinates (OS LandRanger maps).

Contents

PAGE 2 Guide to Symbols
3 Welcome
4 Handbook Guide
6 Your Membership
7 Admission Charges
8 About Us
9 English Heritage at Work
12 Supporting Us
14 National Monuments Record
15 Hiring Venues
16 Books and Gifts
17 Events
18 Planning your Visit
20 London
38 South East
80 South West
118 East of England
142 East Midlands
160 West Midlands
182 Yorkshire
206 North West
222 Hadrian's Wall
232 North East
250 Scotland, the Isle of Man and Wales
254 Church Partnerships
264 Maps
278 Index

Audley End House and Gardens

Your Membership

Making a difference

Every penny from your membership makes a difference to our work in conserving England's historic environment. We appreciate your support, and urge you to continue helping us to preserve England's heritage for future generations. In return, we hope you'll gain a great deal of enjoyment from your membership.

The benefits of membership

English Heritage has over 400 historic properties in its care, and as a member you are entitled to visit them all for free as many times as you may wish. But the benefits of membership don't end there; you are also entitled to free or reduced-price entry at more than 100 other historic attractions and a wealth of events, and you will receive our award-winning quarterly magazine, *Heritage Today*.

Children go free

English Heritage believes in encouraging an enjoyment of history early, and this is reflected in our children go free policy. This allows free entry for up to six accompanying children (under 19) per member, within the family group. Children should be carefully supervised, as historic sites can be hazardous.

For non-members, discounted family tickets are available.

Enjoy Britain's heritage

Whether you're on holiday or in your local area, you can use your membership card to visit more than 100 historic properties in Scotland, Wales and the Isle of Man. During your first year of English Heritage membership, you pay just half-price entry to properties in the care of Cadw (Welsh Historic Monuments), Historic Scotland and Manx National Heritage. Each year after that entry is completely free. For listings of these properties, see pages 250-253.

More places in England

Your membership card will also give you free or discounted entry to many other sites in England. Please see the Other Historic Attractions section in each region.

Please note: discounts will not apply on days when events are held at these properties.

Contact us

If you have comments or views to share, contact Customer Services on **0870 333 1181**. Please note that national call charges apply. Alternatively, write to us at:

English Heritage
Customer Services
PO Box 569
Swindon SN2 2YP

Or email **customers@english-heritage.org.uk**

i

English Heritage membership makes a lovely gift.

Call 0870 333 1182 or visit **www.english-heritage.org.uk/gift** for more details.

Kenilworth Castle

Admission Charges

Members
Entry to English Heritage sites is free to all members on presentation of a valid membership card. You will also be entitled to free or reduced entry at a range of events and other historic attractions (listed at the back of each regional section).

Children
All children under five gain free entry to our properties. Members can also take up to six children (under 19), within the family group, into our properties for free. Unaccompanied children aged 16 or over can gain free entry on production of their parents' membership card. There may be a charge for children at the non-English Heritage properties listed in this guide.

Events
Please note you may be charged a supplement fee when events are being held at a property (check in *Heritage Today* or on our website for details of events). Opening times may also vary when a public or private event is held, so please check with the property before you travel.

Non-Members
There are three levels of charges for non-members shown in the handbook.

For example:

Adult	£2.50
Concession	£1.90
Children (under 16)	£1.30

The concessions apply to senior citizens, jobseekers and students with relevant ID. Prices may vary from the example shown above.

Families
Family tickets are available at some of our larger properties, and in most cases family tickets are valid for two adults and three children. This may vary at sites not managed by English Heritage; please call in advance to confirm their policy.

Groups
Discounts of 15% (10% at Stonehenge) are available for groups of eleven or more visitors paying together.

Call Customer Services on 0870 333 1181 for a copy of our *Group Visits Guide*.

We recommend that groups of visitors book in advance when planning to visit a property.

Overseas Visitor Pass
An Overseas Visitor Pass (OVP) allows unlimited free access to over 100 English Heritage properties for one or two weeks.

With your OVP you enjoy free entry to all English Heritage properties listed in this handbook marked with the OVP symbol, plus free or reduced entry to hundreds of exciting events.

There may be a charge for some events taking place at our properties (check the events leaflet available at our sites). The OVP does not entitle you to free admission at sites not managed by English Heritage and not marked with the OVP symbol. For more information please call 0870 333 1181 or visit **www.english-heritage.org.uk/ovp**

About Us

Introduction to English Heritage

Who are we?

English Heritage was established in 1983 as the Historic Buildings and Monuments Commission for England. We are the Government's leading adviser on the historic environment and are sponsored by the Department for Culture Media & Sport (DCMS).

As well as working closely with the DCMS, we operate with other Government departments, including the Office of the Deputy Prime Minister (ODPM) and the Departments for the Environment, Food & Rural Affairs (DEFRA) and Trade & Industry (DTI).

What do we do?

The history of England is preserved in the many ancient buildings and sites throughout the country – our job is to protect and promote this historic environment. From the earliest traces of human settlement to the most significant buildings of our own time, we want every important historic site to get the care and attention it deserves. By employing the best architects, archaeologists and historians, we aim to help people understand and appreciate why their historic environment matters.

Who are the people?

Sir Neil Cossons is Chairman and Simon Thurley is Chief Executive. A team of 16 commissioners, who change every four years and come from a wide variety of backgrounds, help them.

If you want to find out more about what happens at our Commission meetings, you can look up the minutes at **www.english-heritage. org.uk/minutes**

How are we funded?

English Heritage is funded partly by the Government, and partly by revenue earned from our historic properties. Over a quarter of our income comes from membership, donations, fund-raising and the Lottery. Every penny counts, and there are many ways in which you can support us. Choose to pay your membership by direct debit as this keeps administration costs low. Sign up to Gift Aid, which enables us to recoup 28 pence from every pound given. Purchase a gift of membership as a wonderful present, or introduce a friend to English Heritage, by taking them along to a site or enjoying one of our many events together.

Why is our work important?

We believe that future generations should have the chance to enjoy England's historic environment. This can only happen if we begin to preserve and protect our historic sites now. As well as undertaking the work ourselves, we are able to provide assistance to others.

We are also an organisation that campaigns to improve and preserve the historic environment. Our recent policy document 'The Future of Historic Schools' sets out an approach to understanding the value of these important historic buildings when considering change, in order to safeguard their most important aspects. Download a copy of the document at **www.english-heritage.org.uk/upload/pdf/HELMSchools.pdf** for more information.

We hope that the information we provide at our sites, as well as through our Learning programmes, will encourage people to value the importance of England's historic environment.

Through our role in the planning system, we are able to ensure that any changes made to England's architectural heritage serve to enhance and protect it.

How are we different from The National Trust?

English Heritage is partly funded by the government and has a wider remit than The National Trust, including national and local government responsibilities. Our role is to preserve the extraordinary legacy of buildings, ancient sites and monuments which without attention would otherwise be overlooked and fall into disrepair.

i We welcome approaches for filming and commercial photography at our sites, which often appear in films, television programmes and photo shoots. All queries and requests should be made to Sarah Eastel Locations on 01225 858100 or email info@film-locations.co.uk www.film-locations.co.uk

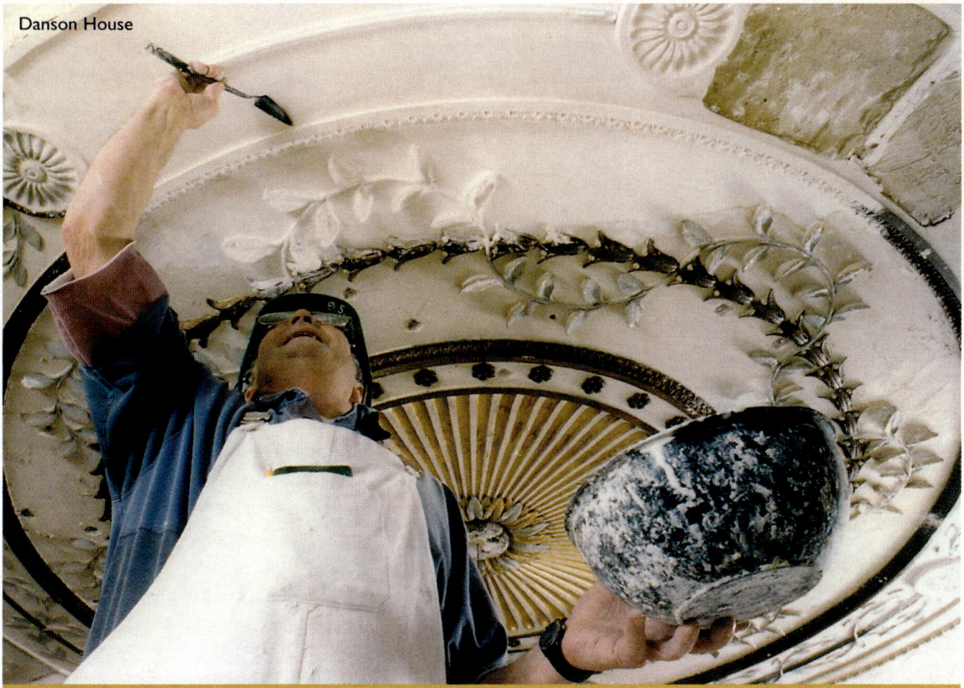

Danson House

English Heritage at Work

A guide to the different types of work we do

Archaeology

As the national archaeology service for England, we set standards, promote innovation and provide detailed archaeological knowledge of the historic environment.

In 2002, we took on responsibility for the historic wrecks and submerged landscapes in, on or under the seabed within 12 miles of the English coast. Our policy paper on the management of maritime archaeology, *Taking to the Water*, is available on our website.

More information on our archaeological work can be found at **www.english-heritage.org.uk/archaeology**

Blue Plaques

What do Sir Christopher Wren and John Lennon have in common? They both have Blue Plaques erected in their honour.

The Royal Society of Arts began the Blue Plaques Scheme in London in the 19th century, and it passed to London County Council in 1901. English Heritage has been running the scheme since 1986, and we are now extending it across the country on a region-by-region basis. To qualify for a Blue Plaque, a person must have been dead for 20 years or have passed the centenary of their birth.

If you would like to know how to nominate someone for a Blue Plaque, go to **www.english-heritage.org.uk/blueplaques**

Conservation

In addition to listing buildings, we also designate monuments and landscapes for protection. For example, monuments such as ruins, earthworks or burial sites may be scheduled as a monument and subject to special control.

We also work with Local Authorities on designating Conservation Areas. These are usually areas characterised by architectural and historic features that are worth preserving or enhancing.

England is fortunate to be home to a number of World Heritage Sites, including Stonehenge and Hadrian's Wall. We work with UNESCO to devise management plans for these unique places.

Battlefields are also important sources of archaeological and historic interest. There are over 40 such landscapes on the *English Heritage Register of Historic Battlefields*. We keep a similar register for parks and gardens, which includes the country's most important green spaces from country house gardens to hospital grounds.

Find out more about our conservation work at **www.english-heritage.org.uk/conservation**

Learning

We encourage people of all ages and abilities to understand, value and enjoy the historic environment. We recently launched our new cutting-edge strategy for learning, bringing together our education, outreach and events programmes.

Education

Each year we welcome over 500,000 pupils and school teachers to our sites completely free of charge. Our expert advice and inspiring resources, courses and events support teachers at all levels, and link to history, citizenship and other curriculum subjects. We recently launched a programme of workshops, tours and other activities for schools at our properties, led by specialist educators.

Outreach

Our team of Outreach Officers is leading a range of exciting, creative projects with hard-to-reach audiences across the country, including young people, ethnic communities and people with disabilities. We are committed to engaging new audiences in learning from, enjoying and valuing the historic environment, through projects ranging from oral history projects to community archaeology digs, youth theatre projects and creating community heritage gardens. The team also works with the Civic Trust to broaden participation in Heritage Open Days.

For more details contact the Learning Department on 020 7973 3385 or visit our website **www.english-heritage.org.uk/learning**

Grants

We give grants to individuals, Local Authorities and voluntary organisations to undertake urgent repairs and to conserve and enhance the historic environment. We also advise the Heritage Lottery Fund on the allocation of Lottery money to worthwhile schemes which do not fit our own grant criteria.

Find out more at **www.english-heritage.org.uk/grants**

Listed Buildings

We recommend buildings of special architectural or historic interest to the Secretary of State for Culture, Media and Sport for listing. Listing means that any changes made to either the internal or external structure of a building are subject to stricter planning regulations.

Most listed buildings date from before 1840, but we also recommend some buildings from after this date. Modern buildings need to be of significant importance, and normally over 30 years old before they are likely to be listed.

There are three categories of listing: Grade I, Grade II* and Grade II. Grade I and Grade II* buildings are of outstanding architectural or historic interest, and of particularly great importance to the nation's built heritage.

More information on current listed buildings and how to suggest a building for listing can be found at **www.english-heritage.org.uk/heritageprotection**

View details and images of England's listed buildings at **www.imagesofengland.org.uk**

Policies

One of our key responsibilities is to develop robust policies to enable national and local decision makers to protect and promote the historic environment.

We gather the evidence to support these policies. Published annually as *Heritage Counts*, it can be viewed at **www.heritagecounts.org.uk**

We play an important role in international conservation, advising the Government on the designation and management of World Heritage Sites in the UK, and campaigning in Brussels and Strasbourg on behalf of the historic environment.

Statutory Advice

We advise Local Planning Authorities on listed building planning applications. Buildings need to change to thrive in the modern world, and we work proactively with these Local Authorities to ensure that this change recognises the historic potential of the building.

We publish an annual *Buildings at Risk Register*, with information on listed buildings and scheduled monuments which are 'at risk' from neglect and decay. We also award grants to Local Authorities, to undertake urgent repairs to these buildings where necessary.

Properties

We currently look after over 400 historic sites, which are open to the public. Our properties include historic country houses, palaces, ruined abbeys, prehistoric settlements, burial sites, castles, statues and Roman remains. Full details are listed in this Handbook.

At many of these sites we provide visitor centres, exhibitions and educational resources. England has an extraordinary array of important historic monuments, and our property list includes Stonehenge, Hadrian's Wall, Dover Castle, Apsley House and Rievaulx Abbey.

Publishing

We publish a wide range of commercial books on a variety of subjects – including general history, gardening, cookery, architecture, photography and children's books. To order a New Titles catalogue call Customer Services on 0870 333 1181 or view all our books at **www.english-heritage .org.uk/books**

Research

Our research and training programmes increase understanding of the historic environment, helping us guide its management in an informed and sustainable way. We concentrate our fieldwork and analysis on poorly understood building types, as well as on specific sites and areas.

For more information email **buildingshistory@english-heritage.org.uk**

Training: Craft & Skills

Traditional skills are at risk of dying out in the UK, and there are currently only 86,000 craftspeople with the necessary specialist skills to maintain our historic buidlings. English Heritage is developing training for these essential skills, including thatching and stonemasonry.

This means there will always be a continuing reservoir of skilled craftspeople to help maintain England's half million listed historic buildings and *Buildings at Risk*.

For more information on any issues relating to English Heritage, please visit our website **www.english-heritage.org.uk** or call Customer Services on **0870 333 1181**.

Supporting English Heritage

How you can help

We depend increasingly on donations from individuals and voluntary support from the private sector and the Heritage Lottery Fund. We are very grateful to all our members and supporters; last year you raised £38.5m to help us conserve and restore some of this country's most culturally important and iconic sites. Thank you.

Donations from members and visitors have helped us to make significant improvements to many of our properties over recent years. One such property is Bolsover Castle in Derbyshire. The series of historic paintings 'The Twelve Caesars' had been previously held in store at Audley End House, Essex. Funding raised through donations has enabled English Heritage to install the paintings in the second floor rooms at Bolsover Castle, and to use them to tell the story of the castle's later history.

If you would like to make a donation, you can do so when you renew your membership, or at any of our sites. You can also now donate online at **www.english-heritage.org.uk/supportus**

There are many ways you can help; from making a donation to pledging a legacy for the future. Visit the Membership and Support Us pages on our website at **www.english-heritage.org.uk/supportus**, telephone our Development Department on 020 7973 3798 or email us at **development@english-heritage.org.uk** to discuss how your gift can support our priority projects.

Titus – one of the Twelve Caesars at Bolsover Castle

Projects supported by the Development Fund
The following is a list of projects currently being supported by donations and legacies:

Great Yarmouth Heritage Youth Club
New youth and community project for young people and local families

Carisbrooke Castle
Development of Edwardian style privy garden with seating, events area and interpretation panels

Osborne House
Woodland restoration with the Forestry Commission

Pendennis Castle
New furniture and ICT equipment for the education suite

Brodsworth Hall
Illuminating gardens for the winter months

Tilbury Fort
Renovation of the West Powder Magazine to create a multipurpose community space

Housesteads Roman Fort
Museum refurbishment including the display of more original artefacts and hands-on exhibits

Kenilworth Castle
Conservation and re-opening of the Gatehouse, including a permanent exhibition on Elizabeth I, matching a grant from the Wolfson Foundation

Learning Programmes
A new range of learning materials for every school in England

Photo: Peter Richardson

Osborne House

National Monuments Record

English Heritage archive

The National Monuments Record, English Heritage's extensive archive based in Swindon, is open to the public. It includes an amazing collection of over eight million photographs of historic buildings, streetscapes, gardens and archaeological sites from the ground and from the air.

The pictures cover the whole of England and date from the 1840s to the present day.

The archive also holds a database of more than a quarter of a million archaeological monuments and excavations in England, as well as thousands of plans, drawings and reports.

This is a public resource, and English Heritage is delighted to welcome visitors to consult these records and our reference library, by visiting our search room in Swindon. Please pre-book your visit to ensure material is available.

Our Outreach team holds workshops and tours to help you make the most of our material. Please call 01793 414797 for details.

Access

If you can't make it to Swindon, there are many other ways you can access our resources:

www.english-heritage.org.uk/viewfinder – view historic images from our collections.

www.imagesofengland.org.uk – view images and descriptions of England's listed buildings.

www.english-heritage.org.uk/pastscape – view information on England's archaeology and historic buildings.

To find out more or to place a remote enquiry please call 01793 414600 or visit our website at **www.english-heritage.org.uk/nmr**

Crystal Palace

OPENING TIMES

Public search room:
Tue-Fri 9.30am-5pm
(tel 01793 414600 for details)

HOW TO FIND US

Direction: Kemble Drive, Swindon, SN2 2GZ

Train: Swindon ¼ mile

MAP Page 265 (2J)
OS Map 173 (ref SU 145850)

Audley End House and Gardens

Hiring a property

Create a memorable occasion for your historic day

What could be a more stunning setting for a wedding, birthday celebration, anniversary dinner or corporate event than an historic English Heritage property?

Celebrations can now be arranged at selected English Heritage properties. Experienced staff are on hand to help fine-tune arrangements and ensure your event will provide special memories for years to come.

Properties available for hire are marked with a 🍸 throughout the Handbook. Those also licensed for civil wedding ceremonies are marked with a 🔔.

Queen Mother's Garden – Walmer Castle

For more information on exclusive hire, please contact the Hospitality Manager on the telephone number below or visit the website: **www.english-heritage.org.uk/hospitality**

Properties available for hire 🍸

Venues licensed for civil wedding ceremonies 🔔

Region	Property	Telephone	Available for hire	Licensed for civil weddings
East of England	Audley End House and Gardens, Essex	Tel: 01799 529403	🍸	🔔
East Midlands	Bolsover Castle Derbyshire	Tel: 01246 856456	🍸	🔔
London	Chiswick House	Tel: 020 7973 3292	🍸	🔔
London	Eltham Palace	Tel: 020 8294 2577	🍸	🔔
London	Jewel Tower	Tel: 020 7973 3292	🍸	
London	Marble Hill House	Tel: 020 7973 3416	🍸	🔔
London	Rangers House	Tel: 020 8894 2577	🍸	
London	Wellington Arch	Tel: 020 7973 3292	🍸	
South East	Bishop's Waltham Palace, Hampshire	Tel: 01424 775705	🍸	🔔
South East	Deal Castle, Kent	Tel: 01304 209889	🍸	🔔
South East	Dover Castle Kent	Tel: 01304 209889	🍸	🔔
South East	Osborne House & Gardens, Isle of Wight	Tel: 01983 203055	🍸	
South East	Walmer Castle and Gardens, Kent	Tel: 01304 209889	🍸	🔔
South West	Old Wardour Castle, Wiltshire	Tel: 01305 820539	🍸	🔔
South West	Pendennis Castle Cornwall	Tel: 01326 310106	🍸	🔔
South West	Portland Castle Dorset	Tel: 01305 820539	🍸	🔔
South West	St Mawes Castle Cornwall	Tel: 01326 310106	🍸	🔔

Books and Gifts

Inspired by the properties in our care

Books

The new *Heritage Unlocked* series aims to encourage visitors to explore some of our lesser-known free sites. Each book covers one area of England and includes features on the area's history and culture, as well as entries on each site. The seven books in the series are: Cornwall and the Isles of Scilly; Devon, Dorset and Somerset; Bristol, Gloucestershire and Wiltshire; The South East; The East of England; Yorkshire and the North East; The North West.

To order these and any other English Heritage books and guidebooks please call 01761 452966 or visit our online bookshop at **www.english-heritage.org.uk/books**

Gifts

We have shops at many of our properties, selling a wide selection of gifts, books, toys and souvenirs. Below is just a selection of some of the ranges available. To view other items in our collection, visit our website at **www.english-heritage.org.uk/shopping**. To order any of these gifts, please call 01761 452966 or order online.

Stonehenge

The great and ancient stone circle of Stonehenge is one of the wonders of the world. Stonehenge's orientation in relation to the rising sun has always been one of its most remarkable features.

Jewellery

Our exclusive jewellery collection of pendants, earrings and charms take its inspiration from the stones, the landscape and astronomical significance of Stonehenge.

Left: Alignment Pendant (17mm diameter) Code 10376 £9.99

Stationery

Exclusively designed print portfolios, journals, notecards and memo blocks have been created using stunning photography and 18th-century engravings.

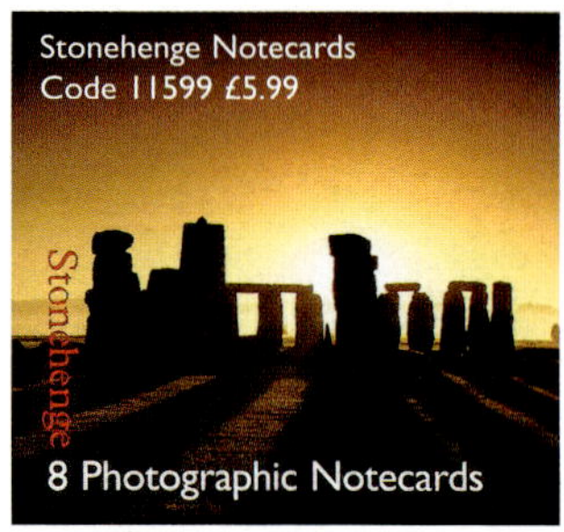

Stonehenge Notecards Code 11599 £5.99

Blue Plaques

The famous English Heritage Blue Plaques Scheme has come to life through these contemporary mugs. Choose from 17 characters, ranging from Mozart to Hendrix. Made in England from bone china, each stylish mug is gift boxed and retails at £10. Visit our website to see the full range.

Members' Offers

English Heritage also works with a number of partners to bring new and exciting offers to our members and customers.

For every booking or purchase made, each partner gives a donation to English Heritage to help us in our work of protecting the historic environment.

Visit our website and look out for offers in our quarterly magazine, *Heritage Today*.

English Heritage Events

Bringing history to life

The Knights' Tournament

From music, drama, outdoor cinema and historic tours, to battle spectaculars and tournaments, English Heritage brings you top quality entertainment in magnificent historic settings.

The highlight of the English Heritage events programme is the ***Festival of History*** on 12-13 August 2006 at Kelmarsh Hall, Northamptonshire.

Celebrating over 2,000 years of history from the Romans to the Swinging Sixties, the Festival offers something for all the family to enjoy. Marvel at spectacular WWI aerial displays and dramatic battle re-enactments. Wander through the colourful living history encampments, barter in the traditional street market and enjoy music, dance and an unrivalled celebrity lecture programme.

Now in its second year, ***The Knights' Tournament*** brings back the days of chivalry, romance and royal sporting entertainment.

Follow your team's progress over the summer, as they are put through their paces in jousting, archery, sword-fighting and mounted skill-at-arms (see p.277 for details).

For fans of historical action, a series of battles are played out at sites across the country, including the most famous of all – the ***Battle of Hastings*** on 14-15 Oct 2006.

For those who want to get their hands on history, an ***English Heritage Experience Day*** provides the ideal opportunity to explore an authentic pastime or learn a new skill. History-lovers who enjoy walking will also enjoy our superb series of guided ***Battlefield Hikes*** to the sites of some of England's most significant battles. For those who prefer a more leisurely encounter with the past, our fully-guided ***Tours Through Time*** are ideal. These exclusive tours include expert commentary, luxury coach travel, and on overnight trips, bed and breakfast with dinner included. Tours Through Time is run in conjunction with Brookland Travel (phone: 0845 212 2863).

All English Heritage events are suitable for families. Events specially designed for children, including fun days, craft workshops and trails, are held during the school holidays at many English Heritage properties.

i

For details of our events, tours and members' activities, check the latest issue of Heritage Today, visit our website **www.english-heritage.org.uk/events** or call Customer Services on **0870 333 1183**.

Planning Your Visit

Essential tips before you visit

Access

We are committed to ensuring that our properties are enjoyed by and are accessible to all. In this handbook we have used the ♿ symbol to indicate that at least some areas of a property are accessible by wheelchair.

For a more thorough guide to accessibility and the special facilities at many of our properties, please refer to our *Access Guide*, which is available free of charge and offers an honest assessment of those landscapes and buildings which have the most to offer visitors with disabilities. For example, sites with alternative routes for wheelchair users, or with features such as scented gardens, tactile objects/displays and specially created audio tours. Information on parking and drop-off points is also included in the guide, as well as an indication of some of the obstacles you may encounter around each site, such as steep steps to a castle keep or grounds that may become waterlogged in wet weather.

Some of these features and facilities will also be of interest to families and carers with young children, or to those who like to include both children and grandparents in their days out.

If you have any questions about a particular site, we encourage you to call in advance. Companions of visitors with disabilities are admitted free to all English Heritage properties.

Information on our sites can also be obtained by fax. For individual site fax numbers, please telephone or email Customer Services.

The *Access Guide* is available in large type, braille, on tape and on disc by region, or on our website. Visit **www.english-heritage.org.uk/accessguide** to download your free copy. Alternatively, please call 0870 333 1181 or minicom 01793 414878, or email **customers@english-heritage.org.uk**

Kenilworth Castle

Catering

Refreshments are available at restaurants and tearooms at some sites, and these are often attractively located within the historic buildings themselves. Visitors are also welcome to picnic in the grounds of many sites. Please check individual listings for details of catering and picnic facilities.

Displays, Exhibitions and Visitor Centres

At many sites, there are display panels explaining how the property appeared in the past, often with the help of reconstruction drawings or interactive displays. Other sites play host to temporary exhibitions of paintings and sculptures.

Dogs

Dogs on leads are welcome wherever possible. Please see listings for individual restrictions. Guide and hearing dogs are welcome everywhere.

Educational Group Visits

Visiting historic sites is an important way of inspiring school children and adult learners about history.
We actively encourage these visits by providing free entry to our sites for pre-booked educational groups. We also provide a range of resources to enable teachers and students to get the most out of their visit.

English Heritage follows the Department for Education and Skills' Guidelines on Health and Safety on Educational Visits. We require you to have at least one adult to every six children in a group containing pupils of school years one to three. The ratio could go up to one to fifteen for years seven and above. For further information or a copy of the new learning pack call 020 7973 3385 or visit **www.english-heritage.org.uk/learning**

Families and Children

We welcome families with children of all ages. Many of our sites include special features, exhibitions or educational facilities suitable for children.

Some properties offer baby-changing facilities. For safety reasons, babies cannot be carried in back carriers at certain properties. Health and Safety guidelines recommend that up to six children can be accompanied by one adult, with a lower ratio for pre-school children. However, you are responsible for the children's supervision and safety at all times, and we would advise that judgement is used with regard to a sensible adult to child ratio, especially at more hazardous sites marked with a ⚠ symbol in this guide.

Family Learning

Look out for the exciting range of resources we are developing at many of our sites. Already featuring at over 50 sites, the resources range from free children's activity sheets and back packs to book boxes, and 'very big books' for younger children – as well as interactive Discovery Centres. Properties which have these resources available are marked with a [icon] throughout this Handbook.

Guides and Tours

Audio guides are available at more than 50 of our sites. In exceptional circumstances, for instance when an event is taking place in key areas of the property, audio guides may not be available. To check for special events see the *Events* section of *Heritage Today* magazine or visit **www.english-heritage.org.uk/events** or call Customer Services. Guidebooks are also on sale at staffed properties or through our postal service – call 0870 429 6658.

Holiday Cottages

Why not spend a special break at one of our new Holiday Cottages, located at our historic properties? For a brochure and reservations, call 0870 333 1187, or visit our website **www.english-heritage.org.uk/holidaycottages**

Photography

Non-commercial photography is welcome in all our grounds. For conservation reasons, it is not permitted inside some properties.

Public Transport and Cycling

All public transport information is correct at time of going to press. We are grateful to Barry Doe for providing this information. If you have any comments or suggestions, please call 01202 528707. Details of all bus travel in England is available from Traveline on 0870 608 2608 or online at **www.traveline.org.uk**

Call Sustrans on 0117 929 0888 or visit **www.sustrans.org.uk** for cycle route information.

Safety

Due to their historic nature, some of our sites have features which could be hazardous – such as steep slopes, sheer drops, slippery or uneven surfaces, steep/uneven steps and deep/fast-flowing water. Please pay attention to all safety notices on site.

We have inserted a ⚠ symbol against these sites in this handbook, but if you are in any doubt about the layout or features, please call the property before you visit. We want you to enjoy our properties, so please take care when you visit and remember to wear suitable footwear.

Our staff are always willing to advise on safety issues. Please prevent fires and do not climb on monuments at any of our sites.

We encourage children to have fun, but please ensure they are supervised at all times.

Smoking

Smoking is not permitted inside any English Heritage property.

Toilets

Toilets are available on or near many English Heritage sites. Please check individual listings.

Find out the latest information by visiting our website **www.english-heritage.org.uk/visits** or call Customer Services on **0870 333 1181**.

Statue of the goddess Psyche, Eltham Palace – see page 28

London

*'Earth has not anything to show more fair:
Dull would he be of soul who could pass by
A sight so touching in its majesty'*

From 'Composed upon Westminster Bridge, September 3, 1802' by William Wordsworth

www.english-heritage.org.uk/london

Properties

See individual listings for details

Camden
Kenwood House

Greenwich
Eltham Palace,
Wernher Collection at
Ranger's House

Hounslow
Chiswick House

Kingston-Upon-Thames
Coombe Conduit

Richmond
Marble Hill House

Southwark
Winchester Palace

Tower Hamlets
London Wall

Westminster
Apsley House, Chapter House and Pyx Chamber, Jewel Tower, Wellington Arch

Comprehensive
map of our sites
Page 266-267

For bus and public transport information, call Transport for London on **020 7222 1234**.

Wellington Arch – see page 35

The Flower of Cities, For All

Some of the most famous poems in praise of London were written by 'outsiders': William Wordsworth was a Cumbrian more often associated with the Lake District. They are a reminder that London, the capital of England and indeed the largest and most important town in Britain since Roman times, has long been regarded as a city for all.

Everybody who was anybody therefore wanted at least a foothold in this centre of government, finance and fashion: many of these great London 'town houses' are now truly open to all – and free of charge to English Heritage members. Much the oldest is **Winchester Palace**, whose rose window recalls the lost glories of medieval magnates' London dwellings. Then comes a splendid array of great Georgian mansions fringing the capital: Robert Adam interiors at **Kenwood**, home of the Earls of Mansfield and surrounded by Humphry Repton's parkland; **Chiswick House** with its Classical gardens, decorated by William Kent as a combination of home, club and picture-gallery for the ultra-fashionable Earl of Burlington; **Marble Hill House**, the Arcadian retreat in Richmond where Henrietta Howard presided over her coterie of wits and connoisseurs; and **Ranger's House** in Greenwich Park, now home of the glorious Wernher Collection.

All these mansions, indeed, house wonderful displays of art and sculpture as well as architecture. So too does 'Number 1 London', last of the true 'town houses' – **Apsley House**, home of the first Duke of Wellington and still the residence of his successors. Opposite stands **Wellington Arch**, originally designed as an outer portal of Buckingham Palace, recalling that part of London's attraction is its status as the seat of monarchy.

Here too, then, English Heritage members can visit the **Chapter House and Pyx Chamber** of the great royal abbey of Westminster, and nearby the **Jewel Tower**, almost the last surviving remnant of the medieval royal palace which became the Houses of Parliament. **Eltham Palace** also began as a medieval royal residence, though now better known for its metamorphosis into a fabulous Art Deco mansion of the 1930s.

Apsley House Hyde Park – W1J 7NT

Apsley House, home of the first Duke of Wellington and his descendants, stands right in the heart of London at Hyde Park Corner. For over 200 years, this great metropolitan mansion has been known colloquially as 'Number 1 London', because it was the first house encountered after passing the tollgates at the top of Knightsbridge.

The Waterloo Gallery

Apsley House was originally designed and built by Robert Adam between 1771 and 1778 for Baron Apsley – from whom it takes its name. It passed to the Wellesley family in 1807, being first owned by Richard and then his younger brother Arthur Wellesley – the Duke of Wellington.

Wellington is most famous for defeating Napoleon at the Battle of Waterloo in 1815, but this was only the culmination of a brilliant military career. He was also a major politician, rising from representing a small Irish constituency in 1790 to Prime Minister in 1828.

The current appearance of Apsley House is the result of alterations made by the Wellesley family, who twice extended the brick Adam house and encased it in stone. The Corinthian portico and two bays of the west wing were added in 1828. Perhaps more importantly, many rooms were redesigned to reflect the Duke of Wellington's rising status, and remain important survivals of Regency interiors. They provided the perfect backdrop for entertaining, particularly at the annual Waterloo Banquets which commemorated the great victory.

Inside Apsley House you will see many aspects of the first duke's life and work, outstandingly his amazing art collection. Paintings

Napoleon Bonaparte by Robert LeFeure

by many famous artists are hung throughout the first floor, many of them part of the Spanish Royal Collection which came into Wellington's possession after the Battle of Vitoria in 1813. A colossal nude statue of Napoleon by Canova dominates the stairwell at the centre of the house.

Throughout his military career, the duke was presented with a vast collection of silver plate and unique porcelain as trophies from grateful nations. Many of these can be seen in the Museum Room. Wellington's victories are celebrated in the fine British craftsmanship of the magnificent Wellington Shield, designed by Thomas Stothard, and the impressive candelabra presented by the Merchants and Bankers of the City of London.

When the seventh Duke of Wellington gave the house to the nation in 1947, the family retained the private rooms, which they still use today. This makes Apsley House not only the last surviving great London town house open to the public, but also the only property managed by English Heritage in which the original owner's family still live.

A comfortable seating area has now been created in the Inner Hall, where visitors can browse through leather-bound albums of images of Wellington, his descendants, and Apsley House. The new 'Wellington Boot' activity pack, for children aged 5-11, is filled with activity sheets and puzzles.

Wellington enthusiasts may also be interested in visiting the spectacular Wellington Arch opposite Apsley House (see p.35), and elegant Walmer Castle (see p.72), the duke's residence when he was Lord Warden of the Cinque Ports.

www.english-heritage.org.uk/apsleyhouse

NON-MEMBERS

APSLEY HOUSE	
Adult	£5.10
Concession	£3.80
Child	£2.60
JOINT TICKET WITH WELLINGTON ARCH	
Adult	£6.50
Concession	£4.90
Child	£3.30
Family ticket	£16.30

OPENING TIMES

1 Apr-31 Oct, Tue-Sun & Bank Hols	10am-5pm
1 Nov-31 Mar, Tue-Sun	10am-4pm
Closed	24-26 Dec and 1 Jan

HOW TO FIND US

Direction: 149 Piccadilly, Hyde Park Corner

Train: Victoria ½ mile

Bus: From surrounding areas.

Tube: Hyde Park Corner, adjacent

Tel: 020 7499 5676

OVP

New guidebook.

MAP Page 266 (4E)
OS Map 176 (ref TQ 284799)

Chapter House and Pyx Chamber

Westminster Abbey

Built by the royal masons in 1250, the Chapter House of Westminster Abbey was originally used in the 13th century by Benedictine monks for their daily meetings. It later became a meeting place of the King's Great Council and the Commons, predecessors of today's Parliament.

A beautiful octagonal building with a vaulted ceiling and delicate central column, it offers rarely seen examples of medieval sculpture, an original floor of glazed tiles and spectacular wall paintings. A door within the vestibule dating from c. 1050 is thought to be the oldest in England. The 11th-century Pyx Chamber also has a medieval tiled floor, and was used as a monastic and royal treasury. It contains a 13th-century stone altar that survived the Reformation.

Chapter House free to EH members. Under the care and management of the Dean and Chapter of Westminster.

OPENING TIMES

Throughout the year;
Mon-Sun 10am-4pm
Closed Good Fri, 24-26 Dec & 1 Jan
May be closed at short notice on state and religious occasions

HOW TO FIND US

Direction: Through the cloister from Dean's Yard if you only want to visit the Chapter House. Turn into Dean's Yard off Broad Sanctuary. Turn left along the square and go through the entrance-way into the cloister

Train: Victoria and Charing Cross both ¾ mile, Waterloo 1 mile

Bus: From surrounding areas

Tube: Westminster and St James's Park stations both ¼ mile

Tel: 020 7654 4834

MAP Page 267 (4F)
OS Map 177 (ref TQ 299795)

Chiswick House

See feature opposite

Coombe Conduit

Kingston-Upon-Thames

Coombe Conduit is made up of two small Tudor buildings connected by an underground passage. Water was once supplied to Hampton Court Palace via this tunnel.

Managed by the Kingston Society.

OPENING TIMES

Apr-Sep, every 2nd Sun 2pm-4pm

HOW TO FIND US

Direction: Coombe Lane on the corner of Lord Chancellor's Walk

Train: Norbiton ¾ mile

Bus: 57 Kingston – Streatham

Tel: 020 8942 1296

MAP Page 266 (4E)
OS Map 176 (ref TQ 204698)

Eltham Palace

See feature – Page 28

i

You can find out more about the work of English Heritage at **www.english-heritage.org.uk/aboutus**

Chiswick House

Chiswick – W4 2RP

Chiswick House is one of the most glorious examples of 18th-century British architecture. The third Earl of Burlington (1694-1753), who designed this elegant Classical villa, drew inspiration from his 'grand tours' of Italy.

A promoter of the Palladian style originally pioneered in Britain by Inigo Jones, Burlington sought to create the kind of villa and garden found in the suburbs of ancient Rome. To do so, he employed William Kent to create sumptuous interiors to contrast with the pure exterior.

The intimate Bedchamber Closet has also now been redecorated, with paintings and prints providing an insight into the Burlington family. A double portrait of Lord and Lady Burlington, by William Aikman, hangs alongside charming paintings of their two young daughters. Further exciting loans of Old Master paintings have been newly displayed to enhance the pictures in the Red and Green Velvet rooms, emphasising the artistic diversity which characterised Burlington's combination of home, private gallery and club.

The Classical gardens are a perfect complement to the house. There is level access to most of the grounds (except for Terrace Walk, owing to a gradient). Wander among the statues in the Italianate gardens, and look out for the buildings hidden in the trees.

The Chiswick House & Gardens Trust (reg. charity 1109239) has been set up to lead a major restoration project. This will include new opportunities for education and improved facilities throughout the site.

www.english-heritage.org.uk/chiswickhouse

NEW FOR 2006 **Eight Old Master paintings, including a newly discovered work by Rubens, are on display in the Red Velvet Room.**

Available for corporate and private hire.

Licensed for civil wedding ceremonies.

NON-MEMBERS

Adult	£4.00
Concession	£3.00
Child	£2.00
Family ticket	£10.00

OPENING TIMES

1 Apr-31 Oct, Wed-Sun & Bank Hols. 10am-5pm

Closes at 2pm on Sat

1 Nov-31 Mar Pre-booked appointments only.

HOW TO FIND US

Direction: Burlington Lane, W4

Train: Chiswick ½ mile

Bus: TfL 190 Hammersmith – Richmond; E3 Greenford – Chiswick

Tube: Turnham Green ¾ mile

Tel: 020 8995 0508

OVP

Disabled access (ground floor; wheelchair stair-climber to first floor, please call to confirm use prior to visit).

Dogs on leads (restricted areas only).

Parking (off westbound A4).

MAP Page 266 (4E)
OS Map 176 (ref TQ 210775)

Eltham Palace Greenwich – SE9 5QE

When textile magnates Stephen and Virginia Courtauld built their 1930s Art Deco mansion by the Great Hall of medieval Eltham Palace, they created a masterpiece of 20th-century design.

Dining room leading to the entrance hall

Completed in 1936, the exterior of the house was built in sympathy with the older building, using a red brick design inspired by Hampton Court Palace. But the interior was and remains a showpiece of glamorous 1930s design. Visitors can revel in the eclectic mix of French-influenced Art Deco, ultra-smart ocean-liner style and cutting-edge Swedish design.

The dining room is a tour-de-force, with pink leather-upholstered chairs, bird's-eye maple veneered walls and a silver ceiling. It is entered through black-and-silver doors portraying animals and birds, drawn from life at London Zoo.

Even more exotic is Virginia Courtauld's vaulted bathroom, lined with onyx and gold mosaic, complete with gold-plated bath taps and a statue of the goddess Psyche. Luxury also emanates from the centrally heated sleeping quarters of the Courtaulds' pet ring-tailed lemur, Mah-Jongg.

A house with all the latest modern conveniences, the Courtaulds' home came with underfloor heating, a centralised vacuum cleaner and a built-in audio system.

The Spotlight display brings together discoveries from the Courtauld era, including original furniture and family photographs.

Entrance hall

Virginia Courtauld's bathroom

As you leave the opulent 1930s house and enter the medieval palace, the interior presents a striking contrast. The Great Hall was built for Edward IV in the 1470s, and Henry VIII spent much of his childhood here.

The 19 acres of beautiful gardens surrounding the palace include both 20th century and medieval elements. These include a rock garden sloping down to the moat, a medieval bridge, herbaceous borders inspired by modern designer Isabelle Van Groeningen, a sunken rose garden and plenty of picnic areas. The garden is special at any time of year, but visitors will delight in the spring bulbs display and the wisteria cascading over the classical pergola in summer.

The Gathering Storm and Stephen Fry's *Bright Young Things*.

www.english-heritage.org.uk/elthampalace

Available for corporate and private hire.

Licensed for civil wedding ceremonies.

The stone bridge

NON-MEMBERS HOUSE AND GARDEN

Adult	£7.60
Concession	£5.70
Child	£3.80
Family ticket	£19.00

NON-MEMBERS GARDEN ONLY

Adult	£4.80
Concession	£3.60
Child	£2.40

OPENING TIMES

1 Apr-31 Oct, Sun-Wed 10am-5pm

1 Nov-20 Dec, Sun-Wed 10am-4pm

21 Dec-3 Feb Closed

4 Feb-31 Mar, Sun-Wed 10am-4pm

HOW TO FIND US

Direction: Off Court Rd SE9, Junction 3 on the M25, then A20 to Eltham

Train: Eltham and Mottingham, both ½ mile

Bus: From surrounding areas

Tel: 020 8294 2548

OVP

Disabled access (and parking via Court Yard entrance).

Parking (signed off Court Rd).

Pushchairs and large rucksacks need to be left at reception.

MAP Page 267 (4F)
OS Map 177 (ref TQ 424740)

Kenwood Hampstead – NW3 7JR

Set in leafy grounds beside Hampstead Heath, this outstanding house was remodelled by Robert Adam between 1764 and 1779. He transformed the original brick building into a majestic villa for the great judge, Lord Mansfield. The richly decorated library is one of Adam's great masterpieces, a feast for the eyes.

The dining room

Brewing magnate Edward Cecil Guinness, first Earl of Iveagh, bought Kenwood House and gardens in 1925. When he died in 1927, he bequeathed the estate and part of his collection of pictures to the nation. The Iveagh Bequest includes important paintings by many great artists, including Rembrandt, Vermeer, Turner, Reynolds and Gainsborough. Now they have been joined by Constable's *Hampstead Heath with Pond and Bathers*, appropriately displayed close to the place where it was originally painted. The paintings beautifully complement Kenwood's sumptuous interiors.

OPENING TIMES

1 Apr-31 Oct, daily	11am-5pm
1 Nov-31 Mar, daily	11am-4pm
Closed	24-26 Dec and 1 Jan

The Park stays open later, please see site notices. House and grounds free; donations welcome. Pre-booked group tours available.

HOW TO FIND US

Direction: Hampstead Lane, NW3

Train: Hampstead Heath 1½ miles

Bus: Tfl 210 Finsbury Park – Golders Green

Tube: Archway and Golders Green, then 210 bus

Tel: 020 8348 1286

Disabled access (ground floor only; toilets).

Dogs on leads (restricted areas only).

Garden shop and house shop.

Parking (charge. Disabled bays. Mobility service available on request).

Restaurant (The Brew House Café open all year; serves home-made food throughout the day).

Please note: Kenwood hosts regular events, garden tours and acclaimed summer concerts.

MAP Page 266 (3E)
OS Map 176 (ref TQ 271874)

The first floor displays a very different array of paintings. The Suffolk Collection includes magnificent portraits of Elizabethan and Stuart men and women by William Larkin, Van Dyck and Lely, given by the Hon. Mrs Greville Howard in 1974.

The parkland surrounding Kenwood was particularly influenced by the great English landscape gardener, Humphry Repton. Set high on a hill, the views of London from these tranquil grounds are stunning. Visitors can also enjoy the lakeside walks and meandering woodland paths, which provide a superb backdrop for the famous summer concerts.

Most of the grounds are accessible by gravel path and grass, but wheelchair users will need strong pushers to manage the slopes. The Brew House Café is a great place to stop for lunch or a cup of tea.

Antechamber

Notting Hill, *Mansfield Park* and *101 Dalmatians*.

www.english-heritage.org.uk/kenwoodhouse

NEW FOR 2006 **A variety of guided tours for a small charge: please call the house for details.**

Jewel Tower

Westminster – SW1P 3JX

The Jewel Tower, or 'King's Privy Wardrobe', was built c.1365 to house Edward III's treasures. One of only two buildings of the original Palace of Westminster to survive the fire of 1834, the tower features a 14th-century ribbed vault. It displays 'Parliament Past and Present', a fascinating exhibition about the history of Parliament.

The second floor now includes new illustrated panels, telling the story of this small but important building.

The remains of a moat and medieval quay are still visible outside.

Available for corporate and private hire.

NON-MEMBERS	
Adult	£2.70
Concession	£2.00
Child	£1.40

OPENING TIMES

1 Apr-31 Oct, daily	10am-5pm
1 Nov-31 Mar, daily	10am-4pm

May close for hospitality functions. Please call to check before travelling.

Closed 24-26 Dec & Jan 1

HOW TO FIND US

Direction: Located on Abingdon Street, opposite the southern end of the Houses of Parliament (Victoria Tower)

Train: Charing Cross ¾ mile, Victoria and Waterloo, both 1 mile

Bus: From surrounding areas

Tube: Westminster ¼ mile

Tel: 020 7222 2219

OVP

MAP Page 267 (4F)
OS Map 177 (ref TQ 301793)

Check *Heritage Today* for news and information on forthcoming events and exclusive members' offers.

Kenwood House

See feature – Page 30

London Wall

Tower Hill

This is the best-preserved remnant of the Roman wall which once formed part of the eastern defences of Roman Londinium. Built c. AD 200, the wall defined the shape and size of London for over a millennium.

OPENING TIMES

Free access

HOW TO FIND US

Direction: Located outside Tower Hill Underground station, EC3

Train: Fenchurch Street ¼ mile

Bus: From surrounding areas

Tube: Tower Hill, adjacent

MAP Page 267 (3F)
OS Map 177 (ref TQ 336807)

Sign-up on-line for our email Members' Newsletter at **www.english-heritage.org.uk/newsletter**

Ranger's House – The Wernher Collection

Greenwich Park – SE10 8QX

Ranger's House is an elegant Georgian villa built in 1723, which became the official residence of the 'Ranger of Greenwich Park' after 1815, when the post was held by Princess Sophia Matilda, niece of George III. It remained an aristocratic and then royal home until 1902.

The house stands on the borders of Greenwich Park, and the Meridian Line passes through its grounds. Today it houses the Wernher Collection – an astounding display of medieval and Renaissance works of art, all purchased by the diamond magnate Sir Julius Wernher (1850-1912).

Arranged within the panelled interiors of this graceful mansion, the Wernher Collection presents a glittering spectacle – a sumptuous arrangement of silver and jewels, paintings and porcelain.

Nearly 700 works of art are on display, including early religious paintings and Dutch Old Masters, minute carved Gothic ivories, fine Renaissance bronzes and silver treasures. Together these pieces reveal the genius of medieval craftsmen, and the unparalleled quality of Renaissance decorative arts.

With the Cutty Sark, Greenwich and Blackheath all nearby, Ranger's House makes a great day out.

www.english-heritage.org.uk/rangershouse

Available for weddings and corporate and private events.

NON-MEMBERS	
Adult	£5.50
Concession	£4.10
Child	£2.80

OPENING TIMES

1 Apr-30 Sep, Sun-Wed 10am-5pm	
1 Oct-31 Mar, by appointment only	
Closed	23 Dec-28 Feb

HOW TO FIND US

Direction: Chesterfield Walk, Blackheath SE10

DLR: Cutty Sark

Train: Blackheath, Greenwich, Lewisham and Maze Hill, all ¾ mile

Bus: 53 Trafalgar Sq – Plumstead

River: Greenwich Pier

Tel: 020 8853 0035

P OVP

Toilets (including disabled).

MAP Page 267 (4F)
OS Map 177 (ref TQ 388769)

Marble Hill House

Richmond – TW1 2NL

Marble Hill is the last complete survivor of the elegant villas and gardens which bordered the Thames between Richmond and Hampton Court in the 18th century. It was begun in 1724 for the remarkable Henrietta Howard, mistress of King George II when he was Prince of Wales, and friend of some of the cleverest men in England. The house and gardens were planned by a coterie of fashionable connoisseurs, including Lord Herbert and Mrs Howard's neighbour, the poet Alexander Pope.

A lovely Palladian villa still set in 66 acres of riverside parkland, Marble Hill was intended as an Arcadian retreat from crowded 18th-century London. It became renowned as a salon of literary wits, gathered round their learned hostess. Some of its original contents, dispersed in 1824, have been re-assembled from as far afield as Philadelphia and Melbourne, Australia. There is also a fine collection of early Georgian paintings, including portraits of Mrs Howard and her circle.

A new display recreates the Chinese wallpaper Henrietta Howard hung in the Dining Room in 1751. Using historical references and motifs, a unique

paper has been designed to fit the room, each sheet different and, like the originals, hand painted by Chinese artists.

NEW FOR 2006 To celebrate the exotic paper, 'Chinoiserie' will be Marble Hill's theme for 2006. 'Hands-on' wallpaper albums and textile samples will allow visitors to enjoy the feel of handmade papers and silks. A printed 'walking tour' highlights the eastern connections of objects in the house, including ceramics and lacquer furniture, showing how China produced exciting new items for the European market, and how each culture influenced the other.

Available for corporate and private hire.

Licensed for civil wedding ceremonies.

NON-MEMBERS

Adult	£4.00
Concession	£3.00
Child	£2.00
Family ticket	£10.00

OPENING TIMES

1 Apr-31 Oct, Sat	10am-2pm
Sun & Bank Hols	10am-5pm
Tours on Tue & Wed	12pm & 3pm
1 Nov-31 Mar by appointment only	
Closed	22 Dec-7 Feb

HOW TO FIND US

Direction: Richmond Rd, Twickenham

Train: St Margarets ½ mile

Bus: From surrounding areas

Tube: Richmond 1 mile

Tel: 020 8892 5115

OVP

Café (Coach House Café, March-Oct).

Disabled access (exterior & ground floor only; toilets).

Dogs (restricted areas only).

MAP Page 266 (4E)
OS Map 176 (ref TQ 173736)

Ranger's House – The Wernher Collection

See feature – Page 33

Wellington Arch

See feature opposite

Winchester Palace

Southwark

Part of the great hall of Winchester Palace, built in the early 13th century as the London house of the Bishops of Winchester, including the striking rose window which adorns the west gable. Most of the palace was destroyed by fire in 1814.

OPENING TIMES

Free access

HOW TO FIND US

Direction: Next to Southwark Cathedral and the Golden Hinde replica ship; corner of Clink St and Storey St, SE1

Train/Tube: London Bridge ¼ mile

Bus: From surrounding areas

MAP Page 267 (4F)
OS Map 177 (ref TQ 325803)

Wellington Arch

Hyde Park – W1J 7JZ

Set in the heart of Royal London at Hyde Park Corner, Wellington Arch is a landmark for Londoners and visitors alike. George IV originally commissioned this massive monument as a grand outer entrance to Buckingham Palace. It was completed in 1830 by architect Decimus Burton, and moved to its present site in 1882.

Take a lift to the balconies just below the spectacular bronze sculpture which tops the imposing monument, for glorious views over London's Royal Parks and the Houses of Parliament. The statue is the largest bronze sculpture in Europe, and depicts the angel of peace descending on the chariot of war.

Inside the Arch, three floors of exhibits tell its fascinating history, including its time as London's smallest Police Station.

Apsley House, opposite the Wellington Arch, was the London home of the Duke of Wellington, and is also managed by English Heritage.

www.english-heritage.org.uk/wellingtonarch

Available for corporate and private hire.

Display inside the Arch

NON-MEMBERS

Adult	£3.10
Concession	£2.30
Child	£1.60

OPENING TIMES

1 Apr-31 Oct, Wed-Sun & Bank Hols 10am-5pm

1 Nov-31 Mar, Wed-Sun 10am-4pm

May close for hospitality functions. Please call to check before travelling.

Closed 24-26 Dec and 1 Jan

HOW TO FIND US

Direction: Hyde Park Corner, W1J

Train: Victoria ¾ mile

Bus: From surrounding areas

Tube: Hyde Park Corner, adjacent

Tel: 020 7930 2726

OVP

Please note: Exclusive group tours are available every Mon, with talk, slide presentation and refreshments on request (small charge).

MAP Page 266 (4E)
OS Map 176 (ref TQ 284798)

Marble Arch

London Statues

In 1999 English Heritage assumed responsibility for the maintenance of 47 statues and monuments within central London, including the Wellington Arch, which you are invited to explore (see p.35).

Statues provide a fascinating insight into the preoccupations of the period. Many of them are associated with wars and military campaigns, such as the Napoleonic Wars, the Boer War and the two World Wars. Royalty is also well represented, with examples throughout the city from Charles I, 1633, to Edward VII, 1921.

A leaflet giving more information about the intriguing history of London's statues and memorials is available free of charge from English Heritage. To obtain a copy of Kings and Queens: Royal Statues & Memorials in London, call English Heritage on 0870 333 1181.

Statue of King George III

The Capital's Monuments

Viscount Alanbrooke	Whitehall, SW1
Queen Anne	Queen Anne's Gate, SW1
Belgian War Memorial	Victoria Embankment
Simon Bolivar	Belgrave Square, SW1
Duke of Cambridge	Whitehall, SW1
Colin Campbell	Waterloo Place, SW1
Carabiniers Memorial	Chelsea Embankment, SW3
Edith Cavell	St Martin's Place, WC2
Cenotaph	Whitehall, SW1
King Charles I	Whitehall, SW1
Queen Charlotte	Queen Square, WC1
Clive of India	King Charles St, SW1
Christopher Columbus	Belgrave Square, SW1
Crimea Memorial	Waterloo Place, SW1
Thomas Cubitt	St George's Drive, Pimlico, SW1
Lord Curzon	Carlton House Terrace, SW1
Duke of Devonshire	Whitehall, SW1
Edward VII	Waterloo Place, SW1
General Eisenhower	Grosvenor Square, W1
Sir John Franklin	Waterloo Place, SW1
General de Gaulle	Carlton Gardens, SW1
King George II	Golden Square, W1
King George III	Cockspur St, SW1
General Gordon	Victoria Embankment
Earl Haig	Whitehall, SW1
Sir Arthur Harris	St Clement Danes, WC2
Lord Herbert	Waterloo Place, SW1
King James II	National Gallery, Trafalgar Square, WC2
Duke of Kent	Crescent Gardens (locked), Portland Place, W1
Baron Lawrence	Waterloo Place, SW1
Machine Gun Corps	Apsley Way, W1
Montgomery	Whitehall, SW1
Lord Napier of Magdala	Queen's Gate, SW7
Marble Arch	W1
Florence Nightingale	Waterloo Place, SW1
Samuel Plimsoll	Victoria Embankment
Lord Portal	Victoria Embankment
Sir Walter Raleigh	Old Royal Naval College, Greenwich, SE10
Royal Artillery Memorial	Apsley Way, SW1
General de San Martin	Belgrave Square, SW1
Captain Scott	Waterloo Place, SW1
Viscount Slim	Whitehall, SW1
Lord Trenchard	Victoria Embankment
George Washington	Trafalgar Square, WC2
Duke of Wellington	Apsley Way, W1
Wellington Arch and Quadriga	Apsley Way, W1
King William III	St James's Square, SW1

Other Historic Attractions

Discounted entry to our members (discounts may not apply on event days)

The Albert Memorial

Kensington – SW1

Her Majesty the Queen reopened the Albert Memorial in 1998, after one of the most ambitious conservation projects ever undertaken by English Heritage. It took four years to repair structural damage to the memorial, which involved stripping the monument to its cast-iron core and rebuilding it with all the original elements conserved. A fully-guided tour provides exclusive access behind the railings of the site.

Managed by the Royal Parks.

ENTRY

Tour (EH members) £4.00

Discount does not extend to EH Corporate Partners

OPENING TIMES

Mar-Dec, guided tours only on 1st Sun of every month at 2pm & 3pm.

Call to book tours. Group bookings at other times by prior arrangement.

HOW TO FIND US

Train: Paddington 1¼ miles, Victoria 1½ miles

Bus: From surrounding areas

Tube: Knightsbridge ½ mile, South Kensington ½ mile

Tel: 020 7495 0916 (10am-4pm)

MAP Page 266 (4E)
OS Map 176 (ref TQ 265797)

Danson House

Kent – DA6 8HL

The most significant building at risk in London in 1995, now restored for the nation by English Heritage and opened to the public for the first time in 30 years by Bexley Heritage Trust. Built for Sir John Boyd, this is one of Sir Robert Taylor's finest villas, with additions by Sir William Chambers. The restored 1760s interiors include a magnificent dining room scheme of 19 paintings by Charles Pavilion, and a rare George England organ.

ENTRY

A 25% discount on entry to English Heritage Members, accompanied children free (one with each paying adult)

OPENING TIMES

Good Friday-30 Oct
Wed, Thur, Sun and Bank Hols

Guided Tours 11am-5pm
Last entry 4.15pm

HOW TO FIND US

Train: Welling Station 1 mile

Bus: TfL B13 from New Eltham, B16 from Kidbrooke, 89 from Lewisham, 486 from Greenwich

Tel: 020 8303 6699

MAP Page 267 (4F)
OS Map 177 (ref TQ 473752)

Kensal Green Cemetery

Kensal Green – NW10

Kensal Green Cemetery is one of seven cemeteries established to cope with the huge population explosion which London experienced at the height of the Industrial Revolution. It houses some spectacular pieces of Victorian Gothic mausoleum architecture and some illustrious residents, including Prince Augustus Frederick, Duke of Sussex (the sixth son of King George III) and his sister Princess Sophia. English Heritage manages the cemetery buildings, and has recently restored the Dissenters' Chapel. There are plans to restore the Anglican Chapel and some of the monuments. Tours, arranged by the Friends of Kensal Green Cemetery, are given every Sunday at 2pm. These include a visit to the catacombs on the first and third Sunday of every month (under 12s not admitted to the catacombs).

ENTRY

Tour (EH members) £4.00

Discount does not extend to EH Corporate Partners

OPENING TIMES

Daily

HOW TO FIND US

Train/Tube: Kensal Green, adjacent

Tel: 07951 631001

MAP Page 266 (3E)
OS Map 176 (ref TQ 231825)

Upnor Castle – see pag

South East

'Trackway and Camp and City lost,
Salt Marsh where now is corn,
Old Wars, old Peace, old Arts that cease,
And so was England born!'

From 'Puck's Song' by Rudyard Kipling, 1906

www.english-heritage.org.uk/southeast

Properties

See individual listings for details

West Berkshire
Donnington Castle

Hampshire
Bishop's Waltham Palace, Calshot Castle, Flowerdown Barrows, Fort Brockhurst, Fort Cumberland, Hurst Castle, Itchen Abbas Roman Villa, King James's and Landport Gates, Medieval Merchant's House, Netley Abbey, Northington Grange, Portchester Castle, Royal Garrison Church, Silchester Roman City Walls and Amphitheatre, Southwick Priory, Titchfield Abbey, Wolvesey Castle (Old Bishop's Palace)

Kent
Bayham Old Abbey, Deal Castle, Dover Castle and the Secret Wartime Tunnels, Dymchurch Martello Tower, Eynsford Castle, Faversham Stone Chapel, The Home of Charles Darwin (Down House), Horne's Place Chapel, Kit's Coty House and Little Kit's Coty House, Knights Templar Church, Lullingstone Roman Villa, Maison Dieu, Milton Chantry, Old Soar Manor, Richborough Roman Amphitheatre, Richborough Roman Fort, Reculver Towers and Roman Fort, Rochester Castle, St Augustine's Abbey and Conduit House, St Augustine's Cross, St John's Commandery, St Leonard's Tower, Sutton Valence Castle, Temple Manor, Upnor Castle, Walmer Castle and Gardens, Western Heights

Oxfordshire
Abingdon County Hall, Deddington Castle, Minster Lovell Hall and Dovecote, North Hinksey Conduit House, North Leigh Roman Villa, Rollright Stones, Wayland's Smithy, Uffington Castle, White Horse and Dragon Hill

Surrey
Farnham Castle Keep, Waverley Abbey

East Sussex
1066 Battle of Hastings, Abbey and Battlefield, Camber Castle, Pevensey Castle

West Sussex
Boxgrove Priory, Bramber Castle

Isle of Wight
Appuldurcombe House, Carisbrooke Castle, Osborne House, St Catherine's Oratory, Yarmouth Castle

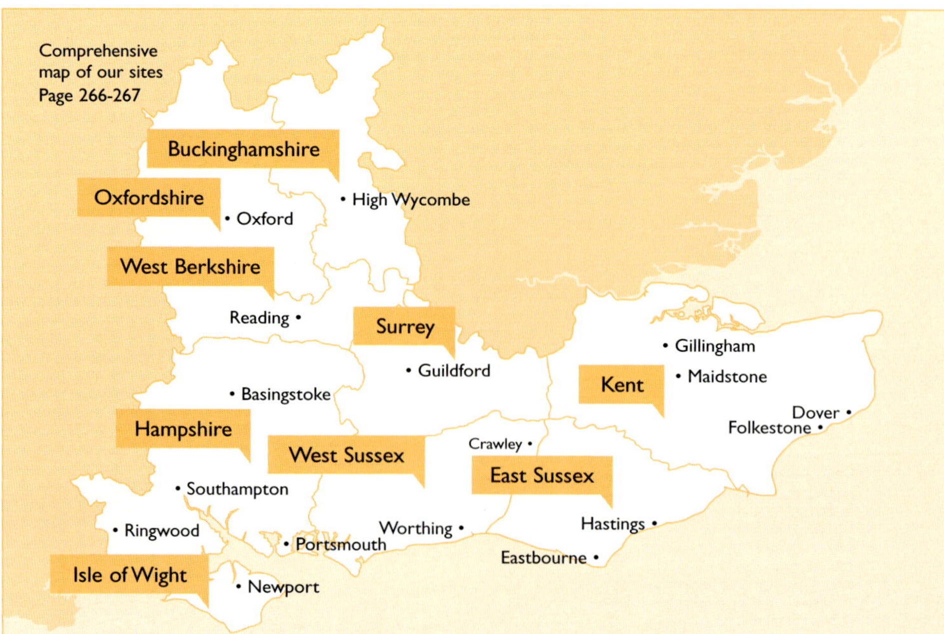

Dover Castle – see page 50

The Gateway of England

In Rudyard Kipling's famous Edwardian children's books, the Sussex nature-spirit Puck conjures up a prehistoric flint-worker, a Roman centurion, a Saxon thegn, a Norman knight, and many others who helped make the long history of the South East. English Heritage members too can easily conjure up memories of these history-makers, at the varied sites of a region which has always been the 'Gateway of England'.

As the area nearest the European mainland, this gateway was from Roman times until the 20th century often hammered at by invaders, and sometimes broken open by them – but just as often held fast shut. Both invaders and defenders have left their mark here, for instance in Roman forts like **Richborough** – once literally the site of the Roman portal to Britain; **Portchester Castle** and other bastions against sea-raiders; or **Pevensey Castle**, where William the Conqueror landed to defeat the Saxons at Hastings – an event whose 940th anniversary is commemorated this year at **1066 Battle of Hastings, Abbey and Battlefield**.

The Normans and their medieval successors in turn raised their great castles here – **Rochester Castle** guarding the road to London; **Carisbrooke Castle** watching over the Isle of Wight; and of course **Dover Castle**, 'the Key of England' which locked the gate right up until World War II. Henry VIII's new fortifications for cannon – **Deal**, **Walmer**, **Camber**, **Hurst** and **Yarmouth Castles** and their sisters – updated the gateway's defences against new threats, as later did **Dymchurch Martello Tower**, the Victorian defences around Portsmouth and – coming full circle – the World War II pillboxes camouflaged among the Roman and Norman ruins of Pevensey Castle.

Yet the 'Gateway of England' was always open to new ideas, which often reached the South East before any other part of England. Here the Romans built their first villas, like **Lullingstone Roman Villa** and **Fishbourne Roman Palace**; here the Christian missionary St. Augustine first landed, founding **St. Augustine's Abbey**, the progenitor of **Bayham**, **Netley** and **Titchfield Abbeys** and the other fine monasteries of the South East; and here swept in the architectural fashions which inspired pioneering mansions like **Appuldurcombe House** and **Northington Grange**, and Queen Victoria's beloved **Osborne House**. Here, too, English Heritage members can visit the cradle of the theories which revolutionised not just the South East, but the whole world – **The Home of Charles Darwin, Down House**.

Abingdon County Hall

Oxfordshire – OX14 3HG

This 17th-century building housed the Assize Courts, which judged the more serious crimes such as murder. Today it is home to the Abingdon Museum.

Managed by Abingdon Town Council.

OPENING TIMES

Daily 10.30am-4pm

Closed 24-26 Dec, Bank Hols (except during August) and during exhibition changeovers

Roof-top visits – spring to autumn, Sats only. Adult £1.00, Child £0.50. Only children over 6 years admitted

HOW TO FIND US

Direction: In Abingdon, 7 miles south of Oxford; in Market Place

Train: Radley 2½ miles

Bus: Oxford Bus 35/A/B from Oxford (passes ⇌ Radley)

Tel: 01235 523703

MAP Page 266 (3C)
OS Map 164 (ref SU 498971)

Appuldurcombe House

Isle of Wight – PO38 3EW

The shell of Appuldurcombe, once the grandest house on the Isle of Wight and still an important example of English Baroque architecture: the 1701 south front has now been restored. It stands in 'Capability' Brown-designed grounds. An exhibition of photographs and prints depict the house and its history.

You can also visit the Freemantle Gate (part of the 1770s neo-Classical additions to the estate) on the nearby public footpath, and the adjacent Falconry Centre (not managed by English Heritage).

Managed by Mr and Mrs Owen.

NON-MEMBERS

Adult	£3.00
Concession	£2.75
Child	£2.00
Family ticket	£9.00

Please note there is an additional charge for members and non-members for the Falconry Centre

OPENING TIMES

1 Apr-30 Jun, daily	10am-4pm
1 Jul-31 Aug, daily	10am-5pm
1 Sep-31 Oct, daily	10am-4pm

Last entry 1 hour before closing

HOW TO FIND US

Direction: Wroxall ½ mile, off B3327

Train: Shanklin 3½ miles

Bus: Southern Vectis 3/A W Cowes – Ventnor; 7/A Ryde – Yarmouth

Ferry: Ryde 11 miles (Wightlink 0870 582 7744; Hovercraft 01983 811000); West Cowes 12 miles, East Cowes 12 miles (both Red Funnel – 0870 444 8898)

Tel: 01983 852484

MAP Page 266 (7C)
OS Map 196 (ref SZ 543800)

1066 Battle of Hastings, Abbey and Battlefield

See feature – Page 44

Bayham Old Abbey

Kent – TN3 8DE

The impressive ruins of an abbey of Premonstratensian 'white canons', on the Kent-Sussex border. They include much of the 13th to 15th-century church, the chapter house, and a picturesque 14th-century gatehouse. Now set in an 18th-century landscape designed by Humphry Repton, the famous landscape gardener who also planned the grounds of Kenwood House in London. Two rooms in the 'Georgian Gothick' dower house are also open to visitors.

NON-MEMBERS

Adult	£3.50
Concession	£2.60
Child	£1.80

OPENING TIMES

1 Apr-30 Sep, daily 11am-5pm

HOW TO FIND US

Direction: 1¾ miles W of Lamberhurst, off B2169

Train: Frant 4 miles

Bus: Arriva 256 Tunbridge Wells – Wadhurst (passes ⇌ Tunbridge Wells)

Tel: 01892 890381

OVP

Disabled access (grounds only).

MAP Page 267 (5G)
OS Map 188 (ref TQ 650365)

Bishop's Waltham Palace

Hampshire – SO32 1DH

The ruins of a medieval palace (together with later additions) used by the bishops and senior clergy of Winchester as they travelled through their diocese. Winchester was the richest diocese in England, and its properties were grandiose and extravagantly appointed. Much of what can be seen today is the work of William Wykeham, who was bishop from 1367. There is an exhibition on the Winchester bishops on the first floor of the farmhouse.

Other palaces of the Bishops of Winchester include Farnham Castle Keep and Wolvesey Castle (Old Bishop's Palace).

Available for corporate and private hire.

Licensed for civil wedding ceremonies.

NON-MEMBERS

Adult	£2.80
Concession	£2.10
Child	£1.40

Admission fee applies only on days when farmhouse is open

OPENING TIMES

Grounds:
1 May-30 Sep, Sun-Fri 10am-5pm

Bishop's Waltham Palace

Farmhouse & Grounds:
1 May-30 Sep, Sun and Bank Hols 10am-5pm

HOW TO FIND US

Direction: In Bishop's Waltham

Train: Botley 3½ miles

Bus: Stagecoach in Hampshire 69 Winchester-Fareham – Southsea (passes close to Winchester and Fareham); Solent Blue Line 8 from Eastleigh (passes Botley)

Tel: 01489 892460

OVP

Disabled access (grounds only).

Dogs on leads (restricted areas only).

MAP Page 266 (6C)
OS Map 185 (ref SU 552174)

Boxgrove Priory

West Sussex

The guest house and other remains of a Benedictine priory: much of the fine 12th to 14th-century monastic church survives as the parish church.

OPENING TIMES

Any reasonable time

HOW TO FIND US

Direction: N of Boxgrove; 4 miles E of Chichester, on minor road off A27

Train: Chichester 4 miles

Bus: Stagecoach in the South Downs 55 from Chichester

Boxgrove Priory

MAP Page 266 (6D)
OS Map 197 (ref SU 908076)

Bramber Castle

West Sussex

The remains of a Norman castle on the banks of the River Adur, founded by William de Braose c. 1075. The earthworks are dominated by a towering wall of the keep gatehouse.

OPENING TIMES

Any reasonable time

HOW TO FIND US

Direction: On W side of Bramber village, off A283

Train: Shoreham-by-Sea 4½ miles

Bus: Brighton & Hove 2A Brighton – Steyning (passes Shoreham-by-Sea)

Parking (limited).

MAP Page 266 (6E)
OS Map 198 (ref TQ 185107)

i

Sign-up on-line for our email Members' Newsletter at **www.english-heritage.org.uk/newsletter**

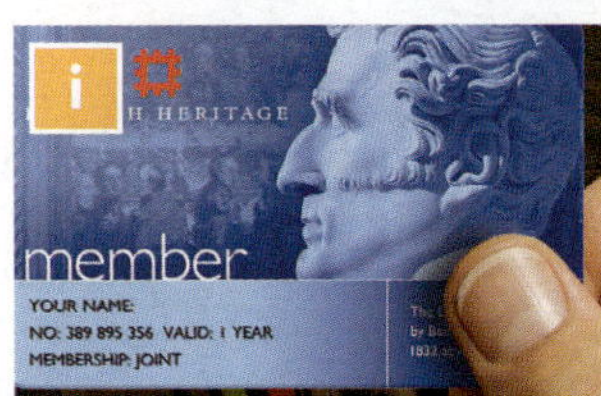

English Heritage membership makes a lovely gift.

Call 0870 333 1181 or visit **www.english-heritage.org.uk/gift** for more details.

1066 Battle of Hastings, Abbey and Battlefield

East Sussex – TN33 0AD

Everyone knows at least one date in English history – 1066, the year the invading Normans defeated the Anglo-Saxons at the Battle of Hastings. In fact the two armies did not fight at Hastings, but at a place by the town now named Battle. In the ruins of Battle Abbey, which King William later built to commemorate the event, you can stand on the very spot where the defeated King Harold fell.

South end of the dorter range

The battlefield – later part of the abbey's Great Park – and the abbey were purchased for the nation in 1976.

A substantial portion of the abbey buildings remain, but little of the early Norman structure is left. Best preserved and most impressive is the Great Gatehouse, rebuilt c. 1338 and arguably the finest of all surviving medieval abbey entrances. The west range of the monastic cloister, incorporating the medieval Great Hall of the abbots, was adapted as a country house by Tudor and Georgian owners after Henry VIII's Dissolution of the Monasteries.

The museum in the gatehouse takes a look at the monastic history of the site, and includes artefacts uncovered in excavations over the years.

Visit the Discovery Centre, housing an activity-based exhibition available to pre-booked school parties and open to families at weekends and throughout the school holidays. There is also a themed childrens' outdoor play area.

The interactive audio tour re-creates the sounds of the battle as you stand where the Saxon army watched the Normans advancing towards them. The battle raged for some hours with neither side gaining an advantage, until the Normans pretended to flee, but then turned back to cut down the Saxons who had broken ranks in pursuit. Open battle raged until the death of Harold, perhaps struck in the eye by an arrow as depicted in the famous Bayeux Tapestry. The spot where he is thought to have fallen was marked by the high altar of the abbey, founded by William the Conqueror c. 1070 to give thanks for his victory.

Why not while away a pleasant afternoon in Battle town: it has a Town Trail, museum, plenty of antique shops, and hosts medieval fayres, events and farmers' markets. From Battle you can take the 1066 Walk to Pevensey Castle (one of Britain's oldest strongholds) where William first landed before moving to Hastings (see p.60).

Find out about other places in the area by visiting the tourist information centre in the site shop, which is accessible from Battle High Street. Don't miss one of the highlights of the national events calendar, a spectacular re-enactment of the Battle of Hastings on 14-15 October 2006 – 940 years on from the most famous date in English history. For more details call 01424 775705 or visit www.english-heritage.org.uk/events

www.english-heritage.org.uk/battleabbey

NEW FOR 2006 **From Oct 2006 visitors can enjoy a state-of-the-art interactive presentation which brings to life the story of the Battle of Hastings and how England was transformed by this dramatic and bloody conflict. The exhibition is housed in a new visitor centre, which also contains a café.**

NON-MEMBERS	
Adult	£5.50
Concession	£4.10
Child	£2.80
Family ticket	£13.80

New prices will be introduced in October 2006:

Adult	£6.30
Concession	£4.70
Child	£3.20
Family	£15.80

OPENING TIMES	
1 Apr-30 Sep, daily	10am-6pm
1 Oct-31 Mar, daily	10am-4pm
Closed	24-26 Dec and 1 Jan

HOW TO FIND US

Direction: In Battle, at south end of High St. Take the A2100 off the A21

Train: Battle ½ mile. Inclusive rail and admission tickets package available; ask at any station

Bus: Arriva Kent & Sussex 4/5 Maidstone – Hastings

Tel: 01424 773792

Local Tourist Information: Battle (01424 773721) and Hastings (01424 781111)

Audio tours (interactive, also available for the visually impaired, those in wheelchairs or with learning difficulties, and in French, Spanish, German and Japanese; braille guides in English only). Interactive tours will not be issued on special events days.

Disabled access (some steps).

Dogs on leads (restricted areas only).

Parking (charge payable for members and non-members).

Toilets (temporary until Oct; thereafter in new building).

Tearoom (opens Oct 2006).

MAP Page 267 (6G)
OS Map 199 (ref TQ 749157)

Calshot Castle

Hampshire – SO4 1BR

This artillery fort, built by Henry VIII to defend the sea passage to Southampton, was recently used as a Navy and RAF base.

Managed by Hampshire County Council.

NON-MEMBERS	
Adult	£2.50
Concession	£1.80
Child	£1.50
Family ticket	£6.00

OPENING TIMES

1 Apr-31 Oct, daily 10am-4pm

HOW TO FIND US

Direction: On spit, 2 miles SE of Fawley, off B3053

Bus: Solent Blue Line X9, 38 Southampton – Calshot (passes Southampton), to within 1 mile

Tel: 02380 892023; when castle is closed, please call 02380 892077

Disabled access (Keep: ground floor only; toilets).

MAP Page 266 (6C)
OS Map 196 (ref SU 489025)

Camber Castle

East Sussex – TN31 7RS

The ruins of an unusually unaltered artillery fort, built by Henry VIII to guard the port of Rye. There are monthly guided walks round Rye Harbour Nature Reserve, including the castle. Contact the Reserve Manager for further details.

www.naturereserve.ryeharbour.org

Managed by Rye Harbour Nature Reserve.

NON-MEMBERS	
Adult	£2.00
Concession	£1.00

(Accompanied children free)

OPENING TIMES

1 Jul-30 Sep, Sat-Sun 2pm-5pm (subject to change, please call to check) (last entry 4.30pm)

HOW TO FIND US

Direction: 1 mile walk across fields, off the A259; 1 mile S of Rye, off Harbour Road. No vehicle access.

Train: Rye 1¼ miles

Bus: From surrounding areas to Rye, then 1¼ miles

Tel: 01797 223862

MAP Page 267 (6H)
OS Map 189 (ref TQ 922185)

Carisbrooke Castle

See feature – Page 48

Deal Castle

Kent – CT14 7BA

Deal Castle is one of the finest Tudor artillery castles in England. It is among the earliest and most elaborate of a chain of coastal forts, which also includes Calshot, Camber, Walmer and Pendennis Castles. Most were built at great speed between 1539 and 1542 by order of King Henry VIII, who feared an invasion by the Catholic powers of Europe. Its squat, rounded turrets were designed to deflect incoming cannon balls, and acted as platforms from which to fire barrages from increasingly sophisticated artillery pieces. The fort guarded the sheltered anchorage of 'the Downs' – the stretch of water between the shore and the hazardous Goodwin Sands, a graveyard of ships. Today you can explore the whole of the castle from the storerooms to the first-floor captain's residence. A pleasant cycle path links Deal and Walmer Castles along the beachfront.

Available for corporate and private hire.

Licensed for civil wedding ceremonies.

NON-MEMBERS	
Adult	£3.90
Concession	£2.90
Child	£2.00

OPENING TIMES

1 Apr-30 Sep, daily 10am-6pm
Open for events during October half term, please call 01304 211067 for details

HOW TO FIND US

Direction: SW of Deal town centre

Train: Deal ½ mile

Bus: From surrounding areas

Deal Castle

Tel: 01304 372762

OVP

Audio tours (also available in French, German and Dutch).

Disabled access (courtyards and ground floor only, parking available).

MAP Page 267 (4J)
OS Map 179 (ref TR 378522)

Deddington Castle

Oxfordshire

Extensive earthworks marking the site of an 11th-century motte and bailey castle.

Managed by Deddington Parish Council.

OPENING TIMES

Any reasonable time

HOW TO FIND US

Direction: S of B4031 on E side of Deddington; 17 miles N of Oxford

Train: King's Sutton 5 miles

Bus: Stagecoach in Banbury 59 Oxford – Banbury, to within ½ mile

MAP Page 266 (2C)
OS Map 151 (ref SP 472316)

Donnington Castle

West Berkshire

The striking twin-towered 14th-century gatehouse of this castle, later the focus of a Civil War siege and battle, survives amid impressive earthworks.

Donnington Castle

OPENING TIMES

Any reasonable time; exterior viewing only

HOW TO FIND US

Direction: 1 mile N of Newbury, off B4494

Train: Newbury 1¼ miles

Bus: Newbury Buses 6, 118, Four Valleys 99, 107 from Newbury

Disabled access (steep slopes within grounds).

MAP Page 266 (4C)
OS Map 174 (ref SU 461692)

Dover Castle and the Secret Wartime Tunnels

See feature – Page 50

Down House – see the Home of Charles Darwin

See feature – Page 54

Dymchurch Martello Tower

Kent – TN29 0TJ

Fully restored and re-equipped with its cannon, this is one of 103 ingeniously-designed artillery towers, built at vulnerable points around the south and east coasts to resist threatened Napoleonic invasion.

NON-MEMBERS

Adult	£2.50
Concession	£1.90
Child	£1.30

OPENING TIMES

Open August Bank Hol and Heritage Open Days 7-10 Sep

Dymchurch Martello Tower

HOW TO FIND US

Direction: In Dymchurch, from High St only

Train: Sandling 7 miles; Dymchurch (Romney, Hythe and Dymchurch Railway) adjacent

Bus: Stagecoach in East Kent 12, Stagecoach in Hastings 711 Dover – Hastings (passes close to Folkestone Central)

OVP

MAP Page 267 (5H)
OS Map 189 (ref TR 102292)

Eynsford Castle

Kent – DA44 0AA

The remains of one of the earliest Norman stone castles, built c. 1100 and little changed afterwards, including the full-height motte wall and part of the hall.

Please check opening times – the castle will be closed 13 Jul-8 Aug for performances of the musical 'Oliver'. Performances: 25-30 Jul and 1-6 Aug, 6pm-11pm; Sat 29 Jul and 5 Aug, matinee 1pm onwards. Call 01322 864879 for details.

OPENING TIMES

1 Apr-12 Jul, daily	10am-6pm
Closed	13 Jul-8 Aug (see above)
9 Aug-30 Sep, daily	10am-6pm
1 Oct-30 Nov, daily	10am-4pm
1 Dec-31 Jan, Wed-Sun	10am-4pm
1 Feb-31 Mar, daily	10am-4pm
Closed	24-26 Dec and 1 Jan

HOW TO FIND US

Direction: In Eynsford, off A225

Train: Eynsford 1 mile

Bus: Arriva, 413/5 Eynsford – Dartford

MAP Page 267 (4F)
OS Map 177 (ref TQ 542658)

Carisbrooke Castle Isle of Wight – PO30 1XY

Crowning a hilltop south of Newport, Carisbrooke Castle has held the dominant defensive position on the Isle of Wight for over 900 years.

The gatehouse and bridge

With its keep, battlements and working well house, Carisbrooke Castle is an exciting site for the whole family to explore. There has been a fortress here since at least Saxon times, but the present castle was built on this site in c. 1100, when the island was granted to the de Redvers family.

When the Spanish Armada passed alarmingly close in 1588, Carisbrooke became enormously significant for the defence of the realm. It was suspected that the Spanish might attempt to seize the island, and in response the castle was transformed into an artillery fortress.

Charles I was imprisoned here in 1647. He was comfortably accommodated in the Constable's Lodging, and a bowling green was constructed for his recreation. Nevertheless he made two attempts to escape: the first was foiled only when he became wedged in the window bars. Today the Charles I room is furnished as a typical bedroom of the Stuart period.

The well house and tread wheel are still in working order and open to visitors. Prisoners may have originally worked the wheel, but from the late 17th century donkeys were used. These hard-working animals can now be found giving demonstrations.

The on-site Carisbrooke Museum (managed by the Carisbrooke Museum Trust) provides more historical information about the castle, as well as memorabilia and artefacts relating to Charles I.

www.english-heritage.org.uk/carisbrookecastle

Two cannons on the west bulwark

A Carisbrooke donkey

NON-MEMBERS

Adult	£5.50
Concession	£4.10
Child	£2.80
Family ticket	£13.80

OPENING TIMES

1 Apr-30 Sep, daily	10am-5pm
1 Oct-31 Mar, daily	10am-4pm
Closed	24-26 Dec and 1 Jan

HOW TO FIND US

Direction: 1¼ miles SW of Newport. Follow signs for Carisbrooke village and then the castle

Train: Ryde Esplanade 9 miles; Wootton (Isle of Wight Steam Railway) 5 miles

Bus: Southern Vectis 6, 7, 7A, 7B, 38 from Newport, West Wight and Ventnor, all to within ¼ mile

Ferry: West Cowes 5 miles, East Cowes 6 miles (Red Funnel – 0870 444 8898); Fishbourne 6 miles, Ryde 8 miles, Yarmouth 9 miles (Wightlink 0870 582 7744; Hovercraft Ryde 01983 811000)

Tel: 01983 522107

Local Tourist Information: 01983 813813

E P OVP

Disabled access (grounds and lower levels only).

Tearooms (open Apr-Oct).

MAP Page 266 (7C)
OS Map 196 (ref SZ 486878)

Dover Castle and the Secret Wartime Tunnels

Kent – CT16 1HU

Pivotal to the defence of England's shores right into the 20th century, Dover Castle tells the tale of the evolution of a fortress.

Telephone exchange in the Secret Wartime Tunnels

No fortress in England boasts a longer history than Dover Castle. Commanding the shortest sea crossing between England and the continent, the site has served as a vital strategic centre since Roman times.

William the Conqueror strengthened the existing Anglo-Saxon fortress in 1066, both Henry II and Henry VIII made their own additions, and Vice Admiral Ramsay famously oversaw the Dunkirk evacuations from the tunnels built into the cliffs beneath the castle.

Dover's wartime secret

The White Cliffs are one of England's most celebrated sights, yet hidden inside them is a fascinating and secret world. Deep underground lies an extensive network of tunnels – first dug during the Napoleonic Wars, but so strategically useful that they continued to be used right through to the 20th century.

Dunkirk evacuation – Operation Dynamo

In May 1940 these tunnels provided the nerve centre for Vice Admiral Ramsay to plan Operation Dynamo – the evacuation of British and allied troops from the Dunkirk beaches of northern France.

The Upper Chapel

This evacuation proved crucial in saving the British army from total defeat and capture. The best estimate was that only 45,000 troops could be evacuated, yet on 4 June Sir Winston Churchill announced to the House of Commons that 338,000 troops had been saved, despite the operation itself coming under fierce attack.

Today you can tour the Secret Wartime Tunnels and experience life as it was lived by the 700 personnel based here in the worst days of World War II. You can see the Command Centre where Sir Winston Churchill viewed the Battle of Britain, and relive the drama as a surgeon

The Secret Wartime Tunnels

struggles to save the life of an injured pilot in the underground hospital. Sounds, smells and film clips from the time realistically recreate the atmosphere of wartime Britain.

Outside, Admiralty Look-out stands on the edge of the cliff, offering a tremendous view of the White Cliffs and across to France. (No public access to viewing platform during some of 2006, due to conservation works). To the west of the look-out you can see a statue of Vice Admiral Ramsay, and read about his key role in both the Dunkirk evacuations and the 1944 Normandy landings.

The key to medieval England
The Norman castle was transformed by Henry II during the 1170s-80s. Around the core of his massive new keep, he raised a double circuit of concentric and strongly-towered walls, creating a fortress then unparalleled in western Europe. The Avranches Tower, purpose-built to control an angle in the eastern defences, has two tiers of over 50 arrow-loops for archers and provides views over the moat and outer defences. Tours are available on the first Friday of every month (additional charge payable).

Graffiti in underground tunnel

Bay window

The 1216 Siege Experience, a stunning presentation using light, film and sound technology, highlights the stronghold's key role in resisting invasion. It recounts the epic sieges of 1216-17, when Dover Castle held out almost alone for King John against rebel barons and their French ally Prince Louis.

Henry VIII's visit

Following the annulment of his marriage to Catherine of Aragon, his excommunication by the Pope and the 1538 peace treaty between France and Spain, Henry VIII was isolated in Europe and a Catholic invasion of England seemed inevitable. The King commissioned a great chain of coastal artillery forts, coming to Dover in 1539 to inspect the work personally. An exciting exhibition at the castle offers a tableau of the preparations for Henry VIII's visit. Very close to Dover you will find two of Henry's coastal defences, Deal Castle and Walmer Castle.

Also of interest at the site are the Princess of Wales's Royal Regiment Museum; one of the best-preserved Roman light-houses in Europe; and the most complete Saxon church in Kent.

The Stone Hut, originally built in 1912 for the Royal Garrison Artillery, has now been converted and is being used as an archaeological store for the South East. On the first Friday of every month (or by pre-arranged booking), visitors can view changing exhibitions of treasures from across the region, including Roman coins and pots, as well as artefacts from both World War II and the Cold War.

Films: Zeffirelli's *Hamlet*, starring Mel Gibson, and *To Kill a King*, starring Dougray Scott.

www.english-heritage.org.uk/dovercastle

Available for corporate and private hire.

Licensed for civil wedding ceremonies.

Holiday cottage available to let.

NON-MEMBERS

Adult	£9.50
Concession	£7.10
Child	£4.80
Family ticket	£23.80

Includes Secret Wartime Tunnels tour. Additional charges for members and non-members may apply on event days

OPENING TIMES

1 Apr-31 Jul, daily	10am-6pm
1-31 Aug, daily	9.30am-6pm
1-30 Sep, daily	10am-6pm
1-31 Oct, daily	10am-5pm
1 Nov-31 Jan, Thu-Mon	10am-4pm
1 Feb-31 Mar, daily	10am-4pm

The keep closes at 5pm on Sat if a hospitality event is booked. Last admission ½ hr before closing time. Last Secret Wartime Tunnel tour 1 hour before closing time.

Closed 24-26 Dec & 1 Jan

HOW TO FIND US

Direction: E of Dover town centre

Train: Dover Priory 1½ miles

Bus: Stagecoach in East Kent, 90C, and 113 from Dover Priory

Tel: 01304 211067

Local Tourist Information Dover 01304 205108

E P OVP

Disabled access (courtyard, grounds and basement. There is good access for wheelchair users to the tunnels, although entry is down a steep slope. Mobility scooters, wheelchair routes and guides are available on site).

Dogs on leads (restricted areas only).

MAP Page 267 (5J)
OS Map 179 (ref TR 325419)

The Home of Charles Darwin, Down House

Kent – BR6 7JT

It was at Down House that Charles Darwin worked on his scientific theories, and wrote *On the Origin of Species by Means of Natural Selection* – the book which both scandalised and revolutionised the Victorian world when it was published in 1859.

Built in the early 18th century, the house remains much as it was when Darwin lived here. The rooms on the ground floor have been furnished to reflect the domestic life of the family, while the study holds his writing desk, chair and numerous objects connected with his work. The first floor offers an interactive exhibition on his life, his research and his discoveries.

The study

English Heritage has recently restored the gardens to their appearance in Darwin's time. Some of his experiments on natural selection are recreated in the garden, and visitors can stroll around the famous Sandwalk, the path Darwin paced as he worked out his ideas.

You can discover more about Darwin and his family from our inclusive audio tour, which is narrated by Sir David Attenborough.

www.english-heritage.org.uk/downhouse

NEW FOR 2006 **'Darwin's Children' – a charming photographic exhibition of Charles and Emma Darwin's children and their relatives, many of which were taken by the Darwins' eldest son, William.**

NON-MEMBERS

Adult	£6.90
Concession	£5.20
Child	£3.50
Family ticket	£17.30

OPENING TIMES

1 Apr-16 Jul, Wed-Sun & Bank Holidays	10am-6pm
17 Jul-31 Aug, daily	10am-6pm (house open 11am-5pm)
1-30 Sep, Wed-Sun	10am-6pm
1-31 Oct, Wed-Sun	10am-5pm
1 Nov-17 Dec, Wed-Sun	10am-4pm
18 Dec-6 Feb	Closed
7 Feb-31 Mar, Wed-Sun	10am-4pm

HOW TO FIND US

Direction: Luxted Rd, Downe; off A21 or A233

Train: Orpington 3¾ miles

Bus: 146 from Bromley North and South railway station; R8 from ⇌ Orpington

Tel: 01689 859119

OVP

Audio tours (English by David Attenborough; also in French, German and Japanese, and for those with sight or hearing impairment).

Parking (plus space for one coach).

MAP Page 267 (4F)
OS Map 177 (ref TQ 431611)

Farnham Castle Keep

Surrey – GU6 0AG

The impressive shell-keep and other defences of a castle founded in 1138 and redeveloped by Henry II after 1155. Long a residence of the wealthy bishops of Winchester, the medieval fortress itself was abandoned after Civil War service, but the later attendant buildings remain in occupation.

NON-MEMBERS

Adult	£2.80
Concession	£2.10
Child	£1.40

OPENING TIMES

1 Apr-30 Sep, Fri-Sun and Bank Hols 12pm-5pm

HOW TO FIND US

Direction: ½ mile N of Farnham town centre, on A287

Train: Farnham ¾ mile

Bus: From surrounding areas

Tel: 01252 713393

OVP

MAP Page 266 (5D)
OS Map 186 (ref SU 837473)

Faversham Stone Chapel

Kent

The remains of a small medieval church, which incorporated the remnants of a 4th-century Romano-British pagan mausoleum.

Managed by The Faversham Society.

OPENING TIMES

Any reasonable time

HOW TO FIND US

Direction: 1¼ miles W of Faversham on A2

Train: Faversham 1½ miles

Bus: Arriva 333, Jaycrest 335 Maidstone – Faversham (passes Faversham)

Tel: 01795 534542

MAP Page 267 (4H)
OS Map 178 (ref TQ 992613)

Flowerdown Barrows

Hampshire

Three Bronze Age burial mounds, including the largest and finest 'disc barrow' in Hampshire, once part of a larger 'barrow cemetery'.

OPENING TIMES

Any reasonable time

HOW TO FIND US

Direction: Off B3049, out of Winchester to Littleton; at crossroads in centre of village

Train: Winchester 2 miles

Bus: Stagecoach in Hampshire 86 from Winchester (passes Winchester)

MAP Page 266 (5C)
OS Map 185 (ref SU 459320)

Fort Brockhurst

Hampshire – PO12 4DS

One of a number of forts built in the 1850s to protect Portsmouth and its vital harbour. Largely unaltered, the parade ground, gun ramps and moated keep can all be viewed. Portchester Castle – which acted as a prison during the Napoleonic Wars – is nearby.

OPENING TIMES

The fort opens occasionally for pre-booked tours, Heritage Open Days 7-10 Sep and is available for private hire, please call 02392 378291

HOW TO FIND US

Direction: Off A32, in Gunner's Way, Elson; on N side of Gosport

Train: Fareham 3 miles

Bus: First 81-7 Fareham – Gosport Ferry (passes Fareham; also Gosport Ferry links with Portsmouth & Southsea)

Disabled access (grounds and ground floor only).

Dogs on leads (restricted areas only).

MAP Page 266 (6C)
OS Map 196 (ref SU 596021)

Fort Cumberland

Hampshire – PO4 9LD

Perhaps England's most impressive piece of 18th-century defensive architecture, Fort Cumberland was reconstructed in pentagonal form by the Duke of Cumberland between 1785 and 1810, and designed to protect Langstone Harbour. Southsea beach is nearby.

OPENING TIMES

The fort opens occasionally for pre-booked guided tours and Heritage Open Days 7-10 Sep; please call 02392 378291

HOW TO FIND US

Direction: In Portsmouth's Eastney district on the estuary approach, via Henderson Rd off Eastney Rd, or from the Esplanade

Train: Fratton 2 miles

Bus: First 15, 16/A ⇌ Portsmouth Harbour – Hayling Ferry

⚠

MAP Page 266 (6C)
OS Map 196 (ref SZ 683993)

The Home of Charles Darwin, Down House

See feature – Page 54

Horne's Place Chapel

Kent

A rare survival of a fine domestic chapel, built for William Horne in 1366 and attached to his timber-framed manor house, which was attacked during the Peasants' Revolt of 1381. The house and chapel are privately owned.

OPENING TIMES

By arrangement; please call 01304 211067

Horne's Place Chapel

HOW TO FIND US

Direction: 1½ miles N of Appledore

Train: Appledore 2½ miles

Parking (nearby).

MAP Page 267 (5H)
OS Map 189 (ref TQ 958309)

Hurst Castle

Hampshire – SO41 0TP

One of the most advanced of the artillery fortresses built by Henry VIII: used as a prison for eminent 17th-century captives, and later strengthened during the 19th and 20th centuries. It commands the narrow entrance to the Solent.

Managed by Hurst Castle Services.

NON-MEMBERS

Adult	£3.00
Concession	£2.80
Child	£1.80

OPENING TIMES

1 Apr-31 Oct, daily 10.30am-5.30pm

HOW TO FIND US

Direction: 1½ mile walk on shingle spit from Milford-on-Sea. Best approached by ferry from Keyhaven – call 01590 642500 for ferry details and fares

Train: Lymington Town 4½ miles to Keyhaven, 6½ miles to site

Bus: Wilts & Dorset 123/4 Bournemouth – Lymington (passes ⇌ New Milton), to within 2½ miles, or 1 mile to ferry

Hurst Castle

Tel: 01590 642344

⚠

Dogs on leads (restricted areas only).

Tearoom/restaurant (Castle Café, not managed by EH. Open Apr-May weekends only, Jun-Sep daily).

Parking (charge payable, at Milford seafront or Keyhaven)

MAP Page 266 (7B)
OS Map 196 (ref SZ 318897)

Itchen Abbas Roman Villa

Itchen, Hampshire

The remains of a prehistoric settlement and a Roman villa, including enclosures, ditches and trackways visible in the form of cropmarks. Pottery dating from the Iron Age and a Roman hypocaust system for underfloor heating have been found here.

OPENING TIMES

No public access. For more information call 01424 775705

MAP Page 266 (5C)
OS Map 185 (ref SU 528343)

King James's and Landport Gates, Portsmouth

Hampshire – PO1 2EJ

Two ornamental gateways, once part of Portsmouth's defences. King James's Gate (of 1687) has been moved, but Landport Gate, designed by Hawksmoor (1760) as the principal entrance to Portsmouth, remains in its original position.

OPENING TIMES

Any reasonable time; exterior viewing only

King James's and Landport Gates

HOW TO FIND US

Direction: King James's Gate forms the entrance to United Services Recreation Ground (officers), Burnaby Rd; Landport Gate as above, men's entrance on St George's Road

Train: Portsmouth Harbour ¼ mile

Bus: From surrounding areas

MAP Page 266 (6C)
OS Map 196 (King James's Gate ref SZ 636999, Landport Gate ref SZ 634998)

Kit's Coty House and Little Kit's Coty House

Kent

The remains of two megalithic 'dolmen' burial chambers. Impressive Kit's Coty has three uprights and a massive capstone: Little Kit's Coty, alias the Countless Stones, is now a jumble of sarsens.

OPENING TIMES

Any reasonable time

HOW TO FIND US

Direction: W of A229 2 miles N of Maidstone.

Train: Aylesford 2½ miles

Bus: Arriva 101 Maidstone East – Gillingham.

MAP Page 267 (4G)
OS Map 188 (Kit Coty's House ref TQ 745608, Little Kit Coty's House ref TQ 744604)

Knights Templar Church, Dover

Kent

The foundations of a small medieval church, traditionally the site of King John's submission to the Papal Legate in 1213.

OPENING TIMES

Any reasonable time

Knights Templar Church, Dover

HOW TO FIND US

Direction: On the Western Heights above Dover

Train: Dover Priory ¾ mile

Tel: 01304 211067

Dogs on leads (restricted areas only).

MAP Page 267 (5J)
OS Map 179 (ref TR 313407)

Lullingstone Roman Villa

Kent – DA4 0JA

A most exciting archaeological find. The villa was built c. AD 75, and extended several times during 300 years of Roman occupation: it includes a room decorated with Christian symbols, among the earliest evidence for Christianity in Britain. Much is still visible today, including mosaic-tiled floors, wall paintings, and the extensive 4th-century bath complex, built when the villa was at its most prosperous. There is also a display of the skeletal remains found on site.

NON-MEMBERS	
Adult	£3.90
Concession	£2.90
Child	£2.00

OPENING TIMES

1 Apr-30 Sep, daily	10am-6pm
1 Oct-30 Nov, daily	10am-4pm
1 Dec-31 Jan, Wed-Sun	10am-4pm
1 Feb-31 Mar, daily	10am-4pm
Closed	24-26 Dec and 1 Jan

Lullingstone Roman Villa

HOW TO FIND US

Direction: ½ mile SW of Eynsford; off A225; off junction 3 of M25

Train: Eynsford ¾ mile

Tel: 01322 863467

Local Tourist Information: Clacketts La 01959 565063

OVP

Audio tours (also available for the visually impaired and for those with learning difficulties, and in French and German).

MAP Page 267 (4F)
OS Map 177 (ref TQ 530651)

Maison Dieu

Kent – ME13 8NS

Originating as a 13th-century wayside hospital, this flint and timber-framed building now displays Roman artefacts from nearby sites.

Managed by The Faversham Society.

NON-MEMBERS	
Adult	£1.00
Concession	£0.80
Child	£0.50

OPENING TIMES

14 Apr-31 Oct, Sat-Sun, Good Friday and Bank Hols 2pm-5pm

HOW TO FIND US

Direction: In Ospringe on A2; ½ mile W of Faversham

Train: Faversham ¾ mile

Bus: Arriva 333, Jaycrest 335 Maidstone – Faversham (passes Faversham)

Tel: 01795 534542

MAP Page 267 (4H)
OS Map 179 (ref TR 313407)

Medieval Merchant's House

Hampshire – SO1 0AT

John Fortin, a merchant who traded with Bordeaux, started building this house c. 1290. A residence and place of business, it stood on one of the busiest streets in medieval Southampton. It has now been restored to its mid-14th-century appearance by the removal of later additions. The house stands near the medieval town wall, built to defend Southampton against seaborne attacks. Netley Abbey, Calshot Castle and Hurst Castle are all within reasonable travelling distance.

NON-MEMBERS	
Adult	£3.50
Concession	£2.60
Child	£1.80

OPENING TIMES

1 Apr-30 Sep, Sat-Sun, Good Friday and Bank Hols 10am-5pm

HOW TO FIND US

Direction: 58 French St, ¼ mile S of city centre, just off Castle Way (between High St and Bugle St)

Train: Southampton ¾ mile

Bus: First 17/A from ⇌ Southampton

Medieval Merchant's House

Tel: 02380 221503

OVP

Audio tours (also available for the visually impaired and those with learning difficulties).

Disabled access (one step).

MAP Page 266 (6B)
OS Map 196 (ref SU 419112)

Milton Chantry

Kent – DA12 2BH

Mainly encased in brick but still retaining its 14th-century timber roof, this was in turn part of a hospital, a chantry chapel, a pub, and a Georgian barracks, before its basement became a World War II gas decontamination chamber.

Managed by Gravesham Borough Council.

NON-MEMBERS	
Adult	£1.50
Concession	£0.75
Child	£0.75

OPENING TIMES

1 Apr-30 Sep, Wed-Sat	12pm-5pm
Sun and Bank Hols	10am-5pm
1 Oct-17 Dec, Sat-Sun	12pm-4pm
Closed	Jan & Feb
1-31 Mar, Sat	12pm-4pm
Sun	10am-4pm

HOW TO FIND US

Direction: In New Tavern Fort Gardens; E of central Gravesend, off A226

Train: Gravesend ¾ mile

Bus: From surrounding areas

Tel: 01474 321520

MAP Page 267 (4G)
OS Map 177 (ref TQ 653743)

Minster Lovell Hall and Dovecote

Oxfordshire

The extensive and picturesque ruins of a 15th-century riverside manor house, including a fine hall, south-west tower, and complete nearby dovecote. The home of Richard III's henchman Lord Lovell.

OPENING TIMES

Any reasonable time.

Dovecote – exterior only

HOW TO FIND US

Direction: Adjacent to Minster Lovell church; 3 miles W of Witney, off A40

Train: Charlbury 7 miles

Bus: Stagecoach in Oxford 102/3 Witney – Carterton with connections from ⇌ Oxford

MAP Page 266 (2B)
OS Map 164 (ref SP 325113)

Netley Abbey

Hampshire

The most complete surviving Cistercian monastery in southern England, with almost all the walls of its 13th and 14th-century church still standing, along with many monastic buildings. Though under royal patronage, maritime

Netley Abbey

Netley was never wealthy, allegedly due to the demands and depredations of mariners. After the Dissolution, the buildings were adapted as a mansion, now vanished: later attempts to demolish the church were abandoned when falling masonry crushed the wrecker.

OPENING TIMES

1 Apr-30 Sep, daily	10am-6pm
1 Oct-31 Mar, daily	10am-4pm

HOW TO FIND US

Direction: In Netley; 4 miles SE of Southampton, facing Southampton Water

Train: Netley 1 mile

Bus: First 16 ⇌ Southampton – Hamble; Solent Blue Line 9A Eastleigh – Hamble (passing ⇌ Southampton Airport Parkway)

Tel: 02392 378291

Toilets (nearby, across the road near the estuary).

MAP Page 266 (6C)
OS Map 196 (ref SU 453090)

North Hinksey Conduit House

Oxfordshire

Roofed conduit for Oxford's first water mains, constructed during the early 17th century.

OPENING TIMES

Exterior viewing only	10am-4pm

HOW TO FIND US

Direction: In North Hinksey off A34; 1½ miles W of Oxford. Located off track leading from Harcourt Hill; use the footpath from Ferry Hinksey Lane (near railway station).

Train: Oxford 1½ mile

MAP Page 266 (3C)
OS Map 164 (ref SP 495050)

North Leigh Roman Villa

Oxfordshire

The remains of a large, well-built Roman courtyard villa. The most important feature is a near complete mosaic tile floor, patterned in reds and browns.

OPENING TIMES

Grounds – any reasonable time. There is a viewing window for the mosaic tile floor. Pedestrian access only from main road – 550 metres (600 yards)

HOW TO FIND US

Direction: 2 miles N of North Leigh; 10 miles W of Oxford, off A4095

Train: Hanborough 3½ miles

Bus: Stagecoach in Oxford 11 Oxford – Witney, to within 1½ miles

Parking (lay-by, not in access lane).

MAP Page 266 (2B)
OS Map 164 (ref SP 397154)

Northington Grange

Hampshire

Set like a lakeside temple in a landscaped park, Northington Grange is the foremost example of the Greek Revival style in England. Created between 1804 and 1809 when William Wilkins encased an earlier house in Classical facades, most strikingly the 'Parthenon portico' on twelve

gigantic columns. It provides a stunning backdrop for the opera evenings which take place here in the summer; call 01962 868600 for details.

The 1999 film, *Onegin*, with Ralph Fiennes, was filmed here.

OPENING TIMES

Exterior only:

1 Apr-31 May, daily	10am-6pm
1 Jun-31 Jul, daily	10am-3pm
1 Aug-30 Sep, daily	10am-6pm
1 Oct-31 Mar, daily	10am-4pm

Closes 3pm June and July for opera evenings

Closed 24-26 Dec and 1 Jan

HOW TO FIND US

Direction: Located 4 miles N of New Alresford, off B3046 along a farm track – 450 metres (493 yards)

Train: Winchester 8 miles

Bus: Cango C41/2 Basingstoke-Alresford (booked on 0845 602 4135)

Tel: 01424 775705

Disabled access (with assistance, steep steps to terrace).

MAP Page 266 (5C)
OS Map 185 (ref SU 562362)

Don't forget your membership card when you visit any of the properties listed in this handbook.

Old Soar Manor

Kent – TN15 0QX

A small but complete portion of a stone manor house built c. 1290. The first floor 'solar' private chamber, with attendant chapel and garderobe, stands over a vaulted undercroft.

Maintained, managed and owned by The National Trust.

OPENING TIMES

1 Apr-28 Sep, Sat-Thu	10am-6pm

HOW TO FIND US

Direction: 1 mile E of Plaxtol

Train: Borough Green and Wrotham 2½ miles

Bus: New Enterprise 222 ⇌ Tunbridge Wells – ⇌ Borough Green (passing ⇌ Tonbridge); Kent Passenger Services 404 from ⇌ Sevenoaks. On both, alight at the E end of Plaxtol, then ¾ mile by footpath

Tel: 01732 810378

Parking (limited).

MAP Page 267 (5G)
OS Map 179 (ref TR 228693)

Osborne House

See feature – Page 62

Pevensey Castle

East Sussex – BN24 5LE

With a history stretching back over sixteen centuries, Pevensey Castle chronicles more graphically than any other fortress the story of Britain's south coast defences. Beginning in the 4th century as one of the last and strongest of the Roman 'Saxon Shore' forts – two-thirds of whose towered walls still stand – it was the landing place of William the Conqueror's army in 1066.

Pevensey Castle

During the decades after the Conquest the fort was converted into a full-scale Norman castle, with a great stone keep and towered bailey wall occupying one corner. Later a twin-towered gatehouse was added, and later still it was strengthened and modernised to face the threat of the Armada in 1588. This was not Pevensey's last military service: during World War II, pillboxes and machine gun posts were cunningly camouflaged among its ancient walls.

An exhibition with artefacts found on-site and an audio tour tell the story of the castle.

NON-MEMBERS

Adult	£3.90
Concession	£2.90
Child	£2.00

OPENING TIMES

1 Apr-30 Sep, daily	10am-6pm
1-31 Oct, daily	10am-4pm
1 Nov-31 Mar, Sat-Sun	10am-4pm

HOW TO FIND US

Direction: In Pevensey off A259

Train: Pevensey & Westham or Pevensey Bay, both ½ mile

Bus: Stagecoach in Hastings 710 from Eastbourne

Tel: 01323 762604

OVP

Dogs on leads (restricted areas only).

Parking (charge payable).

Tearooms (call 01424 775705 for opening arrangements).

Toilets (nearby).

MAP Page 267 (6G)
OS Map 199 (ref TQ 645048)

Portchester Castle

See feature – Page 66

Reculver Towers and Roman Fort

Kent

An imposing landmark, the twin 12th-century towers of the ruined church stand amid the remains of an important Roman 'Saxon Shore' fort and a Saxon monastery. Richborough Roman Fort is nearby.

OPENING TIMES

Any reasonable time; external viewing only

HOW TO FIND US

Direction: At Reculver; 3 miles E of Herne Bay

Train: Herne Bay 4 miles

Bus: Stagecoach in East Kent 7 from Herne Bay

Tel: 01227 740676

Disabled access (grounds only – long slope up from car park).

MAP Page 267 (4J)
OS Map 179 (ref TR 228693)

Richborough Roman Fort and Amphitheatre

Kent – CT13 9JW

Evocatively sited amid the East Kent marshes, Richborough is perhaps the most symbolically important of all Roman sites in Britain, witnessing both the beginning and almost the end of Roman rule here. Though now two miles from the sea, in AD 43 the site overlooked a sheltered lagoon harbour. Here, all but certainly, the invading Roman forces first landed and established a bridgehead. This event was later commemorated by a mighty triumphal arch, whose cross-shaped foundations still survive here. Proclaiming that the Roman conquest of Britain was complete, this also provided an impressive gateway for arrivals at what became the province's main entry port.

By the mid-3rd century, however, Roman Britain was under attack by sea-borne Saxon and other raiders. The once-prosperous commercial port of Rutupiae was hastily fortified, first by the digging of the great triple ditches and ramparts still visible round the site of the arch. But within a decade or so the defences were completely revamped, and Richborough was provided with its circuit of towered stone walls and outer ditches, becoming one of the most important of the 'Saxon Shore' forts. It was also among the last to be regularly occupied: there is evidence of a large Roman population here in the early 5th century, some of them worshipping in the little Early Christian church discovered in one corner of the fort.

You can choose to reach the fort as the Romans would have done, by boat. Boats sail from Sandwich, but not every day: please contact the site to check times.

NON-MEMBERS

Adult	£3.90
Concession	£2.90
Child	£2.00

Richborough Roman Fort and Amphitheatre

OPENING TIMES

Fort:
1 Apr-30 Sep, daily 10am-6pm
Amphitheatre: Any reasonable time, access across grazed land from footpath; please call 01304 612013 for details

HOW TO FIND US

Direction: At the A256/A257 roundabout, take the road for Sandwich and then turn left at the fire station

Train: Sandwich 2 miles

Tel: 01304 612013

OVP

Dogs on leads (restricted areas only).

MAP Page 267 (4J)
OS Map 179 (ref TR 324602)

Rochester Castle

Kent – ME1 1SW

Strategically placed astride the London Road, guarding an important crossing of the River Medway, this imposing fortress has a complex history of destruction and rebuilding. Its mighty Norman tower-keep of Kentish ragstone was built c. 1127 by William of Corbeil, Archbishop of Canterbury, with the encouragement of Henry I. Consisting of three floors above a basement, it still stands 113 feet high. Attached is a tall protruding forebuilding, with its own set of

defences to pass through before the keep itself could be entered at first floor level.

In 1215, garrisoned by rebel barons, the castle endured an epic siege by King John. Having first undermined the outer wall, John used the fat of 40 pigs to fire a mine under the keep, bringing its southern corner crashing down. Even then the defenders held out within the building, until they were eventually starved out after a resistance of nearly two months.

Rebuilt under Henry III and Edward I, the castle remained a viable fortress in the 15th century, but a century later it was decaying. Today it stands repaired as a proud reminder of the history of Rochester, along with the nearby cathedral and Dickensian cobbled streets.

Managed by Medway Council.

NON-MEMBERS

Adult	£4.00
Concession	£3.00
Child	£3.00
Family ticket	£11.00

OPENING TIMES

1 Apr-30 Sep, daily	10am-6pm
1 Oct-31 Mar, daily	10am-4pm
Closed	24-26 Dec and 1 Jan

HOW TO FIND US

Direction: By Rochester Bridge (A2); junction 1 of M2 and junction 2 of M25

Train: Rochester ½ mile

Bus: From surrounding areas

Tel: 01634 402276

OVP

Audio tours (small charge).

Toilets (in castle grounds).

MAP Page 267 (4G)
OS Map 178 (ref TQ 741686)

Osborne House Isle of Wight – PO32 6JY

After her marriage to Prince Albert in 1840, Queen Victoria felt the need for a family residence in the country. To use her words, 'a place of one's own – quiet and retired'.

The Andromeda Fountain

The Billiard Room.

Queen Victoria knew and liked the Isle of Wight after visiting as a child, and she and the Prince Consort were both determined to buy a property there.

'It is impossible to imagine a prettier spot,' wrote the Queen after a visit to Osborne House. In 1845 the royal couple purchased the property with an estate of 342 acres, plus the adjacent Barton Manor to house equerries and grooms and to serve as the home farm.

Before the deeds had even changed hands, architect Thomas Cubitt had been approached – firstly to build a new wing and then to demolish the old house and add further wings. Once all the work was complete, an exquisite pair of Italianate towers dominated the landscape and looked out over passing ships in the nearby Solent.

Artistic interiors

The interiors of Osborne House abound with opulence in both architectural design and decoration. Marble sculptures, commissioned by Victoria and Albert, line the classically designed Grand Corridor of the house and recall the royal couple's love of the arts. Portraits and frescos adorn the walls, serving as a reminder of the family's links to the crowned heads of Europe, and of the unrivalled supremacy of the British

>

Copy of the Medici lion

Osborne House

View from the upper terrace

Empire. Family photographs on the desks of Queen Victoria and Prince Albert offer a further insight into the way they lived.

Queen Victoria's role as Empress of India is celebrated in the richly decorated Durbar Room. Constructed from 1890-91, the room served as an elaborate banqueting hall and every surface, from floor to ceiling, is ornately embellished.

The walls are decorated with symbols from India, including Ganesh – the elephant god of good fortune – and the deeply coffered ceiling is composed of fibrous plaster. The completion of the room coincided with the introduction of electricity, so the Indian-influenced lamp stands were designed to take full advantage of this emerging technology.

Italianate gardens

Prince Albert worked with Cubitt on the Italianate designs for the terraced formal gardens which complement the house. Visitors can now enjoy the Walled Garden much as Victoria and Albert did, since English Heritage has restored it as part of the Contemporary Heritage Gardens Scheme.

The grounds also contain a children's play area, a summerhouse, a museum, and a miniature fort and barracks, as well as the Swiss Cottage, originally built as an educational tool where the royal children could learn

The Swiss Cottage

domestic skills. There is a beautiful wild flower meadow near the Swiss Cottage, and rare red squirrels can be seen throughout the gardens. There is a courtesy minibus, with wheelchair access, to Swiss Cottage.

Queen Victoria loved to stroll through the gardens, and the primroses in the woods were her particular favourites. Most of the gardens are accessible on tarmac and compacted gravel paths. Horse and carriage rides are also available (extra charge).

The Terrace Restaurant has wonderful views across the terrace gardens down to the Solent. It has waiter-served lunches and afternoon teas. The new café in the Petty Officer's Quarters serves lighter meals. (Please note: for non-members, a minimum grounds charge applies).

Guided Tours

From Nov-Mar, the house is open for pre-booked guided tours only, allowing visitors to see the Royal Apartments and private rooms at a quieter time of year in the company of one of our expert guides. From mid-Nov to the New Year, we run themed Christmas tours.

www.english-heritage.org.uk/osbornehouse

NEW FOR 2006 **The Petty Officer's Quarters will house a new café, shop and exhibition which covers various aspects of the sumptuously furnished house and magnificent grounds, as well as the lives and personalities of the Victorian royal family and the servants who cared for them.**

Available for corporate and private hire.

Holiday cottage available to let.

NON-MEMBERS
HOUSE AND GROUNDS

Adult	£9.50
Concession	£7.10
Child	£4.80
Family ticket	£23.80

NON-MEMBERS
GROUNDS ONLY

Adult	£5.50
Concession	£4.10
Child	£2.80
Family ticket	£13.80

OPENING TIMES

1 Apr-30 Sep, daily	10am-5pm
1-31 Oct, daily	10am-4pm
1 Nov-31 Mar, Wed-Sun	10am-4pm

Prebooked guided tours only (last tour is 2.30pm. During the Christmas tour season 11 Nov-7 Jan, last tour time is 3pm)

Closed 24-26 Dec & 1 Jan

On 22-23 Jul, 28-29 Jul & 3 Aug the house closes at 3pm (grounds 4pm) for special events. Please call for details.

HOW TO FIND US

Direction: 1 mile SE of East Cowes

Bus: Southern Vectis 4, Ryde – E Cowes; 5 Newport – E Cowes

Train: Ryde Esplanade 7 miles; Wootton (Isle of Wight Steam Railway) 3 miles

Ferry: East Cowes 1½ mile (Red Funnel – 0870 4448898); Fishbourne 4 miles; Ryde 7 miles (Wightlink 0870 5827744; Hovercraft: Ryde 01983 811000)

Tel: 01983 200022

Local Tourist Information: Cowes and Newport 01983 813818

E OVP

Disabled access (Access for wheelchair users to the first floor, by an existing lift. Whilst we endeavour to provide this service whenever the house is open, there will be occasions when wheelchair access to the first floor is not available).

MAP Page 266 (7C)
OS Map 196 (ref SZ 516948)

Portchester Castle **Hampshire – PO16 9QW**

There are sweeping views from Portchester Castle, and on a clear day you can see across to Portsmouth, Southsea and Hayling Island. This commanding location has made Portchester Castle a major factor in the Solent's defences for hundreds of years.

The most impressive and best-preserved of the Roman 'Saxon Shore' forts, Portchester Castle was built in the late 3rd century, possibly by the breakaway 'Emperor' Carausius. It is the only Roman stronghold in northern Europe whose walls still mainly stand to their full original height, complete with nearly all their originally 20 towers. Subsequently housing a Saxon settlement – which may have directly succeeded Roman abandonment – the huge waterside fortress became a Norman castle in the 12th century. A formidable tower-keep was built in one corner, used by Henry I as a secure lodging and safe depository for treasury bullion.

In 1215 the French allies of rebellious barons captured the castle from supporters of King John. Its demolition was ordered by his successor, Henry III, but it was retained as a bastion against further invasion and to store munitions for wars against France.

Throughout the Hundred Years War, Portchester Castle was thus in the front line, serving as a staging-post for expeditions and repelling raids from across the Channel. When Richard II made temporary peace with France in 1396, he transformed part of the castle into a palace: but when war was renewed, Henry V used it as a departure point for the Agincourt campaign in 1415. Thereafter it was superseded by Portsmouth and saw little action. It was used to house troops in the Civil War, and prisoners of war during the Dutch and Napoleonic Wars: graffiti from the late 18th and early 19th centuries can still be seen.

Roman intaglio of Mercury

Southwest keep spiral staircase

An exhibition in the keep interprets the long history of the castle and the development of Portchester manor and village, as well as the extensive archaeological finds excavated on site.

www.english-heritage.org.uk/portchestercastle

NON-MEMBERS

Adult	£3.90
Concession	£2.90
Child	£2.00

OPENING TIMES

1 Apr-30 Sep, daily	10am-6pm
1 Oct-31 Mar, daily	10am-4pm
Closed	24-26 Dec and 1 Jan

HOW TO FIND US

Direction: On the S side of Portchester off A27; Junction 11 on M27

Train: Portchester 1 mile

Bus: First 1/A, 5 Fareham – Southsea to within ¼ mile

Tel: 02392 378291

OVP

Disabled access (grounds and lower levels only).

Dogs on leads (restricted areas only).

Toilets (facilities are in the car park, operated by Fareham District Council).

MAP Page 266 (6C)
OS Map 196 (ref SU 625046)

Rollright Stones

Oxfordshire

The Rollright Stones consist of three groups of stones; the King's Men, the Whispering Knights and the King Stone. They span nearly 2,000 years of Neolithic and Bronze Age development.

Managed by The Rollright Trust.

OPENING TIMES

All the stones are accessible sunrise to sunset, 'The Whispering Knights' and 'The King Stone' via a footpath; entry to 'The King's Men' is courtesy of the owner, who may levy a charge (Adult 50p, Child 25p).

HOW TO FIND US

Direction: Off unclassified road between A44 and A3400; 3 miles NW of Chipping Norton, near villages of Little Rollright and Long Compton

Train: Moreton-in-Marsh 6½ miles

Tel: 01553 631330

Parking (in lay-by).

MAP Page 266 (2B)
OS Map 151 (ref SP 297309)

Royal Garrison Church, Portsmouth

Hampshire – PO1 2NJ

Royal Garrison Church

Royal Garrison Church was constructed around 1212 as a hospital. Although the church was badly damaged in a 1941 fire-bomb raid on Portsmouth, the chancel was saved.

Managed by the Friends of the Royal Garrison.

OPENING TIMES

1 Apr-30 Sep, Mon-Sat 11am-4pm (contact the key keeper in winter 02392 378291)

HOW TO FIND US

Direction: In Portsmouth; on Grand Parade S of High St

Train: Portsmouth Harbour ¾ mile

Bus: From surrounding areas

Tel: 02392 378291

Parking (nearby).

MAP Page 266 (6C)
OS Map 196 (ref SZ 633992)

St Augustine's Abbey

Kent – CT1 1TF

This great abbey, marking the rebirth of Christianity in southern England, was founded in AD 597 by St Augustine. Originally created as a burial place for the Anglo-Saxon kings of Kent, it is part of the Canterbury World Heritage Site, along with the cathedral and St Martin's Church.

St Augustine's Abbey

The impressive abbey is situated outside the city walls and is sometimes missed by visitors. At the abbey, you can also enjoy the museum and free interactive audio tour.

NON-MEMBERS

Adult	£3.90
Concession	£2.90
Child	£2.00

OPENING TIMES

1 Apr-30 Sep, daily	10am-6pm
1 Oct-31 Mar, Wed-Sun	10am-4pm
Closed	24-26 Dec and 1 Jan

HOW TO FIND US

Direction: In Canterbury, ¼ mile E of Cathedral Close

Train: Canterbury East and West, both ¾ mile

Bus: From surrounding area

Tel: 01227 767345

Local Tourist Information: Canterbury 01227 766567

Audio tours (interactive).

Disabled access (all site can be viewed, but some steps).

Parking (nearby).

MAP Page 267 (4J)
OS Map 179 (ref TR 155578)

St Augustine's Abbey Conduit House

Kent

The Conduit House is part of the monastic waterworks which supplied nearby St Augustine's Abbey.

OPENING TIMES

Any reasonable time; exterior viewing only

St Augustine's Abbey Conduit House

HOW TO FIND US

Direction: In King's Park. Approx. 5-10 min walk from St Augustine's Abbey. Please call or ask at the abbey for directions.

Train: Canterbury East or West, both 1½ miles

MAP Page 267 (4J)
OS Map 179 (ref TR 159580)

St Augustine's Cross

Kent

This 19th-century cross of Saxon design marks what is traditionally thought to have been the site of St Augustine's landing on the shores of England in AD 597. Accompanied by 30 followers, Augustine is said to have held a mass here before moving on.

OPENING TIMES

Any reasonable time

HOW TO FIND US

Direction: 2 miles E of Minster off B29048

Train: Minster 2 miles

Bus: Stagecoach in East Kent 37, Eastonways E42 from Ramsgate

MAP Page 267 (4J)
OS Map 179 (ref TR 340642)

St Catherine's Oratory

Isle of Wight

A tall medieval octagonal tower, allegedly a lighthouse, built here in 1328 as penance for stealing church property from a wrecked ship. Affectionately known as the Pepperpot, it stands on one of the highest parts of the Isle of Wight.

St Catherine's Oratory

It is part of the Tennyson Heritage Coast, a series of linked cliff-top monuments. A later lighthouse and several monuments can be seen nearby.

Maintained and managed by The National Trust.

OPENING TIMES

Any reasonable time

HOW TO FIND US

Direction: E of Blackgang roundabout, off A3055

Train: Shanklin 9 miles

Bus: Southern Vectis 6 Ventnor – Newport; 7/A Yarmouth – Ryde, to within 1 mile

Ferry: West Cowes 14 miles, East Cowes 14 miles (both Red Funnel – 0870 444 8898); Yarmouth 15 miles (Wightlink – 0870 582 7744)

MAP Page 266 (7C)
OS Map 196 (ref SZ 494773)

St John's Commandery

Kent

The flint-walled 13th-century chapel and hall of a 'Commandery' of Knights Hospitallers, later converted into a farmhouse. It has a fine moulded-plaster ceiling and a remarkable timber roof.

OPENING TIMES

Any reasonable time for exterior viewing. Internal viewing by appointment only; please call 01304 211067 for details

HOW TO FIND US

Direction: 2 miles NE of Densole, off A260

Train: Kearsney 4 miles

St John's Commandery

Bus: Stagecoach in East Kent 16/A Folkestone Central – Canterbury, to within 1 mile

Tel: 01553 631330

MAP Page 267 (5J)
OS Map 179 (ref TR 232440)

St Leonard's Tower

Kent

An early and well-preserved example of a small free-standing Norman tower keep, surviving almost to its original height. It was probably built c. 1080 by Gundulf, Bishop of Rochester, and takes its name from a chapel of St Leonard which once stood nearby.

Managed by West Malling Parish Council.

OPENING TIMES

Any reasonable time for exterior viewing. Internal viewing by appointment only; please call 01732 870872.

HOW TO FIND US

Direction: Nr West Malling, on unclassified road W of A228

Train: West Malling 1 mile

Bus: Arriva 70 from Maidstone, 151 from Chatham

Disabled access (grounds only).

MAP Page 267 (4G)
OS Map 188 (ref TQ 676571)

Silchester Roman City Walls and Amphitheatre

Hampshire

In the Iron Age, the region in which Silchester is located was part of the tribal territory of the Atrebates. During the Roman period their tribal centre became known as Calleva Atrebatum, growing into a substantial settlement of over 400,000 square metres (100 acres). Though none of the ancient buildings are visible today, archaeological investigations have given us an idea of the town's overall layout and how this would have changed over time. On the edge of the Roman town, outside the walls, are the remains of a rural amphitheatre built AD 50-75 and able to seat about 3,000 people.

OPENING TIMES

Any reasonable time

HOW TO FIND US

Direction: On a minor road, 1 mile E of Silchester

Train: Bramley or Mortimer, both 2¾ miles

Bus: Reading Buses 143 from [rail] Reading to within ½ mile

MAP Page 266 (4C)
OS Map 175 (ref SU 639624)

Southwick Priory

Hampshire

Scanty remains of a wealthy priory of Augustinian canons, transferred from Portchester: once a famous place of pilgrimage.

OPENING TIMES

No public access. For more information call 01424 775705

Southwick Priory

MAP Page 266 (6C)
OS Map 196 (ref SU 628084)

Sutton Valence Castle

Kent

The ruins of a small 12th-century Norman keep, with panoramic views over the Weald.

OPENING TIMES

Any reasonable time

HOW TO FIND US

Direction: 5 miles SE of Maidstone; in Sutton Valence village, on A274

Train: Headcorn 4 miles, Hollingbourne 5 miles

Bus: Arriva 12 Maidstone – Tenterden (passes [rail] Headcorn)

MAP Page 267 (5G)
OS Map 188 (ref TQ 815491)

Temple Manor

Kent

Part of a manor house of the Knights Templar, built in about 1240, with a fine first floor hall displaying traces of wall paintings.

Managed by Medway Council.

OPENING TIMES

1 Apr-30 Sep, Sun only	10am-6pm
1-31 Oct, Sun only	10am-4pm

(For group visits please call 01634 843666).

HOW TO FIND US

Direction: Located in Strood (Rochester), off A228

Train: Strood ¾ mile

Bus: From surrounding areas

Disabled access (grounds only).

MAP Page 267 (4G)
OS Map 178 (ref TQ 733685)

Titchfield Abbey

Hampshire – PO15 5RA

The ruins of a 13th-century Premonstratensian abbey, part of its church converted into a grand turreted Tudor gatehouse.

OPENING TIMES

1 Apr-30 Sep, daily	10am-6pm
1-31 Oct, daily	10am-5pm
1 Nov-31 Mar, daily	10am-4pm
Closed	25 Dec

HOW TO FIND US

Direction: Located ½ mile N of Titchfield, off A27

Train: Fareham 2 miles

Bus: First 26 Fareham-Hedge End (passing [rail] Fareham)

Tel: 01424 775705

MAP Page 266 (6C)
OS Map 196 (ref SU 542067)

Uffington Castle, White Horse and Dragon Hill

Oxfordshire

These atmospheric sites lie along the Ridgeway. Uffington 'Castle' is a large Iron Age hillfort, Dragon Hill a natural mound associated in legend with St George. The famous and enigmatic White Horse is the oldest chalk-cut hill figure in Britain, and may be more than 2,500 years old.

Owned and managed by The National Trust.

Uffington Castle, White Horse and Dragon Hill

OPENING TIMES

Any reasonable time

HOW TO FIND US

Direction: S of B4507, 7 miles W of Wantage

MAP Page 266 (3B)
OS Map 174 (ref SU 301866)

Upnor Castle

Kent – ME2 4XG

Set in tranquil grounds adjoining a riverside village, this rare example of an Elizabethan artillery fort was begun in 1559 and redeveloped in 1599-1601, to protect warships near the new Chatham dockyards. It entirely failed to do so in 1667, when the Dutch sailed past it to burn or capture the English fleet at anchor.

Managed by Medway Council.

NON-MEMBERS

Adult	£4.00
Concession	£3.00
Child	£3.00
Family ticket	£11.00

OPENING TIMES

1 Apr-30 Sep, daily	10am-6pm
1-31 Oct, daily	10am-4pm

Upnor Castle

HOW TO FIND US

Direction: At Upnor, on unclassified road off A228

Train: Strood 2 miles

Bus: ASD 197 from Chatham; Arriva 191-3, 196 Chatham – Hoo, alight Wainscott, then 1 mile

Tel: 01634 718742 or 01634 338110 when castle is closed

Disabled access (grounds only).

Dogs on leads (restricted areas only).

Parking (at a slight distance from castle – park before village).

MAP Page 267 (4G)
OS Map 178 (ref TQ 759706)

Walmer Castle and Gardens

See feature – Page 72

Waverley Abbey

Surrey

Fragments of the church and monastic buildings of the first Cistercian abbey in England, founded in 1128.

OPENING TIMES

Any reasonable time

HOW TO FIND US

Direction: 2 miles SE of Farnham, off B3001; off Junction 10 of M25

Train: Farnham 2 miles

Bus: Stagecoach in Hants & Surrey 46 Guildford – Aldershot (passing Farnham)

Parking (limited).

MAP Page 266 (5D)
OS Map 186 (ref SU 868453)

Wayland's Smithy

Oxfordshire

A fine and atmospheric Neolithic chambered long barrow 2km along the Ridgeway from the Uffington White Horse: it was once believed to be the habitation of the Saxon smith-god Wayland.

Managed by The National Trust.

OPENING TIMES

Any reasonable time

HOW TO FIND US

Direction: On the Ridgeway; ¾ mile NE of B4000, Ashbury – Lambourn Road

Parking (may be a charge).

MAP Page 266 (3B)
OS Map 178 (ref TQ 759706)

Western Heights, Dover

Kent

A huge fortification begun during the Napoleonic Wars and completed in the 1860s, designed to protect Dover from French invasion. Only the moat can be visited.

Part of the White Cliffs Countryside Project.

OPENING TIMES

Any reasonable time

HOW TO FIND US

Direction: Above Dover town on W side of harbour

Train: Dover Priory ¾ mile

Tel: 01304 211067

MAP Page 267 (5J)
OS Map 179 (ref TR 312408)

Walmer Castle and Gardens Kent – CT14 7LJ

Originally built during the reign of Henry VIII as part of a chain of coastal artillery defences against Catholic attack from Europe, Walmer Castle has evolved over time into an elegant residence.

View across the Broadwalk to the ca

The Duke of Wellington's bedroom

Walmer Castle became the official residence of the Lord Warden of the Cinque Ports in 1708. When visiting, it is easy to imagine why the Duke of Wellington, who held the post of Lord Warden for 23 years, enjoyed his time here so much.

The spirit of Napoleon's nemesis and the victor of Waterloo still lives on at Walmer, and the yellow chintz armchair in which he died on 14 September 1852 can still be seen here. Wellington preferred unsophisticated surroundings, and his campaign bed – with its original horsehair mattress and bedding – remains on display as a testament to his spartan tastes. A pair of original 'Wellington boots' can also be seen, alongside a great many personal effects in the fascinating on-site Wellington museum.

The honorary title of Lord Warden of the Cinque Ports – the ancient 'five ports' of the south-east coast – is the oldest military honour England can give, and is still awarded today. Admiral Sir Michael Boyce GCB was appointed Lord Warden in 2004.

Successive Lords Warden have left their mark on Walmer Castle's buildings and gardens. Thus Lady Hester Stanhope used local militia to create new landscaping as a surprise for her uncle William Pitt, Lord Warden and Prime Minister: while Lord Warden W.H. Smith – member of the famous stationers family – saved many of the valuable furnishings now on display throughout the site. >

The greenhouse

Walmer Castle and Gardens

In recent years, Lords Warden of the Cinque Ports have been provided with private apartments above the gatehouse and, although these were never used by Sir Winston Churchill during his tenure, both Sir Robert Menzies (former Australian Prime Minister) and Her Majesty Queen Elizabeth the Queen Mother made regular visits and stop-overs at the castle. Some of the rooms used by the Queen Mother are open to visitors, as is her magnificent garden, designed by Penelope Hobhouse and given to Her Majesty on her 95th birthday.

There are beautiful gardens surrounding the house, including a commemorative lawn, woodland walk, croquet lawn and a working kitchen garden, as well as a double herbaceous border flanked by mature yew hedges. The remainder of the grounds are mostly wildlife gardens, and are a great place to spot birds.

When you need a break, home-made lunches and teas are available at the Lord Warden's Tearoom, and the well-stocked gift shop is well worth a visit. An audio tour is available at the site and, for those inspired by the magnificent gardens, plants are on sale.

Queen Mother's Garden

There is a pleasant cycle path along the beachfront between Deal and Walmer Castles.

Duke of Wellington enthusiasts may also be interested in two other properties managed by English Heritage. Apsley House (see p.24) was the Duke's impressive London residence, and the spectacular Wellington Arch (see p.35), opposite Apsley House, originally had a large statue of the Duke of Wellington erected on the top.

Available for corporate and private hire.

Licensed for civil wedding ceremonies.

www.english-heritage.org.uk/walmercastle

Wellington Boots

Queen Victoria's bedroom

NON-MEMBERS

Adult	£6.20
Concession	£4.70
Child	£3.10
Family ticket	£15.50

OPENING TIMES

1 Apr-30 Sep, daily (closes at 4pm Sat)	10am-6pm
1-31 Oct, Wed-Sun	10am-4pm
1-31 Mar, daily	10am-4pm
Closed 7-9 Jul (when Lord Warden is in residence)	

HOW TO FIND US

Direction: On coast S of Walmer, on A258; Junction 13 of M20 or from M2 to Deal

Train: Walmer 1 mile

Bus: From surrounding areas

Tel: 01304 364288

Local Tourist Information Deal 01304 369576 and Dover 01304 205108

P OVP

Audio tours (also in French, Dutch and German).

Disabled access (courtyard and garden only; parking available).

Parking (near approach to castle).

MAP Page 267 (5J) OS Map 179 (ref TR 378501)

Wolvesey Castle (Old Bishop's Palace)

Hampshire

Begun as a 12th-century Norman keep and bailey castle, the palace was the chief residence of the Bishops of Winchester. Situated next to Winchester Cathedral, its extensive ruins reflect their importance and wealth. The last great occasion at Wolvesey was on 25 July 1554, when Queen Mary and Philip of Spain held their wedding breakfast in the East Hall.

OPENING TIMES

1 Apr-30 Sep, daily	10am-5pm

HOW TO FIND US

Direction: ¾ mile SE of Winchester Cathedral, next to the Bishop's Palace; access from College St

Train: Winchester ¾ mile

Bus: From surrounding areas

Tel: 02392 378291

MAP Page 266 (5C)
OS Map 185 (ref SU 484291)

Yarmouth Castle

Isle of Wight – PO41 0PB

This last and most sophisticated addition to Henry VIII's coastal defences was completed after his death in 1547, with the first new-style 'arrowhead' artillery bastion built in England. Also a magnificent picnic spot, with views over the Solent.

Other artillery forts built by Henry VIII include Deal Castle, Hurst Castle and Pendennis Castle.

There is a waterbus link to Hurst Castle. Call Hurst Castle Ferries on 01590 642500 for details.

NON-MEMBERS

Adult	£2.80
Concession	£2.10
Child	£1.40

OPENING TIMES

1 Apr-30 Sep, Sun-Thu	11am-4pm

HOW TO FIND US

Direction: In Yarmouth, adjacent to car ferry terminal

Bus: Southern Vectis 7, 7A, 7B from Newport

Ferry: Wightlink – 0870 582 7744 (Lymington-Yarmouth)

Yarmouth Castle

Tel: 01983 760678

OVP

Disabled access (ground floor only).

Parking (coaches and cars 200 metres (220 yards) limited to 1 hour only).

MAP Page 266 (7B)
OS Map 196 (ref SZ 354898)

Check *Heritage Today* for news and information on forthcoming events and exclusive members' offers.

English Heritage members can take up to 6 children, as part of a family group, into our properties at no extra cost (see page 6).

Other Historic Attractions

Discounted entry to our members (discounts may not apply on event days)

Anne of Cleves House

Lewes, East Sussex – BN7 1JA

This 16th-century timber framed Wealden hall-house was given to Anne as part of her divorce settlement from Henry VIII.

Managed by Sussex Past.

ENTRY

Adult	£3.10
Concession	£2.80
Child	£1.55

Half price for EH members

OPENING TIMES

Mar-Oct, daily	
Remainder of year, Tue-Sat	
Closed	24-26 Dec

Tel: 01273 474610

www.sussexpast.co.uk

MAP Page 267 (6F)
OS Map 198 (ref TQ 411096)

Dover Museum & Bronze Age Boat Gallery

Dover, Kent – CT16 1PB

This modern interactive museum tells the story of Dover's rich history, and displays the world's oldest prehistoric seagoing boat, discovered nearby.

Managed by Dover District Council and Heritage Projects Ltd.

ENTRY

Adult	£2.50
Concession	£1.50
Child	£1.50

Half price for EH members

Dover Museum & Bronze Age Boat Gallery

OPENING TIMES

Mon-Sat	10am-5.30pm
Sun (Apr-Sep only)	1pm-5pm
Closed	25-26 Dec & 1 Jan

Tel: 01304 201066

www.dovermuseum.co.uk

MAP Page 267 (5J)
OS Map 179 (ref TR 319414)

Fishbourne Roman Palace

Chichester, West Sussex – PO19 3QR

The remains of a military supply base, built at the time of the Roman invasion in AD 43, and a sumptuous palace, constructed AD 75, with 20 spectacular mosaic floors in various states of completeness.

Managed by Sussex Past.

ENTRY

Adult	£6.50
Concession	£5.50
Child	£3.40

Half price for EH members

OPENING TIMES

1 Feb-15 Dec, daily	
Remainder of year, Sat-Sun only	
Closed	25 Dec

Tel: 01243 785859

www.sussexpast.co.uk

MAP Page 266 (6D)
OS Map 197 (ref SU 839048)

The Historic Dockyard

Chatham, Kent – ME4 4TZ

The only virtually complete dockyard surviving from the Trafalgar era, The Historic Dockyard is among the world's

The Historic Dockyard

most significant and fascinating maritime heritage sites. The 80-acre site displays both spectacular architecture and exciting naval exhibits.

Managed by The Historic Dockyard Trust.

ENTRY

Admission charges apply. Please call for details. 20% reduction for EH members

OPENING TIMES

11 Feb-29 Oct, daily	10am-6pm
Closes 6pm or dusk if earlier	
Weekends only in November	
Last entry: Nov-March,	3pm
Apr-Oct,	4pm

Tel: 01634 823807

www.thedockyard.co.uk

MAP Page 267 (4G)
OS Map 178 (ref TQ 75969)

Leeds Castle

Nr Maidstone, Kent – ME17 1PL

Listed in the Domesday Book, Leeds Castle has been a Norman stronghold, a royal residence for six of England's medieval queens and a palace of Henry VIII. The site attractions include a dog collar museum, aviary, maze and grotto, vineyard, toddlers' play area and daily falconry displays.

Managed by Leeds Castle Enterprises Ltd.

ENTRY

Adult	£13.50
Concession	£11.00
Child	£8.00

20% reduction for EH members

Leeds Castle

OPENING TIMES

Daily from 10am, except 24 Jun, 1 Jul, 4 Nov & 25 Dec. Please check website for closing times as they vary seasonally

Tel: 01622 765400

www.leeds-castle.com

MAP Page 267 (5G)
OS Map 188 (ref TQ 837533)

Lewes Castle and Barbican House Museum

Lewes, East Sussex – BN7 1YE

Begun in the 1070s, this castle was finally completed 300 years later. Its history is told in 'The Story of Lewes Town' at the Barbican House Museum.

Managed by Sussex Past.

ENTRY

Adult	£4.50
Concession	£4.00
Child	£2.25

Half price for EH members

OPENING TIMES

Daily, except Mondays in Jan

Closed 24-26 Dec

Tel: 01273 486290

www.sussexpast.co.uk

MAP Page 267 (6F)
OS Map 198 (ref TQ 413101)

Marlipins Museum

Shoreham-By-Sea, West Sussex – BN43 5DA

A c. 14th-century building with a knapped flint and Caen stone chequer-work façade, containing a fully accessible museum with many exhibits of local interest.

Managed by Sussex Past.

ENTRY

Adult	£2.50
Concession	£2.00
Child	£1.50

Half price for EH members

OPENING TIMES

2 May-31 Oct, Tue-Sat & Bank Hols

Tel: 01273 462994

www.sussexpast.co.uk

MAP Page 266 (6E)
OS Map 198 (ref TQ 215050)

Michelham Priory

Nr Hailsham, East Sussex – BN27 3QS

Part of a 13th-century priory – later converted into a Tudor mansion – surrounded by seven acres of wonderful gardens and England's longest water-filled medieval moat.

Managed by Sussex Past.

ENTRY

Adult	£5.60
Concession	£4.70
Child	£2.90

Half price for EH members

OPENING TIMES

Mar-Jul, Tue-Sun & Bank Hols

Aug, daily

Sep-Oct, Tue-Sun

Tel: 01323 844224

www.sussexpast.co.uk

MAP Page 267 (6F)
OS Map 199 (ref TQ 559093)

Penshurst Place

Penshurst, Kent – TN11 8DG

Magnificent ancestral home of the Sidney family since 1552, set amidst tranquil Tudor gardens and parkland. Medieval Barons' Hall dating from 1341, and Staterooms containing a wonderful collection of furniture, tapestries, portraits, porcelain and armour. Venture playground, toy museum, woodland trail, garden tearoom and gift shop.

HOUSE & GROUNDS

Adult	£7.50
Concession	£7.00
Child	£5.00

GROUNDS ONLY

Adult	£6.00
Concession	£5.50
Child	£4.50

EH members get free entry to the house when purchasing a grounds only ticket.

OPENING TIMES

Please call 01892 870307

MAP Page 267 (5F)
OS Map 188 (ref TQ 528440)

The Priest House

West Hoathly, West Sussex – RH19 4PP

The Priest House

Standing in the beautiful surroundings of a traditional cottage garden on the edge of Ashdown Forest, The Priest House is an early 15th-century timber-framed hall-house with a dramatic roof of Horsham stone. Inside the house are many interesting exhibits, while outside is a delightful formal herb garden.

Managed by Sussex Past.

ENTRY

Adult	£2.90
Concession	£2.60
Child	£1.45

Half price for EH members

OPENING TIMES

Mar-Jul, Tue-Sun & Bank Hols

Aug, daily

Sep-Oct, Tue-Sun

Tel: 01342 810479

www.sussexpast.co.uk

MAP Page 267 (5F)
OS Map 187 (ref TQ 362325)

Royal Pavilion

Brighton, East Sussex – BN1 1EE

This Regency palace was the magnificent seaside residence of King George IV. The exterior, which was inspired by Indian architecture, contrasts with interiors decorated in Chinese taste.

Managed by Brighton and Hove City Council.

ENTRY

Adult	£6.10
Concession	£4.30
Child (age 5-15)	£3.60

Prices subject to change. Adult EH members are entitled to a group discount rate

Royal Pavilion

OPENING TIMES

Apr-Sep, daily	9.30am-5.45pm
Oct-Mar, daily	10am-5.15pm

Last admission 45 mins before closing

Closed 25-26 Dec (closes 24 Dec 2.30pm)

Tel: 01273 290900

www.royalpavilion.org.uk

MAP Page 267 (6F)
OS Map 198 (ref TQ 313042)

Rycote Chapel

Oxfordshire – 0X9 2PE

This 15th-century chapel has original furniture, including exquisitely carved and painted woodwork.

Owned by Mr and Mrs Bernard Taylor and managed by the Rycote Buildings Charitable Foundation.

ENTRY

Adult	£3.50
Concession	£2.50
Child	£1.50

Prices subject to change

OPENING TIMES

1 Apr-30 Sep, Fri-Sun 2pm-6pm

Times may change at short notice – please ring for details

Directions: 3 miles SW of Thame off A329

Bus: Arriva the Shires 260, 280 Oxford – Aylesbury (passes ⇌ Haddenham and Thame Parkway), to within ½ mile

Rycote Chapel

Train: Haddenham and Thame Parkway 5 miles

Tel: 01844 210210/07742 925512

MAP Page 266 (3C)
OS Map 187 (ref TQ 362325)

Weald and Downland Open Air Museum

Nr Chichester, West Sussex – PO18 0EU

England's leading museum of historic buildings, set in 50 acres of beautiful Sussex countryside.

Managed by the Weald and Downland Open Air Museum.

ENTRY

Adult	£7.95
Concession	£6.95
Child	£4.25

Half price entry for EH members

OPENING TIMES

1 Apr-31 Oct, daily	10.30am-6pm
1 Nov-21 Dec, daily	10.30am-4pm
26 Dec-1 Jan, daily	10.30am-4pm
3 Jan-18 Feb, Wed, Sat & Sun only	10.30am-4pm
19 Feb-31 Mar, daily	10.30am-4pm

Tel: 01243 811348

www.wealddown.co.uk

MAP Page 266 (6D)
OS Map 197 (ref SU 874128)

Deal Castle Kent
Walmer Castle & Gardens Kent
Dover Castle Kent

Bust of Christ, Old Wardour Castle – see page 99

Photo: Paul Highnam

South West

'They bide their time off serpentine
Green lanes, in fields, with railings
Round them and black cows; tall, pocked
And pitted stones, grey, ochre-patched
With moss, lodgings for lost spirits.
Long Meg, Five Kings, Nine Maidens,
Twelve Apostles: with such familiar names
We make them part of ordinary lives.
On callow pasture-land
The Shearers and The Hurlers stand.'

From 'Ancient Monuments' by John Ormond, 1923-90

www.english-heritage.org.uk/southwest

Properties

See individual listings for details

Bristol & Bath
Sir Bevil Grenville's Monument, Stanton Drew Circles and Cove, Stoney Littleton Long Barrow, Temple Church

Cornwall
Ballowall Barrow, Carn Euny Ancient Village, Chysauster Ancient Village, Dupath Well, Halliggye Fogou, Hurlers Stone Circles, King Doniert's Stone, Launceston Castle, Pendennis Castle, Penhallam, Restormel Castle, St Breock Downs Monolith, St Catherine's Castle, St Mawes Castle, Tintagel Castle, Tregiffian Burial Chamber, Trethevy Quoit

Devon
Bayard's Cove Fort, Berry Pomeroy Castle, Blackbury Camp, Dartmouth Castle, Grimspound, Hound Tor Deserted Medieval Village, Kirkham House, Lydford Castle and Saxon Town, Merrivale Prehistoric Settlement, Okehampton Castle, Royal Citadel (Plymouth), Totnes Castle, Upper Plym Valley

Dorset
Abbotsbury Abbey Remains, Christchurch Castle and Norman House, Fiddleford Manor, Jordan Hill Roman Temple, Kingston Russell Stone Circle, Knowlton Church and Earthworks, Lulworth Castle, Maiden Castle, The Nine Stones, Portland Castle, St Catherine's Chapel, Sherborne Old Castle, Winterbourne Poor Lot Barrows

Gloucestershire
Belas Knap Long Barrow, Blackfriars, Cirencester Amphitheatre, Great Witcombe Roman Villa, Greyfriars, Hailes Abbey, Kingswood Abbey Gatehouse, Notgrove Long Barrow, Nympsfield Long Barrow, Odda's Chapel, Offa's Dyke, Over Bridge, St Briavel's Castle, St Mary's Church, Uley Long Barrow (Hetty Pegler's Tump), Windmill Tump Long Barrow

Isles of Scilly
Bant's Carn Burial Chamber and Halangy Down Ancient Village, Cromwell's Castle, Garrison Walls, Harry's Walls, Innisidgen Lower and Upper Burial Chambers, King Charles's Castle, Old Blockhouse, Porth Hellick Down Burial Chamber

Somerset
Butter Cross, Cleeve Abbey, Farleigh Hungerford Castle, Gallox Bridge, Glastonbury Tribunal, Meare Fish House, Muchelney Abbey, Nunney Castle, Yarn Market

Wiltshire
Alexander Keiller Museum, Avebury, Avebury Stone Circles, Bradford-on-Avon Tithe Barn, Bratton Camp and White Horse, Chisbury Chapel, Hatfield Earthworks, Ludgershall Castle and Cross, Netheravon Dovecote, Old Sarum, Old Wardour Castle, The Sanctuary, Silbury Hill, Stonehenge, West Kennet Avenue, West Kennet Long Barrow, Windmill Hill, Woodhenge

Comprehensive map of our sites Page 264-265

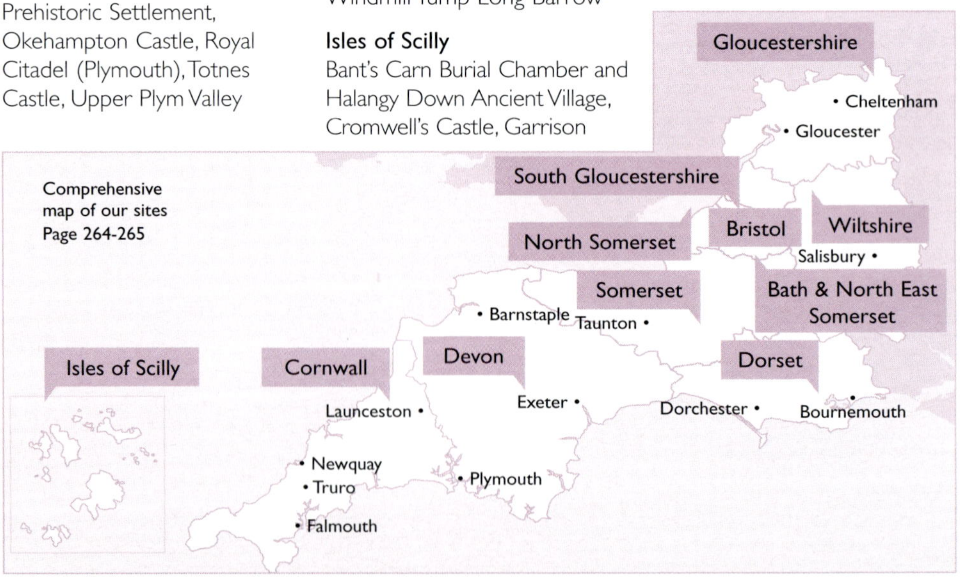

Stonehenge – see page 106

Varied Treasures

The South West region stretches from the Gloucestershire Cotswolds, via Wiltshire, Bristol, Somerset and Dorset, through Devon to Land's End in Cornwall, and beyond to the Isles of Scilly. It contains more (and perhaps more extensively varied) individual sites than any other English Heritage region.

Undoubtedly the most internationally renowned of these are the great prehistoric monuments of the **Stonehenge** and **Avebury** complexes, a World Heritage Site. The South West indeed is without rival for the richness of its visible and visitable prehistory, ranging from the distinctive monuments of Cornwall and the **Scillies** – including villages and 'fogou' passages – through the clustering sites of **Dartmoor**, to the 'long barrows' of the Cotswold-Severn area, so often dramatically positioned. Some of these ancient sites (like **Stanton Drew Circles** or **Silbury Hill** or **Hurlers Stone Circles**) are outstandingly impressive: others unobtrusively 'bide their time off serpentine green lanes.' All preserve the mystery of their precise original use and purpose, save that they were connected with beliefs we can now only guess at.

The South West is likewise rich in Christian religious sites, notably the monasteries of **Cleeve Abbey** with its wonderfully complete cloister buildings; **Hailes Abbey**; and **Muchelney Abbey** with its abbot's lodging, a medieval manor house in miniature and a companion for **Fiddleford Manor** and **Kirkham House** in Paignton.

Many of the region's sites have more warlike origins: the mighty Iron Age hillfort of **Maiden Castle** has many successors in the South West's fine array of medieval castles. Cornwall boasts **Launceston**, **Restormel** and legend-haunted **Tintagel Castles**; Devon romantically-sited **Berry Pomeroy**, **Okehampton** and **Totnes Castles**. Dorset has **Sherborne Old Castle**; Somerset holds **Nunney Castle** and **Farleigh Hungerford Castle**, with its lurid family history; there are **Old Wardour Castle** and the fascinating multi-period fortress of **Old Sarum** in Wiltshire; and **St Briavels Castle** in Gloucestershire.

Nor did fortress-building end with the Middle Ages in the South West, whose long coast remained vulnerable to invaders until the 20th century. **Dartmouth Castle**, the first purpose-built artillery fort in England, was succeeded by Henry VIII's coastal castles – including **Pendennis**, **St Mawes** and **Portland Castles**, themselves frequently updated as recently as World War II. But this introduction can only summarise the South West's varied treasures: English Heritage members are recommended to turn to the site gazetteer, or better still visit the sites themselves.

Avebury

Wiltshire

Avebury rivals – some would say exceeds – Stonehenge as the largest, most impressive and most complex prehistoric site in Britain. Built and altered over many centuries from about 2850 BC – 2200 BC, it now appears as a huge circular bank and ditch, enclosing an area of 28.5 acres (11.5 hectares), including part of Avebury village. Within this 'henge' ditch is an inner circle of great standing stones, enclosing two more stone circles, each with a central feature.

The site's present appearance owes much to the marmalade-heir Alexander Keiller, who excavated and re-erected many stones during the 1930s, and whose archaeological collections are displayed in the nearby museum. Associated with pagan devil-worship, many stones had been broken or buried in medieval and later times, one crushing its destroyer as it fell.

Avebury did not stand alone either, being linked to several other Neolithic ritual sites in English Heritage care. West Kennet Avenue joined it to The Sanctuary, and another stone avenue connected it with Beckhampton. West Kennet Long Barrow and Windmill Hill are also nearby, as is huge and mysterious Silbury Hill. This extraordinary assemblage of sites seemingly formed a huge 'sacred landscape', whose use and purpose can still only be guessed at. Avebury and its surroundings have, with Stonehenge, achieved international recognition as a World Heritage Site.

Managed by The National Trust.

Avebury Stone Circles

Originally erected 4,500 years ago, many of the stones were located and re-erected in the 1930s by Alexander Keiller. The Circles and henge encircle part of the village.

Part of the Avebury World Heritage Site. Owned and managed by The National Trust.

OPENING TIMES

Any reasonable time

Usual facilities may not be available around the Summer Solstice 20-22 June. Please check before you visit

HOW TO FIND US

Direction: 7 miles W of Marlborough

Train: Pewsey 10 miles; Swindon 11 miles

Bus: Stagecoach in Swindon/First 49 Swindon – Trowbridge; Wilts & Dorset 5/6 Salisbury – Swindon (all services pass close to ⇌ Swindon)

Avebury Stone Circles

Parking (Visitor car park free to EH members. S of Avebury off A4361. Free disabled visitors' parking in village car park).

MAP Page 265 (3J)
OS Map 173 (ref SU 099700)

Alexander Keiller Museum, Avebury

Wiltshire – SN8 1RF

One of the most important prehistoric archaeological collections in Britain. The admission fee includes access to The National Trust's Barn Gallery – an interpretation gallery using interactive exhibits and CD-ROMs to tell the story of the landscape and its people over the past 6,000 years.

Part of the Avebury World Heritage Site. The museum collection is managed by The National Trust.

NON-MEMBERS	
Adult	£4.20
Child	£2.10

OPENING TIMES	
1 Apr-31 Oct	10am-6pm
1 Nov-31 Mar	10am-4pm
Closed	24-25 Dec

HOW TO FIND US

Direction: In Avebury, 7 miles W of Marlborough

Train: Pewsey 10 miles; Swindon 11 miles

Bus: Stagecoach in Swindon/ First 49 Swindon – Trowbridge; Wilts & Dorset 5/6 Salisbury – Swindon (all services pass close to ⇌ Swindon)

Parking (visitor car park free to EH members. S of Avebury off A4361. Free disabled visitors' parking in village car park).

MAP Page 265 (3J)
OS Map 173 (ref SU 099700)

Abbotsbury Abbey Remains

Dorset

Part of a monastic building, perhaps the abbot's lodging, of Benedictine Abbotsbury abbey. St Catherine's Chapel (see p.101) is within half a mile.

OPENING TIMES

Any reasonable time

HOW TO FIND US

Direction: Located in Abbotsbury, off B3157, near a churchyard

Train: Upwey 7½ miles

Bus: First X53 Poole – Exeter (passes close to ≡ Weymouth)

Parking (charged).

MAP Page 265 (5H)
OS Map 194 (ref SY 578852)

Alexander Keiller Museum, Avebury

See opposite page

Avebury & Avebury Stone Circles

See opposite page

Ballowall Barrow

Cornwall

In a spectacular cliff-edge position, this large Bronze Age chambered tomb had a long and complex history as a sacred site. Seen as excavated by the Victorians.
Managed by The National Trust.

OPENING TIMES

Any reasonable time

HOW TO FIND US

Direction: 1 mile W of St Just, near Carn Gloose

Train: Penzance 8 miles

Bus: First 17/A Penzance – St Just, then 1 mile

MAP Page 264 (7A)
OS Map 203 (ref SW 355312)

Bayard's Cove Fort

Devon

A small early Tudor artillery fort, built to defend Dartmouth harbour entrance.

OPENING TIMES

Any reasonable time

HOW TO FIND US

Direction: Located in Dartmouth, on the riverside

Train: Paignton, 7 miles; Kingswear (Paignton & Dartmouth Railway) few minutes walk, both by ferry

Bus: Stagecoach in Devon 120 Paignton – Kingswear, then ferry to Dartmouth; First 111 Torquay – Dartmouth

MAP Page 265 (6F)
OS Map 202 (ref SX 879509)

Belas Knap Long Barrow

Gloucestershire

A particularly fine example of a Neolithic long barrow of c. 3000 BC, with the mound restored and surrounded by a stone wall. The tomb chambers, where the remains of 31 Stone Age people were found, have been opened up for visitors to view.

Managed by Gloucestershire County Council.

OPENING TIMES

Any reasonable time

HOW TO FIND US

Direction: Near Charlton Abbots; ½ mile on Cotswold Way

Train: Cheltenham 9 miles

Bus: Castleways from Cheltenham, to within 1¾ miles of site

MAP Page 265 (1J)
OS Map 163 (ref SP 021254)

Berry Pomeroy Castle

Devon – TQ9 6NJ

Tucked away in a steep wooded valley, Berry Pomeroy Castle is the perfect romantic ruin. Within the 15th-century defences of the Pomeroy family castle looms the dramatic four-storey shell of the great Elizabethan mansion of the Seymours. On the wall of the gatehouse chamber is a 15th-century painting of the Three Kings bearing gifts to Christ. The mansion was begun in c. 1560, and was massively enlarged in c. 1600, becoming the most spectacular house in Devon – a match for Audley End or Longleat. Abandoned by 1700, it became the focus of blood-curdling ghost stories, recounted in the audio tour. Tea shop: woodland walks from the car park (including steep tracks) provide fine views of the ruins from below.

NON-MEMBERS	
Adult	£3.60
Concession	£2.70
Child	£1.80

OPENING TIMES	
1 Apr-30 Jun, daily	10am-5pm
1 Jul-31 Aug, daily	10am-6pm
1-30 Sep, daily	10am-5pm
1-31 Oct, daily	10am-4pm

Berry Pomeroy Castle

HOW TO FIND US

Direction: 2½ miles E of Totnes off A385

Train: Totnes 3½ miles

Bus: First 111 Torquay – Dartmouth (passes ⇌ Totnes)

Tel: 01803 866618

OVP

Disabled access (grounds and ground floor only).

Parking (no coach access), at end of long drive (approx ¾ mile).

Tearoom (not managed by EH).

MAP Page 265 (6F)
OS Map 202 (ref SX 839623)

Blackbury Camp

Devon

An Iron Age hillfort with impressive ramparts, now surrounded by woodland.

OPENING TIMES

Any reasonable time

HOW TO FIND US

Direction: Off B3174/A3052

Train: Honiton 6½ miles

MAP Page 265 (5G)
OS Map 173 (ref ST 823604)

Blackfriars, Gloucester

Gloucestershire

One of the most complete surviving friaries of Dominican 'black friars' in England, later converted into a Tudor house and cloth factory. Notable features include the church and the fine scissor-braced dormitory roof.

ENTRY

Non-Member	£3.50
EH Members and Children	£3.00

Blackfriars, Gloucester

OPENING TIMES

Access by guided tour only

Jul-Aug, Sun	3pm
Heritage Open Days (Free), 9-10 Sep	12.30pm & 3pm

HOW TO FIND US

Direction: In Blackfriars Lane, off Ladybellegate St, off Southgate St, Gloucester

Train: Gloucester ½ mile

Bus: From surrounding areas

Parking (adjacent. Charge applies, not managed by EH).

MAP Page 265 (2J)
OS Map 163 (ref SP 021254)

Bradford-On-Avon Tithe Barn

Wiltshire

A spectacular 14th-century monastic stone barn, 51 metres (168 ft) long, with an amazing timber-cruck roof.

OPENING TIMES

Daily	10.30am-4pm
Closed	25 Dec

HOW TO FIND US

Direction: Located ½ mile S of town centre off B3109

Train: Bradford-on-Avon ¼ mile

Bus: First/Wilts & Dorset X4/5 Bath – Salisbury

Parking (adjacent, not managed by EH - charge applies).

MAP Page 265 (3H)
OS Map 173 (ref ST 823604)

Bratton Camp and White Horse

Wiltshire

Below an Iron Age hillfort, enclosing a much earlier long barrow, stands the Westbury White Horse. Cut into the hillside in 1778, this replaced an older horse, possibly commemorating King Alfred's nearby victory over the Vikings.

OPENING TIMES

Any reasonable time

HOW TO FIND US

Direction: 2 miles E of Westbury off B3098, 1 mile SW of Bratton

Train: Westbury 3 miles

Bus: First 87/8 Trowbridge – Devizes (passes ⇌ Westbury)

MAP Page 265 (3J)
OS Map 173 (ref ST 823604)

Butter Cross, Dunster

Somerset

The transplanted stump of a medieval stone cross, once a meeting-place for butter-sellers. Gallox Bridge and the Yarn Market are nearby.

Managed by The National Trust.

OPENING TIMES

Any reasonable time

HOW TO FIND US

Direction: Beside minor road to Alcombe, 350 metres (400 yards) NW of Dunster parish church

Train: Dunster (West Somerset Railway) 1 mile

Bus: First 28 ⇌ Taunton – Minehead; 38 from Minehead to within ½ mile

MAP Page 265 (4F)
OS Map 173 (ref ST 823604)

Carn Euny Ancient Village

Cornwall

Among the best preserved ancient villages in the south-west, occupied from Iron Age until late Roman times. It includes the foundations of stone houses, and an intriguing 'fogou' underground passage.

Managed by the Cornwall Heritage Trust.

OPENING TIMES

Any reasonable time

HOW TO FIND US

Direction: 1¼ miles SW of Sancreed off A30

Train: Penzance 6 miles

Bus: First 17/A Penzance – St Just, to within 2 miles of the site

Parking (600 metres (660 yards) away in Brane).

MAP Page 264 (7A)
OS Map 2033 (ref SW 402288)

Chisbury Chapel

Wiltshire

A pretty thatched and flint-walled 13th-century chapel, later used as a barn.

OPENING TIMES

Any reasonable time

HOW TO FIND US

Direction: Off unclassified road, ¼ mile E of Chisbury, off A4; 6 miles E of Marlborough

Train: Bedwyn 1 mile

MAP Page 265 (3K)
OS Map 174 (ref SU 280660)

Christchurch Castle and Norman House

Dorset

The remains of Christchurch Castle include parts of the mound-top keep, and more unusually the 12th-century riverside chamber block or 'Constable's House'. This very early example of domestic architecture includes a rare Norman chimney.

OPENING TIMES

Any reasonable time

HOW TO FIND US

Direction: Located in Christchurch, near the Priory

Train: Christchurch ¾ mile

Bus: From surrounding areas

MAP Page 265 (5K)
OS Map 195 (ref SZ 160927)

Chysauster Ancient Village

Cornwall – TR20 8XA

This Iron Age settlement was originally occupied almost 2,000 years ago. The village consisted of eight stone-walled homesteads known as 'courtyard houses', found only on the Land's End peninsula and the Isles of Scilly. The houses line a 'village street', and each had an open central courtyard surrounded by a number of thatched rooms. There are also the remains of an enigmatic 'fogou' underground passage.

NON-MEMBERS

Adult	£2.40
Concession	£1.80
Child	£1.20

Chysauster Ancient Village

OPENING TIMES

1 Apr-30 Jun, daily	10am-5pm
1 Jul-31 Aug, daily	10am-6pm
1-30 Sep, daily	10am-5pm
1-31 Oct, daily	10am-4pm

HOW TO FIND US

Direction: Located 2½ miles NW of Gulval, off B3311

Train: Penzance 3½ miles

Bus: First 16 Penzance – St Ives, to within 1½ miles

Tel: 07831 757934

OVP

MAP Page 264 (7B)
OS Map 203 (ref SW 472350)

Cirencester Amphitheatre

Gloucestershire

The earthwork remains of one of the largest Roman amphitheatres in Britain, built in the early 2nd century. It served the Roman city of Corinium (now Cirencester), then second only in size and importance to London, and had a capacity of around 8,000 spectators. Later fortified against Saxon invaders.

OPENING TIMES

Any reasonable time

HOW TO FIND US

Direction: Located W of Cirencester, next to the bypass. Access from the town, or along Chesterton Lane from the W end of the bypass, on to Cotswold Ave

Train: Kemble 4 miles

Bus: Stagecoach in the Cotswolds 881/Beaumont 55 from Kemble; Beaumont 55 from Moreton-in-Marsh

MAP Page 265 (2J)
OS Map 163 (ref SP 020014)

Dartmouth Castle

Photo: Peter Anderson

Dartmouth Castle

Devon – TQ6 0JN

This well-preserved and beautifully sited castle juts out into the narrow entrance of the Dart Estuary.

Begun in the late 14th century, a defence called 'the Fortalice' was intended to protect the homes of Dartmouth merchants from shipborne attack. By 1491 it had been reinforced by a gun tower, probably the very first fortification in England purpose-built to mount heavy cannon.

It is said that Chaucer based the 'Shipman' character in his *Canterbury Tales* on John Hawley – the colourful merchant and Mayor of Dartmouth who began the first castle. Today, you can enjoy other tales of the castle as you journey through time from the Tudor period and the Civil War to World War II. Displays on the castle's 600-year history add to the experience.

Make it a full day out. Why not take a boat trip from the quayside at Dartmouth, which lands you just a short walk from the castle entrance.

www.english-heritage.org.uk/dartmouthcastle

NON-MEMBERS	
Adult	£3.70
Concession	£2.80
Child	£1.90

OPENING TIMES	
1 Apr-30 Jun, daily	10am-5pm
1 Jul-31 Aug, daily	10am-6pm
1-30 Sep, daily	10am-5pm
1-31 Oct, daily	10am-4pm
1 Nov-31Mar, Sat-Sun	10am-4pm
Closed	24-26 Dec and 1 Jan

HOW TO FIND US

Direction: 1 mile SE of Dartmouth off B3205, narrow approach road

Train: Paignton 8 miles via ferry

Bus: Stagecoach in Devon 120 Paignton – Kingswear, then a ferry to Dartmouth; First 111 Torquay – Dartmouth (passing Totnes). On both, alight Dartmouth, then 1 mile walk or ferry to site

Tel: 01803 833588

Local Tourist Information Dartmouth Tel: 01803 834224

OVP

Parking (not owned by EH, small charge).
Tearooms (not managed by EH).
Toilets (not managed by EH).

MAP Page 265 (6F)
OS Map 202 (ref SX 887503)

Cleeve Abbey

Somerset – TA23 0PS

The picturesque Cistercian abbey of Cleeve boasts the most impressively complete and unaltered set of monastic cloister buildings in England, standing roofed and two storeys high. They include the gatehouse, the 15th-century refectory with its glorious angel roof, an unusual 'painted chamber', and now protected, the floor of an earlier refectory, decked from end to end with 13th-century heraldic tiles. The great dormitory is one of the finest examples in the country: beneath it are the vaulted warming room, and the sacristy with more early 13th-century tilework and decoration.

Displays interpret the features of monastic life, while the exhibition 'Our Painted Past' illustrates wall-paintings from English Heritage properties throughout the country.

www.english-heritage.org.uk/cleeve

NON-MEMBERS

Adult	£3.40
Concession	£2.60
Child	£1.70

OPENING TIMES

1 Apr-30 Jun, daily	10am-5pm
1 Jul-31 Aug, daily	10am-6pm
1-30 Sep, daily	10am-5pm
1-31Oct, daily	10am-4pm
Closed	1 Nov-31 Mar

Cleeve Abbey

HOW TO FIND US

Direction: Located in Washford, ¼ mile S of A39

Train: Washford ½ mile (West Somerset Railway)

Bus: First 28 Taunton – Minehead; 38 from Minehead

Tel: 01984 640377

OVP

Disabled access (grounds & ground floor only, plus toilet).

Dogs on leads (restricted areas only).

MAP Page 265 (4F)
OS Map 181 (ref ST 047407)

Dartmouth Castle

See feature opposite

Dupath Well

Cornwall

This charming and almost complete well-house of c. 1500 stands over an ancient holy well, believed to cure whooping cough. Built of granite blocks, it houses the remains of an immersion bath for cure-seekers.

Managed by the Cornwall Heritage Trust.

OPENING TIMES

Any reasonable time

HOW TO FIND US

Direction: 1 mile E of Callington off A388

Train: Gunnislake 4½ miles

Bus: First 76 Plymouth – Launceston, then 1 mile

MAP Page 264 (6D)
OS Map 201 (ref SX 375692)

Farleigh Hungerford Castle

Somerset – BA2 7RS

Farleigh Hungerford was begun in the 1370s by Sir Thomas Hungerford, Speaker of the Commons, and extended in the 15th century by his son Walter, Lord Hungerford, Agincourt veteran and distinguished medieval statesman. The remains of their fortress, built in the most up-to-date and fashionable quadrangular style of the time, include two tall corner towers, along with a walled outer court incorporating a complete castle chapel and attendant priest's house.

Crowded with fine family monuments and bedecked with wall paintings, the chapel stands above a crypt where the lead coffins of 16th and 17th-century Hungerfords are still visible. These have 'death masks' of the deceased indented into them, and are probably the best examples of their type in Britain. The colourful Hungerford family included two members executed during the Wars of the Roses and another – who imprisoned his wife here for four years – beheaded for alleged treason and witchcraft by Henry VIII. One Lady Hungerford was hanged for murdering her first husband and burning his body in the castle's kitchen oven, another was charged with adultery and attempted poisoning.

The chequered history of Farleigh and its owners is told in new interpretation panels, extensive new displays in the Priests' House, and a new audio tour. Much improved facilities for disabled visitors include a touch-screen virtual tour, while new family and educational facilities include a 'book box', a schools base and examples of historic costumes.

www.english-heritage.org.uk/farleighhungerford

NON-MEMBERS

Adult	£3.50
Concession	£2.60
Child	£1.80

OPENING TIMES

1 Apr-30 Jun, daily	10am-5pm
1 Jul-31 Aug, daily	10am-6pm
1-30 Sep, daily	10am-5pm
1-31 Oct, daily	10am-4pm
1 Nov-31 Mar, Sat & Sun	10am-4pm
Closed	24-26 Dec & 1 Jan

HOW TO FIND US

Direction: In Farleigh Hungerford, 9 miles SE of Bath; 3½ miles W of Trowbridge on A366

Train: Avoncliffe 2 miles; Trowbridge 3½ miles

Bus: Bodmans 96 from Trowbridge (passes close to ⇌ Trowbridge) then 1½ mile

Tel: 01225 754026

OVP

Disabled access (Chapel and Priest's House, ground floor only. Disabled toilet).

New guidebook (2006).

MAP Page 265 (3H)
OS Map 173 (ref ST 801576)

Fiddleford Manor

Dorset

The principal parts of a small stone manor house, probably begun c. 1370 for William Latimer, Sheriff of Somerset and Dorset. The hall and solar chamber display outstandingly fine timber roofs.

Please note
The adjoining building is a private residence and is not open to visitors.

OPENING TIMES

1 Apr-30 Sep, daily	10am-6pm
1 Oct-31 Mar, daily	10am-4pm
Closed	24-26 Dec and 1 Jan

HOW TO FIND US

Direction: 1 mile E of Sturminster Newton off A357

Bus: Damory 310 from Blandford

Disabled access (ground floor only – with 1 step).

Parking (no coach access).

MAP Page 265 (4H)
OS Map 162 (ref ST 801136)

Gallox Bridge, Dunster

Somerset

This ancient stone bridge – originally 'gallows bridge'– once carried packhorses bringing fleeces to Dunster market. The Yarn Market and Butter Cross are nearby.

Managed by The National Trust.

OPENING TIMES

Any reasonable time

HOW TO FIND US

Direction: Located off A396 at the S end of Dunster village

Train: Dunster ¾ mile (West Somerset Railway)

Bus: First 28 ⇌ Taunton – Minehead, also 38 from Minehead, to within ¼ mile of site

MAP Page 265 (4F)
OS Map 181 (ref SS 989432)

Glastonbury Tribunal

Somerset – BA6 9DP

A fine late 15th-century stone town house, with an early Tudor façade and panelled interiors. Now contains a Tourist Information Centre and the Glastonbury Lake Village Museum.

Managed by Glastonbury Tribunal Ltd.

NON-MEMBERS – MUSEUM

Adult	£2.00
Concession	£1.50
Child	£1.50
Senior	£1.00

OPENING TIMES

1 Apr-30 Sep,	Sun-Thu	10am-5pm
	Fri-Sat	10am-5.30pm
1 Oct-31 Mar,	Sun-Thu	10am-4pm
	Fri-Sat	10am-4.30pm
Closed		25-26 Dec and 1 Jan

HOW TO FIND US

Direction: In Glastonbury High St

Bus: First 375/6 ⇌ Bristol Temple Meads – Street

Tel: 01458 832954

Disabled access (ground floor – 2 steps).

Parking (charged).

MAP Page 265 (4H)
OS Map 182 (ref ST 499389)

Great Witcombe Roman Villa

Gloucestershire

The remains of a large and luxurious villa built c. AD 250, with a bathhouse complex and possibly the shrine of a water spirit.

OPENING TIMES

Exterior: Reasonable daylight hours

HOW TO FIND US

Direction: Located 5 miles SE of Gloucester off A46; ½ mile S of reservoir in Witcombe Park; 400 metres (440 yards) from Cotswold Way National Trail

Train: Gloucester 6 miles

Bus: Stagecoach in Gloucester 10 from Gloucester, to within 1½ miles of site

Parking (no access for coaches. No parking permitted in the lane to or beyond the car park).

MAP Page 265 (2J)
OS Map 163 (ref SO 899142)

Greyfriars, Gloucester

Gloucestershire

Substantial remains of an early Tudor friary church of Franciscan 'grey friars'.

OPENING TIMES

Any reasonable time

HOW TO FIND US

Direction: On Greyfriars Walk

Train: Gloucester ½ mile

Bus: From surrounding areas

MAP Page 265 (2J)
OS Map 162 (ref SO 832184)

Grimspound

Devon

The best known of many Dartmoor prehistoric settlements, Grimspound dates from the late Bronze Age. The remains of 24 stone houses survive within a massive boundary wall.

Managed by Dartmoor National Park Authority.

OPENING TIMES

Any reasonable time

HOW TO FIND US

Direction: 6 miles SW of Moretonhampstead, off B3212

Bus: First 82 Exeter St David's – Plymouth, to within 2 miles of the site

MAP Page 264 (5E)
OS Map 191 (ref SX 701809)

Hailes Abbey

Gloucestershire – GL54 5PB

The Cistercian abbey of Hailes was founded in 1246 by Richard of Cornwall, in thanksgiving for deliverance from shipwreck, and dissolved on Christmas Eve 1539. Though never housing large numbers of monks, it had

extensive and elaborate buildings, financed by pilgrims visiting its renowned relic, 'the Holy Blood of Hailes' – allegedly a phial of Christ's own blood. Sculptures, stonework and other site finds are displayed in the museum: an audio tour helps you to learn even more about the site. The adjacent parish church has medieval wall paintings. Plant sales throughout the season.

www.english-heritage.org.uk/hailes

Owned by The National Trust, managed and maintained by English Heritage.

NON-MEMBERS

Adult	£3.30
Concession	£2.50
Child	£1.70

National Trust members admitted free, but charged for audio tours (£1.50) and special events

OPENING TIMES

1 Apr-30 Jun, daily	10am-5pm
1 Jul-31 Aug, daily	10am-6pm
1-30 Sep, daily	10am-5pm
1-31 Oct, daily	10am-4pm
Closed	1 Nov-31 Mar

HOW TO FIND US

Direction: 2 miles NE of Winchcombe off B4632. On the Cotswold Way National Trail

Train: Cheltenham 10 miles

Bus: Castleways from Cheltenham, to within 1½ miles of site

Tel: 01242 602398

OVP

Audio tours (also for visually impaired and those with learning difficulties).

Disabled access (ramp to museum, disabled toilet).

MAP Page 265 (1J)
OS Map 150 (ref SP 050300)

Halliggye Fogou

Cornwall

Roofed and walled in stone, this complex of passages is the largest and best-preserved of several mysterious underground tunnels associated with Cornish Iron Age settlements. The purpose of such 'fogous' – a Cornish-language word meaning 'cave' – is unknown: refuges, storage chambers or ritual shrines have all been suggested.

Free entry to the fogou. Entry to the rest of the Trelowarren Estate is charged.

Managed by the Trelowarren Estate.

OPENING TIMES

Reasonable daylight hours Apr-Oct, but completely blocked Nov-Mar, inclusive

HOW TO FIND US

Direction: 5 miles SE of Helston off B3293. E of Garras on Trelowarren Estate

Train: Penryn 10 miles

Bus: Truronian T2/3 from Truro

Parking (free to members producing a membership card).

Visitors are advised to bring a torch.

MAP Page 264 (7B)
OS Map 203 (ref SW 713239)

Hatfield Earthworks

Wiltshire

The earthworks of a Neolithic henge and monumental mound, by a loop in the River Avon.

OPENING TIMES

Any reasonable time

HOW TO FIND US

Direction: 5½ miles SE of Devizes, off A342; NE of village of Marden

Hatfield Earthworks

Train: Pewsey 5 miles

MAP Page 265 (3J)
OS Map 173 (ref SU 092583)

Hound Tor Deserted Medieval Village

Devon

The remains of four 13th-century stone farmsteads, on land originally farmed in the Bronze Age. This isolated Dartmoor hamlet was probably abandoned in the early 15th century.

Managed by the Dartmoor National Park Authority.

OPENING TIMES

Any reasonable time

HOW TO FIND US

Direction: 1½ miles S of Manaton, ½ mile from the Ashburton road

Parking (½ mile walk across moor to monument).

MAP Page 264 (5E)
OS Map 191 (ref SX 746788)

Hurlers Stone Circles

Cornwall

Three fine late Neolithic or early Bronze Age stone circles arranged in a line, a grouping unique in England. Probably the best examples of ceremonial circles in the south west, they are traditionally the remains of men petrified for playing 'hurling' on a Sunday.

Managed by the Cornwall Heritage Trust.

OPENING TIMES

Any reasonable time

HOW TO FIND US

Direction: Located ½ mile NW of Minions, off B3254

Hurlers Stone Circles

Train: Liskeard 7 miles

MAP Page 264 (6D)
OS Map 201 (ref SX 258714)

Jordan Hill Roman Temple

Dorset

The foundations of a 4th-century Romano-Celtic temple.

OPENING TIMES

Any reasonable time

HOW TO FIND US

Direction: Located 2 miles NE of Weymouth, off A353

Train: Upwey or Weymouth, both 2 miles

Bus: First 4/A, 31, 500/3, from Weymouth

MAP Page 265 (5H)
OS Map 194 (ref SY 699821)

King Doniert's Stone

Cornwall

Two richly carved pieces of a 9th-century 'Celtic' cross, with an inscription commemorating Dumgarth, British King of Dumnonia, who drowned c. AD 875.

Managed by the Cornwall Heritage Trust.

OPENING TIMES

Any reasonable time

HOW TO FIND US

Direction: 1 mile NW of St Cleer, off B3254

Train: Liskeard 7 miles

Bus: Western Greyhound 573 Callington-Looe (passing Liskeard) to within ½ mile

Parking (in lay-by).

MAP Page 264 (6D)
OS Map 201 (ref SX 236688)

Kingston Russell Stone Circle

Dorset

A late Neolithic or early Bronze Age circle of 18 fallen stones, on a hilltop overlooking Abbotsbury and the sea.

OPENING TIMES

Any reasonable time

HOW TO FIND US

Direction: Located 2 miles N of Abbotsbury; 1 mile along a footpath off a minor road to Hardy Monument

Train: Dorchester South or West, both 8 miles

Limited parking on road verge at access to farm. Access to Stone Circle on foot only via public footpaths, off minor roads. 1¾ miles, no off-road vehicle access.

MAP Page 265 (5H)
OS Map 194 (ref SY 578878)

Kingswood Abbey Gatehouse

Gloucestershire

This 16th-century gatehouse, one of the latest monastic buildings in England, displays a richly sculpted mullioned window. It is the sole survivor of this Cistercian abbey.

OPENING TIMES

Exterior: any reasonable time

Interior: key available from 3 Wotton Road, Abbey St 10am-3.30pm weekdays only

HOW TO FIND US

Direction: In Kingswood, off B4060; 1 mile SW of Wotton-under-Edge

Train: Yate 8 miles

Bus: First 309 Bristol – Dursley

Public toilets near to monument.

MAP Page 265 (2H)
OS Map 162 (ref ST 747920)

Kirkham House, Paignton

Devon

This late medieval stone house, afterwards split into three cottages, was restored in the 1960s. Furnished with modern furniture, illustrating traditional craftsmanship and the original use of the rooms.

Guided tours of medieval Paignton available on open days: first at 2.15pm, thereafter on request.

Managed in association with the Paignton Preservation & Local History Society.

OPENING TIMES

14 Apr, 17 Apr, 1 May, 29 May, 28 Aug and every Sun in Jul-Aug 2pm-5pm

Heritage Open Days 9-10 Sep 11am-4pm

HOW TO FIND US

Direction: Located in Kirkham St, off Cecil Rd, Paignton

Train: Paignton ½ mile

Bus: From surrounding areas

MAP Page 265 (6F)
OS Map 202 (ref SX 885610)

Knowlton Church and Earthworks

Dorset

The siting of this ruined medieval church at the centre of a Neolithic ritual henge earthwork symbolises the transition from pagan to Christian worship.

OPENING TIMES

Any reasonable time

HOW TO FIND US

Direction: SW of Cranborne on B3078

MAP Page 265 (4J)
OS Map 195 (ref SU 024103)

Launceston Castle

Cornwall – PL15 7DR

Launceston Castle's keep is set on the high motte of a stronghold built soon after the Norman Conquest. Its North gate was famously used as a gaol for George Fox during the reign of Charles II. As the venue for the county assizes and gaol, the castle witnessed the trials and hangings of numerous criminals. The last execution was in 1821. A hands-on display at the castle traces 1,000 years of history, with finds from site excavations.

NON-MEMBERS

Adult	£2.30
Concession	£1.70
Child	£1.20

OPENING TIMES

1 Apr-30 Jun, daily	10am-5pm
1 Jul-31 Aug, daily	10am-6pm
1-30 Sep, daily	10am-5pm
1-31 Oct, daily	10am-4pm
Closed	1 Nov-31 Mar

HOW TO FIND US

Direction: In Launceston

Bus: First X8, 76 Plymouth – Bude

Tel: 01566 772365

OVP

Disabled access (outer bailey).

MAP Page 264 (5D)
OS Map 201 (ref SX 331846)

Ludgershall Castle and Cross

Wiltshire

The ruins and earthworks of a royal castle dating mainly from the 12th and 13th centuries, frequently used as a hunting lodge. The remains of the medieval cross stand in the centre of the village.

OPENING TIMES

Any reasonable time

HOW TO FIND US

Direction: Located on the N side of Ludgershall, off A342

Train: Andover 7 miles

Bus: Stagecoach in Hampshire/ Wilts & Dorset 7-9 Andover – Salisbury

Disabled access (part of site only and village cross).

Parking (limited).

MAP Page 265 (3K)
OS Map 184 (ref SU 264512)

Lulworth Castle

Dorset – BH20 5QS

A 17th-century hunting lodge set in extensive parkland. Following a fire in 1929, the exterior has been restored to its former glory: the walls, interior and displays revealing past secrets. Stunning views across the World Heritage Coast.

Owned and managed by the Lulworth Estate.

Lulworth Castle

ENTRY

Adult	£7.00 (£8.50)*
Concession	£6.00 (£7.00)*
Child	£4.00 (£4.50)*
(Children under 5 go free)	

(*Bracketed figure indicates entry fee for jousting season: 23 Jul-28 Aug inclusive)

Family ticket	
(2 adults and 3 children)	£21.00
(1 adult and 3 children)	£14.00

Only the castle is free to members. Half-price admission to the Chapel, Woodland Walk, Play Area, Animal Farm and Park.

Members will be charged full entry price for special event days : 15-17 Apr, 30 Apr-1 May, 28/29 May, 29/30 Jul. During the jousting season (23 Jul-28 Aug), half-price admission is on offer to members for the whole estate and joust.

Available for corporate hire, wedding ceremonies and celebrations. Please call the Castle and ask for the Wedding Organiser.

OPENING TIMES

26 Mar-29 Sep, Sun-Fri 10.30am-6pm

1 Oct-23 Mar, Sun-Fri 10.30am-4pm

Closed 24-25 Dec and on Saturdays throughout the year except Easter weekend and 7-20 Jan 2007

HOW TO FIND US

Direction: Located in E Lulworth off B3070; 3 miles NE of Lulworth Cove

Train: Wool 4 miles

Bus: First 103 Wool – Dorchester

Tel: 0845 450 1054

Disabled access (limited).

Cafe (not managed by EH).

MAP Page 265 (5J)
OS Map 194 (ref SY 853822)

Lydford Castle and Saxon Town

Devon

Beautifully sited on the fringe of Dartmoor, Lydford boasts three defensive features. Near the centre is a 13th-century tower keep on a mound, later a prison notorious for harsh punishments – 'the most annoyous, contagious and detestable place within this realm.' To the south is an earlier Norman earthwork castle: to the north, Saxon town defences.

Managed by The National Trust.

OPENING TIMES

Any reasonable time

HOW TO FIND US

Direction: In Lydford off A386; 8 miles S of Okehampton

Bus: First 86 Plymouth – Barnstaple (passes Plymouth)

MAP Page 264 (5E)
OS Map 201 (SX 509848)

Maiden Castle

Dorset

Among the largest and most complex Iron Age hillforts in Europe, Maiden Castle's huge multiple ramparts enclose an area equivalent to 50 football pitches, protecting several hundred residents. Excavations in the 1930s and 1980s revealed the site's 4000 year history, reaching its apogee at a time of inter-tribal rivalry in the 2nd century BC. They also produced dramatic evidence of the hillfort's final fall to Roman invaders in AD 44, including stores of sling-stones and the bones of a defender killed by a Roman ballista bolt.

OPENING TIMES

Any reasonable time

HOW TO FIND US

Direction: 2 miles S of Dorchester, off A354, N of bypass

Train: Dorchester South or West, both 2 miles

MAP Page 265 (5H)
OS Map 194 (ref SY 669884)

Meare Fish House

Somerset

The only surviving monastic fishery building in England, this housed the Abbot of Glastonbury's water bailiff and provided facilities for fish-salting and drying.

OPENING TIMES

Any reasonable time. Key available from Manor House farm

HOW TO FIND US

Direction: In Meare village, on B3151

Bus: First 668 Cheddar – Street

MAP Page 265 (4G)
OS Map 182 (ref ST 458417)

Merrivale Prehistoric Settlement

Devon

The remains of a Bronze Age settlement, side by side with a 'ritual landscape' of sacred sites – three stone rows, a stone circle, standing stones and burial cairns – probably constructed over a long period between c. 2500 BC – 1000 BC.

Managed by Dartmoor National Park Authority.

OPENING TIMES

Any reasonable time

HOW TO FIND US

Direction: 1 mile E of Merrivale

Train: Gunnislake 10 miles

Bus: DAC 98 Yelverton – Tavistock (with connections from Plymouth)

MAP Page 264 (6E)
OS Map 191 (ref SX 554748)

Muchelney Abbey

Somerset – TA10 0DG

Muchelney, the atmospheric and once-remote 'great island' amid the Somerset Levels, has many rewards for visitors. Beside the clearly laid out foundations of the wealthy medieval Benedictine abbey (and its Anglo-Saxon predecessor) stands a complete early Tudor house in miniature. Originally the abbots' lodgings, this charming building includes a magnificent great chamber with ornate fireplace, carved settle

and stained glass; two rooms with time-faded walls painted to resemble cloth hangings; and a pair of kitchens with fine timber roof. Parts of the richly decorated cloister walk and refectory are incorporated, and nearby is the thatched two-storey monks' lavatory, unique in Britain.

Plant sales throughout the season.

Exhibitions illustrate monastic life with a fascinating collection of site finds, including decorated tiles and stonework. Much improved facilities for disabled visitors include a touch-screen tour of less accessible areas.

www.english-heritage.org.uk/muchelney

The fine adjacent parish church and the medieval Priest's House are not managed by English Heritage.

NON-MEMBERS	
Adult	£3.20
Concession	£2.40
Child	£1.60

OPENING TIMES	
1 Apr-30 Jun, daily	10am-5pm
1 Jul-31 Aug, daily	10am-6pm
1-30 Sep, daily	10am-5pm
1-31 Oct, daily	10am-4pm
Closed	1 Nov-31 Mar

HOW TO FIND US

Direction: In Muchelney, 2 miles S of Langport via Huish Episcopi

Bus: First 54 Taunton – Yeovil to within 1 mile of site

Tel: 01458 250664

OVP

Disabled access (grounds and most of ground floor, adapted toilet).

MAP Page 265 (4G)
OS Map 193 (ref ST 429249)

Netheravon Dovecote

Wiltshire

A charming 18th-century brick dovecote, still with most of its 700 or more nesting boxes.

OPENING TIMES

Exterior viewing only

HOW TO FIND US

Direction: In Netheravon, 4½ miles N of Amesbury on A345

Train: Pewsey 9 miles, Grateley 11 miles

Bus: Wilts & Dorset 5/6 Salisbury – Swindon (passes close to Salisbury and Swindon)

MAP Page 265 (3J)
OS Map 184 (ref SU 147484)

Notgrove Long Barrow

Gloucestershire

A grassed-over Neolithic long barrow containing stone-lined burial chambers, on the crest of a high Cotswold ridge.

Managed by Gloucestershire County Council.

OPENING TIMES

Any reasonable time

HOW TO FIND US

Direction: Located 1½ miles NW of Notgrove, on A436

Bus: Pulham's Moreton-in-Marsh – Cheltenham (passes close to Moreton-in-Marsh)

MAP Page 265 (1J)
OS Map 163 (ref SP 096212)

Nunney Castle

reduced by Parliamentarian cannon in 1645: but not until Christmas Day 1910 did the gun-damaged portion of the wall collapse.

OPENING TIMES

Any reasonable time

HOW TO FIND US

Direction: Located in Nunney, 3½ miles SW of Frome, off A361 (no coach access)

Train: Frome 3½ miles

Bus: First 161/2 Frome – Wells

Disabled access (exterior only).

MAP Page 265 (3H)
OS Map 183 (ref ST 737457)

The Nine Stones

Dorset

A small prehistoric circle of nine standing stones constructed approx. 4,000 years ago, in a wooded glade. Winterbourne Poor Lot Barrows are nearby.

OPENING TIMES

Any reasonable time

HOW TO FIND US

Direction: 1½ miles SW of Winterbourne Abbas, on A35

Train: Weymouth 4½ miles

Bus: First 31 Weymouth – Axminster (passing Dorchester South)

Parking (in small lay-by opposite, next to barn).

Warning: cross road with care.

MAP Page 265 (5H)
OS Map 194 (ref SY 611904)

Nunney Castle

Somerset

The striking and picturesque moated castle of Nunney was built in the 1370s by Sir John de la Mere, who had seemingly served in the French wars. Certainly it was designed in the latest French style, resembling a miniature version of the famous Paris Bastille.

Held for the King during the Civil War, it was quickly

Nympsfield Long Barrow

Gloucestershire

A large Neolithic burial mound with spectacular vistas over the Severn Valley. Its internal burial chambers are uncovered for viewing.

Managed by Gloucestershire County Council.

OPENING TIMES

Any reasonable time

HOW TO FIND US

Direction: Located 1 mile NW of Nympsfield on B4066

Train: Stroud 5 miles

MAP Page 265 (2H)
OS Map 162 (ref SO 794013)

Odda's Chapel

Gloucestershire

One of the most complete surviving Saxon churches in England, this chapel was built in 1056 by Earl Odda, and rediscovered in 1865 subsumed into a farmhouse. Nearby is the equally famous Saxon parish church.

Managed by Deerhurst Parish Council.

OPENING TIMES

1 Apr-31 Oct, daily	10am-6pm
1 Nov-31 Mar, daily	10am-4pm
Closed	24-26 Dec and 1 Jan

HOW TO FIND US

Direction: Located in Deerhurst off B4213, at Abbots Court; SW of parish church

Train: Cheltenham 8 miles

Bus: Swanbrook 351 Gloucester-Upton-upon-Severn (passing close to Gloucester)

Parking (not EH, charges applies).

MAP Page 265 (1J)
OS Map 150 (ref SO 869298)

Offa's Dyke

Gloucestershire

A three-mile section of the great earthwork boundary dyke built along the Anglo-Welsh border by Offa, King of Mercia, probably during the 780s. This especially impressive wooded stretch includes the Devil's Pulpit, with fine views of Tintern Abbey.

Offa's Dyke

OPENING TIMES

Any reasonable time

HOW TO FIND US

Direction: Located 3 miles NE of Chepstow, off B4228. Via Forest Enterprise Tidenham car park, 1 mile walk (waymarked) down to The Devil's Pulpit on Offa's Dyke (access is suitable only for those wearing proper walking shoes and is not suitable for the very young, old or infirm)

Train: Chepstow 7 miles

Bus: Stagecoach in South Wales; Welcome 69 Chepstow – Monmouth, to within ½ mile

MAP Page 265 (2H)
OS Map 162 (ref SO 546011-ST 549975)

Okehampton Castle

Devon – EX20 1JB

The remains of the largest castle in Devon, in an outstandingly picturesque setting on a wooded spur above the rushing River Okement. Begun soon after the Norman Conquest as a motte and bailey castle with a stone keep, it was converted into a sumptuous residence in the 14th century by Hugh Courtenay, Earl of Devon, much of whose work survives. After the last Courtenay owner fell foul of Henry VIII in 1538, it declined into an allegedly haunted ruin. Riverside picnic area and woodland walks nearby.

Okehampton Castle

NON-MEMBERS

Adult	£3.00
Concession	£2.30
Child	£1.50

OPENING TIMES

1 Apr-30 Jun, daily	10am-5pm
1 Jul-31 Aug, daily	10am-6pm
1-30 Sep, daily	10am-5pm
Closed	1 Oct-31 Mar

HOW TO FIND US

Direction: Located 1 mile SW of Okehampton town centre

Train: Okehampton (summer Sundays only) ½ mile

Bus: First X9/10 Exeter – Bude; 86 Plymouth – Barnstaple

Tel: 01837 52844

OVP

Audio tours (also available for the visually impaired and those with learning difficulties).

MAP Page 264 (5E)
OS Map 191 (ref SX 583942)

Old Sarum

See feature – Page 98

Old Wardour Castle

See feature – Page 99

English Heritage properties turn any private or corporate function into a truly historic occasion. See page 16 for a list of properties which are available for hire.

Photo: Skyscan Balloon Photography

Old Sarum

Wiltshire – SP1 3SD

The great earthwork of Old Sarum stands near Salisbury on the edge of Wiltshire's chalk plains. Its mighty ramparts were raised in about 500 BC by Iron Age peoples, and later occupied by the Romans, the Saxons and, most importantly, the Normans.

William the Conqueror paid off his army here in 1070, and in 1086 summoned all the great landowners of England here to swear an oath of loyalty. A Norman castle was built on the inner mound, joined soon afterwards by a royal palace. By the middle of the 12th century a new town occupied much of the great earthwork, complete with a noble new Norman cathedral, the mother church of a huge diocese.

But Norman Sarum was not destined to thrive. Soldiers and priests quarelled, and life on the almost waterless hilltop became intolerable. The solution was a move downhill to the new settlement now known as Salisbury, where a new cathedral was founded in 1220. Thereafter Old Sarum went into steep decline: its cathedral was demolished, its castle eventually abandoned. But the largely uninhabited site continued to 'elect' two MPs, becoming the most notorious of the 'Rotten Boroughs' swept away by the 1832 Reform Act.

Today, the remains of the prehistoric fortress and of the Norman palace, castle and cathedral evoke memories of thousands of years of history: they are interpreted by graphic panels throughout the site.

Contact the site for details of special events in 2006.

www.english-heritage.org.uk/oldsarum

NON-MEMBERS

Adult	£2.90
Concession	£2.20
Child	£1.50

OPENING TIMES

1 Apr-30 Jun, daily	10am-5pm
1 Jul-31 Aug, daily	9am-6pm
1-30 Sep, daily	10am-5pm
1-31 Oct, daily	10am-4pm
1 Nov-28 Feb, daily	11am-3pm
1-31 Mar, daily	10am-4pm
Closed	24-26 Dec and 1 Jan

HOW TO FIND US

Direction: 2 miles N of Salisbury, off A345

Train: Salisbury 2 miles

Bus: Wilts & Dorset/Stagecoach in Hampshire 3, 5-9 from Salisbury

Tel: 01722 335398

Local Tourist Information Salisbury: 01722 334956

OVP

Disabled access (outer bailey and grounds only, disabled toilet).

New guidebook.

MAP Page 265 (4J)
OS Map 184 (ref SU 138327)

Old Wardour Castle

Wiltshire – SP3 6RR

Beautifully sited beside a lake, Old Wardour Castle was built in the late 14th century by John Lord Lovel as a lightly fortified but showy and luxurious residence. A hexagonal tower house ranged round a central courtyard, its form is unique in England.

After decorative updating in 1570, the castle was besieged in turn by both sides during the Civil War, and badly damaged. Restored to Lord Arundell of Wardour, in the 18th century it was incorporated as a romantic ruin into the landscaped grounds of New Wardour House (not managed by EH, no public access). The castle's setting in a Registered Landscape indicates the significance of this hidden jewel.

An audio tour brings the castle's long history to life: it was the setting for part of the film *Robin Hood, Prince of Thieves.*

Please contact the site for details of special events.

www.english-heritage.org.uk/oldwardourcastle

Available for corporate and private hire.

Licensed for civil wedding ceremonies.

NON-MEMBERS	
Adult	£3.20
Concession	£2.40
Child	£1.60

OPENING TIMES	
1 Apr-30 Jun, daily	10am-5pm
1 Jul-31 Aug, daily	10am-6pm
1-30 Sep, daily	10am-5pm
1-31 Oct, daily	10am-4pm
1 Nov-31 Mar, Sat-Sun	10am-4pm
Closed	24-26 Dec & 1 Jan

HOW TO FIND US

Direction: Located off A30 2 miles SW of Tisbury. Also accessible from A350

Train: Tisbury 2½ miles

Bus: Wilts & Dorset 26 Salisbury – Shaftesbury (passes Tisbury)

Tel: 01747 870487

P OVP

Disabled access (grounds and ground floor only).

MAP Page 265 (4J)
OS Map 184 (ref ST 939263)

Over Bridge

Gloucestershire

A single-arch stone bridge spanning the River Severn, built in 1825-30 by the great engineer Thomas Telford.

OPENING TIMES

Any reasonable time

HOW TO FIND US

Direction: 1 mile NW of Gloucester, at junction of A40 (Ross) and A417 (Ledbury)

Train: Gloucester 2 miles

Bus: From [rail] Gloucester

[icons]

Parking (in lay-by).

MAP Page 265 (1H)
OS Map 162 (ref SO 816196)

Pendennis Castle

See feature – Page 102

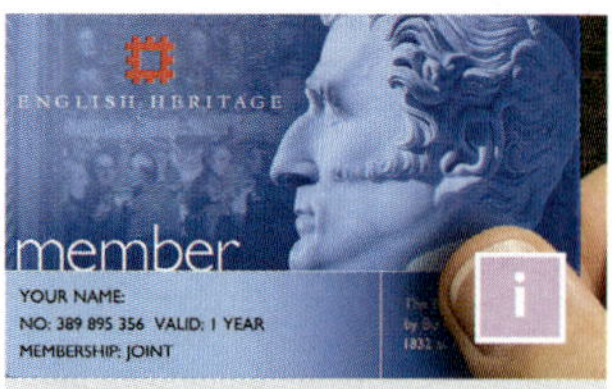

Penhallam Manor

Cornwall

The low and grass-covered but complete ground-plan of a moated 13th-century manor house, in a delightful woodland setting.

OPENING TIMES

Any reasonable time

HOW TO FIND US

Direction: Signposted from Week St Mary, off a minor road off A39 from Treskinnick Cross (10 minutes' walk from the car park on the forest track)

[icons]

Parking (limited).

MAP Page 264 (5D)
OS Map 190 (ref SX 224974)

Portland Castle

See feature – Page 104

Restormel Castle

Cornwall – PL22 0BD

Restormel Castle

Built in c. 1300, the great circular shell-keep of Restormel survives in good condition. It stands on an earlier Norman mound surrounded by a deep dry ditch, atop a high spur beside the River Fowey. Twice visited by the Black Prince, it finally saw action during the Civil War in 1644. A favourite picnic spot.

NON-MEMBERS

Adult	£2.40
Concession	£1.80
Child	£1.20

OPENING TIMES

1 Apr-30 Jun, daily	10am-5pm
1 Jul-31 Aug, daily	10am-6pm
1-30 Sep, daily	10am-5pm
1-31 Oct, daily	10am-4pm

HOW TO FIND US

Direction: Located 1½ miles N of Lostwithiel, off A390

Train: Lostwithiel 1½ miles

Tel: 01208 872687

[icons] OVP

Access (via a stock grazing area so appropriate footwear must be worn. There are three steps on the entrance path, so disabled visitors may want to call the site in advance to arrange alternative access).

MAP Page 264 (6C)
OS Map 200 (ref SX 104614)

Royal Citadel, Plymouth

Devon

A dramatic 17th-century fortress built to defend the coastline from the Dutch, and still in use by the military today. Viewing is only by weekly tours led by Blue Badge Guides.

ENTRY

Non-member	£3.50
EH members and children	£3.00

Royal Citadel, Plymouth

OPENING TIMES

By guided tour only, May-Sep:
Tue & Thu only 2.30pm

HOW TO FIND US

Direction: At E end of Plymouth Hoe

Train: Plymouth 1 mile

Bus: From surrounding areas

plymouthukbbg@hotmail.com

MAP Page 264 (6E)
OS Map 201 (ref SX 480538)

St Breock Downs Monolith

Cornwall

Originally 5 metres (16 ft) high and weighing some 16.75 tonnes, this is Cornwall's largest and heaviest prehistoric monolith. It stands on the summit of the St Breock Downs, offering wonderful views.

Managed by the Cornwall Heritage Trust.

OPENING TIMES

Any reasonable time

HOW TO FIND US

Direction: Located on St Breock Downs; 3½ miles SW of Wadebridge off unclassified road to Rosenannon

Train: Roche 5½ miles

MAP Page 264 (6C)
OS Map 200 (ref SW 968683)

St Briavels Castle

Gloucestershire

The fine twin-towered gatehouse of this castle, built by Edward I in 1292, once defended a factory making crossbow bolts from Forest of Dean iron. Long a prison, it is now a youth hostel in marvellous walking country.

St Briavels Castle

OPENING TIMES

Exterior: any reasonable time

Bailey: 1 Apr-30 Sep, daily 1pm-4pm

HOW TO FIND US

Direction: In St Briavels; 7 miles NE of Chepstow off B4228

Train: Chepstow 8 miles

Tel: 01594 530272

MAP Page 265 (2H)
OS Map 162 (ref SO 559046)

St Catherine's Castle

Cornwall

One of a pair of small artillery forts built by Henry VIII in the 1530s to defend Fowey Harbour, consisting of two storeys with gun ports at ground level.

OPENING TIMES

Any reasonable time

HOW TO FIND US

Direction: 1½ miles SW of Fowey, along a woodland footpath off A3082

Train: Par 4 miles

Bus: First 25/B St Austell-Fowey to within ½ mile

P

Parking (Ready Money Cove Car Park, Fowey ¾ mile walk).

MAP Page 264 (6C)
OS Map 200 (ref SX 119509)

St Catherine's Chapel, Abbotsbury

Dorset

Set high on a hilltop overlooking Abbotsbury Abbey (see p.85), this sturdily buttressed and barrel-vaulted 14th-century chapel was built by the monks as a place of pilgrimage and retreat.

St Catherine's Chapel, Abbotsbury

OPENING TIMES

Any reasonable time

HOW TO FIND US

Direction: ½ mile S of Abbotsbury; by path from village, off B3157. Path leads off signposted lane to Swannery

Train: Upwey 7 miles

Bus: First X53 Poole – Exeter

MAP Page 265 (5H)
OS Map 194 (ref SY 573848)

St Mary's Church, Kempley

Gloucestershire

A delightful Norman church, displaying one of the most outstandingly complete and well-preserved sets of medieval wall paintings in England, dating from the 12th and 14th centuries.

Managed by the Friends of Kempley Church.

OPENING TIMES

1 Apr-31 Oct, daily 10am-6pm

Telephone for appointment in winter.

HOW TO FIND US

Direction: 1 mile N of Kempley off B4024; 6 miles NE of Ross-on-Wye

Train: Ledbury 8 miles

Tel: 01531 660214

MAP Page 265 (1H)
OS Map 149 (ref SO 670313)

Pendennis Castle Cornwall – TR11 4LP

Constructed between 1540 and 1545, Pendennis and its sister St Mawes Castle form the Cornish end of the chain of coastal castles built by Henry VIII to counter a threat from France and Spain. Thereafter Pendennis was frequently adapted to face new enemies over 400 years, right through until World War II.

In 1598, during Elizabeth I's reign, a new type of defensive wall was added around the original fort. The castle was strengthened again prior to the Civil War and played host to the future Charles II in 1646, before he sailed to the Isles of Scilly. It then withstood five months of siege, before becoming the penultimate Royalist garrison on the British mainland to surrender.

Pendennis continued to play a vital role in Cornwall's defences throughout the late 19th and early 20th centuries, and saw significant action during World War II. Evidence of its fascinating history is on show throughout the site; the Noonday Gun is fired every day during July and August, and the Guardhouse has been returned to its World War I appearance. You can also visit the underground magazines and tunnels, including the World War II Half Moon Battery, as well as the original 16th-century keep with its recreated Tudor gun deck.

NEW FOR 2006 **The refurbished 1901 Royal Artillery Barracks now houses a new interactive exhibition, tracing the history of the castle, its people, and its links with Falmouth and the trade routes of the British Empire. A key feature is a hands-on scale model of the castle: with the aid of special effects, children will also now be able to step into the shoes of a soldier on kit parade. The new education suite, with two large child-friendly education rooms and a wet room for creative workshops, can accommodate up to 120 children.**

The new hospitality area is not only a fully-equipped conference centre but also an exceptional wedding venue, with the sea as a stunning backdrop.

www.english-heritage.org.uk/pendenniscastle

Available for corporate and private hire.

Licensed for civil wedding ceremonies.

Holiday cottage available to let.

Barrack Block

NON-MEMBERS

Adult	£4.80
Concession	£3.60
Child	£2.40
Family ticket	£12.00

OPENING TIMES

1 Apr-30 Jun, daily	10am-5pm*
1 Jul-31 Aug, daily	10am-6pm*
1-30 Sep, daily	10am-5pm*
1 Oct-31 Mar, daily	10am-4pm
Closed	24-26 Dec and 1 Jan

*Closes at 4pm on Saturdays. The keep also closes for 1 hour at lunch on Saturdays when events are booked.

HOW TO FIND US

Direction: On Pendennis Headland, 1 mile SE of Falmouth

Train: Falmouth Docks ½ mile

Bus: First 309 from Falmouth, Jun-Aug only

Tel: 01326 316594

Local Tourist Information: 01326 313457

OVP

Disabled access (wheelchair access to the grounds, there are steep steps or drops in places).

Tearooms (open Apr-Oct, daily; Nov-Mar, Wed-Sun).

MAP Page 264 (7C)
OS Map 204 (ref SW 824318)

Portland Castle

Dorset – DT5 1AZ

The history of this fortress, which overlooks Portland harbour, is diverse and fascinating. Built by Henry VIII to defend Weymouth against possible French and Spanish invasion, its squat appearance is typical of the artillery forts built in the early 1540s.

Unusually for a fortress of this period, the castle has survived largely unaltered. It first witnessed serious fighting during the Civil War, when it was seized by both Parliamentarians and Royalists.

It became a Seaplane Station during World War I, and was in the forefront of the D-Day preparations which helped to end World War II.

The Governor's Garden, designed by Christopher Bradley-Hole as part of the Contemporary Heritage Garden series, contains an impressive circular amphitheatre made from local Portland stone, with two-level seating for about 200 people.

This perfectly sheltered spot is a great place to relax and enjoy the dramatic sea and harbour views.

Portland Castle offers accessibility for all – there are audio tours and a Touch Tour for the visually impaired. You can even come face-to-face with Henry VIII in the Great Hall. When you need a break, the recently refurbished tearoom is the ideal place for a light lunch or a cup of tea.

Contact the site for details of special summer 2006 events.

www.english-heritage.org.uk/portlandcastle

Enjoy a refreshing sea journey to Portland Castle from Weymouth aboard 'My Girl', a World War II veteran boat. 10% discount for EH members – valid April to October 2006. Tel 01305 785000 or visit www.whitemotorboat.freeuk.com

Available for corporate and private hire.

Licensed for civil wedding ceremonies.

NON-MEMBERS

Adult	£3.70
Concession	£2.80
Child	£1.90

OPENING TIMES

1 Apr-30 Jun, daily	10am-5pm
1 Jul-31 Aug, daily	10am-6pm
1-30 Sep, daily	10am-5pm
1-31 Oct, daily	10am-4pm
Closed	1 Nov-31 Mar

HOW TO FIND US

Direction: Overlooking Portland Harbour in Castletown, Isle of Portland

Train: Weymouth 4½ miles

Bus: First 1, 501 from Weymouth (passing close to Weymouth)

Ferry: From Weymouth Harbour, Good Fri-end Sep (weather permitting). Call the castle for details.

Tel: 01305 820539

OVP

Disabled access (Captain's House, ground floor of the castle and Governor's Garden).
Captain's House Tearooms (table service & outdoor servery).

MAP Page 265 (6H)
OS Map 194 (ref SY 685744)

St Mawes Castle

Cornwall – TR2 3AA

The best preserved and most elaborately decorated of Henry VIII's coastal fortresses, St Mawes was built to counter invasion threats from France and Spain: its counterpart was Pendennis, on the other side of the Fal Estuary (see p.102).

The clover-leaf shaped fort fell easily to landward attack by Parliamentarian forces in 1646, and was not properly refortified until the late 19th and early 20th centuries. Other coastal forts built by Henry VIII include Portland, Deal and Walmer Castles.

Available for corporate and private hire.

Licensed for civil wedding ceremonies.

Holiday cottage available to let.

NON-MEMBERS

Adult	£3.60
Concession	£2.70
Child	£1.80

OPENING TIMES

1 Apr-30 Jun, Sun-Fri	10am-5pm*
1 Jul-31 Aug, Sun-Fri	10am-6pm*
1-30 Sep, Sun-Fri	10am-5pm*
1-31 Oct, daily	10am-4pm
1 Nov-31 Mar, Fri-Mon	10am-4pm

*Closed Sat. May close 4pm on Sun & Fri for private events

Closed	24-26 Dec & 1 Jan

Castle closed between 1-2pm in winter

St Mawes Castle

HOW TO FIND US

Direction: In St Mawes on A3078

Train: Penmere, 4 miles via Prince of Wales Pier and ferry

Bus: First 50 Truro – St Mawes to within ½ mile

Tel: 01326 270526

Dogs on leads (grounds only).

MAP Page 264 (7C)
OS Map 204 (ref SW 841328)

The Sanctuary

Wiltshire

Begun in about 3000 BC, the Sanctuary became a complex of timber post rings and stone circles: its components are now indicated by concrete slabs. A place of great ritual significance, it was later linked to Avebury by West Kennet Avenue.

Managed by The National Trust.
Part of the Avebury World Heritage Site.

OPENING TIMES

Any reasonable time.

Usual facilities may not be available around the Summer Solstice June 20-22. Please check before you visit.

HOW TO FIND US

Train: Pewsey 9 miles, Bedwyn 12 miles

Bus: Wilts and Dorset 5/6 Salisbury – Swindon (passes close to Swindon)

Parking (in lay-by).

MAP Page 265 (3J)
OS Map 173 (ref SU 118680)

Sherborne Old Castle

Dorset – DT9 3SA

Built by Bishop Roger of Salisbury in the 12th century as a strongly defended palace, Sherborne Old Castle became a powerful Royalist base during the Civil War. Described as 'malicious and mischievous' by Cromwell, it fell in 1645 after a fierce eleven-day siege.

www.english-heritage.org.uk/sherborne

NON-MEMBERS

Adult	£2.40
Concession	£1.80
Child	£1.20

Joint ticket for Sherborne Castle and Grounds £5.50. Members' discounts: see page 117

OPENING TIMES

1 Apr-30 Jun, daily	10am-5pm
1 July-31 Aug, daily	10am-6pm
1-30 Sep, daily	10am-5pm
1-31 Oct, daily	10am-4pm
Closed	1 Nov-31 Mar

HOW TO FIND US

Direction: Located ½ mile E of Sherborne, off B3145

Train: Sherborne ¾ mile

Tel: 01935 812730

MAP Page 265 (4H)
OS Map 183 (ref ST 648168)

Stonehenge Wiltshire – SP4 7DE

The great and ancient stone circle of Stonehenge is one of the wonders of the world. What visitors see today are the substantial remnants of the last in a sequence of such monuments erected between c. 3000 BC and 1600 BC. Each monument was a circular structure, aligned with the rising of the sun at the solstice.

Stonehenge in the snow

Stonehenge at sunrise

There has always been intense debate over quite what purpose Stonehenge served. Certainly it was the focal point in a landscape filled with prehistoric ceremonial structures. It also represented an enormous investment of labour and time. A huge effort and great organisation was needed to carry the stones tens – and sometimes hundreds – of miles by land and water, and then to shape and raise them. Only a sophisticated society could have mustered so large a workforce, and the design and construction skills necessary to produce Stonehenge and its surrounding monuments.

The Stone Circle viewed from the 'Slaughter Stone'

Stonehenge's orientation in relation to the rising and setting sun has always been one of its most remarkable features. Whether this was because its builders came from a sun-worshipping culture or because – as some scholars have asserted – the circle and its banks were part of a huge astronomical calendar, remains a mystery.

What cannot be denied is the ingenuity of the builders of Stonehenge. With only very basic tools at their disposal, they shaped the stones and formed the mortises and tenons that linked uprights to lintels.

Using antlers and bones, they dug the pits to hold the stones and made the banks and ditches that enclosed them.

There are direct links with the people who built Stonehenge in their tools, artefacts, pottery and even the contents of their graves. Some of these are displayed in the museums at Salisbury and Devizes.

The first monument in the Stonehenge landscape consisted of a circular bank and ditch with a ring of 56 wooden posts, the pits for which are now known as Aubrey Holes. Later monuments all used and reused the great stones we see today, many of which were brought from some distance away. The final phase comprised the construction of an outer circle of huge standing stones – super-hard sarsens, from the Marlborough Downs. These were topped by lintels, forming a ring. Inside this stood a horseshoe of five still-larger constructions, known as trilithons: pairs of uprights with a lintel across each. All the stones were connected using mortise-and-tenon joints. Smaller bluestones, from the Preseli Mountains in South Wales, were arranged in a ring and a horseshoe, within the great circle and horseshoe of sarsen stones. In an earlier phase, these bluestones had been erected in a different arrangement.

Burial mounds, possibly containing the graves of ruling families, are also integral to the landscape. Neolithic long barrows and the various types of circular barrows which came later are still visible. So too are other earthworks and monuments. Some remain enigmatic, such as the long oval earthwork to the north, the Cursus – once thought to be a chariot racecourse. You can visit the Cursus and other parts of the Stonehenge landscape. Woodhenge, two miles to the north east, was a wooden oval-post structure, also aligned with the Solstice sunrise. It is believed to be contemporary with the first phase of Stonehenge.

A World Heritage Site, Stonehenge and all its surroundings remain powerful witnesses to the once great civilisations of the Stone and Bronze Ages, between 5,000 and 3,000 years ago.

Stonehenge is surrounded by 1,500 acres of land owned by The National Trust, with excellent walks.

www.english-heritage.org.uk/stonehenge

Stone Circle access outside normal opening hours by advance booking only. Book during weekday office hours.

NON-MEMBERS

Adult	£5.90
Concession	£4.40
Child	£3.00
Family ticket	£14.80

National Trust members admitted free

Aerial view

OPENING TIMES

16 Mar-31 May, daily	9.30am-6pm
1 Jun-31 Aug, daily	9am-7pm
1 Sep-15 Oct, daily	9.30am-6pm
16 Oct-15 Mar, daily	9.30am-4pm
Closed	24-26 Dec and 1 Jan

Opening times from 20 to 22 June may be subject to change due to Summer Solstice. Please check with Customer Services before your visit.

Recommended last admission time no later than 30 minutes before the advertised closing time. Stonehenge will close promptly 20 minutes after the advertised closing time.

When weather conditions are bad, access may be restricted and visitors may not be able to use the walkway around the stone circle.

HOW TO FIND US

Direction: 2 miles W of Amesbury on junction of A303 and A344/A360

Train: Salisbury 9½ miles

Bus: Wilts & Dorset 3 from Salisbury

Tel: 0870 333 1181 (Customer Services)

Local Tourist Information Amesbury: 01980 622833; and Salisbury: 01722 334956

Stone Circle Access Line: 01722 343834, advance booking only

OVP

Audio tours (complimentary – available in nine languages & hearing loop: subject to availability).

Catering (Stonehenge Kitchen, open all year).

Guidebooks (also available in French, German, Spanish and Japanese; large print and braille guides in English only).

No dogs allowed (except guide and hearing dogs).

Parking (free for members. Seasonal charge for non-members, refundable on entry).

New guidebook.

MAP Page 265 (4J)
OS Map 184 (ref SU 122422)

Silbury Hill

Wiltshire

The largest man-made mound in Europe, huge and mysterious Silbury Hill is comparable in height and volume to the roughly contemporary Egyptian pyramids.

Probably completed by about 2350 BC and part of the Avebury 'sacred landscape', it apparently contains no burial or shrine, and was clearly important in itself: but its purpose and significance remain enigmatic.

Part of the Avebury World Heritage Site.

OPENING TIMES

Viewing area at any reasonable time. Strictly no access to the hill itself

Usual facilities may not be available around the Summer Solstice 20-22 June. Please check before you visit.

HOW TO FIND US

Direction: 1 mile W of West Kennet on A4

Train: Pewsey 9 miles, Swindon 13 miles

Bus: Stagecoach in Swindon/First 49 Swindon – Trowbridge; Wilts & Dorset 5/6 Salisbury – Swindon (all pass within ¾ mile and pass close to ⇌ Swindon)

Disabled access (viewing area).

MAP Page 265 (3J)
OS Map 173 (ref SU 100685)

Sir Bevil Grenville's Monument

Bath & NE Somerset

Erected to commemorate the heroism of a Royalist commander and his Cornish pikemen at the Battle of Lansdown, 1643.

OPENING TIMES

Any reasonable time

HOW TO FIND US

Direction: Located 4 miles NW of Bath on the N edge of Lansdown Hill, near the road to Wick

Train: Bath Spa 4½ miles

Bus: Ebley 620 ⇌ Bath Spa – Tetbury

P

Parking (in lay-by).

MAP Page 265 (3H)
OS Map 172 (ref ST 722703)

Stanton Drew Circles and Cove

Bath & NE Somerset

Though the third largest collection of prehistoric standing stones in England, the three circles and three-stone 'cove' of Stanton Drew are surprisingly little-known. Recent surveys have revealed that they were only part of a much more elaborate ritual site.

Stanton Drew Circles and Cove

OPENING TIMES

Cove: any reasonable time. Two main stone circles; access at the discretion of the landowner, who may levy a charge.

HOW TO FIND US

Direction: Cove: located in the garden of the Druid's Arms public house. Circles: located E of Stanton Drew village

Train: Bristol Temple Meads 7 miles

Bus: First 672 ⇌ Bristol Temple Meads – Cheddar

MAP Page 265 (3H)
OS Map 172 (cove ref ST 597631, circles ref ST 601633)

Stonehenge

See feature – Page 106

Stoney Littleton Long Barrow

Bath & NE Somerset

One of the finest accessible examples of a Neolithic chambered tomb, with its multiple burial chambers open to view.

OPENING TIMES

Any reasonable daylight hours

HOW TO FIND US

Direction: 1 mile S of Wellow off A367

Train: Bath Spa 6 miles

P

Parking (limited).

Note: visitors are advised to bring a torch, and that there may be mud on approach and interior floor.

MAP Page 265 (3H)
OS Map 172 (ref ST 735572)

Temple Church

Bristol

The 'leaning tower' and walls of this large late medieval church survived bombing during World War II. The graveyard is now a public garden.

OPENING TIMES

Exterior only: any reasonable time

HOW TO FIND US

Direction: Located in Temple St, off Victoria St

Train: Bristol Temple Meads ¼ mile

Bus: From surrounding areas

MAP Page 265 (3H)
OS Map 172 (ref ST 593727)

Tintagel Castle

See feature – Page 112

Totnes Castle

Devon – TQ9 5NU

Photo: Peter Anderson

A classic Norman motte and bailey castle, founded soon after the Conquest to overawe the Saxon town. A well-preserved later shell-keep crowns its steep mound, giving sweeping views across the town rooftops to the River Dart.

Keep accessible only via steep steps.

NON-MEMBERS

Adult	£2.40
Concession	£1.80
Child	£1.20

OPENING TIMES

1 Apr-30 Jun, daily	10am-5pm
1 Jul-31 Aug, daily	10am-6pm
1-30 Sep, daily	10am-5pm
1-31 Oct, daily	10am-4pm

HOW TO FIND US

Direction: In Totnes, on a hill overlooking the town

Train: Totnes ¼ mile

Tel: 01803 864406

OVP

Parking (charged, 64 metres (70 yards); cars only, narrow approach roads).

MAP Page 264 (6E)
OS Map 202 (ref SX 800605)

Tregiffian Burial Chamber

Cornwall

A Neolithic or early Bronze Age chambered tomb with an entrance passage, walled and roofed with stone slabs, leading into the central chamber.

Managed by the Cornwall Heritage Trust.

OPENING TIMES

Any reasonable time

HOW TO FIND US

Direction: Located 2 miles SE of St Buryan, on B3315

Train: Penzance 5½ miles

MAP Page 264 (7B)
OS Map 203 (ref SW 431244)

Trethevy Quoit

Cornwall

This well-preserved and impressive Neolithic 'dolmen' burial chamber stands 2.7 metres (8.9 ft) high. There are five standing stones, surmounted by a huge capstone.

Managed by Cornwall Heritage Trust.

OPENING TIMES

Any reasonable time

HOW TO FIND US

Direction: 1 mile NE of St Cleer, near Darite; off B3254

Train: Liskeard 3½ miles

Bus: Western Greyhound 573 Callington – Looe (passes Liskeard) within ½ mile

MAP Page 264 (6D)
OS Map 201 (ref SX 259688)

Uley Long Barrow (Hetty Pegler's Tump)

Gloucestershire

A partly reconstructed Neolithic chambered mound, 37 metres (120 ft) long, atmospherically sited overlooking the Severn Valley. 'Hetty Pegler' was its 17th-century landowner.

Managed by Gloucestershire County Council.

OPENING TIMES

Any reasonable time

HOW TO FIND US

Direction: Located 3½ miles NE of Dursley, on B4066

Train: Stroud 6 miles

Bus: Stagecoach in the Cotswolds 20 Stroud – Uley (passes close to Stroud), then 1 mile

MAP Page 265 (2H)
OS Map 162 (ref SO 790000)

Upper Plym Valley

Devon

Some 300 Bronze Age and medieval sites, covering 15.5 square kilometres (6 square miles) of Dartmoor landscape.

Managed by The National Trust.

OPENING TIMES

Any reasonable time

HOW TO FIND US

Direction: 4 miles E of Yelverton

MAP Page 264 (6E)
OS Map 202 (ref SX 580660)

West Kennet Avenue

Wiltshire

An 'avenue', originally of around 100 pairs of prehistoric standing stones, raised to form a winding 1.5 mile ritual link between the pre-existing monuments of Avebury and The Sanctuary.

Part of the Avebury World Heritage Site.

Owned and managed by The National Trust.

OPENING TIMES

Any reasonable time.

Usual facilities may not be available around the Summer Solstice 20-22 Jun. Please check before you visit.

West Kennet Avenue

HOW TO FIND US

Direction: Runs alongside B4003

Train: Pewsey 9 miles, Swindon 12 miles

Bus: Stagecoach in Swindon/ First 49 Swindon – Trowbridge; Wilts and Dorset 5/6 Salisbury – Swindon (all pass close to Swindon)

Disabled access (on roadway).

MAP Page 265 (3J)
OS Map 173 (ref SU 105695)

West Kennet Long Barrow

Wiltshire

One of the largest, most impressive and most accessible Neolithic chambered tombs in Britain. Built in around 3400 BC, and used by a whole community for at least a thousand years.

Part of the Avebury World Heritage Site.

Managed by The National Trust.

OPENING TIMES

Any reasonable time.

Usual facilities may not be available around the Summer Solstice 20-22 Jun. Please check before you visit.

West Kennet Long Barrow

HOW TO FIND US

Direction: ¾ mile SW of West Kennet, along footpath off A4

Train: Pewsey 9 miles, Swindon 13 miles

Bus: Stagecoach in Swindon/ First 49 Swindon – Trowbridge; Wilts and Dorset 5/6 Salisbury – Swindon (all pass close to Swindon)

Parking (in lay-by).

MAP Page 265 (3J)
OS Map 173 (ref SU 105677)

Windmill Hill

Wiltshire

The classic Neolithic 'causewayed enclosure', with three concentric but intermittent ditches. Large quantities of animal bones found here indicate feasting, animal trading or rituals here, or perhaps all three.

Part of the Avebury World Heritage Site.

Managed by The National Trust.

OPENING TIMES

Any reasonable time

HOW TO FIND US

Direction: 1¼ mile NW of Avebury

Train: Swindon 11 miles

Bus: Stagecoach in Swindon/ First 49 Swindon – Trowbridge; Wilts and Dorset 5/6 Salisbury – Swindon (all pass close to Swindon)

MAP Page 265 (3J)
OS Map 173 (ref SU 087714)

Tintagel Castle **Cornwall – PL34 0HE**

With its spectacular location on one of England's most dramatic coastlines, Tintagel is an awe-inspiring and romantic spot, a place of legends.

Joined to the mainland by a narrow neck of land, Tintagel Island faces the full force of the Atlantic. On the mainland itself, the gaunt remains of the medieval castle represent only one phase in a long history of occupation. Even before Richard Earl of Cornwall built his castle, Tintagel was already associated with the conception of King Arthur. The connection was later renewed by Alfred, Lord Tennyson, in his *Idylls of the King*.

After a period as a Roman settlement and military outpost, Tintagel is thought to have been a trading settlement of Celtic kings during the 5th and 6th centuries. Legend has it that one of these was King Mark, whose nephew Tristan fell in love with Yseult (or Isolde). Their doomed romance is part of Tintagel's story.

The remains of the 13th-century castle are breathtaking. Steep stone steps, stout walls and rugged windswept cliff edges encircle the Great Hall, where Richard Earl of Cornwall once feasted.

There are many unanswered questions and legends surrounding Tintagel. The castle has an amazing capacity to surprise us, even after years of investigation.

In June 1998, excavations were undertaken under the direction of Professor Chris Morris of the University of Glasgow, on a relatively sheltered and small site on the eastern side of the island, first excavated in the 1930s. Pottery from the 5th and 6th centuries was found, as well as some fine glass fragments believed to be from 6th or 7th-century Málaga in Spain. Even more remarkable was a 1,500-year-old piece of slate on which remained two Latin inscriptions. The second inscription reads: 'Artognou, father of a descendant of Coll, has had [this] made.' Who exactly Artognou was continues to be a subject for lively speculation.

'Searching for King Arthur', a magical mystery audio visual tour through the ages, introduces visitors to the castle, its legends and history.

The bridge giving access to the 'The Island Ward'

During the summer you can also enjoy a special introductory talk. The site offers a newly refurbished shop and visitor facilities.

Access to the castle is difficult for disabled visitors (via over 100 steep steps). There is a Land Rover service from the village which can take visitors to the exhibition and shop (Apr-Oct only). Contact the site for service information.

www.english-heritage.org.uk/tintagelcastle

NON-MEMBERS	
Adult	£4.30
Concession	£3.20
Child	£2.20

OPENING TIMES	
1 Apr-30 Sep, daily	10am-6pm
1-31 Oct, daily	10am-5pm
1 Nov-31 Mar, daily	10am-4pm
Closed	24-26 Dec and 1 Jan

HOW TO FIND US

Direction: On Tintagel Head, ½ mile along uneven track from Tintagel; no vehicles except Land Rover Service

Bus: Western Greyhound 524 Bude – Wadebridge, 594 Bude – Truro (with connections on 555 at Wadebridge to ⇄ Bodmin Parkway)

Tel: 01840 770328

Local Tourist Information Tintagel Visitors' Centre: 01840 779084; Camelford (summer only): 01840 212954
Padstow: 01841 533449

OVP

Disabled access (limited via Land Rover service to castle Apr-Oct, extra charge).

Parking (600 metres (660 yards) in the village).

MAP Page 264 (5C)
OS Map 200 (ref SX 049891)

Windmill Tump Long Barrow, Rodmarton

Gloucestershire

A Neolithic chambered tomb with an enigmatic 'false entrance'.

Managed by Gloucestershire County Council.

OPENING TIMES

Any reasonable time

HOW TO FIND US

Direction: 1 mile SW of Rodmarton

Train: Kemble 5 miles

Bus: Stagecoach in the Cotswolds 881 from Kemble

MAP Page 265 (2J)
OS Map 163 (ref ST 933973)

Winterbourne Poor Lot Barrows

Dorset

A 'cemetery' of 44 Bronze Age burial mounds of varying types and sizes, straddling the A35 main road.

OPENING TIMES

Any reasonable time

HOW TO FIND US

Direction: 2 miles W of Winterbourne Abbas, S of junction of A35 with a minor road to Compton Valence. Access via Wellbottom Lodge – 180 metres (200 yards) E along A35 from junction

Train: Dorchester West or South, both 7 miles

Bus: First 31 Weymouth – Axminster (passes Dorchester South)

No adjacent parking.
Warning; cross road with care.

MAP Page 265 (5H)
OS Map 194 (ref SY 590907)

Woodhenge

Wiltshire

Neolithic monument, dating from about 2300 BC, with concrete markers replacing six concentric rings of timber posts, once possibly supporting a ring shaped building.

Part of the Stonehenge World Heritage Site.

OPENING TIMES

Any reasonable time.

Usual facilities may not be available around the Summer Solstice 20-22 Jun. Please check before you visit.

HOW TO FIND US

Direction: 1½ miles N of Amesbury, off A345, just S of Durrington

Train: Salisbury 9 miles

Bus: Wilts & Dorset 5/6 Salisbury – Swindon (passes close to Salisbury and Swindon); 16 from Amesbury

MAP Page 265 (4J)
OS Map 184 (ref SU 151434)

Yarn Market, Dunster

Somerset

This fine 17th-century timber-framed octagonal market hall is a monument to Dunster's once-flourishing cloth trade. Gallox Bridge and the Butter Cross are nearby.

Managed by The National Trust.

OPENING TIMES

Any reasonable time

HOW TO FIND US

Direction: In Dunster High St

Train: Dunster (West Somerset Railway) ½ mile

Bus: First 28 Taunton – Minehead, to within ¼ mile; 38 from Minehead

MAP Page 265 (4F)
OS Map 181 (ref SS 992438)

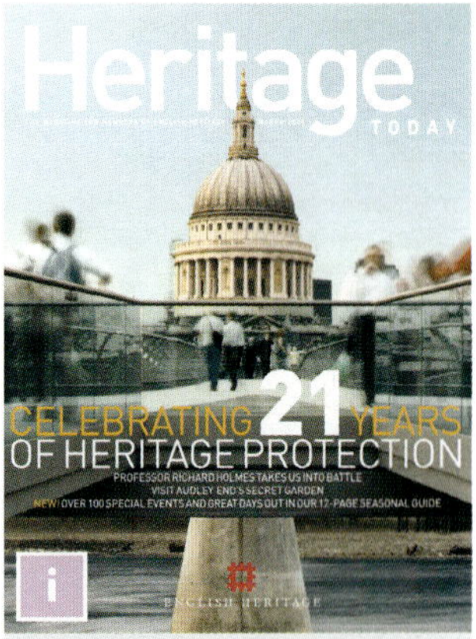

Check *Heritage Today* for news and information on forthcoming events and exclusive members' offers.

Looking for a unique present?

Why not browse our online shop at **www.english-heritage.org.uk/shopping**

Tresco with Old Blockhouse in the distance

The Heritage of Scilly

Isles of Scilly

The stunningly beautiful Isles of Scilly hold vast arrays of archaeological riches both above and below sea level. English Heritage recognises the importance of promoting this unique cultural landscape, and provides expert advice and significant funding to regeneration and conservation projects throughout the Isles.

This compact archipelago of about 100 islands lies around 28 miles to the south-west of Land's End. None of them is any bigger than three miles across and only five are inhabited. Despite their landmass of only 16 square kilometres (10 square miles), these islands contain a remarkable number of historic sites. These range from traditional farmhouses and dwellings to ritual burial monuments, cist grave cemeteries and Romano-Celtic shrines. Early settlements provide evidence of a distinctive Scillonian culture which thrived in the island group 2,000 years ago. More recently, defensive monuments constructed during the Civil War and World War II stand as testament to the strategic importance of the islands. The Gulf Stream keeps the climate warm, enabling exotic plants and wildlife to thrive.

OPENING TIMES

All EH properties on the Scillies are open at any reasonable time

HOW TO FIND US

Direction: See individual property entries on page 116 for access details

Tel: 0117 9750700
(Regional office)

Bant's Carn Burial Chamber and Halangy Down Ancient Village

St Mary's, Isles of Scilly

In a wonderfully scenic location, on a hill above the site of the ancient Iron Age village, stands this Bronze Age burial mound with entrance passage and inner chamber.

OPENING TIMES

Any reasonable time

HOW TO FIND US

Direction: 1 mile N of Hugh Town

MAP Page 264 (5B)
OS Map 203 (ref SV 910123)

Cromwell's Castle

Tresco, Isles of Scilly

Standing on a rocky promontory guarding the lovely anchorage between Bryher and Tresco, this round tower is one of the few surviving Cromwellian fortifications in Britain, built after the conquest of the Royalist Scillies in 1651.

OPENING TIMES

Any reasonable time

HOW TO FIND US

Direction: On the shoreline, approach with care, ¾ mile NW of New Grimsby

MAP Page 264 (4A)
OS Map 203 (ref SV 882159)

Garrison Walls

St Mary's, Isles of Scilly

You can enjoy a two-hour walk alongside the ramparts of these defensive walls and earthworks, dating from the 16th to 18th centuries.

OPENING TIMES

Any reasonable time

HOW TO FIND US

Direction: Around the headland W of Hugh Town

MAP Page 264 (5A)
OS Map 203 (ref SV 898104)

Harry's Walls

St Mary's, Isles of Scilly

An unfinished artillery fort, built above St Mary's Pool harbour in 1551.

OPENING TIMES

Any reasonable time

HOW TO FIND US

Direction: ¼ mile NE of Hugh Town

MAP Page 264 (5B)
OS Map 203 (ref SV 909109)

Innisidgen Lower and Upper Burial Chambers

St Mary's, Isles of Scilly

Two Bronze Age communal burial cairns of particularly Scillonian type, with fine views. The upper cairn is the best preserved in the islands.

OPENING TIMES

Any reasonable time

HOW TO FIND US

Direction: 1¾ miles NE of Hugh Town

MAP Page 264 (5B)
OS Map 203 (ref SV 922127)

King Charles's Castle

Tresco, Isles of Scilly

The ruins of a mid 16th-century coastal artillery fort, later garrisoned – hence the name –

by Civil War Royalists. Reached from New Grimsby by footpath.

OPENING TIMES

Any reasonable time

HOW TO FIND US

Direction: Located ¾ mile NW of New Grimsby. Coastal location, approach with care

MAP Page 264 (4A)
OS Map 203 (ref SV 882161)

Old Blockhouse

Tresco, Isles of Scilly

Substantial remains of a small 16th-century gun tower protecting Old Grimsby harbour, vigorously defended during the Civil War.

OPENING TIMES

Any reasonable time

HOW TO FIND US

Direction: Located on Blockhouse Point, at the S end of Old Grimsby harbour

MAP Page 264 (4A)
OS Map 203 (ref SV 897155)

Porth Hellick Down Burial Chamber

St Mary's, Isles of Scilly

A large and imposing 'Scillonian' Bronze Age entrance grave, with kerb, inner passage and burial chamber all clearly visible.

OPENING TIMES

Any reasonable time

HOW TO FIND US

Direction: 1¾ miles E of Hugh Town

MAP Page 264 (5B)
OS Map 203 (ref SV 928108)

Other Historic Attractions

Discounted entry to our members (discounts may not apply on event days)

The Arthurian Centre

Cornwall – PL32 9TT

Walk through newly exposed archaeology to 'King Arthur's Stone' and Camlann battlefield. Lots to see and learn for all ages, including 'Grail Trail' and unique exhibition.

ENTRY

20% discount for EH members

Discount does not extend to EH Corporate Partners

OPENING TIMES

Easter-31 Oct, daily 10am-5pm

HOW TO FIND US

Directions: On B3314 at Slaughterbridge, Camelford

Tel: 01840 213947

www.arthur-online.co.uk

MAP Page 264 (5C)
OS Map 200 (ref SX 109857)

Coldharbour Mill Museum

Devon – EX15 3EE

This 200 year old woollen mill still produces knitting yarns and woven tartans, and tells the story of the once flourishing West Country woollen industry. It houses a restored waterwheel, steam-powered mill engines and a 1910 Lancashire boiler, which are still operated on special steam-up days.

Coldharbour Mill Museum

Owned and managed by the Coldharbour Mill Trust.

NON-MEMBERS

Adult	£6.25
Concession	£5.75
Child	£2.95
Family	£17.00

EH members, and up to 6 children within their family group, get free entry. Discount does not extend to EH Corporate Partners or Cadw and Historic Scotland members. For tour times and special events details please call 01884 840960

OPENING TIMES

Mar-Oct, daily 10.30am-5pm (last tour 3.30pm)

Nov-Feb 11am-4pm (last tour 3pm)

HOW TO FIND US

Direction: Located just off B3440 as it enters Uffculme from Willand. 2 miles south-east of J27 on M5.

Train: Tiverton Parkway 2 miles

Bus: Stagecoach in Devon 1/B Exeter – Tiverton (passes ≹ Tiverton Parkway); First 92/A Taunton – Exeter/Tiverton

Tel: 01884 840960

www.coldharbourmill.org.uk

Disabled access (partial).
Dogs on leads (grounds only).

MAP Page 265 (5F)
OS Map 181 (ref ST 062122)

Sherborne Castle

Dorset – DT9 3PY

A great Elizabethan and Jacobean mansion begun by Sir Walter Raleigh, set in 20 acres of lakeside landscaped gardens.

Sherborne Castle

ENTRY

£2.50 entry to grounds for EH members, except on special event days. Discount does not extend to EH Corporate Partners

OPENING TIMES

1 Apr-30 Oct, Sat-Sun & Tue-Thu & Bank Hols 11am-5pm

Last admission 4.30pm. Castle interior opens 2.30pm on Saturdays.

HOW TO FIND US

Directions: E of Sherborne, off A30

Tel: 01935 813182

MAP Page 265 (4H)
OS Map 183 (ref ST 649164)

Woodchester Mansion

Gloucestershire – GL10 3TS

Woodchester Mansion was abandoned by its builders before it was completed, and has been virtually untouched by time since the mid-1870s. A wonderful opportunity to explore a neo-Gothic building 'frozen' in mid-assembly.

ENTRY

£4.00 for EH members

Discount does not extend to EH Corporate Partners

OPENING TIMES

Please call for details.

HOW TO FIND US

Directions: B4066, 5 miles south of Stroud

Tel: 01453 861541

www.woodchestermansion.org.uk

MAP Page 265 (2H)
OS Map 183 (ref SO 809014)

Audley End House – see page 122

Photo: John Critchley

East of England

'As on the highway's quiet edge
He mows the grass beside the hedge
The old man has for company
The distant, grey, salt-smelling sea
A poppied field, a cow and calf
The finches on the telegraph'

From 'The Coast: Norfolk', by Frances Cornford, 1886-1960

www.english-heritage.org.uk/eastofengland

Properties

See individual listings for details

Bedfordshire
Bushmead Priory, De Grey Mausoleum, Houghton House, Wrest Park

Cambridgeshire
Denny Abbey and the Farmland Museum, Duxford Chapel, Isleham Priory Church, Longthorpe Tower

Essex
Audley End House and Gardens, Hadleigh Castle, Hill Hall, Lexden Earthworks and Bluebottle Grove, Mistley Towers, Prior's Hall Barn, St Botolph's Priory, St John's Abbey Gate, Tilbury Fort, Waltham Abbey Gatehouse and Bridge

Hertfordshire
Berkhamsted Castle, Old Gorhambury House, Roman Wall of St Albans

Norfolk
Baconsthorpe Castle, Berney Arms Windmill, Binham Priory, Binham Market Cross, Blakeney Guildhall, Burgh Castle, Caister Roman Site, Castle Acre: Bailey Gate, Castle Acre Castle and Castle Acre Priory, Castle Rising Castle, Church of the Holy Sepulchre, Cow Tower in Norwich, Creake Abbey, Great Yarmouth Row Houses & Greyfriars' Cloisters, Grime's Graves, North Elmham Chapel, St Olave's Priory, Thetford Priory, Thetford Warren Lodge, Weeting Castle

Suffolk
Bury St Edmunds Abbey, Framlingham Castle, Landguard Fort, Leiston Abbey, Lindsey/St James's Chapel, Moulton Packhorse Bridge, Orford Castle, Saxtead Green Post Mill

Comprehensive map of our sites Page 268-269

Framlingham Castle – see page 128

Pilgrims, Barons and Merchants

This is the country of the East Angles – with their 'north folk' and 'south folk' in Norfolk and Suffolk – and the East Saxons, with the three inland counties of Cambridgeshire, Bedfordshire and Hertfordshire. Much of it is now deeply rural: but its many ancient churches, pretty villages, historic farmhouses and merchants' guildhalls still testify that this was among the most populous and prosperous regions of pre-industrial England.

Here too stood some of medieval England's most famous pilgrimage centres: the Virgin's shrine at **Walsingham**; **Bury St Edmunds Abbey**, shrine of a martyred East Anglian king, once patron saint of all England; and Our Lady's statue at **Thetford Priory**. The remains of many other east-country monasteries are also in English Heritage's care: among them **Binham Priory**; **Denny Abbey** with its unusual history and farmland museum; **Waltham Abbey**; Colchester's **St Botolph's Priory** and **St John's Abbey Gate**; **Leiston Abbey**; and **Castle Acre Priory** on the pilgrims' road, accompanied by its Norman planned town and the mighty earthworks of **Castle Acre Castle**.

The region indeed boasts some of England's finest castles: **Castle Rising** with its spectacular keep; great baronial **Framlingham Castle** and its royal rival **Orford Castle**, with one of the best-preserved keep interiors in the country; Norfolk's **Baconsthorpe Castle**, Hertfordshire's **Berkhamsted Castle** and Essex's **Hadleigh Castle**. **Tilbury Fort**, guarding the Thames approach to London, is the most complete surviving 17th-century artillery fortress in Britain, successor to a long line of coastal defences stretching back to Roman **Burgh Castle**.

This was also from Roman times a region of prosperous towns: Roman and earlier remains can be seen at both Colchester and St Albans. Norwich – with **Cow Tower** among its defences – was the biggest walled city in medieval England, London included; and imaginatively-interpreted **Great Yarmouth Row Houses** testify to that town's long reign as England's greatest fishing port.

Then there are the East of England's great houses. Imposing **Audley End** with its wonderful interiors; **Wrest Park**, whose owners lie beneath serried monuments at **De Grey Mausoleum**; **Houghton House**, the 'House Beautiful' of 'Pilgrim's Progress'; **Hill Hall** with its wall-paintings; the remains of once-extravagant **Old Gorhambury House**. And for the venturesome, one of this region's sites is especially worth experiencing – **Grime's Graves**, the only place in Britain where you can descend into a prehistoric flint mine.

Audley End House & Gardens Essex – CB11 4JF

Sir Thomas Audley was given the lands of Walden Abbey by Henry VIII, and adapted the abbey buildings as his mansion. His grandson Thomas, first Earl of Suffolk, rebuilt this mansion between 1610 and 1614. The new Audley End was truly palatial in scale, but Suffolk fell from power after 1618.

Charles II bought the house in 1668, using it as a base for attending Newmarket races. By the 1680s, Sir Christopher Wren was warning of the need for major repairs. The cost of these caused William III to return Audley End to the Suffolk family. When the Suffolk line died out in 1745, it was bought by the Countess of Portsmouth for her nephew and heir, Sir John Griffin Griffin. Following his inheritance, Griffin Griffin – also the fourth Baron Howard de Walden and first Baron Braybrooke – made changes to the house, adding a suite of neo-Classical rooms designed by Robert Adam and a Gothic chapel. Meanwhile, 'Capability' Brown had been employed to remodel the grounds.

Today, the house's interior is largely the result of ownership by the third Baron Braybrooke, who inherited it in 1825. He installed his extensive picture collection and filled the rooms with furnishings. The fourth Baron Braybrooke's natural history collection also remains an appealing feature of the house.

After nearly 30 years in store, a rare set of English tapestries by the Soho weaver Paul Saunders has been conserved and displayed in the Tapestry Room. Depicting figures in a landscape with ruined buildings, they were originally supplied to Audley End in 1767. Following paint research, the room has also been redecorated in the warm stone colour used when the tapestries were first installed there.

The Gardens

Much has been done recently to restore the park and the fine Victorian gardens to their former glory. An artificial lake, created with water from the River Cam, runs through delightful 18th-century parkland. The Classical Temple of Concorde, built in 1790 in honour of George III, and the restored 19th-century formal parterre garden dominate the views from the back of the house.

Visitors can see Robert Adam's ornamental garden buildings, and the Elysian Garden cascade. The thriving organic walled Victorian Kitchen Garden – with its box-edged paths, trained fruit and 52m (170ft) long vine house, still as it was in its Victorian heyday – is a memorable part of any visit. Also worth visiting are the historic kitchen and dry laundry.

Please note:
In some rooms, light levels are reduced to preserve vulnerable textiles and other collections. No photography or stiletto heels allowed in the house. Please call the site for special events information.

www.english-heritage.org.uk/audleyend

Available for corporate and private hire.

Licensed for civil wedding ceremonies.

NON-MEMBERS
HOUSE & GARDENS

Adult	£8.95
Concession	£6.70
Child	£4.50
Family ticket	£22.40

NON-MEMBERS
GARDENS ONLY

Adult	£4.80
Concession	£3.60
Child	£2.40
Family ticket	£12.00

OPENING TIMES

House:

4-26 Mar, Sat-Sun	10am-4pm
Behind The Scenes Tours	
1 Apr-30 Jun, Wed-Sun	11am-5pm
(closes 3pm Sat)	
Guided Historical Tours	
1 Jul-31 Aug, Wed-Sun	11am-5pm
(closes 3pm Sat)	
1 Sep-1 Oct, Wed-Sun	11am-5pm
(closes 3pm Sat)	
Guided Historical Tours	
7-29 Oct, Sat-Sun	10am-4pm
Behind The Scenes Tours	
3-31 Mar, Sat-Sun	10am-4pm
Behind The Scenes Tours	

Note: Last admission 1 hour before closing

Gardens:

4-26 Mar Sat-Sun	10am-5pm
1 Apr-1 Oct, Wed-Sun & Bank Hols	10am-6pm
7-29 Oct, Sat-Sun	10am-5pm
3-31 Mar, Sat-Sun	10am-5pm

At certain times of the year, access to the house is by 'Behind The Scenes Tours' and 'Guided Historical Tours'. In Mar and Oct, tours will be 'Behind The Scenes Tours' only. Some rooms will not be open to the public throughout the season. Please call for details.

HOW TO FIND US

Direction: 1 mile W of Saffron Walden on B1383 (M11 exit 8 or 10)

Train: Audley End 1¼ miles. Note: Footpath is beside busy main road.

Bus: Hedingham/Four Counties 59, Stansted Transit 301 from Audley End

Tel: 01799 522399 (info line)

Disabled access: Tel 01799 522842

Local Tourist Information
Saffron Walden: 01799 510444
Cambridge: 01223 464732

E OVP

Disabled access (ground floor & gardens only). Information sheets in French, Dutch, German, Spanish and Japanese.

MAP Page 269 (5F)
OS Map 154 (ref TL 525382)

Baconsthorpe Castle

Norfolk

The extensive ruins of a late medieval and Tudor fortified manor house, its knapped flint walls reflected in the lake enlarged from its original moat. Baconsthorpe is the work of several generations of the locally powerful (but somewhat disreputable) Heydon family. Sir John Heydon probably built the strong inner gatehouse and curtain wall, equipped for artillery, during the Wars of the Roses. In more peaceful times a descendant converted part of the house into a textile factory, and in c. 1560 Sir Christopher Heydon added the turreted outer gateway, inhabited until 1920.

OPENING TIMES

Any reasonable time

HOW TO FIND US

Direction: 3/4 mile N of village of Baconsthorpe off unclassified road, 3 miles E of Holt

Train: Sheringham 4½ miles

MAP Page 269 (1H)
OS Map 133 (ref TG 121382)

Berkhamsted Castle

Hertfordshire

The substantial remains of a strong and important motte and bailey castle dating from the 11th to 13th centuries, with surrounding walls, ditches and earthworks.

OPENING TIMES

All year, daily, Summer	10am 6pm
Winter	10am-4pm
Closed	25 Dec and 1 Jan

HOW TO FIND US

Direction: Near Berkhamsted

Bus: From surrounding areas

Train: Berkhamsted, adjacent

MAP Page 268 (6D)
OS Map 165 (ref SP 995082)

Berney Arms Windmill

Norfolk

One of Norfolk's best and largest extant marsh mills, built to grind a constituent of cement and in use until 1951, finally pumping water to drain surrounding marshland.

NON-MEMBERS

Adult	£2.40
Concession	£1.80
Child	£1.20

OPENING TIMES

1 May-31 Aug. Pre-booked guided tours only.
Tel: 01799 522842

Berney Arms Windmill

HOW TO FIND US

Direction: 3½ miles NE of Reedham on the N bank of River Yare. Accessible by hired boat, or by footpath from Halvergate (3½ miles). ¼ mile walk from train

Train: Berney Arms ¼ mile

MAP Page 269 (3K)
OS Map 134 (ref TG 465049)

Binham Priory

Norfolk

The most complete and impressive monastic ruins in Norfolk, of a Benedictine priory with a well-documented but scandalous history. The nave, with its splendid 13th-century west front, is now the parish church, displaying a screen with medieval saints overpainted with Protestant texts.

Managed by Binham Parochial Church Council.

OPENING TIMES

Any reasonable time

HOW TO FIND US

Direction: ¼ mile NW of village of Binham-on-Wells on road off B1388

Bus: Sanders 45/6 Norwich-Fakenham

Tel: 01328 830362

MAP Page 269 (1H)
OS Map 132 (ref TF 982399)

Binham Market Cross

Norfolk

The tall shaft of a 15th-century cross, on the site of an annual fair held from the 1100s until the 1950s.

Managed by Binham Parochial Church Council.

OPENING TIMES

Any reasonable time

HOW TO FIND US

Direction: Located on the Binham village green adjacent to the Priory

Bus: Sanders 45/6 Norwich-Fakenham

MAP Page 269 (1H)
OS Map 132 (ref TF 984396)

Blakeney Guildhall

Norfolk

The fine 15th-century brick-vaulted undercroft of the guildhall of Blakeney's prosperous fish merchants.

Managed by Blakeney Parish Council.

OPENING TIMES

Any reasonable time

HOW TO FIND US

Direction: In Blakeney off A149

Train: Sheringham 9 miles

Bus: Norfolk Green 36 Sheringham – Hunstanton

Tel: 0845 300 6116

MAP Page 269 (1H)
OS Map 133 (ref TG 028441)

Burgh Castle

Norfolk

The imposing stone walls, with added towers for catapults, of a Roman 3rd-century Saxon Shore fort. Panoramic views over Breydon Water, into which the fourth wall long since collapsed.

Managed by Norfolk Archaeological Trust.

OPENING TIMES

Any reasonable time

HOW TO FIND US

Direction: At far W end of Breydon Water on unclassified road, 3 miles W of Great Yarmouth

Train: Great Yarmouth 5 miles

Bus: First 6/7 from Great Yarmouth

MAP Page 269 (3K)
OS Map 134 (ref TG 475047)

Bury St Edmunds Abbey

Suffolk

The extensive ruins of the wealthiest and most powerful Benedictine monastery in England, shrine of St Edmund. They include the noble 14th-century Great Gate, the Norman Tower, and the ground plan and altered west front of the immense church.

Managed by St Edmundsbury Borough Council.

OPENING TIMES

Any reasonable time

HOW TO FIND US

Direction: E end of town centre

Train: Bury St Edmunds 1 mile

Bus: From surrounding areas

Tel: 01284 764667

MAP Page 269 (4G)
OS Map 155 (ref TL 857642)

Bushmead Priory

Bedfordshire – MK44 2LD

A rare survival of the complete refectory of an Augustinian priory, with fine timber roof and notable 14th-century wall paintings.

NON-MEMBERS

Adult	£2.00
Concession	£1.50
Child	£1.00

OPENING TIMES

1 May-31 Aug. Pre-booked guided tours only

Telephone: 01799 522842

HOW TO FIND US

Direction: Located off B660, 2 miles S of Bolnhurst

Train: St Neots 6 miles

P

MAP Page 268 (4E)
OS Map 153 (ref TL 115607)

Caister Roman Site

Norfolk

The partial remains of a Roman Saxon Shore fort, operating in partnership with Burgh Castle, including wall and ditch sections and building foundations.

Managed by Great Yarmouth Borough Council.

OPENING TIMES

Any reasonable time

HOW TO FIND US

Direction: Near Caister-on-Sea, 3 miles N of Great Yarmouth

Train: Great Yarmouth 3 miles

Bus: First Bus 1, 3, 8 from Great Yarmouth

MAP Page 269 (2K)
OS Map 134 (ref TG 517123)

Castle Acre Priory, Castle and Bailey Gate

Norfolk

The delightful village of Castle Acre boasts an extraordinary wealth of history.

Situated on the Peddar's Way, a major trade and pilgrim route to Thetford, Bromholm Priory and Walsingham, it is a very rare and complete survival of a Norman planned settlement, including a castle, town, parish church and associated monastery. All this is the work of a great Norman baronial family, the Warennes, mainly during the 11th and 12th centuries.

First came the castle, founded soon after the Conquest by the first William de Warenne, initially as a stone 'country house'. During the first half of the 12th century, however, more disturbed conditions prompted its progressive conversion into a strong keep, further defended by stone walls and an immense system of ditched earthworks. Still impressively visible, these are perhaps the finest castle earthworks in England.

Meanwhile, the 'planned town' deliberately established outside the castle was also protected by ditched earthwork defences with stone gates. The north or Bailey Gate of c. 1200 still survives, with the main road into the village still running between its towers.

Visitors to Castle Acre can likewise trace the ancient street layout of this now peaceful village, lined with attractive flint or brick houses, before exploring both the great castle earthworks and the extensive priory remains.

Castle Acre Castle and Bailey Gate

Norfolk

OPENING TIMES

Any reasonable time

HOW TO FIND US

Direction: Located at the E end of Castle Acre, 5 miles N of Swaffham

(Castle only)

MAP Page 269 (2G)
OS Map 132 (ref TF 819152)

Castle Acre Priory

See feature opposite

Castle Rising Castle

Norfolk – PE31 6AH

One of the largest, best-preserved and most lavishly decorated keeps in England, surrounded by 20 acres of mighty earthworks. Begun in 1138 by William d'Albini for his new wife, the widow of Henry I, in the 14th century it became the luxurious exile-place of Queen Isabella, widow (and alleged murderess) of Edward II.

Owned and managed by Lord Howard of Rising.

NON-MEMBERS	
Adult	£3.85
Concession	£3.10
Child	£2.20
Family ticket	£11.50

OPENING TIMES

1 Apr-1 Nov, daily	10am-6pm
Closes at dusk if earlier in Oct	
2 Nov-31 Mar, Wed-Sun	10am-4pm
Closed	24-26 Dec

HOW TO FIND US

Direction: Located 4 miles NE of King's Lynn off A149

Train: King's Lynn 4½ miles

Bus: First 410/1 King's Lynn-Hunstanton

Tel: 01553 631330

Audio tours (charged).

Disabled access (exterior, only toilets).

Dogs on leads (restricted areas).

MAP Page 269 (2G)
OS Map 132 (ref TF 666246)

Castle Acre Priory

Norfolk – PE32 2XD

One of the largest and best-preserved monastic sites in England, the foundation of Castle Acre Priory in about 1090 sprang directly from a visit by William de Warenne II and his wife Gundrada to the great French monastery of Cluny. So impressed were they by its beauty and holiness that they vowed to introduce the Cluniac order of monks to England.

The Cluniac love of decoration is everywhere reflected in the extensive ruins of Castle Acre Priory, whose great 12th-century church directly imitated that of Cluny itself. Its beautiful west end, standing almost to its full height, displays tiered ranks of intersecting round arches: it forms an attractive group with the late medieval porch, part timber-framed and part flint-chequered, and the extremely well-preserved prior's lodging. A mansion in itself, this includes a first floor chapel retaining traces of wall paintings, and a private chamber with two fine oriel windows.

There is much more to see at the priory, including the substantial remains of many of the buildings round the cloister. The recreated herb garden next to the visitor centre grows herbs which the monks would have used for medicinal, culinary and decorative purposes.

NEW FOR 2006 **New exhibits in the dairy illustrate how one powerful family created Castle Acre, and how three orders of men – nobles, priests and peasants – fought, prayed or worked. Beautiful carvings and other artefacts from the site and medieval period are also on show. New audio tour and orientation leaflet.**

NON-MEMBERS	
Adult	£4.50
Concession	£3.40
Child	£2.30
Family ticket	£11.30

OPENING TIMES

1 Apr-30 Sep, daily		10am-6pm
1 Oct-31 Mar, Thu-Mon		10am-4pm
Closed	24-26 Dec and 1 Jan	

HOW TO FIND US

Direction: ¼ mile W of village of Castle Acre, 5 miles N of Swaffham

Tel: 01760 755394

OVP

Disabled access (ground floor and grounds only).

MAP Page 269 (2G)
OS Map 132 (ref TF 814148)

Framlingham Castle

Suffolk – IP13 9BP

Framlingham is a magnificent example of a late 12th-century castle. Built by Roger Bigod, Earl of Norfolk, the castle, together with Framlingham Mere, was designed both as a stronghold and as a symbol of power and status – as befitted one of the most influential people at the court of Henry II. Architecturally, the castle is notable for its curtain wall and mural towers, an early example of this design.

The castle fulfilled a number of roles. It was at the centre of the struggle between the Bigod barons and the Crown, and Mary Tudor mustered her supporters here in 1553, before being crowned Queen. At the end of the 16th century it was a prison; later still a poorhouse and school were built in the grounds. Today the imposing stone walls and crenellated towers with their ornate Tudor chimneys dominate, while the grassy earthworks around the castle are subdued reminders of busier times. To the west, the Mere provides a stunning setting.

While visiting, why not take a walk around the magnificent Framlingham Mere and the castle's outer courts and moats? Or perhaps negotiate the impressive wall-walk and take in the beautiful views of the surrounding countryside, or enjoy one of Framlingham's many pubs or tearooms.

Please note

Entry also includes access to the Lanman Trust's Museum of local history.

www.english-heritage.org.uk/framlinghamcastle

Late medieval stone head

NON-MEMBERS

Adult	£4.50
Concession	£3.40
Child	£2.30
Family ticket	£11.30

OPENING TIMES

1 Apr-30 Sep, daily	10am-6pm
1 Oct-31 Mar, Thu-Mon	10am-4pm
Closed	24-26 Dec and 1 Jan

The property may close early if an event is booked, please ring in advance for details.

HOW TO FIND US

Direction: In Framlingham on B1116

Train: Wickham Market 6½ miles; Saxmundham 7 miles

Bus: First 64A, Gemini 164 from Ipswich (passes Woodbridge); Beeston 118/9 from Ipswich

Tel: 01728 724189

Local Tourist Information Woodbridge: 01394 382240

OVP

Disabled access (grounds and ground floor only).

MAP Page 269 (4J)
OS Map 156 (ref TM 287637)

Church of the Holy Sepulchre, Thetford

Norfolk

The only surviving remains in England of a priory of Canons of the Holy Sepulchre, who aided pilgrims to Christ's tomb: the ruined nave of their 14th-century church, later used as a barn. Thetford Priory (see p.137) is within walking distance.

OPENING TIMES

Any reasonable time

HOW TO FIND US

Direction: Located on the W side of Thetford off B1107

Bus: From surrounding areas

Train: Thetford ¾ mile

MAP Page 269 (3H)
OS Map 144 (ref TL 865831)

Cow Tower, Norwich

Norfolk

One of the earliest purpose-built artillery blockhouses in England, this brick tower was built in c. 1398-9 to command a strategic point in Norwich's city defences.

Managed by Norwich City Council.

OPENING TIMES

Any reasonable time

Cow Tower, Norwich

HOW TO FIND US

Direction: In Norwich, near cathedral (approx. 1 mile walk)

Bus: From surrounding areas

Train: Norwich ½ mile

Tel: 01603 213434

MAP Page 269 (2J)
OS Map 134 (ref TG 240092)

Creake Abbey

Norfolk

The ruined church of an Augustinian abbey, reduced in size after fire and plague.

OPENING TIMES

Any reasonable time

HOW TO FIND US

Direction: N of North Creake off B1355

MAP Page 269 (1H)
OS Map 132 (ref TF 856395)

De Grey Mausoleum, Flitton

Bedfordshire

Among the largest sepulchral chapels attached to any English church, this cruciform mausoleum houses a remarkable sequence of 17 sculpted and effigied monuments spanning nearly three centuries (1615-1899), to the De Grey family of Wrest Park.

De Grey Mausoleum, Flitton

OPENING TIMES

Weekends only. Contact the keykeeper in advance: Mrs Stimson, 3 Highfield Road, Flitton (01525 860094)

HOW TO FIND US

Direction: Through Flitton, attached to the church, on an unclassified road 1½ miles W of A6 at Silsoe

Train: Flitwick 2 miles

MAP Page 268 (5E)
OS Map 153 (ref TL 059359)

Denny Abbey and the Farmland Museum

Cambridgeshire – CB5 9PQ

Denny Abbey has a unique and fascinating history. Founded in 1159 as a Benedictine monastery, it then became a retirement home for elderly Knights Templars. After the Templars' suppression for alleged heresy in 1308, it next passed to the Countess of Pembroke, who converted part into a house and established in the rest a convent of 'Poor Clare' Franciscan nuns. This in turn was dissolved by Henry VIII in 1539, whereafter the buildings became a farm until the 1960s, with the nuns' great refectory as its barn. Among its tenants was Thomas Hobson, the horse-hirer whose refusal to allow customers to select their mounts gave rise to the expression 'Hobson's choice'.

Denny Abbey and the Farmland Museum

All these changes are still traceable in the building: they are now interpreted for visitors by new graphic panels illustrated by local artist Anne Biggs, together with a time-line tracing the site's history from 4000 BC, a new viewing platform and displays of site-finds. New family-friendly activities include imaginative hands-on interactives about medieval tiles, stained glass and arches.

Denny's later farming story is continued by 'Walnut Tree Cottage', furnished as a labourer's home of the 1940s. The site's Farmland Museum also features a fenman's hut, blacksmith's and wheelwright's workshops, a village shop display and many other aspects of Cambridgeshire rural life.

Please note: There is a charge of £2.40 for EH members and OVP holders for entry to the museum.

Managed by the Farmland Museum Trust.

ENTRY MUSEUM AND ABBEY NON-MEMBERS

Adult	£3.80
Concession	£3.00
Child	£1.70
Children under 5	Free
Family ticket	£9.60

OPENING TIMES

1 Apr-31 Oct, daily	12pm-5pm

i

Sign-up on-line for our email Members' Newsletter at **www.english-heritage.org.uk**

Denny Abbey and the Farmland Museum

HOW TO FIND US

Direction: Located 6 miles N of Cambridge on A10

Train: Waterbeach 3 miles

Bus: Stagecoach in Cambridge 19 Cambridge-Ely

Tel: 01223 860489/860988

OVP

Disabled access (museum and abbey ground floor only).

Dogs on leads (restricted areas only).

Tearooms/restaurant (weekends only).

MAP Page 269 (4F)
OS Map 154 (ref TL 492685)

Duxford Chapel

Cambridgeshire

A modest but complete and attractive 14th-century chantry chapel, perhaps originally a hospital.

Managed by South Cambridgeshire District Council.

OPENING TIMES

Any reasonable time

HOW TO FIND US

Direction: Adjacent to Whittlesford station off A505

Train: Whittlesford, adjacent

MAP Page 269 (4F)
OS Map 154 (ref TL 485473)

Framlingham Castle

See feature – Page 128

Great Yarmouth Row Houses & Greyfriars' Cloisters

Norfolk – NR30 2RQ

Living space was very much at a premium in early 17th-century Great Yarmouth, then among the most prosperous fishing ports in England. Hence the inhabitants crowded into the town's distinctive 'Rows', a network of narrow alleyways linking Yarmouth's three main thoroughfares. Many 'Row houses' were damaged by Word War II bombing or demolished during post-War clearances, but two surviving properties in the care of English Heritage show what these characteristic dwellings looked like at various stages in their history.

Both Row 111 and the Old Merchant's House were originally built in the early 17th century as wealthy merchant's residences, but later sub-divided into tenements. The Old Merchant's House, which has spectacular Jacobean plaster ceilings in two of its rooms, is presented as it was in about 1870, when the Atkins and Rope families of fishermen – represented by models of family members at work or rest – shared the property. Adjacent Row 111 house is shown as it was in about 1942 (just before it received a direct hit from an incendiary bomb), likewise with

Great Yarmouth Row Houses & Greyfriars' Cloisters

figures of the three families which then occupied parts of it. Both houses also display a wonderful collection of fixtures and fittings – including painted panels, elaborate wall-ties and door-knockers – rescued from other now-demolished Row dwellings, a treasure trove for lovers of period decoration.

Nearby stands Greyfriars Cloister, the remains of a 13th-century friary of Franciscan 'grey friars', later swallowed up by Row development and converted into a number of dwellings large and small. Traces of their interior features can still be seen on the brick-built walls of parts of the cloister and church, laid bare by wartime bombing. Early 14th-century wall-paintings were discovered here in the 1960s. (Enquire at Row 111 for arrangements to view the paintings.)

NON-MEMBERS	
Adult	£3.40
Concession	£2.60
Child	£1.70

OPENING TIMES

1 Apr-30 Sep, daily 12pm-5pm

Free guided tour of Greyfriars' Cloisters at 10.30am on the first Wed of every month. Please call site for details.

HOW TO FIND US

Direction: Great Yarmouth, follow signs for Historic Quay

Train: Great Yarmouth ½ mile

Bus: From surrounding areas

Tel: 01493 857900

OVP

MAP Page 269 (2K)
OS Map 134 (Houses ref TG 525072, Cloisters ref TG 524073)

Grime's Graves

See feature – Page 132

Hadleigh Castle

Essex

The romantic ruins of a once-royal castle overlooking the Essex marshes. Hadleigh was begun in about 1230 by Hubert de Burgh, but extensively refortified as a strong royal residence in 1360-70 by Edward III. The barbican and the two striking eastern drum towers – one seemingly used by Georgian revenue men looking out for smugglers – are his work. Recent archaeological research has also discovered evidence of Roman activity here.

OPENING TIMES

Any reasonable time

HOW TO FIND US

Direction: ¾ mile S of A13 at Hadleigh

Train: Leigh-on-Sea 1½ miles by footpath

Bus: First and Arriva Southend services from surrounding areas to within ½ mile

Disabled access (hilly).

MAP Page 269 (7G)
OS Map 154 (ref TL 485473)

Don't forget your membership card when you visit any of the properties listed in this handbook.

Hill Hall

Essex – CM6 7QQ

This fine Elizabethan mansion features some of the earliest external Renaissance architectural detail in the country, and two rare and outstanding sets of 16th-century wall paintings of mythical and Biblical subjects. Hill Hall has now been divided into private houses, but parts remain open to the public by prior arrangement.

NON-MEMBERS	
Adult	£3.00
Concession	£2.50
Child	£1.50

OPENING TIMES

1 Apr-30 Sep Pre-booked guided tours on Wed only

Tel: 01799 522842

HOW TO FIND US

Direction: 3 miles SE of Epping. Entrance ½ mile N of Theydon Mount

Underground: Epping 2½ miles

MAP Page 269 (6F)
OS Map 167 (ref TQ 489995)

Grime's Graves

Norfolk – IP26 5DE

Grime's Graves is the only Neolithic flint mine open to visitors in Britain. A grassy lunar landscape of over 400 shafts, pits, quarries and spoil dumps, they were first named Grim's Graves – meaning the pagan god Grim's quarries, or 'the Devil's holes' – by the Anglo-Saxons. It was not until one of them was excavated in 1870 that they were found to be flint mines dug over 5,000 years ago, during the later Neolithic and early Bronze Ages.

What the prehistoric miners sought here was the fine quality jet-black flint 'floorstone', which occurs some nine metres below surface level. This was prized as an easily 'knapped' material for axes and other tools – and much later elsewhere for well-sparking flintlock muskets. Digging with red-deer antler picks, they sank shafts from which radiated gallery-tunnels, following the seams of flint. Today visitors can descend 9 metres (30 ft) by ladder into one excavated shaft, an unforgettable experience.

The small exhibition area illustrates the history of this fascinating site.

Set amid the distinctive Breckland heath landscape, Grime's Graves is also a Site of Special Scientific Interest, the home of a wide variety of plants and fauna.

NON-MEMBERS	
Adult	£2.70
Concession	£2.00
Child	£1.40
Family ticket	£6.80

No entry to the mines for children under 5 years of age

OPENING TIMES	
3-31 March, Thu-Mon	10am-5pm
1 Apr-30 Sep, daily	10am-6pm
1-31 Oct, Thu-Mon	10am-5pm

HOW TO FIND US

Direction: Located 7 miles NW of Thetford off A134

Train: Brandon 3½ miles

Bus: Burton's 200 Thetford – Newmarket, alight Santon Downham; then 2 miles

Tel: 01842 810656

OVP

Disabled access (exhibition area only; access track rough).

Dogs on leads (restricted areas).

Visitors intending to descend the shaft should wear flat shoes.

MAP Page 269 (3G)
OS Map 144 (ref TL 817899)

Houghton House

Bedfordshire

The shell of a 17th-century mansion with magnificent views, reputedly the inspiration for the 'House Beautiful' in John Bunyan's *Pilgrim's Progress*. Built around 1615 for Mary, Dowager Countess of Pembroke, in a mixture of Jacobean and Classical styles: the ground floors of two Italianate loggias survive, possibly the work of Inigo Jones.

OPENING TIMES

Any reasonable time

HOW TO FIND US

Direction: 1 mile NE of Ampthill off A421, 8 miles S of Bedford

Train: Flitwick or Stewartby, both 3 miles

Bus: Stagecoach in Northants 142, Red Rose 223 Bedford – Flitwick

MAP Page 268 (5E)
OS Map 153 (ref TL 039395)

Isleham Priory Church

Cambridgeshire

The best example in England of a small Norman Benedictine priory church, surviving in a surprisingly unaltered state despite later conversion into a barn.

OPENING TIMES

Any reasonable time. Contact the key-keeper, Mrs R Burton, 18 Festival Road, Isleham – 5 mins walk

HOW TO FIND US

Direction: Located in centre of Isleham, 16 miles NE of Cambridge on B1104

Train: Newmarket 8½ miles, Ely 9 miles

MAP Page 269 (4G)
OS Map 143 (ref TL 642743)

Landguard Fort

Suffolk – IP11 3TX

The site of the last opposed invasion of England in 1667 and the first land battle of the Royal Marines. The current fort was built in the 18th century, and modified in the 19th century with substantial additional 19th/20th century outside batteries.

The nearby submarine mining building houses Felixstowe museum's collections of local interest.

Managed by Landguard Fort Trust.

NEW FOR 2006 **Existing guided tours and audio tours of the fort will be supplemented in 2006 by a DVD presentation of the site's history and by guided tours of the outside batteries.**

NON-MEMBERS

Adult	£3.00
Concession	£2.50
Child	£1.00

Free entry for children under 5 and wheelchair users.

OPENING TIMES

1 Apr-31 May, daily	10am-5pm
1 Jun-30 Sep, daily	10am-6pm
1-27 Oct, daily	10am-5pm

Last admission 1 hour before closing

Tel 07749 695523 to book battery and group tours

HOW TO FIND US

Direction: 1 mile S of Felixstowe town centre – follow signs to Landguard Point

Train: Felixstowe 2½ miles

Bus: First 75-7 Ipswich-Felixstowe Dock to within ¾ mile of site

New guidebook.

MAP Page 269 (5J)
OS Map 169 (ref TM 284319)

Leiston Abbey

Suffolk

One of Suffolk's most impressive monastic ruins, of a 14th-century abbey of Premonstratensian 'white canons', with a 16th-century brick gatehouse.

Managed by Pro Corda College.

OPENING TIMES

Any reasonable time

HOW TO FIND US

Direction: N of Leiston off B1069

Bus: First 64, Gemini 164, Goldline 165 Ipswich-Aldeburgh (pass close Saxmundham)

Train: Saxmundham 5 miles

MAP Page 269 (4K)
OS Map 156 (ref TM 445642)

Lexden Earthworks and Bluebottle Grove

Essex

The banks and ditches of a series of late Iron Age defences protecting the western side of Camulodunum – pre-Roman Colchester. There are also many pre-Roman graves hereabouts, including Lexden Tumulus, allegedly the burial place of the British chieftain Cunobelinus.

Managed by Colchester Borough Council.

OPENING TIMES

Any reasonable time

HOW TO FIND US

Direction: 2 miles W of Colchester off A604. Lexden Earthworks are on Lexden Straight Rd. To visit Bluebottle Grove from Lexden, turn left into Heath Rd, left into Church Lane, right into Beech Hill and follow the brown-and-white tourist signs to the site

Train: Colchester or Colchester Town, both 2½ miles

Bus: Network Colchester 5 from ⇌ Colchester

Tel: 01206 282931

MAP Page 269 (5H)
OS Map 168 (Lexden Earthworks ref TL 965246, Bluebottle Grove ref TL 975245)

Lindsey/St James's Chapel

Suffolk

A pretty thatched 13th-century chapel with lancet windows.

OPENING TIMES

All year: daily 10am-4pm

HOW TO FIND US

Direction: Located on an unclassified road ½ mile E of Rose Green and 8 miles E of Sudbury

Train: Sudbury 8 miles

Disabled access (single step).

MAP Page 269 (5H)
OS Map 156 (ref TM 445642)

Longthorpe Tower

Cambridgeshire – PE1 1HA

Longthorpe displays one of the most complete and important sets of 14th-century domestic wall paintings in northern Europe. This varied 'spiritual encyclopaedia' of worldly and religious subjects includes the Wheel of Life, the Nativity and King David.

NON-MEMBERS

Adult	£2.40
Concession	£1.80
Child	£1.20

OPENING TIMES

1 May-31 Aug, Pre-booked guided tours only

Longthorpe Tower

HOW TO FIND US

Direction: Located 2 miles W of Peterborough on A47

Train: Peterborough 1½ miles

Bus: Stagecoach in Peterborough Citi 2, Kime 9 from city centre (passing ⇌ Peterborough)

Tel: 01799 522842

Parking (not at site).

MAP Page 268 (3E)
OS Map 142 (ref TL 162984)

Mistley Towers

Essex

Two porticoed Classical towers, which stood at each end of a grandiose but highly unconventional Georgian church, designed by Robert Adam in 1776.

Managed by Mistley Thorn Residents' Association.

OPENING TIMES

Key available from Mistley Quay Workshops: 01206 393884

HOW TO FIND US

Direction: Located on B1352, 1½ miles E of A137 at Lawford, 9 miles E of Colchester

Train: Mistley ¼ mile

Bus: First 103/4 Colchester-Harwich

Disabled access (exterior only).
Dogs on leads (restricted areas).

MAP Page 269 (5H)
OS Map 169 (ref TM 116320)

Moulton Packhorse Bridge

Suffolk

A pretty four-arched 15th-century bridge, spanning the River Kennet on the old route from Cambridge to Bury St Edmunds.

OPENING TIMES

Any reasonable time

HOW TO FIND US

Direction: **In Moulton off B1085, 4 miles E of Newmarket**

Train: **Kennett 2 miles**

MAP Page 269 (4G)
OS Map 154 (ref TL 698645)

North Elmham Chapel

Norfolk

A place with an unusual story, told by new graphic panels. The small Norman chapel here stood on the site of an earlier timber church, probably the Saxon cathedral of East Anglia.

In the 14th century it was converted into a fortified manor house by Henry Despenser, the unpopular Bishop of Norwich who brutally suppressed the Peasant's Revolt of 1381.

Managed by North Elmham Parish Council.

OPENING TIMES

Any reasonable time

HOW TO FIND US

Direction: **Located 6 miles N of East Dereham on B1110**

MAP Page 269 (2H)
OS Map 132 (ref TF 988216)

Old Gorhambury House

Hertfordshire

The remains of a once immense mansion built in 1563-8 by Sir Nicholas Bacon, Queen Elizabeth's Lord Keeper, and twice visited by the Queen. Its extravagantly showy two-storey porch survives, with parts of the hall, chapel and clock-tower.

OPENING TIMES

All year (except 1 Jun), any reasonable time

HOW TO FIND US

Direction: **On foot by permissive 2-mile path: any reasonable time. By car (1 May-30 Sep, Thurs pm only), drive to Gorhambury Mansion and walk across the gardens**

Train: **St Albans Abbey 3 miles, St Albans 3½ miles**

Bus: **Arriva 300/1, 340 St Albans-Hemel Hempstead to start of drive**

MAP Page 268 (6E)
OS Map 166 (ref TL 110076)

Orford Castle

Suffolk – IP12 2ND

The unique polygonal tower-keep of Orford Castle stands beside the pretty town and former port which Henry II also developed here in the 1160s. His aim was to counterbalance the power of turbulent East Anglian barons like Hugh Bigod of Framlingham, and to guard the coast against foreign mercenaries called to their aid.

An eighteen-sided drum with three square turrets, and a forebuilding reinforcing its entrance, the keep was built to a highly innovative design. The progress of its construction between 1165 and 1173 is extensively recorded in royal documents. Both exterior and interior survive almost intact, allowing visitors to explore the basement with its vital well, and the lower and upper halls – the latter the principal room of the castle. Round these polygonal rooms is a maze of passages, leading to the chapel, kitchen and other chambers in the turrets. From the roof there are magnificent views seaward to Orford Ness.

Recent archaeological work has provided a clearer ▷

understanding of how the castle worked, and a new painting by Frank Gardiner shows how the keep and its vanished outer defences looked in their heyday. The upper hall now houses a display by the Orford Museum Trust, including local finds of Roman brooches, medieval seals and coins and some of the borough regalia. Graphic panels display maps, documents, pictures and photographs, illustrating Orford's history down to the 20th century.

NON-MEMBERS

Adult	£4.50
Concession	£3.40
Child	£2.30
Family ticket	£11.30

OPENING TIMES

1 Apr-30 Sep, daily	10am-6pm
1 Oct-31 Mar, Thu-Mon	10am-4pm
Closed	24-26 Dec and 1 Jan

HOW TO FIND US

Direction: In Orford on B1084, 20 miles NE of Ipswich

Train: Wickham Market 8 miles

Bus: Country Travel 160, 182 Woodbridge-Orford (passes ⇌ Melton)

Tel: 01394 450472

MAP Page 269 (4J)
OS Map 166 (ref TL 110076)

Prior's Hall Barn, Widdington

Essex

One of the finest surviving medieval barns in eastern England, tree-ring dated to the mid-15th century, with a breathtaking aisled interior and crown post roof, the product of some 400 oaks.

OPENING TIMES

1 Apr-30 Sep, Sat-Sun	10am-6pm

HOW TO FIND US

Direction: In Widdington, on unclassified road 2 miles SE of Newport, off B1383

Train: Newport 2 miles

Bus: Stansted Transit 301 Bishops Stortford-Saffron Walden (passing ⇌ Audley End)

MAP Page 269 (5F)
OS Map 167 (ref TL 537318)

Roman Wall, St Albans

Hertfordshire

A section of the two-mile long wall built between AD 265-270 to defend the Roman city of Verulamium: including the foundations of towers and the London Gate.

OPENING TIMES

Any reasonable time

HOW TO FIND US

Direction: Located on the S side of St Albans, ½ mile from the centre, off the A4147

Train: St Albans Abbey ½ mile, St Albans 1¼ miles

Bus: From surrounding areas

MAP Page 268 (6E)
OS Map 166 (ref TL 137066)

Saxtead Green Post Mill

Suffolk – IP13 9QQ

This corn mill, whose whole body revolves on its base, was one of many built in Suffolk from the late 13th century. Though milling ceased in 1947, it is still in working order. Climb the wooden stairs to the various floors, which are full of fascinating mill machinery.

NON-MEMBERS

Adult	£2.70
Concession	£2.00
Child	£1.40

OPENING TIMES

1 Apr-30 Sep, Fri-Sat & Bank Hols	12pm-5pm

HOW TO FIND US

Direction: 2½ miles NW of Framlingham on A1120

Train: Wickham Market 9 miles

Bus: Country Travel 160, 182 Woodbridge – Orford (passes close to ⇌ Woodbridge)

Tel: 01728 685789

MAP Page 269 (4J)
OS Map 156 (ref TM 253644)

St Botolph's Priory

Essex

The 12th-century nave of the first Augustinian priory church in England, with an impressive west front.

Managed by Colchester Borough Council.

St Botolph's Priory

OPENING TIMES

Any reasonable time

HOW TO FIND US

Direction: Nr Colchester Town station

Train: Colchester Town, adjacent

Bus: From surrounding areas

Tel: 01206 282931

MAP Page 269 (5H)
OS Map 168 (ref TL 999249)

St John's Abbey Gate

Essex

This elaborate pinnacled 15th-century gatehouse, in East Anglian flushwork, is the sole survivor of the Benedictine abbey of St John. It was stormed by Parliamentarian soldiers during the Civil War siege of 1648.

Managed by Colchester Borough Council.

OPENING TIMES

Any reasonable time

HOW TO FIND US

Direction: S side of central Colchester

Train: Colchester Town ¼ mile

Bus: From surrounding areas

Tel: 01206 282931

MAP Page 269 (5H)
OS Map 168 (ref TL 998248)

St Olave's Priory

Norfolk

The wonderfully complete 14th-century brick-vaulted refectory undercroft – later a cottage occupied until 1902 – of a small Augustinian priory.

OPENING TIMES

Any reasonable time

HOW TO FIND US

Direction: Located 5½ miles SW of the town of Great Yarmouth on A143

Train: Haddiscoe 1¼ miles

Dogs on leads (restricted areas only).

MAP Page 269 (3K)
OS Map 134 (ref TM 459996)

Thetford Priory

Norfolk

The extensive remains of one of the most important East Anglian monasteries, the Cluniac Priory of Our Lady of Thetford. Founded in the early 12th century, it owed much of its prosperity to a miraculous appearance of the Virgin Mary, whose statue here was discovered to conceal relics of saints, and became a magnet for pilgrims. Two of the greatest men in early Tudor England, Thomas Howard, victor of Flodden, and Henry Fitzroy, illegitimate son of Henry VIII, were buried near her shrine.

Survivals include the lower walls of the church and cloister, along with the impressive shell of the priors' lodging and, reached by a pathway from the main site, an almost complete 14th-century gatehouse. The Church of the Holy Sepulchre (see p.129) is within walking distance.

OPENING TIMES

Any reasonable time

HOW TO FIND US

Direction: Located on the W side of Thetford, near the station

Train: Thetford ¼ mile

Bus: From surrounding areas

MAP Page 269 (3G)
OS Map 144 (ref TL 866834)

Thetford Warren Lodge

Norfolk

Probably built c.1400 by the Prior of Thetford, this defensible lodge protected gamekeepers and hunting parties against armed poachers. Much later used by the local 'warreners' who harvested rabbits here.

OPENING TIMES

Any reasonable time

HOW TO FIND US

Direction: Located 2 miles W of Thetford off B1107

Train: Thetford 2½ miles

Bus: Burton's 200 Thetford – Newmarket (passes close Thetford)

MAP Page 269 (3G)
OS Map 144 (ref TL 839841)

Wrest Park Bedfordshire – MK45 4HS

This is one of the most magnificent gardens in England, yet one of the least well known. Unlike 'Capability' Brown's natural landscape styling, favoured during the late 18th century, Wrest Park's formal gardens provide a fascinating history of gardening styles, laid out over 150 years and inspired by the great gardens of Versailles in France.

The Pavilion from the Long Water

Wrest Park was the home of the De Grey family – whose serried monuments fill the nearby De Grey Mausoleum – from the 13th century until 1917. The gardens are celebrated for their rare survival of a formal early 18th-century layout of wooded walks and canals, centred on the architectural highlight of the pavilion designed by Thomas Archer in 1710. Subsequent generations added garden buildings such as the Bath House and the Chinese Pavilion, valuing the special atmosphere of the established garden even when more fashionable landscapers would have swept it away.

The old manor house was demolished when the present house was completed by 1834. This was designed by Thomas, Earl de Grey, an enthusiast for 18th-century French architecture. It is set further north than the site of the old house, and new formal gardens were laid out between the mansion and the woodland garden. The Orangery, Italian garden and Parterre with magnificent lead statues date from the 19th century.

Don't miss our English Heritage St George's Day event here, the largest in the country.

Please note
There is no public access to the house. Entry to gardens only.

www.english-heritage.org.uk/wrestpark

NON-MEMBERS	
Adult	£4.50
Concession	£3.40
Child	£2.30
Family ticket	£11.30

OPENING TIMES

1 Apr-30 Sep, Sat-Sun & Bank Hols	10am-6pm
1-31 Oct, Sat-Sun	10am-5pm

HOW TO FIND US

Direction: ¾ mile E of Silsoe off A6, 10 miles S of Bedford

Train: Flitwick 4 miles

Bus: Stagecoach in Northants X1 Bedford – Luton

Tel: 01525 860152

OVP

Buggies available for disabled visitors.

MAP Page 268 (5E)
OS Map 153 (ref TL 091355)

Tilbury Fort

Essex – RM18 7NR

The artillery fort at Tilbury on the Thames estuary protected London's seaward approach from the 16th century through to World War II. Henry VIII built the first fort here, and Queen Elizabeth famously rallied her army nearby to face the threat of the Armada. The present fort was begun in 1672 under Charles II: it is much the best example of its type in England, with its complete circuit of moats and bastioned outworks still substantially surviving. The fort mounted powerful artillery to command the river, as well as landward defences. Later, two magazines were constructed to store vast quantities of gun-powder. In one of these a new exhibition traces the role of the fort in the defence of London. Perhaps because of its strength, Tilbury Fort has never been involved in the kind of action for which it was designed. The worst bloodshed within the fort occurred in 1776, when a fight following a Kent-Essex cricket match left a cricketer and the fort's sergeant dead.

Visitors can now enter one of Tilbury's 19th-century magazines through dark and atmospheric passages in the north east bastion. For those with an interest in military

history there are new displays of guns and gunpowder barrels, and information on advances in military engineering.

The recently revised audio tour includes Elizabeth I's Armada speech, and a description of life at the fort by Nathan Makepiece, the fort's Master Gunner. '*Sharpe*', the TV historical drama set during the Napoleonic Wars, was filmed here.

NEW FOR 2006 New interpretation scheme in the North East Bastion magazine passages and an interactive oral history programme, to provide every visitor with a fascinating new insight into Tilbury.

NON-MEMBERS

Adult	£3.40
Concession	£2.60
Child	£1.70
Family ticket	£8.50

£1.30 to fire anti-aircraft gun

OPENING TIMES

1 Apr-31 Oct, daily	10am-5pm
1 Nov-31 Mar, Thu-Mon	10am-4pm

HOW TO FIND US

Direction: Located ½ mile E of Tilbury off A126. Close to the Port of Tilbury

Train: Tilbury Town 1½ miles

Bus: Rail shuttle ⇌ Tilbury – Tilbury Ferry, then ¼ mile

Ferry: Gravesend-Tilbury Ferry, then ¼ mile

Tel: 01375 858489

OVP

Disabled access (exterior, magazines and fort square).

Dogs on leads (restricted areas).

MAP Page 269 (7G)
OS Map 177 (ref TQ 651753)

Waltham Abbey Gatehouse and Bridge

Essex

A fine 14th-century gatehouse, bridge and other remains of the abbey refounded by Harold, last Saxon King of England.

Managed by Lee Valley Park.

OPENING TIMES

Any reasonable time

HOW TO FIND US

Direction: In Waltham Abbey off A112

Train: Waltham Cross 1¼ miles

Bus: Frequent services by different operators from ⇌ Waltham Cross

Tel: 01992 702200

Sensory trail guide.

MAP Page 269 (6F)
OS Map 166 (Gatehouse ref TL 381007, Harold's Bridge ref TL 382009)

Weeting Castle

Norfolk

The ruins of a substantial early medieval moated manor house, built in local flint.

OPENING TIMES

Any reasonable time

HOW TO FIND US

Direction: Located 2 miles N of Brandon off B1106

Train: Brandon 1¼ miles

MAP Page 269 (3G)
OS Map 144 (ref TL 778891)

Wrest Park

See feature – Page 138

Other Historic Attractions

Discounted entry to our members (discounts may not apply on event days)

Felixstowe Museum

Suffolk

ENTRY

Adult	£1.00
Child	£0.50

20% discount for EH members.

OPENING TIMES

Easter Sun-6 Jun, Sun & Bank Hols	1pm-5.30pm
7 Jun-28 Sep, Wed, Sun & Bank Hols	1pm-5.30pm
29 Sep-31 Oct, Sun & Bank Hols	1pm-5.30pm

Direction: Located 1 mile S of Felixstowe, near the docks

Train: Felixstowe 2½ miles

Bus: First Eastern Counties service 75/7 Ipswich – Felixstowe Dock to within ½ mile of the site

Tel: 01394 674355 for admission prices and further details

MAP Page 269 (5J)
OS Map 169 (ref TM 283320)

Flag Fen Excavations

Cambridgeshire

Britain's Bronze Age centre, including preserved timbers of a 3,000 year old fen causeway, recreated Bronze Age village and museum of excavated finds. Extensive shop, café and events programme.

ENTRY

Adult	£4.25
Concession	£3.75
Child	£3.00
Under 5s	Free
Family	£11.50

20% reduction, including event days, for EH members

Additional prices apply on event days

OPENING TIMES

Daily	10am-5pm
Closed	24 Dec-2 Jan

Last admission 4pm in summer, 3pm in winter

Direction: 2 miles S of Wittlesey Rail Station to the East of Peterborough; 3 miles from Peterborough city centre

Tel: 01733 313414

www.flagfen.com

MAP Page 268 (3E)
OS Map 142 (ref TL 225989)

Time and Tide Museum

Norfolk

Come and find out about Great Yarmouth's fascinating history, its rich maritime and fishing heritage. Wander down a typical 1913 'Row'; experience the heady atmosphere of a 1950s fishwharf; take the wheel of a coastal drifter and hear gripping tales of wreck and rescue. Located in a Victorian herring curing works, there is something for all the family, with lively hands-on displays and free audio guides.

ENTRY

Adult	£5.80
Adult in family group	£5.10
Concession	£5.20
Child	£3.70

25% discount on all ticket categories for EH Members

OPENING TIMES

3 Apr-29 Oct Mon-Sun	10am-5pm
30 Oct-1 Apr Mon-Fri	10am-4pm
Sat & Sun	12pm-4pm

Closed
21-26 Dec and 31 Dec-1 Jan

Tel: 01493 745526

www.museums.norfolk.gov.uk

MAP Page 269 (2K)
OS Map 142 (ref TL 225989)

Peveril Castle – see page 155

East Midlands

'Four Dukes, two Lords, and three rabbit warrens take in half the county…'

Sir George Savile of Rufford Abbey to Lord Rockingham, 1769

www.english-heritage.org.uk/eastmidlands

Properties

See individual listings for details

Derbyshire
Arbor Low Stone Circle and Gib Hill Barrow, Bolsover Castle, Bolsover Cundy House, Hardwick Old Hall, Hob Hurst's House, Nine Ladies Stone Circle, Peveril Castle, Sutton Scarsdale Hall, Wingfield Manor

Leicestershire
Ashby de la Zouch Castle, Jewry Wall, Kirby Muxloe Castle

Lincolnshire
Bolingbroke Castle, Gainsborough Old Hall, Lincoln Medieval Bishops' Palace, Sibsey Trader Windmill, Tattershall College

Northamptonshire
Chichele College, Eleanor Cross Geddington, Kirby Hall, Rushton Triangular Lodge

Nottinghamshire
Mattersey Priory, Rufford Abbey

Rutland
Lyddington Bede House

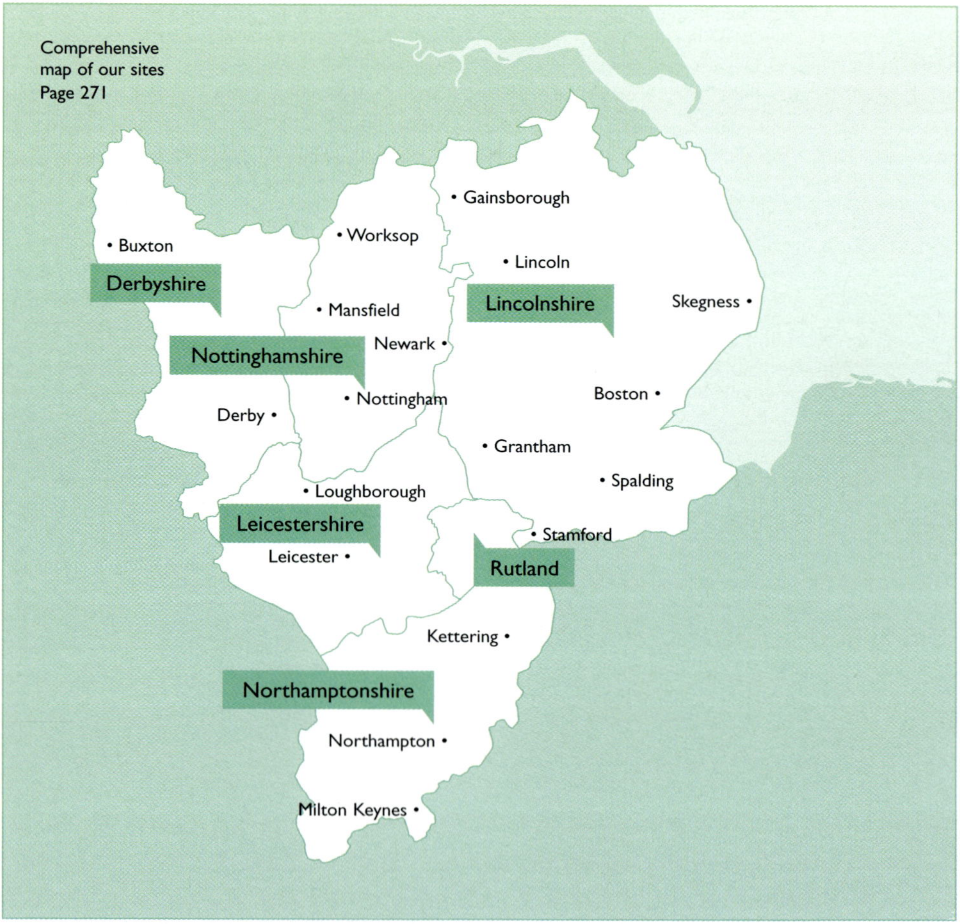

Kirby Hall – see page 153

A Heritage of Great Houses

The East Midlands is a region of very varied landscapes, ranging from the Derbyshire High Peak to the wide-skied fens of south Lincolnshire, and from the Nottinghamshire Trent plain to the rolling limestone hills and pretty villages of Northamptonshire, Leicestershire and Rutland. Each of these areas has its own distinctive English Heritage sites. In the Peak stands medieval **Peveril Castle**, along with enigmatic **Arbor Low Stone Circle** and other prehistoric remains; Lincolnshire has **Bolingbroke Castle**, **Sibsey Trader Windmill** and **Tattershall College**; Northamptonshire boasts Geddington's **Eleanor Cross** and delightful **Rushton Triangular Lodge**.

But what makes the East Midlands particularly attractive for English Heritage members is the region's large number of 'great houses': so famous was this area for lordly estates that part of it is still known as 'the Dukeries.' Much the earliest of these great houses is **Lincoln Medieval Bishops' Palace**, focus of the largest diocese in medieval England: **Lyddington Bede House**, later an Elizabethan almshouse, was also originally a bishops' palace. 15th-century aristocrats likewise built lavishly here. Lord Hastings converted **Ashby de la Zouch Castle** into a luxurious mansion, and had begun **Kirby Muxloe Castle** when he fell foul of Richard III; Sir Thomas Burgh founded **Gainsborough Old Hall**, one of England's most outstanding medieval town mansions; and Ralph Lord Cromwell, not content with Tattershall Castle, also raised huge and now ruined **Wingfield Manor**.

Wingfield Manor later served as one of the many mansion-prisons of Mary Queen of Scots. Her jailer there was the Earl of Shrewsbury, husband of one of the most extraordinary women in English history, 'Bess of Hardwick'. Bess herself was a mansion-builder on an ambitious scale: the ruins of English Heritage's **Hardwick Old Hall**, her remodelled birthplace, stand beside her even grander 'New Hall'. **Bolsover Castle**, only a short trip away, is among the finest of all surviving Stuart great houses: its extravagant 'Little Castle', with recently restored period interiors, looks out across the valley to the dramatic shell of Georgian **Sutton Scarsdale Hall**. 17th-century **Rufford Abbey**, also ruined, now reveals its origins as a Cistercian monastery: and further south, last but by no means least, rise the vast, partly ruined remains of **Kirby Hall**, one of the greatest houses of Elizabethan England.

Arbor Low Stone Circle and Gib Hill Barrow

Derbyshire

The region's most important prehistoric site, Arbor Low is a Neolithic henge monument atmospherically set amid high moorland. Within an earthen bank and ditch, a circle of some 50 white limestone slabs, all now fallen, surrounds a central stone 'cove' – a feature found only in major sacred sites. Nearby is enigmatic Gib Hill, a large burial mound.

Please note: The farmer who owns right of way to property may levy a charge for entry.

Managed by Peak District National Park Authority.

OPENING TIMES

Daily, in summer	10am-6pm
Daily, rest of year	10am-4pm
Closed	24-26 Dec and 1 Jan

HOW TO FIND US

Direction: ½ mile W of A515, 2 miles S of Monyash

Train: Buxton 10 miles

Bus: TM Travel 181 from Sheffield, 202 from Alfreton, Hulleys 171 from Chesterfield, all to Parsley Hay, then 1 mile

Tel: 01629 816200

MAP Page 270 (2E)
OS Map 119 (ref SK 160636)

Ashby De La Zouch Castle

See feature opposite

Bolingbroke Castle

Lincolnshire

The remains of a 13th-century hexagonal castle, birthplace in 1367 of the future King Henry IV, with adjacent earthworks. Besieged and taken by Cromwell's Parliamentarians in 1643.

Managed by Heritage Lincolnshire.

OPENING TIMES

Any reasonable time

HOW TO FIND US

Direction: In Old Bolingbroke, 16 miles N of Boston off A16

Train: Thorpe Culvert 10 miles

Tel: 01529 461499

MAP Page 271 (2J)
OS Map 122 (ref TF 349650)

Bolsover Castle

See feature – Page 148

Bolsover Cundy House

Derbyshire

This charming cottage-like 17th-century conduit house once supplied water to Bolsover Castle. Recently restored, including its vaulted stone-slab roof.

Managed by Bolsover Civic Society.

Bolsover Cundy House

OPENING TIMES

Any reasonable time

HOW TO FIND US

Direction: Off M1 at junction 29, follow signs for Bolsover Castle. In Craggs Road, Bolsover, 6 miles E of Chesterfield on A362

Train: Chesterfield 6 miles

Bus: Stagecoach in Chesterfield service 81-3, Chesterfield - Bolsover

Tel: 01246 822844 (Bolsover Castle)

MAP Page 271 (2F)
OS Map 141 (ref SK 470707)

Chichele College

Northamptonshire

The gatehouse and other remains of a communal residence for priests serving the parish church, founded by local-born Archbishop Chichele in c. 1422. Regularly used to display works of art.

For full details, visit www.eastnorthamptonshire.gov.uk

Managed by Cultural Community Partnerships.

OPENING TIMES

Quadrangle – any reasonable time. For the chapel, contact the keykeeper, Mrs D Holyoak, 12 Lancaster St, Higham Ferrers. Or telephone 01933 314157

HOW TO FIND US

Direction: In Higham Ferrers

Train: Wellingborough 5 miles

Bus: Stagecoach in Northants 46/7 from Wellingborough

Tel 01933 655401

Dogs on leads (restricted areas only).

MAP Page 271 (6G)
OS Map 153 (ref SP 960687)

Ashby De La Zouch Castle

Leicestershire – LE65 1BR

Ashby Castle forms the backdrop to the famous jousting scenes in Sir Walter Scott's classic novel of 1819, *Ivanhoe*. Now a ruin, the castle began as a manor house in the 12th century. It only achieved castle status in the 15th century, by which time the hall and buttery had been enlarged, with a solar to the east and a large integral kitchen added to the west.

Between 1474 and his execution by Richard III in 1483, Edward IV's Chamberlain Lord Hastings added the chapel and the impressive keep-like Hastings Tower – a castle within a castle. Visitors can now climb the 24 metre (78 feet) tower, which offers fine views. Later the castle hosted many royal visitors, including Henry VII, Mary Queen of Scots, James I and Charles I.

A Royalist stronghold during the Civil War, the castle finally fell to Parliament in 1646, and was then made unusable. An underground passage from the kitchen to the tower, probably created during this war, can still be explored today.

www.english-heritage.org.uk/ashbydelazouchcastle

NON-MEMBERS	
Adult	£3.40
Concession	£2.60
Child	£1.70
Family ticket	£8.50

OPENING TIMES	
1 Apr-30 Jun, Thu-Mon	10am-5pm
1 Jul-31 Aug, daily	10am-6pm
1 Sep-31 Oct, Thu-Mon	10am-5pm
1 Nov-31Mar, Thu-Mon	10am-4pm
Closed	24-26 Dec and 1 Jan

HOW TO FIND US

Direction: In Ashby de la Zouch, 12 miles S of Derby on A511. Restricted parking on site, please park in town car park

Train: Burton on Trent 9 miles

Bus: Arriva 9, 25/7 Burton on Trent-Ashby de la Zouch; Arriva 118, 218 Leicester-Swadlincote

Local Tourist Information 01530 411767

Tel: 01530 413343

OVP

Disabled access (grounds only).

Parking (restricted on site, please park in town car park - charge applies).

MAP Page 270 (4E)
OS Map 128 (ref SK 361166)

Bolsover Castle Derbyshire – S44 6PR

'By an unlikely miracle,' wrote the architectural historian Mark Girouard, 'the keep at Bolsover has survived into this century as an almost untouched expression in stone of the lost world of Elizabethan chivalry and romance.'

Photo: Skyscan Balloon Photography

Dominating the countryside from its hilltop, Bolsover occupies the site of a medieval castle built by the Peverel family shortly after the Norman Conquest. Sir Charles Cavendish bought the old castle in 1612 and began work on his 'Little Castle' project. Despite its embattled appearance, his creation was not designed for defence, but for elegant living.

Sir Charles intended the house as a retreat from the world to an imaginary golden age of chivalry and pleasure. His son William, later Duke of Newcastle, inherited the Little Castle in 1616 and set about its completion, assisted by the architect John Smythson. An extraordinary survival, the exquisitely carved fireplaces and recently conserved murals and painted panelling of its interiors take the visitor on an allegorical journey from earthly concerns to heavenly (and erotic) delights.

William also added the vast and stately rooms of the Terrace Range, now a dramatic roofless shell. To show off his achievement, in 1634 he invited the Stuart court to 'Love's Welcome to Bolsover', a masque specially written by Ben Jonson for performance in the Fountain Garden. Finally he constructed the cavernous Riding House with its magnificent roof, perhaps the finest surviving indoor riding school in Britain: here he indulged his passion for training 'great horses'. There is also a Discovery Centre in the Stables, with audio-visual displays.

The castle battlements and the Venus Garden are in the process of being restored, and the fountain, with 23 new statues, plays again for the first time in centuries. A series of 'Caesar paintings' depicting Roman emperors and empresses has also recently returned to Bolsover. These were commissioned by William Cavendish and copied from originals by the great Venetian artist Titian – which have since been destroyed – making the Bolsover versions uniquely important.

Bolsover Castle regularly hosts living history events, open-air concerts and evening plays. It also offers an interactive audio tour. There is reasonable disabled access to the main buildings and good access to the grounds: the Little Castle is not accessible to wheelchairs.

www.english-heritage.org.uk/bolsovercastle

Available for corporate and private hire.

Licensed for civil wedding ceremonies.

The Terrace Range

Satyr on the Venus Fountain

Photo: Andrew Tryner

NON-MEMBERS

Adult	£6.60
Concession	£5.00
Child	£3.30
Family ticket	£16.50

OPENING TIMES

1 Apr-30 Apr, Thu-Mon	10am-5pm*
1 May-30 Sep, daily	10am-6pm*
1-31 Oct, Thu-Mon	10am-5pm*
*Closes at 4pm on Saturday	
1 Nov-31 Mar, Thu-Mon	10am-4pm
Closed	24-26 Dec and 1 Jan

May close early for evening events, or for 1 hour at lunch if a hospitality event has been booked. Please call to check.

HOW TO FIND US

Direction: In Bolsover, 6 miles E of Chesterfield on A632. Off M1 at junction 29 (signposted).

Train: Chesterfield 6 miles

Bus: Stagecoach in Chesterfield 81-3 Chesterfield-Bolsover

Tel: 01246 822844

Local Tourist Information (Chesterfield): 01246 345777

Parking (in Castle car park off main gate, also coach drop-off point).

MAP Page 271 (2F)
OS Map 120 (ref SK 470707)

Eleanor Cross, Geddington

Northamptonshire

In 1290 Eleanor of Castile, the beloved wife of Edward I and mother of his fourteen children, died at Harby in Nottinghamshire. The places where her body rested on the journey south to its tomb in Westminster Abbey were marked by stone crosses. The stately triangular Geddington cross, with its canopied statues surmounted by a slender hexagonal pinnacle, is the best-preserved of only three intact survivors. Other crosses stand at Hardingstone near Northampton, and Waltham Cross, Hertfordshire.

OPENING TIMES

Any reasonable time

HOW TO FIND US

Direction: Located in the village of Geddington, off A43 between Kettering and Corby

Train: Kettering 4 miles

Bus: Stagecoach in Northants 8 Kettering-Corby

MAP Page 271 (5G)
OS Map 141 (ref SP 894830)

Gainsborough Old Hall

Lincolnshire – DN21 2NB

A little-known gem, Gainsborough Old Hall is among the best-preserved medieval manor houses in England. Partly brick and partly timber-framed, and mainly later 15th century with Elizabethan additions, it has a kitchen with an enormous fireplace, a noble great hall, and an imposing lodgings tower.

Managed by Lincolnshire County Council.

NON-MEMBERS

Adult	£3.70
Concession	£2.50
Child	£2.50
Family ticket	£9.99

Small charge to special events for EH members. Discount for groups of 30 or more

OPENING TIMES

2 Apr-29 Oct,	Mon-Sat	10am-5pm
	Sun	1pm-4.30pm
30 Oct-31 Mar,	Mon-Sat	10am-5pm
Closed	24-26 & 31 Dec & 1 Jan	

HOW TO FIND US

Direction: In Gainsborough, opposite the library

Train: Gainsborough Central ½ mile, Gainsborough Lea Road 1mile

Bus: From surrounding areas

Tel: 01427 612669

Disabled access (most of ground floor).

MAP Page 271 (1G)
OS Map 112 (ref SK 813900)

Hardwick Old Hall

Derbyshire – S44 5QJ

The remodelled family home of Bess of Hardwick, one of the richest and most remarkable women of Elizabethan England, stands beside the New Hall she raised later in the 1590s. Though the Old Hall is now roofless, visitors can still ascend four floors to view surviving decorative plasterwork, as well as the kitchen and service rooms. An audio tour tells Bess's story.

Managed by English Heritage and owned by The National Trust.

NEW FOR 2006 **A new exhibition in the West Lodge describes Bess's adventures in architecture, telling how she transformed her birthplace from a medieval manor house into a luxurious Elizabethan mansion: it operated alongside the New Hall as household accommodation for two centuries. New graphic panels focus on the rich interiors Bess created.**

NON-MEMBERS

Adult	£3.50
Concession	£2.60
Child	£1.80
Family ticket	£8.80

National Trust members admitted free, but small charge at EH events. Tickets for the New Hall (The National Trust) and joint tickets for both properties available at extra cost

Hardwick Old Hall

OPENING TIMES

1 Apr-30 Sep, Wed-Thu, Sat-Sun	10am-6pm
1-31 Oct, Wed- Thu, Sat-Sun	10am-5pm

HOW TO FIND US

Direction: 9½ miles SE of Chesterfield, off A6175, from J29 of M1

Train: Chesterfield 8 miles

Bus: Cosy Coaches C1 from Chesterfield (Sun and Thurs, Jun-Aug only); otherwise Stagecoach in Chesterfield 737, 747 Sheffield/Chesterfield-Nottingham, alight Glapwell 'Young Vanish', 1½ miles

Tel: 01246 850431

OVP

MAP Page 271 (2F)
OS Map 120 (ref SK 462637)

Hob Hurst's House

Derbyshire

A square prehistoric burial mound with an earthwork ditch and outer bank. Named after a local goblin.

Managed by the Peak District National Park Authority.

OPENING TIMES

Any reasonable time

HOW TO FIND US

Direction: From unclassified road off B5057, 9 miles W of Chesterfield

Train: Chesterfield 9 miles

Bus: Hulleys 170, TM Travel X67 from Chesterfield to within 2 miles

Tel: 01629 816200

MAP Page 270 (2E)
OS Map 119 (ref SK 287692)

Jewry Wall

Leicestershire

A length of Roman wall over 9 metres (30 feet) high, with a museum displaying the archaeology of Leicester and its region.

OPENING TIMES

Daily, summer	10am-6pm
Daily, rest of year	10am-4pm
Museum: Open Sat only	11am-4.30pm
Closed	24-26 Dec and 1 Jan

HOW TO FIND US

Direction: In St Nicholas St, W of Church of St Nicholas

Train: Leicester ¾ mile

Bus: From surrounding areas

Tel: 01162 254971 (Jewry Wall Museum)

Parking (by museum, within St Nicholas Circle).

MAP Page 271 (4F)
OS Map 140 (ref SK 582045)

Kirby Hall

See feature – Page 153

Kirby Muxloe Castle

Leicestershire – LE9 9MD

Begun in the 1480s by Lord Hastings, but never completed, Kirby Muxloe Castle is currently closed while English Heritage undertakes extensive conservation work to the brickwork and moat bridge. Visitors are welcome to view the work from outside the castle area, around the perimeter of the moat. The conservation work is due to be completed in 2007.

OPENING TIMES

Currently closed

HOW TO FIND US

Direction: 4 miles W of Leicester off B5380; close to M1 junction 21A, northbound exit only

Train: Kettering 11 miles

Bus: Arriva 63, 152-4 from Leicester

Tel: 01162 386886

MAP Page 271 (4F)
OS Map 140 (ref SK 524046)

Lincoln Medieval Bishops' Palace

See feature – Page 154

Lyddington Bede House

Rutland – LE15 9LZ

Set beside the church of a picturesque ironstone village, Lyddington Bede House originated as the late medieval wing of a palace belonging to the Bishops of Lincoln. By 1600 it had passed to Sir Thomas Cecil, son of Queen Elizabeth's chief minister, who converted it into an almshouse for twelve poor 'bedesmen' over 30 years old and two women (over 45), all free of lunacy, leprosy or the French pox. Visitors can wander through the bedesmen's rooms, with their tiny windows and fireplaces, and view the former bishops' Great Chamber with its beautifully carved ceiling cornice. An audio tour reconstructs some of the major changes during the past 700 years, and there is a small herb garden.

NON-MEMBERS

Adult	£3.30
Concession	£2.50
Child	£1.70
Family ticket	£8.30

Lyddington Bede House

OPENING TIMES

1 Apr-31 Oct, Thu-Mon	10am-5pm

HOW TO FIND US

Direction: In Lyddington, 6 miles N of Corby; 1 mile E of A6003, next to the church

Bus: Rutland Flyer 1 Corby – Oakham (passes close to Oakham)

Tel: 01572 822438

OVP

Disabled access (ground floor only).

MAP Page 271 (5G)
OS Map 141 (ref SP 876970)

Mattersey Priory

Nottinghamshire

The remains, mainly the 13th-century refectory and kitchen, of a small monastery for just six Gilbertine canons – the only wholly English monastic order.

OPENING TIMES

Any reasonable time

HOW TO FIND US

Direction: ¾ mile down rough drive, 1 mile E of Mattersey off B6045

Train: Retford 7 miles

MAP Page 271 (1G)
OS Map 112 (ref SK 703896)

Nine Ladies Stone Circle

Derbyshire

A small but apparently complete early Bronze Age stone circle of nine stones, part of a complex of prehistoric circles and standing stones on Stanton Moor.

Managed by Peak District National Park Authority.

Nine Ladies Stone Circle

OPENING TIMES

Any reasonable time

HOW TO FIND US

Direction: From an unclassified road off A6, 5 miles SE of Bakewell

Train: Matlock 4½ miles

Bus: Hulleys 170 Matlock-Bakewell to within 1mile

Tel: 01629 816200

MAP Page 270 (2E)
OS Map 119 (ref SK 249635)

Peveril Castle

See feature – Page 155

Rufford Abbey

Nottinghamshire

The best-preserved remains of a Cistercian abbey west cloister range in England, dating mainly from c. 1170. Incorporated into part of a 17th-century and later mansion, set in Rufford Country Park.

OPENING TIMES

Open all year from	10am-5pm
Jan-Feb	10am-4pm
Closed	25 Dec

For full details of opening times, please call

HOW TO FIND US

Direction: 2 miles S of Ollerton off A614

Train: Mansfield 8 miles

Bus: Stagecoach in Bassetlaw 33 Nottingham-Worksop; F1/2 Heanor/Nottingham-Clumber

Tel: 01623 822944

Occasional charge for members on event days.
Parking (charge applies – not managed by EH).
Shop – craft centre.

MAP Page 271 (2F)
OS Map 120 (ref SK 646648)

Kirby Hall

Northamptonshire – NN17 1AA

Kirby Hall is one of England's greatest Elizabethan and 17th-century houses. Begun by Sir Humphrey Stafford in about 1570, it was purchased six years later by Sir Christopher Hatton, one of Queen Elizabeth's 'comely young men' and later her Lord Chancellor, who hoped in vain to receive the Queen here during one of her annual 'progresses' around the country.

Although this vast mansion is partly roofless, most of its walls survive to their full impressive height: so does the stupendous three-tier inner porch, begun following French pattern books and later further embellished in the Classical style by the sculptor Nicholas Stone. Kirby Hall's exceptionally rich decoration, indeed, proclaims that its successive owners were always in the forefront of new ideas about architecture and design. The Great Hall and state rooms also remain intact, and have been refitted and redecorated to authentic 17th and 18th-century specifications.

Sir Christopher Hatton the Fourth added the great gardens (described as 'ye finest garden in England') in the late 17th century. They are now partly restored and laid out in an elaborate 'cutwork' design.

The gardens and ground floor of the building are both easily accessible by wheelchair.

Jane Austen's *Mansfield Park* was filmed here in 1999.

www.english-heritage.org.uk/kirbyhall

Owned by the Earl of Winchilsea and managed by English Heritage.

NON-MEMBERS	
Adult	£4.50
Concession	£3.40
Child	£2.30
Family ticket	£11.30

OPENING TIMES	
1 Apr-30 Jun, Thu-Mon	10am-5pm
1 Jul-31 Aug, daily	10am-6pm
1 Sep-31 Oct, Thu-Mon	10am-5pm
1 Nov-31 Mar, Thu-Mon	10am-4pm
Closed	24-26 Dec and 1 Jan

HOW TO FIND US

Direction: On an unclassified road off A43, 4 miles NE of Corby

Train: Kettering 9 miles

Tel: 01536 203230

OVP

Disabled access (grounds, gardens and ground floor only).

Dogs on leads (restricted areas).

MAP Page 271 (5G)
OS Map 141 (ref SP 926927)

Lincoln Medieval Bishops' Palace

Lincolnshire – LN2 1PU

Standing almost in the shadow of Lincoln cathedral, with sweeping views over the ancient city and the countryside beyond, the medieval bishops' palace was once among the most important buildings in the country. The administrative centre of the largest diocese in medieval England, stretching from the Humber to the Thames, its architecture reflected the enormous power and wealth of the bishops as princes of the church.

Begun in the late 12th century, the palace's most impressive feature is the undercrofted West Hall, initiated by Bishop St. Hugh and completed in the 1230s. The chapel range and entrance tower were built by Bishop William Alnwick, who modernised the palace in the 1430s. Having hosted visits from Henry VIII and James I, the palace was sacked by Royalist troops during the Civil War.

The vineyard

Built on hillside terraces, the palace also boasts one of the most northerly working vineyards in Europe, and a Contemporary Heritage Garden. Designed by Mark Anthony Walker, its form was inspired by the cathedral's medieval vaulting and the curves of the vines, with trees shaped to echo spires. Award-winning audio tour.

www.english-heritage.org.uk/lincolnbishops

NON-MEMBERS	
Adult	£3.70
Concession	£2.80
Child	£1.90
Family ticket	£9.30

OPENING TIMES	
1 Apr-30 Jun, daily	10am-5pm
1 Jul-31 Aug, daily	10am-6pm
1 Sep-31 Oct, daily	10am-5pm
1 Nov-31 Mar, Thu-Mon	10am-4pm
Closed	24-26 Dec and 1 Jan

HOW TO FIND US

Direction: S side of Lincoln Cathedral, through a tunnel in the wall

Train: Lincoln 1 mile

Bus: From surrounding areas

Tel: 01522 527468

OVP

Parking (limited disabled parking on site).

MAP Page 271 (2H)
OS Map 121 (ref SK 978717)

Peveril Castle

Derbyshire – S33 8WQ

Perched high above the pretty village of Castleton, the castle offers breathtaking views of the Peak District. Founded soon after the Norman Conquest of 1066 by William Peverel, one of King William's most trusted knights, it played an important role in guarding the Peak Forest area.

When 'Castle Peak' (as it was known in the Middle Ages) passed into the hands of Henry II, he made a number of additions. Most notable is the great square keep, with its round-headed windows, built in 1176. Thirteenth-century developments included the great hall, and though by 1400 the fortress had ceased to be of strategic importance, its impregnability guaranteed its continued use as a prison.

Following extensive conservation work on the keep, English Heritage has erected a walk-way at first floor level, enabling visitors to enter two chambers previously inaccessible: a medieval garderobe, and a small room with beautiful views of the surrounding countryside.

A new visitor centre now assures an even warmer welcome. New displays tell the story of Peveril as the focal point of the Royal Forest of the Peak, a hunting preserve for monarchs since the 11th century. There is also improved access, with a lift from the new gift shop to the first floor interpretation room, castle model and toilet facilities.

www.english-heritage.org.uk/peverilcastle

NON-MEMBERS

Adult	£3.50
Concession	£2.60
Child	£1.80
Family ticket	£8.80

OPENING TIMES

1-30 Apr, daily	10am-5pm
1 May-31 Aug, daily	10am-6pm
1 Sep-31 Oct, daily	10am-5pm
1 Nov-31 Mar, Thu-Mon	10am-4pm
Closed	24-26 Dec and 1 Jan

HOW TO FIND US

Direction: Via the market place in Castleton; 15 miles W of Sheffield on A6187

Train: Hope 2½ miles

Bus: First/Stagecoach in Chesterfield 272-4 Sheffield-Castleton, then 1 mile

Tel: 01433 620613

OVP

Parking (in town).

MAP Page 270 (2E)
OS Map 110 (ref SK 149826)

Rushton Triangular Lodge

Northamptonshire – NN14 1RP

This delightful triangular building was designed by Sir Thomas Tresham (father of one of the Gunpowder Plotters) and constructed between 1593 and 1597. It is a testament to Tresham's Roman Catholicism: the number three, symbolising the Holy Trinity, is apparent everywhere. There are three floors, trefoil windows and three triangular gables on each side. On the entrance front is the inscription 'Tres Testimonium Dant' ('there are three that give witness'), a Biblical quotation from St John's Gospel referring to the Trinity. It is also a pun on Tresham's name; his wife called him 'Good Tres' in her letters.

NON-MEMBERS

Adult	£2.40
Concession	£1.80
Child	£1.20

OPENING TIMES

1 Apr-31 Oct, Thu-Mon 10am-5pm

HOW TO FIND US

Direction: 1 mile W of Rushton, on unclassified road; 3 miles from Desborough on A6

Train: Kettering 5 miles

Rushton Triangular Lodge

Bus: Stagecoach in Northants 19 Kettering-Market Harborough, alight Desborough, then 2 miles

Tel: 01536 710761

OVP

Dogs on leads (restricted areas only).
Parking (nearby lay-by).

MAP Page 271 (5G)
OS Map 141 (ref SP 830831)

Sibsey Trader Windmill

Lincolnshire – PE22 0SY

Built in 1877, this restored six-storey mill with complete gear, sails and fantail still works today. The award-winning tearoom sells produce made from the mill's organic, stone-ground flour.

Managed by Ian Ansell. T: 07718 320449.

NON-MEMBERS

Adult	£2.00
Concession	£1.50
Child	£1.00

Sibsey Trader Windmill

OPENING TIMES

1 Apr-31 Oct,	
Sat, Tue & Bank Hols	10am-6pm
Sun	11am-6pm
1 Nov-31 Mar, Sat	11am-5pm
Closed	24-26 Dec and 1 Jan

HOW TO FIND US

Direction: ½ mile W of Sibsey off A16, 5 miles N of Boston

Train: Boston 5 miles

Bus: Various services and operators from Boston to Sibsey, then ½ mile

Tel: 01205 750036/460647

OVP

Disabled access (exterior only).

MAP Page 271 (3J)
OS Map 122 (ref TF 345510)

Sutton Scarsdale Hall

Derbyshire

The imposing shell of a grandiose Georgian mansion built in 1724, with an immensely columned exterior. Roofless since c. 1920, when its interiors were dismantled and some exported to America: but there is still much to discover within, including traces of sumptuous plaster-work. Set amid contemporary garden remains, including ha ha ditch and parish church.

Sutton Scarsdale Hall

OPENING TIMES

Summer, daily	10am-6pm
Rest of year, daily	10am-4pm
Closed	24-26 Dec and 1 Jan

HOW TO FIND US

Direction: Between Chesterfield and Bolsover, 1½ miles S of Arkwright Town

Train: Chesterfield 5 miles

Bus: Stagecoach in Chesterfield 48 from Chesterfield

MAP Page 271 (2F)
OS Map 120 (ref SK 442689)

Tattershall College

Lincolnshire

Remains of a grammar school for church choristers, founded in the mid-15th century by Ralph, Lord Cromwell, the builder of nearby Tattershall Castle (National Trust) and of English Heritage's Wingfield Manor.

The college is managed by Heritage Lincolnshire.

OPENING TIMES

Any reasonable time

HOW TO FIND US

Direction: In Tattershall, 14 miles NE of Sleaford on A153

Train: Ruskington (U) 10 miles

Bus: Brylaine 5 Lincoln-Boston (passing close Lincoln and Boston)

Tel: 01529 461499

MAP Page 271 (2H)
OS Map 122 (ref TF 213578)

Wingfield Manor

Derbyshire – DE55 7NH

The vast and immensely impressive ruins of a palatial medieval manor house arranged round a pair of courtyards, with a huge undercrofted Great Hall and a defensible High Tower 22 metres (72 feet) tall. This monument to late medieval 'conspicuous consumption' was built in the 1440s for the wealthy Ralph, Lord Cromwell, Treasurer of England. Later the home of Bess of Hardwick's husband, the Earl of Shrewsbury, who imprisoned Mary Queen of Scots here in 1569, 1584 and 1585.

Wingfield Manor is contained within a private working farm and partly surrounds the farmhouse. Visitors are asked to respect the privacy of the owners and keep to the official routes. No visits outside listed opening hours.

TV's *Peak Practice* and Zeffirelli's film *Jane Eyre* have been filmed here.

NON-MEMBERS	
Adult	£3.40
Concession	£2.60
Child	£1.70

Wingfield Manor

OPENING TIMES

Pre-booked guided tours only
Telephone: 01246 856456

HOW TO FIND US

Direction: 17 miles N of Derby; 11 miles S of Chesterfield on B5035; ½ mile S of South Wingfield. From M1 junction 28, W on A38, A615 (Matlock Road) at Alfreton, 1½ miles and turn onto B5035

Train: Alfreton 4 miles

Bus: Stagecoach in Chesterfield/ Doyles 140 Matlock-Alfreton

Tel: 01773 832060

OVP

Parking (none on site).
Orientation guide available.

MAP Page 270 (3E)
OS Map 119 (Ref SK 374548)

Sign-up on-line for our email Members' Newsletter at **www.english-heritage.org.uk/newsletter**

English Heritage membership makes a lovely gift.

Call 0870 333 1181 or visit **www.english-heritage.org.uk/gift** for more details.

Don't forget to check opening dates and times before you visit.

Other Historic Attractions

Discounted entry to our members (discounts may not apply on event days)

Althorp

Northamptonshire – NN7 4HQ

Visitors are invited to view the house, grounds and exhibition 'Diana – A Celebration', as well as the island in the Round Oval where Diana, Princess of Wales is laid to rest.

ENTRY

EH members get free entry to the upstairs of the house. Please call for admission prices.

OPENING TIMES

Please call for details of opening times

HOW TO FIND US

Direction: Althorp is located 7 miles North-West of Northampton off the A428. From the North leave M1 at Junction 18, From the South leave M1 at Junction 16, From West leave A14 at Junction 1(west bound only)

Tel: 01604 770107

www.althorp.com

MAP Page 271 (6F)
OS Map 152 (ref SP 682651)

78 Derngate, Northampton

Northamptonshire

A house re-designed by Charles Rennie Mackintosh for model-manufacturer W.J. Bassett-Lowke. Carefully restored to its 1917 appearance in 2003, it is among Mackintosh's last architectural works, and is the only Mackintosh house open in England. Supporting exhibitions explore the Mackintosh designs and celebrate the life and work of Bassett-Lowke.

Managed by the 78 Derngate Northampton Trust.

NON-MEMBERS

Adult	£5.50
Concession, inc. child	£4.00
Family ticket	£13.50
School parties (per head)	£2.50

EH members and up to 6 children within their family group get free entry. Discount does not extend to EH Corporate Partners or members of Cadw and Historic Scotland.

OPENING TIMES

12 Apr-26 Nov, Wed-Sun & Bank Hols	10.30am-5pm
Last admission	3.30pm

Visits must be booked, please call 01604 603407

78 Derngate, Northampton

HOW TO FIND US

Direction: In Northampton, close to Derngate theatre

Train: Northampton ¾ miles

Bus: From surrounding areas

MAP Page 271 (6G)
OS Map 152 (ref SP 759603)

Kelmarsh Hall

Northampton – NN6 9LT

Kelmarsh Hall, built in 1732 to a James Gibbs design, is surrounded by its traditional working estate, grazed parkland and beautiful gardens attributable to Nancy Lancaster, Norah Lindsay and Geoffrey Jellicoe.

ENTRY

Admission charge applies. Please call for details. One EH member free with one (1) paying visitor.

OPENING TIMES

Please call or check our website for details.

HOW TO FIND US

Direction: Junction 2 of A14 on A508 btw Northampton and Market Harborough

Tel: 01604 686543

www.kelmarsh.com

MAP Page 271 (5G)
OS Map 141 (ref SP 736796)

Moira Furnace

Leicestershire – DE12 6AT

An early 19th-century blast furnace which tells the story of the iron making process: short boat trips available.

ENTRY

Adult	£2.50
Concession	£1.50
Child (3-12 yrs)	£1.00

These prices are for guided museum tours lasting 1 hour.

EH members get 2 tickets of the same type for the price of 1 on guided museum tours.

OPENING TIMES

1 Apr-30 Sep, Tue-Sun 10am-5pm

1 Oct-31 Mar, Wed-Sun 11am-4pm

Moira Furnace

HOW TO FIND US

Direction: Moira Furnace is 2 miles away from Ashby de la Zouch and 2 miles away from Swadlincote

Tel: 01283 224667

MAP Page 270 (4E)
OS Map 128 (ref SK 314151)

Papplewick Pumping Station

Nottinghamshire – NG15 9AT

Britain's finest working Victorian water pumping station, with ornate engine house, cooling pot, landscaped grounds, woodland play area, original twin steam engines and six boilers, hands on activities and a miniature railway.

Papplewick Pumpng Station

ENTRY

Prices on steaming days

Adult	£4.50
Concession and students	£3.50
Child	£2.50
Family ticket	£12.00

25% off all ticket categories for EH members.

OPENING TIMES

Please call for details of opening times

HOW TO FIND US

Direction: Off the A60 near Ravenshead, midway between Mansfield and Nottingham

Tel: 01159 632938

MAP Page 271 (3F)
OS Map 120 (ref SK 583521)

Sculpted chapter house entran-
Haughmond Abbey – see page

West Midlands

'What are those blue remembered hills,
What spires, what farms are those?
This is the land of lost content,
I see it shining plain,
Those happy highways where I went
And cannot come again'

From 'A Shropshire Lad' by A.E.Housman, 1896

www.english-heritage.org.uk/westmidlands

Properties

See individual listings for details

Herefordshire
Arthur's Stone, Edvin Loach Old Church, Goodrich Castle, Longtown Castle, Mortimer's Cross Water Mill, Rotherwas Chapel, Wigmore Castle

Shropshire
Acton Burnell Castle, Boscobel House and the Royal Oak, Buildwas Abbey, Cantlop Bridge, Clun Castle, Haughmond Abbey, Iron Bridge, Langley Chapel, Lilleshall Abbey, Mitchell's Fold Stone Circle, Moreton Corbet Castle, Old Oswestry Hill Fort, Stokesay Castle, Wenlock Priory, White Ladies Priory, Wroxeter Roman City

Staffordshire
Croxden Abbey, Wall Roman Site

West Midlands
Halesowen Abbey

Warwickshire
Kenilworth Castle

Worcestershire
Leigh Court Barn, Witley Court

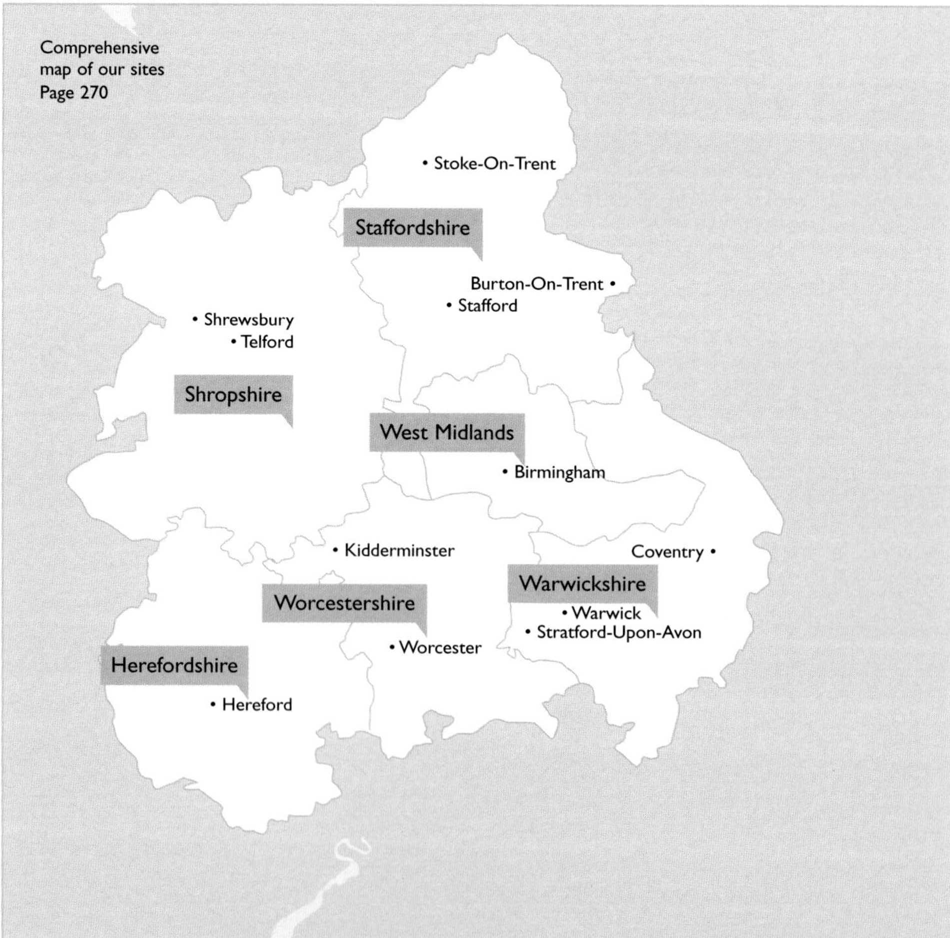

Kenilworth Castle – see page 170

Heartland and Marchland

For the poet Housman, looking west from his home at Bromsgrove in Worcestershire, the 'blue remembered' Welsh Border hills were a symbol of nostalgia for his lost youth. English Heritage members need not take so sombre a view of this attractive region, to whose many fascinating sites they can 'come again' as often as they wish.

Easily accessible from most parts of England, yet in places surprisingly remote-seeming, the West Midlands is a heartland characterised by much delightful countryside and many traditional buildings. Particularly distinctive are those built in the regional speciality, timber-framing: among them **Boscobel House**; the wonderful gatehouse of **Stokesay Castle**; and **Leigh Court Barn**, the largest cruck-framed building in Britain.

For many centuries, however, the western fringe of this now peaceful heartland was also a much fought-over frontier with Wales – the Welsh 'Marches', from an Anglo-Saxon word meaning 'borders'. Here lived the 'Mercians' or 'borderers', whose great King Offa raised his famous 8th-century **Offa's Dyke** as the boundary between English and Welsh territory. The Normans in turn reinforced the frontier with castles, among them **Clun**, **Longtown** and **Goodrich Castles** on its crag above the Wye, and **Wigmore Castle**, unusually preserved as a 'romantic ruin', the home of those most turbulent of 'Marcher Lords', the Mortimers. Further east stands the mighty **Kenilworth Castle** with its Elizabethan associations: a reminder that Warwickshire is the heartland of 'Shakespeare's country'.

The West Midlands also boasts many notable monastic sites, including **Croxden Abbey**, **Haughmond Abbey**, **Lilleshall Abbey**, **Wenlock Priory** and **Buildwas Abbey** (which grew rich from iron-working). Not far away is the **Iron Bridge**, proclaiming that the West Midlands was also a heartland of the Industrial Revolution.

And like all English Heritage's regions, the West Midlands has its 'one-offs', sites with a unique and special appeal. Among these is the vast ruined mansion of **Witley Court**, amid its splendid gardens; **Wroxeter Roman City**, with impressive traces of a lost Roman city; the charmingly unaltered interiors of **Rotherwas Chapel** and remote **Langley Chapel**; and the theatrical Elizabethan shell of **Moreton Corbet Castle**.

Acton Burnell Castle

Shropshire

The red sandstone shell of a semi-fortified tower house, built in 1284-93 by Bishop Burnell, Edward I's Lord Chancellor. Parliaments were twice held here, in 1283 and 1285.

OPENING TIMES

Any reasonable time

HOW TO FIND US

Direction: Located in Acton Burnell, signposted from A49, 8 miles S of Shrewsbury

Train: Shrewsbury or Church Stretton, both 8 miles.

MAP Page 270 (4B)
OS Map 126 (ref SJ 534019)

Arthur's Stone

Herefordshire

An atmospheric Neolithic 'dolmen' burial chamber made of great stone slabs, in the hills above Herefordshire's Golden Valley

OPENING TIMES

Any reasonable time

HOW TO FIND US

Direction: 7 miles E of Hay-on-Wye off B4348 near Dorstone

Bus: Stagecoach in South Wales 39, Yeomans Canyon 40 Hereford – Brecon to within ¾ mile

MAP Page 270 (7B)
OS Map 148 (ref SO 319431)

Boscobel House and The Royal Oak

See feature opposite

Buildwas Abbey

Shropshire – TF8 7BW

The extensive ruins of a Cistercian abbey, including much of its fine 12th-century church. In a woodland setting beside the River Severn, not far from the Iron Bridge.

NON-MEMBERS

Adult	£2.70
Concession	£2.00
Child	£1.40

OPENING TIMES

1 Apr-31 May, Thu-Mon	10am-5pm
1 Jun-31 Aug, daily	10am-6pm
1-30 Sep, Thu-Mon	10am-5pm

HOW TO FIND US

Direction: On S bank of River Severn on A4169, 2 miles W of Ironbridge

Train: Telford Central 6 miles

Bus: Arriva 96 Telford-Shrewsbury (passes close to Telford Central)

Tel: 01952 433274

OVP

Disabled access is limited.

MAP Page 270 (4C)
OS Map 127 (ref SJ 643043)

Cantlop Bridge

Shropshire

A single-span, cast-iron road bridge over the Cound Brook. Designed by the great engineer Thomas Telford, who was instrumental in shaping industrial Shropshire and the West Midlands.

OPENING TIMES

Any reasonable time

HOW TO FIND US

Direction: ¾ mile SW of Berrington on an unclassified road off A458

Train: Shrewsbury 5 miles

MAP Page 270 (4B)
OS Map 126 (ref SJ 517062)

Boscobel House and The Royal Oak

Shropshire – ST19 9AR

Boscobel House was built in about 1632, when John Gifford of Whiteladies converted a timber-framed farmhouse into a hunting lodge. The Gifford family were Roman Catholics, at a time when the religion suffered persecution. Tradition holds that the true purpose of Boscobel was to serve as a secret place for the shelter of Catholics in times of need.

The house was, however, destined for greater fame. Following the execution of King Charles I in 1649, his eldest son made a brave though misguided attempt to regain the throne. In 1651 his hopes were crushed at Worcester in the final conflict of the Civil War. Young Charles was forced to flee for his life.

Initially the future King Charles II set out to cross the River Severn into Wales, but found his way blocked by Cromwell's patrols. He sought refuge instead at Boscobel, hiding first in a tree that is now known as the Royal Oak and then spending the night in a priest-hole in the house's attic. He then travelled on in disguise via other safe houses before escaping to France.

Boscobel later became a much visited place, although it remained a working farm. Visitors can also see the dairy, farmyard, smithy, gardens, and a descendant of the Royal Oak. Tearoom available.

www.english-heritage.org.uk/boscobelhouse

NON-MEMBERS	
Adult	£4.80
Concession	£3.60
Child	£2.40
Family ticket	£12.00

NON-MEMBERS GROUNDS ONLY	
Adult	£1.60
Concession	£1.20
Child	£0.80

The famous Royal Oak

OPENING TIMES

1 Apr-31 May, Thu-Mon	10am-5pm
1 Jun-31 Aug, daily	10am-6pm
1 Sep-31 Oct, Thu-Mon	10am-5pm

Last entry 1 hour before closing.

HOW TO FIND US

Direction: On minor road from A41 to A5, 8 miles NW of Wolverhampton. 5 mins drive from M54 J3

Train: Cosford 3 miles

Tel: 01902 850244

E OVP

Parking (coaches welcome).

MAP Page 270 (4C)
OS Map 127 (ref SJ 838082)

Clun Castle

Shropshire

The dramatic riverside ruins and extensive earthworks of a Welsh Border Norman castle, its tall keep unusually set on the side of its mound.

OPENING TIMES

Any reasonable time

HOW TO FIND US

Direction: In Clun, off A488, 18 miles W of Ludlow

Train: Hopton Heath 6½ miles; Knighton 6½ miles

Guidebooks available from Stokesay Castle.

MAP Page 270 (5B)
OS Map 137 (ref SO 299809)

Croxden Abbey

Staffordshire

Croxden Abbey

The impressive remains of an abbey of Cistercian 'white monks', including towering fragments of its 13th-century church, infirmary and 14th-century abbot's lodging.

OPENING TIMES

All year round	10am-5pm

HOW TO FIND US

Direction: 5 miles NW of Uttoxeter off A522

Train: Uttoxeter 6 miles

MAP Page 270 (3D)
OS Map 128 (ref SK 066397)

Edvin Loach Old Church

Herefordshire

A traditional English churchyard, Edvin Loach contains both a 19th-century church and the remains of an 11th-century church.

OPENING TIMES

Any reasonable time

HOW TO FIND US

Direction: Located 4 miles N of Bromyard on an unclassified road off B4203

MAP Page 270 (6C)
OS Map 149 (ref SO 663584)

Goodrich Castle

See feature – Page 168

Halesowen Abbey

West Midlands – B62 8RJ

Contact Regional Office on 0121 625 6820 for details.

Haughmond Abbey

Shropshire

The extensive remains of an Augustinian abbey, including its abbots' quarters, refectory and cloister. The substantially surviving chapter house has a frontage richly bedecked with 12th and 14th century carving and statuary, and a fine timber roof of c. 1500. New pictorial interpretation boards guide the visitor, and an introductory exhibition displays archaeological finds. Picnic area and light refreshments available.

NON-MEMBERS

Adult	£2.70
Concession	£2.00
Child	£1.40

OPENING TIMES

1 Apr-31 May, Thu-Mon	10am-5pm
1 Jun-31 Aug, daily	10am-6pm
1-30 Sep, Thu-Mon	10am-5pm

Haughmond Abbey

HOW TO FIND US

Direction: Located 3 miles NE of Shrewsbury off B5062

Train: Shrewsbury 3½ miles

Bus: Arriva 519 Shrewsbury – Newport

Tel: 01743 709661

OVP

Disabled access (not easy).

MAP Page 270 (4B)
OS Map 126 (ref SJ 542152)

Iron Bridge

See feature – Page 169

Kenilworth Castle

See feature – Page 170

Langley Chapel

Shropshire

A small chapel tranquilly set all alone in charming countryside. Its atmospheric interior contains a perfect set of 17th-century timber furnishings, including a musicians' pew.

OPENING TIMES

1 Mar-31 Oct, daily	10am-5pm
1 Nov-28 Feb, daily	10am-4pm

HOW TO FIND US

Direction: 1½ miles S of Acton Burnell, on an unclassified road off A49; 9½ miles S of Shrewsbury

Train: Shrewsbury 7½ miles

MAP Page 270 (5B)
OS Map 149 (ref SO 663584)

Leigh Court Barn

Worcestershire

An outstanding display of English medieval carpentry, this mighty timber-framed barn is the largest cruck structure in Britain. Built for Pershore Abbey in the early 14th century, it is 46 metres (150 feet) long, with 18 cruck blades each made from a single oak tree.

OPENING TIMES

1 Apr-30 Sep, Thu-Sun and Bank Hol Mons	10am-6pm

HOW TO FIND US

Direction: 5 miles W of Worcester on an unclassified road off A4103

Train: Worcester Foregate Street 5 miles

Bus: First 417 from Worcester to within 1 mile

MAP Page 270 (6C)
OS Map 150 (ref SO 783535)

Lilleshall Abbey

Shropshire

The extensive, evocative ruins of an abbey of Augustinian canons, notably the remains of the cloister buildings and the 12th and 13th-century church, with its lavishly sculpted processional doorway.

OPENING TIMES

1 Apr-30 Sep, daily	10am-5pm
Closed	1 Oct-31 Mar

HOW TO FIND US

Direction: On an unclassified road off A518, 4 miles N of Oakengates

Train: Oakengates 4½ miles

Bus: Arriva 481 Telford – Stafford (passes close to Telford Central and Stafford) to within 1 mile

Tel: 0121 625 6820 (Regional office)

Guidebooks from Haughmond Abbey, or upon order.

MAP Page 270 (4C)
OS Map 127 (ref SJ 738142)

i

Visit **www.english-heritage.org.uk** for up-to-date events information and the latest news.

i

Sign-up on-line for our email Members' Newsletter at **www.english-heritage.org.uk**

Goodrich Castle

Herefordshire – HR9 6HY

Goodrich stands majestically on a wooded hill commanding the passage of the River Wye into the picturesque valley of Symonds Yat. The castle was begun in the late 11th century, by the English thegn Godric who gave it his name. A generation later the splendidly preserved square keep which still forms its core was added, probably in the time of Richard 'Strongbow' de Clare, Earl of Pembroke and Lord of Goodrich 1148-76.

Under King John, Goodrich was granted with the earldom of Pembroke to the famous William Marshal, a great castle-builder who may have initiated work on the inner ward. Each of the Marshal's four sons inherited the fortress in turn, the last dying childless at Goodrich in 1245.

Thereafter the fortress and earldom passed to Henry III's half-brother, William de Valence, who rebuilt its defences and living quarters in the most up-to-date style. Goodrich still boasts one of the most complete sets of medieval domestic buildings surviving in any English castle. William's widow Countess Joan frequently stayed here with an entourage of up to 200, entertaining her relations and friends in the most lavish style.

During the Civil War, Goodrich was held successively by both sides. Sir Henry Lingen's Royalists eventually surrendered in 1646 under threats of undermining and a deadly Parliamentarian mortar. The famous 'Roaring Meg', the only surviving Civil War mortar, has returned to the castle after over 350 years.

www.english-heritage.org.uk/goodrichcastle

NEW FOR 2006 **From autumn 2006, a new café, shop and visitor facilities will be available.**

NON-MEMBERS

Adult	£4.50
Concession	£3.40
Child	£2.30
Family ticket	£11.30

OPENING TIMES

1 Apr-31 May, daily	10am-5pm
1 Jun-31 Aug, daily	10am-6pm
1 Sep-31 Oct, daily	10am-5pm
1 Nov-28 Feb, Thu-Mon	10am-4pm
1-31 Mar, daily	10am-5pm
Closed	24-26 Dec and 1 Jan

HOW TO FIND US

Direction: 5 miles S of Ross-on-Wye off A40

Bus: Stagecoach in Wye & Dean 34 Monmouth Ross-on-Wye (with connection from Gloucester) to within ½ mile

Tel: 01600 890538

OVP

Parking (400 yards from castle).
Disabled access (limited, please call for details).
New guidebook.

MAP Page 270 (7C)
OS Map 162 (ref SO 577200)

www.britainonview.com/Powel Libera

Iron Bridge

Shropshire

The world's first iron bridge was erected over the River Severn here in 1779. It was cast by local ironmaster Abraham Darby of Coalbrookdale, who had invented a revolutionary process for smelting iron using coke. Perhaps Britain's best known industrial monument, the bridge gave its name to the spectacular wooded gorge which became the cradle of the Industrial Revolution.

Ironbridge Gorge is now a World Heritage Site.

Iron Bridge is the perfect place to begin a tour of the many industrial, ceramic, decorative arts and living history museums of the Gorge, and of the many other English Heritage sites nearby. These include Buildwas Abbey, Wenlock Priory, Wroxeter Roman City and Stokesay Castle.

OPENING TIMES

Any reasonable time

HOW TO FIND US

Direction: Adjacent to A4169

Bus: From Telford (all services pass close to Telford Central and Wellington Telford West)

MAP Page 270 (4C)
OS Map 127 (ref SJ 672034)

Kenilworth Castle Warwickshire – CV8 1NE

Kenilworth Castle has been intimately linked with some of the most important figures in English history. With its impressive Norman keep, John of Gaunt's great hall, and the magnificent buildings raised for Queen Elizabeth I, it is among the largest castle ruins in England.

Photo: Peter Richardson

The castle in its landscape is a remarkable time-capsule of medieval and Tudor history. The massive Norman keep stands at the core of King John's expansion of the defences after 1210, including the curtain walls and defensive towers of the outer court. An enormous mere or shallow lake was created at this time, effectively putting the castle on an island.

Kenilworth was granted to Simon de Montfort by Henry III in 1253. Simon was the leader of a baronial reform campaign, which resulted in civil war and his death in 1265 at the Battle of Evesham. But his supporters famously defended the castle for nearly a year, succumbing only to starvation. In 1326 Edward II was imprisoned here and forced to renounce the throne, before his transfer to Berkeley Castle and alleged murder by red hot poker.

By 1394, John of Gaunt added the splendid great hall and private apartments of the inner court, turning the fortress into a palace. Back in royal ownership, it was favoured by Henry V, who created the Pleasaunce, a summerhouse and water-garden. Elizabeth I's favourite, Robert Dudley, Earl of Leicester, was granted the castle in the 16th century, and added more fine buildings to receive the queen and her court. Kenilworth became the focus of extravagant festivities. In 1575 Elizabeth paid a 19 day visit, being lavishly entertained with music, dancing, hunting and fireworks. The elaborate gatehouse and stables still bear witness to this high point in Kenilworth's history.

The castle never saw such glories again. After the Civil War it was partially demolished, and the great lake was drained away. Saved for the nation in 1938, Kenilworth remains an atmospheric reminder of great leaders, their glories, pleasures and rebellions. It also offers fine countryside views – with the Millennium Trail from the castle to the Pleasaunce one of the best ways to enjoy them.

Tearoom in summer, and gift shop.

www.english-heritage.org.uk/kenilworthcastle

NEW FOR 2006 In the spring, a new admissions building and shop will be open. The fully restored Gatehouse will also open to the public in the summer for the first time in many years. The Gatehouse will house a major new exhibition telling the story of the relationship between Queen Elizabeth I and Robert Dudley, Earl of Leicester. It will also show how the Gatehouse would have looked when it was last inhabited in the 1930s. Also available in the summer will be a new audio tour and exhibition recounting the history of the castle.

NON-MEMBERS

Adult	£5.90
Concession	£4.40
Child	£3.00
Family ticket	£14.80

OPENING TIMES

1 Apr-31 May, daily	10am-5pm
1 Jun-31 Aug, daily	10am-6pm
1 Sep-31 Oct, daily	10am-5pm
1 Nov-28 Feb, daily	10am-4pm
1-31 Mar, daily	10am-5pm

Note: the Gatehouse may close early on Saturdays for private events

Closed 24-26 Dec and 1 Jan

HOW TO FIND US

Direction: In Kenilworth off A46. Clearly signposted from the town centre, off B4103

Train: Warwick and Coventry 5 miles

Bus: Stagecoach in Warwickshire X1 Coventry – Stratford-upon-Avon calls at Castle; otherwise X12, X17, Travel West Midlands 12 Coventry – Leamington Spa to within a few min walk. All pass close to ⇌ Coventry & Leamington Spa

Tel: 01926 852078

Local Tourist Information Kenilworth: 01926 748900

OVP

Audio tours (also in French and German).

Tearoom (Open Easter-Oct daily, Tel: 01926 864376).

New guidebook.

Parking (charge applies – members £1, non-members (including Local Resident Pass Holders) £2.50).

MAP Page 270 (5E)
OS Map 140 (ref SP 278723)

Longtown Castle

Herefordshire

A powerful thick-walled round keep of c. 1200, characteristic of the Welsh Borders, on a large earthen mound amid other castle remains. Set in the beautiful Olchon valley, with magnificent views of the Black Mountains.

OPENING TIMES

Any reasonable time

HOW TO FIND US

Direction: Located 4 miles WSW of Abbey Dore, off B4347

MAP Page 270 (7B)
OS Map 161 (ref SO 321291)

Mitchell's Fold Stone Circle

Shropshire

A Bronze Age stone circle, the focus of many legends, set in dramatic moorland on Stapeley Hill. It once consisted of some 30 stones, 15 of which are still visible.

Managed by Shropshire County Council.

OPENING TIMES

Any reasonable time

HOW TO FIND US

Direction: 16 miles SW of Shrewsbury

Train: Welshpool 10 miles

Bus: Minsterley/Arriva 553 Shrewsbury – Bishop's Castle (passes close to Shrewsbury) to within 1 mile

Tel: 01939 232771

MAP Page 270 (5B)
OS Map 137 (ref SO 304984)

Moreton Corbet Castle

Shropshire

The ruins of the medieval castle and Tudor manor house of the Corbets are dominated by the theatrical shell of an ambitious Elizabethan mansion wing in Italianate style, which was devastated during the Civil War. Fine Corbet monuments fill the adjacent church.

OPENING TIMES

Any reasonable time

HOW TO FIND US

Direction: In Moreton Corbet off B5063 (a turning off A49), 7 miles NE of Shrewsbury

Train: Yorton 4 miles

Bus: Arriva X64 Shrewsbury – Hanley (passes close to Shrewsbury and Stoke-on-Trent) to within 1 mile

Guidebooks from Buildwas and Haughmond Abbeys.

MAP Page 270 (4C)
OS Map 126 (ref SJ 561231)

i

English Heritage membership makes a lovely gift.

Call 0870 333 1181 or visit **www.english-heritage.org.uk/gift** for more details.

Mortimer's Cross Water Mill

Herefordshire – HR6 9PE

A rare one-man-operated 18th-century water mill in part working order. Nearby there are attractive gardens and woodland walks, a stone weir and the significant Aymestrey Limestone Quarry. Special day and evening guided tours for groups are available, and every Bank Holiday Monday is a demonstration grinding day. Please call for details.

NON-MEMBERS

Adult	£4.00
Concession	£3.50
Child	£2.50

OPENING TIMES

Apr-30 Sep, Sun & Bank Holiday Mons 10am-4pm
Other times by arrangement

HOW TO FIND US

Direction: Located 7 miles NW of Leominster on B4362

Train: Leominster 7½ miles

Tel: 01568 708820

Disabled access (exterior and ground floor only).

Warning (there are steep river banks and sluice channels which are hazardous at all times).

MAP Page 270 (6B)
OS Map 148 (ref SO 426637)

Old Oswestry Hill Fort

Shropshire

The most hugely impressive Iron Age hillfort on the Welsh Borders, covering 40 acres, with formidable multiple ramparts.

OPENING TIMES

Any reasonable time

HOW TO FIND US

Direction: 1 mile N of Oswestry, off an unclassified road off A483

Train: Gobowen 2 miles

Bus: Arriva 2, 53, 63 from Gobowen

MAP Page 270 (3B)
OS Map 126 (ref SJ 295310)

Rotherwas Chapel

Herefordshire

The family chapel of the Roman Catholic Bodenham family. The originally simple medieval building has a fine Elizabethan timber roof, a rebuilt 18th-century tower, and a mid-Victorian side chapel and high altar.

OPENING TIMES

Any reasonable time. Key keeper located at nearby filling station

HOW TO FIND US

Direction: 1½ miles SE of Hereford on B4399, left into Chapel Road

Train: Hereford 3½ miles

Bus: First 78 from Hereford

Disabled access (kissing gate).

MAP Page 270 (7B)
OS Map 149 (ref SO 536383)

Stokesay Castle

See feature – Page 174

i

English Heritage members can take up to 6 children, as part of a family group, into our properties at no extra cost (see page 6).

Stokesay Castle Shropshire – SY7 9AH

Stokesay Castle is the finest and best preserved 13th-century fortified manor house in England. It offers visitors a unique glimpse into a distant age, when strength and elegance were combined.

The panelled Solar Chamber

Take the audio tour

Set amid peaceful countryside near the Welsh border, it forms an outstandingly picturesque group with its timber-framed gatehouse and the parish church.

Lawrence of Ludlow, who made his fortune as a wool merchant and set up as a country gentleman, acquired the manor in 1281. Extensive recent tree-ring dating confirms that he had completed virtually the whole of the still-surviving buildings by 1291, the date of his 'licence to crenellate' from Edward I.

The dating also revealed that Stokesay's magnificent open-hearthed great hall, with its fine cruck-built timber roof, shuttered gable windows and precipitous staircase, has scarcely been altered since it was built. The north tower displays an original medieval tiled floor and remains of wall painting, while the south tower – with fine views from its roof – contains a panelled solar chamber added in the 17th century. Its dominating feature is a fireplace with richly carved overmantel, still bearing clear traces of gold, pink, red, green and white painting.

Across the courtyard stands the truly delightful gatehouse, an elaborate example of the regional style of lavishly showy timber-framing, with charming carvings of Adam and Eve. This was built in 1640, a few years before Stokesay's only known military encounter, when it surrendered without fighting during the Civil War.

An audio tour will help you to imagine Stokesay as the centre of medieval life. Its grounds include cottage-style gardens, a tea room in summer, and a gift shop.

www.english-heritage.org.uk/stokesaycastle

NON-MEMBERS	
Adult	£4.80
Concession	£3.60
Child	£2.40
Family ticket	£12.00

OPENING TIMES	
1-30 Apr, Thu-Mon	10am-5pm
1 May-30 Jun, daily	10am-5pm
1 Jul-31 Aug, daily	10am-6pm
1 Sep-31 Oct, Thu-Mon	10am-5pm
1 Nov-28 Feb, Fri-Mon	10am-4pm
1-31 Mar, Thu-Mon	10am-5pm
Closed	24-26 Dec & 1 Jan

HOW TO FIND US

Direction: 7 miles NW of Ludlow off A49

Train: Craven Arms 1 mile

Bus: Whittle 435 Shrewsbury – Ludlow

Tel: 01588 672544

Local Tourist Information Ludlow: 01584 875053

OVP

Disabled access (call site for details).

Entrance to the courtyard is through an historic gate. Unsuitable for motorised scooters and unassisted wheelchair users.

Tearoom (Seasonal: 1 Apr-31 Oct).

MAP Page 270 (5B)
OS Map 148 (ref SO 436817)

Wall Roman Site (Letocetum)

Staffordshire – WS14 0AW

Wall was an important staging post on Watling Street, the Roman military road to North Wales. It provided overnight accommodation for travelling Roman officials and imperial messengers. The foundations of an inn and bathhouse can be seen, and many of the excavated finds are displayed in the on-site museum.

Managed by English Heritage and owned by The National Trust.

NON-MEMBERS

Adult	£3.00
Concession	£2.30
Child	£1.50

National Trust members admitted free, but small charge on EH special events days

OPENING TIMES

1 Apr-31 May, Wed-Sun	10am-5pm
1 Jun-31 Aug, daily	10am-6pm
1 Sep-31 Oct, Wed-Sun	10am-5pm
Closed	1 Nov-31 Mar

HOW TO FIND US

Direction: Off A5 at Wall, near Lichfield

Train: Shenstone 1½ miles

Tel: 01543 480768

Audio tours (£1.50 for National Trust members).

MAP Page 270 (4D)
OS Map 139 (ref SK 098066)

Wenlock Priory

Shropshire – TF13 6HS

Photo: Paul Highnam

The ruins of a large priory of Cluniac monks, whose love of decoration is reflected in the exuberant carving of its Norman chapter house and rare 'lavatorium' – an octagonal wash-house. Parts of the 13th-century church also stand, in grounds bedecked with topiary. Wenlock Priory was part of the immense Europe-wide network of the great French abbey of Cluny.

NON-MEMBERS

Adult	£3.30
Concession	£2.50
Child	£1.70

OPENING TIMES

1-30 Apr, Thu-Mon	10am-5pm
1 May-30 Jun, daily	10am-5pm
1 Jul-31 Aug, daily	10am-6pm
1 Sep-31 Oct, Thu-Mon	10am-5pm
1 Nov-28 Feb, Thu-Sun	10am-4pm
1-31 Mar, Thu-Mon	10am-5pm

HOW TO FIND US

Direction: In Much Wenlock

Train: Telford Central 9 miles

Bus: Shropshire Bus 436/7 Shrewsbury – Bridgnorth (passes close to ⇌ Shrewsbury)

Tel: 01952 727466

MAP Page 270 (5C)
OS Map 127 (ref SJ 625001)

White Ladies Priory

Shropshire

The remains of the late 12th-century church of a small nunnery of 'white ladies' or Augustinian canonesses, surrounded by picturesque woodland near Boscobel House.

OPENING TIMES

1 Apr-31 Oct, daily	10am-5pm
Closed	1 Nov-31 Mar

HOW TO FIND US

Direction: Located 1 mile SW of Boscobel House off an unclassified road between A41 and A5; 8 miles NW of Wolverhampton

Train: Cosford 2½ miles

MAP Page 270 (4C)
OS Map 127 (ref SJ 826076)

Check *Heritage Today* for news and information on forthcoming events and exclusive members' offers.

Wigmore Castle

Herefordshire

Once the stronghold of the turbulent Mortimer family, Wigmore Castle was abandoned by the 17th century. Now it is among the most remarkable ruins in England, largely buried up to first floor level by earth and fallen masonry. Yet many of its fortifications survive to full height, including parts of the keep on its towering mound.

OPENING TIMES

Any reasonable time

HOW TO FIND US

Direction: Located 8 miles W of Ludlow on A4110. Accessible via footpath ¾ mile from the village on Mortimer Way

Train: Bucknell 6 miles, Ludlow 10 miles

Toilets (including disabled) at the Village Hall and also the Compasses Hotel by arrangement.
Tel: 01568 770705.

There are steep steps to the summit, which are hazardous in icy conditions. Children must stay under close control and should not climb the walls or banks. Strong footwear is recommended. There is no custodial presence.

MAP Page 270 (6B)
OS Map 148 (ref SO 408693)

Stokesay Castle – see page 174

Witley Court and Gardens Worcestershire – WR6 6JT

A hundred years ago, Witley Court was one of England's great country houses, hosting many extravagant parties. Today it is a spectacular ruin, the result of a disastrous fire in 1937.

The vast and rambling remains of the palatial 19th-century mansion are surrounded by magnificent landscaped gardens – the 'Monster Work' of William Nesfield – which still contain huge stone fountains. The largest, representing Perseus and Andromeda, which has been restored, was described as making the 'noise of an express train' when fired.

Before 1846, when William Humble Ward (later first Earl of Dudley) inherited Witley Court, the land surrounding the house was laid out in the English landscape style of the mid-18th century. As part of Ward's transformation of the estate, he called in the leading landscape designer of the time, William Andrews Nesfield, whose skills in designing intricate and elegant parterres were complemented by his great ability as an artist and engineer.

Nesfield started work in 1854, creating the south parterre with its great Perseus and Andromeda fountain. His scheme involved elegantly designed plantings of clipped evergreens and shrubs, with parterres enclosed by more clipped evergreens. The central avenue of planting from the house led through the fountains to the Golden Gates, terminating the south parterre. The east parterre garden with its Flora Fountain was designed in the Parterre de Broderie style, meaning that it was intended to have the appearance of embroidery, with box-edged shapes filled with coloured gravel and flowers.

Following the disastrous fire in 1937 the Witley Estate, including its gardens, fell into long decline. English Heritage has now restored the south garden.

The Woodland Walks in the North Park pass many different species of tree and shrub, acquired from all over the world to create a showpiece. A new garden in 'the Wilderness' is part of the Contemporary Heritage Garden project. This provides yet more opportunities for walking within Witley Court's grounds. Attached to Witley Court is Great Witley Church, which has an amazing Italianate Baroque interior (not managed by English Heritage). The church also has a tearoom close by, and Witley Court has a superb gift shop. The Perseus and Andromeda fountain is back in working order, with even the original high cascades operating. The fountain will be firing between April and September. Weekdays: 12pm, 2pm and 4pm. Weekends: on the hour every hour from 11am to 4pm.

www.english-heritage.org.uk/witleycourt

Perseus and Andromeda Fountain

Balustrade

NON-MEMBERS

Adult	£5.20
Concession	£3.90
Child	£2.60
Family ticket	£13.00

OPENING TIMES

1 Apr-31 May, daily	10am-5pm
1 Jun-31 Aug, daily	10am-6pm
1 Sep-31 Oct, daily	10am-5pm
1 Nov-28 Feb, Thu-Mon	10am-4pm
1-31 Mar, daily	10am-5pm
Closed	24-26 Dec and 1 Jan

HOW TO FIND US

Direction: 10 miles NW of Worcester on A443

Train: Worcester Foregate St 9½ miles

Bus: Yarranton 758 Worcester – Tenbury Wells (passes close to Worcester Foregate St)

Tel: 01299 896636

Local Tourist Information Droitwich Spa: 01905 774312

P OVP

Disabled access (exterior and grounds only).

Tearooms open daily, Apr-Sep and Sat and Sun, Oct (not managed by EH).

New audio tour.

MAP Page 270 (6C)
OS Map 150 (ref SO 769649)

North wall of the frigidarium

Photo: Paul Highnam

Wroxeter Roman City

Shropshire – SY5 6PH

Wroxeter (or 'Viroconium') was the fourth largest city in Roman Britain. It began as a legionary fortress and later developed into a thriving civilian city, populated by retired soldiers and traders. Though much still remains below ground, today the most impressive features are the 2nd-century municipal baths, and the remains of the huge wall dividing them from the exercise hall in the heart of the city.

The site museum and audio tour reveal how Wroxeter worked in its heyday, and the health and beauty practices of its 5000 citizens. Dramatic archaeological discoveries provide a glimpse of the last years of the Roman city, and its possible conversion into the headquarters of a 5th-century British or Irish warlord.

www.english-heritage.org.uk/wroxeter

NON-MEMBERS	
Adult	£4.00
Concession	£3.00
Child	£2.00
Family ticket	£10.00

OPENING TIMES	
1 Mar-30 May, daily	10am-5pm
1 Jun-31 Aug, daily	10am-6pm
1 Sep-31 Oct, daily	10am-5pm
1 Nov-28 Feb, Wed-Sun	10am-4pm
Closed	24-26 Dec & 1 Jan

HOW TO FIND US

Direction: Located at Wroxeter, 5 miles E of Shrewsbury on B4380

Train: Shrewsbury 5½ miles; Wellington Telford West 6 miles

Bus: Arriva 96 Telford – Shrewsbury (passes close to Telford Central)

Tel: 01743 761330

OVP

MAP Page 270 (4B)
OS Map 126 (ref SJ 565087)

Other Historic Attractions

Discounted entry to our members (discounts may not apply on event days)

Stoneleigh Abbey

Warwickshire – CV8 2LF

Originally founded for Cistercian monks, Stoneleigh Abbey reflects a rich mix of history. Charles I was entertained here, Jane Austen uses descriptions of it in two of her novels, and Queen Victoria visited it in 1858. The estate includes a medieval gatehouse – one of the few in Britain still standing and complete; the Great West Wing with State Rooms decorated in fine freehand plasterwork; and a Gothic Revival riding school and stables. Tearoom facilities available.

ENTRY (WEST WING & STABLES)	
Adult	£6.00
Senior Citizens	£4.00
Child	£2.50

One child free with each Adult ticket

ENTRY (GROUNDS ONLY)	
Per Person	£2.50

10% discount to EH members
All prices are subject to change and are correct at time of going to print

OPENING TIMES

Good Friday-29 Oct
Tue, Wed, Thu, Sun and Bank Hols

Guided Tours	11am, 1pm, 3pm
Grounds open	10am-5pm

HOW TO FIND US

Direction: B4115 off the A452/A46, just a short journey from Kenilworth Castle

Tel: 01926 858535

www.stoneleighabbey.org

MAP Page 270 (5E)
OS Map 140 (ref SP 318712)

The Barn, Kenilworth Castle – see page 170

Photo: Peter Richardson

'Leda and the Swan', Brodsworth Hall and Gardens – see page 186

Yorkshire

'See all, hear all, say nowt,
Eat all, sup all, pay nowt,
And if tha does owt for nowt,
Allus do it for thissen'.

Old Yorkshire proverb

www.english-heritage.org.uk/yorkshire

Properties

See individual listings for details

East Riding of Yorkshire
Burton Agnes Manor House, Howden Minster, Skipsea Castle

Lincolnshire
Gainsthorpe Medieval Village, St Peter's Church, Thornton Abbey and Gatehouse

North Yorkshire
Aldborough Roman Site, Byland Abbey, Clifford's Tower, Easby Abbey, Fountains Abbey, Helmsley Castle, Kirkham Priory, Marmion Tower, Middleham Castle, Mount Grace Priory, Pickering Castle, Piercebridge Roman Bridge, Richmond Castle, Rievaulx Abbey, St Mary's Church, Scarborough Castle, Spofforth Castle, Stanwick Iron Age Fortifications, Steeton Hall Gateway, Wharram Percy Deserted Medieval Village, Wheeldale Roman Road, Whitby Abbey, York Cold War Bunker

South Yorkshire
Brodsworth Hall and Gardens, Conisbrough Castle, Monk Bretton Priory, Roche Abbey

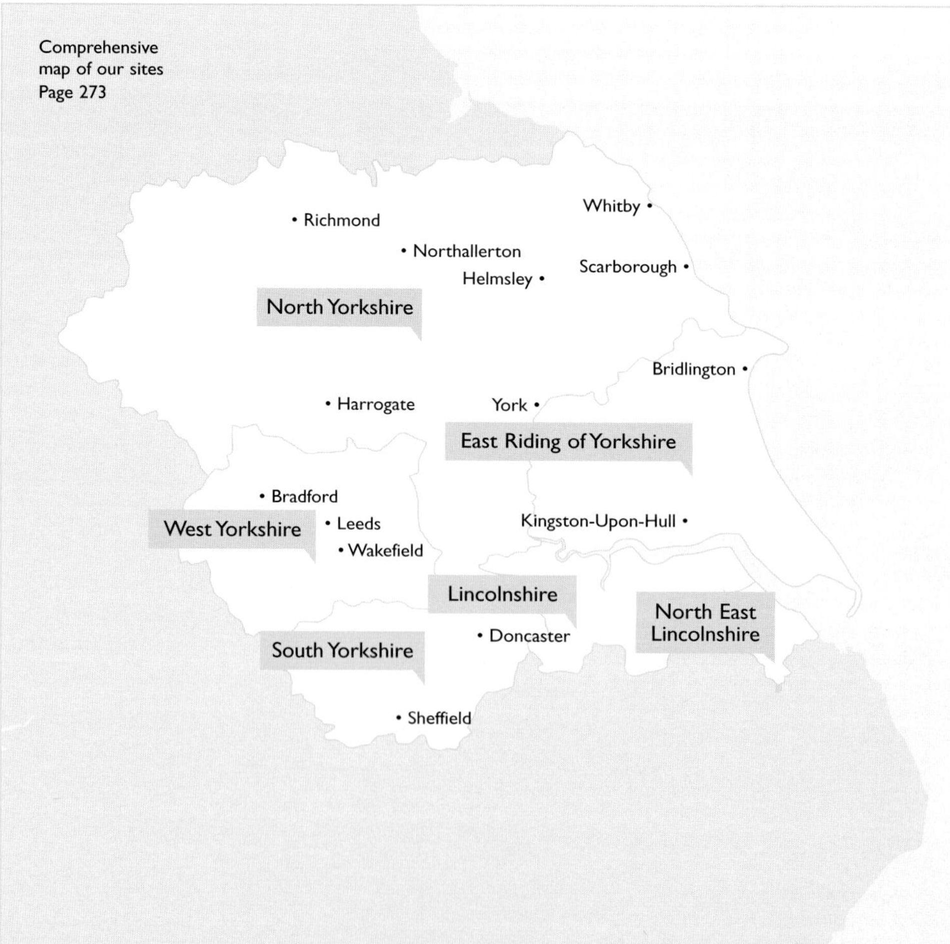

Bronze Age sword, Scarborough Castle – see page 197

Photo: Tony Bartholomew

A Kingdom In Itself

Proudly quoted by Yorkshiremen, this gritty saying (p.183) summarises the reputation for hard-headed independence carefully nurtured by England's biggest county. Large enough to be a kingdom in itself, this was effectively what Yorkshire was for long periods of its history. Much of this history can be traced in English Heritage's many Yorkshire sites.

In pre-Roman times, this was the heartland of Britain's biggest tribe, the Brigantes, whose centres were at Stanwick and later at Aldborough. One of their ancestors perhaps owned the prehistoric sword which has recently returned to dramatic **Scarborough Castle**, itself a multi-period encapsulation of Yorkshire history. Later the county was the core of the kingdom of Northumbria, the cultural power-house of Anglo-Saxon northern Britain, whose story is told at **Whitby Abbey**. It then became an independent realm of Viking settlers, who divided it into the 'thridings' – thirdings – which became the three steadfastly maintained Yorkshire Ridings.

Though subsumed into England after the Norman Conquest and the raising of **Richmond Castle**, medieval Yorkshire remained the domain of independently-minded castle-building barons.

The county's notable fortresses include **Conisbrough Castle** with its cylindrical keep; moors-edge **Pickering Castle**; **Clifford's Tower** in the heart of York; and **Middleham Castle**, home of the Nevilles and Richard III. Walter Espec of **Helmsley Castle**, which was recently enhanced with new displays, was also the founder of **Kirkham Priory** and the impressively complete **Rievaulx Abbey**: Yorkshire's noble monastic ruins are indeed among its chief glories. They include innovative **Byland Abbey**; **Easby Abbey** by Richmond; **Monk Bretton** and **Roche** in the south; **Thornton Abbey** across the Humber; and **Mount Grace Priory** with its unique Carthusian hermit-cells.

The varied landscapes of Yorkshire – wild moorland and agricultural plain, the Pennine Dales, and the chalk Wolds and sea-coast of the East Riding – also contain sites of many other kinds. There are medieval manor houses at **Burton Agnes** and **Spofforth Castle**; and that most evocative of deserted medieval villages, **Wharram Percy**. High Victorian **St Mary's Church, Studley Royal** contrasts with **St Peter's**, Barton-on-Humber, one of England's finest Anglo-Saxon churches. Two very different new sites will also open in 2006: The Abbey Inn at **Byland Abbey**, and the **York Cold War Bunker**. But perhaps the most distinctive of all English Heritage's Yorkshire properties is **Brodsworth Hall** amid its delightful gardens, a Victorian mansion frozen in time.

Brodsworth Hall and Gardens South Yorkshire – DN5 7XJ

Brodsworth Hall was built in the 1860s in the Italianate style also favoured for Queen Victoria's Osborne House, though furnished on a more comfortable and domestic scale. Much of its original scheme survives today, making it one of England's most unaltered Victorian country houses. The gardens, a collection of 'grand gardens in miniature', have been restored to their Victorian splendour, reflecting the desires and aspirations of Victorian country gentry.

The Flower Garden

Brodsworth's builder was Charles Thellusson, whose wealthy family devoted themselves to yachting and horse-racing. The magnificent silver Goodwood Cup, won by a Thellusson ancestor's racehorse in 1835, has recently been purchased by English Heritage to rejoin the racing mementos still on display at Brodsworth.

The house was occupied in unbroken succession by members of the Thellusson family and their accumulated impedimenta, a factor which lends it special charm. The last resident, the indomitable Sylvia Grant-Dalton, fought a losing battle against subsidence and leaking roofs for 56 years. Following her death in 1988, English Heritage then made the bold but highly successful decision to conserve the interiors 'as found' rather than replacing or restoring them,

Garden Statue

recounting the tale of how a once opulent Victorian house grew comfortably old and inviting to all.

Exhibitions offering an insight into life at Brodsworth include 'Maids and Mistresses', 'Serving the House', 'Family Life', 'The Gardens', and 'The Goodwood Cup'.

For Garden Lovers

The family gardens, a series of 'grand gardens in miniature', have been substantially restored since English Heritage took over management of the property in 1990: they are now a fine example of 1860s 'gardening book' design. Many years of pruning and tree removal have opened up vistas last enjoyed before World War I.

The flower garden displays a fine selection of period bedding plants, and the romantic views from the restored summer-house take in the quarry garden, paths, bridges and garden buildings. Of special interest are the restored woodland garden, the statue walks and the fern dell, planted with unusual specimens. The gardens at Brodsworth Hall are a delight in any season, but here are our suggested dates for viewing specific collections. Please bear in mind that exact display times are subject to seasonal variation.

Feb/Mar
180,000 snowdrops and 36 varieties of daffodil.

Apr
14,000 bulbs and 5,000 tulips form the spring bedding.

May
Laburnum Arch in flower.

May/June
Rose display and over 100 historic varieties of geranium at their peak.

July
Summer bedding around the fountain; 250 varieties of ferns at their best.

Sep-Oct
Ornamental trees display their autumn colours.

Oct-Nov
Evening illuminations creating a magical journey around the garden.

Nov-Jan
Over 400 yew trees and many laurels provide shelter for a bracing winter walk.

>

For Families

The garden has picnic tables and large areas of grass for expending energy! The hall has activity sheets to keep youngsters interested throughout the furnished interiors, two family rooms, plus special activities for children in the exhibitions. A baby changing room is available in the toilets. Garden Explorer back-packs help children and families to investigate the gardens. There is a children's story box, and special trails during school holidays.

Mobility around the site

Visitors please note that prams and back carriers for babies are not allowed in the fragile interiors of the hall. Staff can however provide small padded pushchairs and slings for visitors' use. For visitors with mobility needs, the leg-weary or families with young children, a new six-seater electric buggy now operates a shuttle service from the public car parks. The smooth paths and benches throughout the gardens enable visitors to rest and enjoy the atmosphere, although some steps and steep slopes limit access to parts of the garden. The hall is accessed by ramps and has seats along the route for visitors to use, many handrails and a lift to enable visitors to enjoy the first floor.

www.english-heritage.org.uk/brodsworthhall

The dining room

NON-MEMBERS HOUSE & GARDENS:	
Adult	£6.60
Concession	£5.00
Child	£3.30

NON-MEMBERS GARDENS ONLY:	
Adult	£4.60
Concession	£3.50
Child	£2.30

OPENING TIMES

House:

1 Apr-29 Sep, Tue-Sun & Bank Hols 1pm-5pm

30 Sep-29 Oct, Sat-Sun 12pm-4pm

Gardens and Tearoom:

1 Apr-29 Oct, daily 10am-5.30pm

Gardens, Tearoom, Shop & Servants' Wing:

30 Oct-31 Mar, Sat-Sun 10am-4pm

Closed 23-24 Dec & 30-31 Dec

Last admission ½ hour before closing

HOW TO FIND US

Direction: In Brodsworth, 5 miles NW of Doncaster off A635 Barnsley Road; from junction 37 of A1(M)

Train: South Elmsall 4 miles; Moorthorpe 4½ miles; Doncaster 5½ miles

Bus: Yorkshire Traction 211 Doncaster – Barnsley (passing close ≷ Doncaster and passing ≷ South Elmsall & Moorthorpe). Alight at Pickburn, Five Lanes End, then ½ mile walk

Local Tourist Information Doncaster: 01302 734309

Tel: 01302 724969 (info-line)

No cameras (house).

MAP Page 273 (5G)
OS Map 111 (ref SE 506070)

Aldborough Roman Site

N. Yorkshire – YO51 9EP

Aldborough, among the northernmost urban centres in the Roman Empire, succeeded Stanwick (see p.200) as the tribal stronghold of the Romanised Brigantes, the largest tribe in Britain. One corner of the defences is clearly laid out amid the towering trees of a Victorian arboretum, a tranquil place for picnics. Two almost complete mosaic pavements can be viewed in their original position, and the site museum's fine collection of Roman finds make this the best place in Yorkshire to study the Romans. There is a handling collection of real and replica Roman objects, mosaic-making kits, and a 'tree box' for the arboretum.

NON-MEMBERS

Adult	£3.00
Concession	£2.30
Child	£1.50

OPENING TIMES

1 Apr-30 Jun, Sat-Sun	11am-5pm
1 Jul-31 Aug, Thu-Mon	10am-5pm
1-30 Sep, Sat-Sun	11am-5pm

HOW TO FIND US

Direction: Located in Aldborough, ¾ mile SE of Boroughbridge on a minor road off B6265; within 1 mile of junction of A1 and A6055

Bus: Arriva/Harrogate Coach Travel 142 ⇌ York-Ripon

Tel: 01423 322768

OVP

Dogs on leads (restricted areas only).

MAP Page 273 (3G)
OS Map 99 (ref SE 405662)

Brodsworth Hall and Gardens

See feature – Page 186

Burton Agnes Manor House

East Riding of Yorkshire

A medieval manor house interior, with a rare and well-preserved Norman undercroft and a 15th-century roof, all encased in brick during the 17th and 18th centuries.

OPENING TIMES

1 Apr-31 Oct, daily	11am-5pm

The nearby Burton Agnes Hall and Gardens are privately owned and are not managed by English Heritage

HOW TO FIND US

Direction: In Burton Agnes village, 5 miles SW of Bridlington on A166

Train: Nafferton 5 miles

Bus: E Yorkshire 744 ⇌ York – Bridlington

MAP Page 273 (3J)
OS Map 101 (ref TA 102632)

Byland Abbey

N. Yorkshire – YO61 4BD

Byland was one of the great Yorkshire Cistercian abbeys, housing at its zenith well over 200 monks and lay brothers. Much of its huge cathedral-sized church survives, including the whole north side and the greater part of the 13th-century west front. With its mixture of rounded Romanesque and pointed Gothic arches, this proclaims the arrival of the new Gothic style which

Byland pioneered in the north. Its great circular rose window, now surviving only in part, was probably the model for the rose window of York Minster.

Both Rievaulx Abbey and Helmsley Castle are within reasonable travelling distance.

NEW FOR 2006 The updated museum now houses archaeological site finds, including intricate stonework and decorative tiles, plus new graphic interpretation panels. There is also a range of new family-friendly books and activities. The Abbey Inn, a gastro-pub adjoining the Abbey, is now in the care of English Heritage.

NON-MEMBERS

Adult	£3.00
Concession	£2.30
Child	£1.50

OPENING TIMES

1 Apr-31 Jul, Thu-Mon	10am-5pm
1-31 Aug, daily	10am-5pm
1-30 Sep, Thu-Mon	10am-5pm

HOW TO FIND US

Direction: 2 miles S of A170, between Thirsk and Helmsley; near Coxwold village

Train: Thirsk 10 miles

Bus: Stephensons 31/X, Moorsbus M15 York-Helmsley

Tel: 01347 868614

OVP

Parking (opposite the Abbey).

Toilets (Abbey Inn opposite the Abbey).

Restaurant (Abbey Inn opposite the Abbey).

MAP Page 273 (2G)
OS Map 100 (ref SE 549789)

Clifford's Tower, York

N. Yorkshire – YO1 9SA

In 1068-9, William the Conqueror built two motte and bailey castles in York, to strengthen his military hold on the north. Clifford's Tower, an unusual four-lobed keep built in the 13th century atop the mound of William's larger fortress, is now the principal surviving stonework remnant of York's medieval castle. The sweeping views of the city from the tower still show why it played such an important part in controlling northern England.

On summer weekends a costumed interpreter brings to life key events in the history of York and the Tower.

NON-MEMBERS	
Adult	£3.00
Concession	£2.30
Child	£1.50
Family ticket	£7.50

OPENING TIMES

1 Apr-30 Sep, daily	10am-6pm
1-31 Oct, daily	10am-5pm
1 Nov-31 Mar, daily:	10am-4pm
Closed	24-26 Dec and 1 Jan

HOW TO FIND US

Direction: In Tower St, York

Train: York 1 mile

Bus: From surrounding areas

Tel: 01904 646940

Local Tourist Information York: 01904 621756

OVP

Parking (local charge).

MAP Page 273 (3G)
OS Map 105 (ref SE 605515)

Conisbrough Castle

S. Yorkshire – DN12 3BU

The white, cylindrical keep of this 12th-century castle is a spectacular structure. Built of magnesian limestone, it is the only example of its kind in England. Restored, with two new floors and a roof, it is a fine example of medieval architecture, and was one of the inspirations for Sir Walter Scott's classic novel, *Ivanhoe*.

www.conisbroughcastle.org.uk

Managed by The Ivanhoe Trust.

OPENING TIMES

1 Apr-30 Sep, daily (last admission 4.20pm)	10am-5pm
1 Oct-31 Mar, daily (last admission 3.20pm)	10am-4pm

Closed over Christmas period. Please call for details.

EH members admitted free or with a discount during special events.

Guided, evening and school party tours offered. Available for private hire and special events. Castle may close early for private functions on Saturdays in the summer.

HOW TO FIND US

Direction: Located NE of Conisbrough town centre off A630; 4½ miles SW of Doncaster

Train: Conisbrough ½ mile

Bus: From surrounding areas

Tel: 01709 863329

Dogs on leads (restricted areas only). Parking (visitors with disabilities, please call the site to reserve a space).

MAP Page 273 (5G)
OS Map 111 (ref SK 515989)

Easby Abbey

N. Yorkshire

The substantial remains of an abbey of Premonstratensian 'white canons', most notably its lavish roof-height refectory of c. 1300 and other monastic buildings. Within the precinct is the still-active parish church, displaying fine 13th-century wall paintings. In a beautiful setting by the River Swale, Easby can be reached via a pleasant walk from Richmond Castle.

OPENING TIMES

1 Apr-30 Sep, daily	10am-6pm
1-31 Oct, daily	10am-5pm
1 Nov-31 Mar, daily	10am-4pm
Closed	24-26 Dec and 1 Jan

HOW TO FIND US

Direction: 1 mile SE of Richmond, off B6271

Bus: Arriva X26/7, 27/8 Darlington-Richmond (pass close Darlington) then 1½ miles

Guidebooks (from Richmond Castle).

MAP Page 273 (2F)
OS Map 92 (ref NZ 185003)

Gainsthorpe Medieval Village

Lincolnshire

Gainsthorpe Medieval Village

A deserted medieval village, one of the best-preserved examples in England, clearly visible as a complex of grassy humps and bumps. According to legend demolished as a den of thieves, the real reason for its abandonment remains uncertain.

OPENING TIMES

Any reasonable time

HOW TO FIND US

Direction: Located on minor road W of A15; S of Hibaldstow; 5 miles SW of Brigg

Train: Kirton Lindsey 3 miles

MAP Page 273 (5J)
OS Map 112 (ref SE 954011)

Helmsley Castle

See feature – Page 192

Howden Minster

East Riding of Yorkshire

The elaborately decorated ruins of a 14th-century chancel and chapter house (viewable only from the outside), attached to the still operational cathedral-like minster church.

OPENING TIMES

Any reasonable time	
Closed	24-26 Dec and 1 Jan

HOW TO FIND US

Direction: In Howden; 23 miles W of Kingston Upon Hull, 25 miles SE of York, near the junction of A63 and A614

Train: Howden 1½ miles

Bus: East Yorkshire 155/6 Goole-Hull

P

Parking (street parking nearby).

MAP Page 273 (4H)
OS Map 106 (ref SE 748283)

Kirkham Priory

N. Yorkshire – YO60 7JS

The riverside ruins of an Augustinian priory, including a gatehouse bedecked with the heraldry of the Roos family of Helmsley Castle, and a handsome set of monastic washbasins. Picturesquely set in the beautiful Derwent valley near the Yorkshire Wolds. On-site interpretation includes the story of the secret visit of Winston Churchill, and Kirkham's role in preparations for D-Day during World War II.

NON-MEMBERS

Adult	£3.00
Concession	£2.30
Child	£1.50

OPENING TIMES

1 Apr-31 Aug, daily	10am-6pm
1-30 Sep, Thu-Mon	10am-4pm
1-31 Oct, Sat-Sun	10am-4pm

HOW TO FIND US

Direction: 5 miles SW of Malton, on a minor road off A64

Train: Malton 6 miles

Bus: Yorkshire Coastliner 840/2/3/5 Leeds – Scarborough/Whitby (pass York and Malton) to within ¾ mile

Tel: 01653 618768

OVP

MAP Page 273 (3H)
OS Map 100 (ref SE 736658)

Marmion Tower

N. Yorkshire

The fine 15th-century gatehouse of a vanished riverside manor house, with a beautiful oriel window. The monuments of the manor's Marmion family owners grace the adjacent church.

OPENING TIMES

1 Apr-30 Sep, daily	10am-6pm
1-31 Oct, daily	10am-5pm
1 Nov-31 Mar, daily	10am-4pm
Closed	24-26 Dec and 1 Jan

HOW TO FIND US

Direction: On A6108 in West Tanfield

Train: Thirsk 10 miles

MAP Page 273 (3F)
OS Map 99 (ref SE 268787)

You can find out more about the work of English Heritage at **www.english-heritage.org.uk**

Helmsley Castle North Yorkshire – YO62 5AB

Surrounded by spectacular banks and ditches, the great medieval castle's impressive ruins stand beside the attractive market town of Helmsley. The fortress was probably begun after 1120 by Walter Espec – 'Walter the Woodpecker'. Renowned for piety as well as soldiering, this Norman baron of 'gigantic stature' also founded nearby Rievaulx Abbey and Kirkham Priory, both English Heritage properties.

Most of Helmsley's surviving stonework defences were raised during the late 12th and 13th centuries, by the crusader Robert de Roos and his descendants. They include a pair of immensely strong 'barbican' entrances and the high, keep-like east tower, unusually D-shaped in plan, which still dominates the town.

But Helmsley is not only a medieval fortress. During the Elizabethan period the Manners family remodelled the castle's chamber block into a luxurious mansion, whose fine plasterwork and panelling still partly survive. The castle's first and last military trial came during the Civil War. Held for King Charles, it endured a three month siege before being starved out in November 1644 by Parliamentarians under Sir Thomas Fairfax, who was seriously wounded in the fighting. Fairfax then dismantled the defences but spared the mansion, subsequently the home of his daughter and her husband, the profligate Duke of Buckingham.

Demoted to a romantic backdrop when later owners moved to nearby Duncombe Park, Helmsley Castle has recently undergone a thorough makeover by English Heritage, making it more accessible to a wide range of visitors. This includes a brand-new visitor centre also providing tourist information, an audio tour, and an imaginative hands-on exhibition in the mansion range. Displaying a fascinating array of finds from Civil War cannon balls to early tableware, this explores the social and domestic as well as the military aspects of the fortress. New facilities for disabled visitors include full ground level ramping, a virtual tour of less accessible areas, and a tactile model with braille text. Enhanced learning resources include family-friendly books and activities.

Find out about other sites and accommodation in the area from the Tourist Information Centre, which is located in the Visitor Centre.

Rievaulx and Byland Abbeys are both nearby: Rievaulx can be reached on foot via the Cleveland Way (approx. 2.5 miles/1.5 hours each way, strong footwear required).

www.english-heritage.org.uk/helmsleycastle

The South Barbican and outer ditch

Visitor Centre

Exhibition in the West Range

NON-MEMBERS	
Adult	£4.00
Concession	£3.00
Child	£2.00
Family ticket	£10.00

OPENING TIMES

1 Apr-30 Sep, daily	10am-6pm
1-31 Oct, daily	10am-5pm
1 Nov-31 Mar, Thu-Mon	10am-4pm

Closed
27 May 2006, 24-26 Dec and 1 Jan

HOW TO FIND US

Direction: Near the town centre

Bus: Scarborough & District 128 from Scarborough

Tourist Information Centre Tel: 01439 770173

Tel: 01439 770442

OVP

Parking (large car park adjacent to castle; charge payable).

Toilets (in car park and town centre).

MAP Page 273 (2G)
OS Map 100 (ref SE 611836)

Middleham Castle

N. Yorkshire – DL8 4RJ

The childhood and favourite home of Richard III, Middleham Castle was a fortress of the mighty Neville family, Earls of Westmoreland and of Warwick. Around the massive 12th-century central keep, they progressively constructed three ranges of luxurious chambers and lodgings, turning the castle into a fortified palace by the mid-15th century. Though roofless, many of these buildings survive, making Middleham a fascinating castle to explore. Here Richard spent part of his youth, in the guardianship of 'Warwick the Kingmaker'.

An exhibition about notable personalities from the castle's past includes a replica of the beautiful Middleham Jewel, a 15th-century pendant decorated with a large sapphire found near the castle. Family-friendly books and activities.

NON-MEMBERS

Adult	£3.50
Concession	£2.60
Child	£1.80

OPENING TIMES

1 Apr-30 Sep, daily	10am-6pm
1 Oct-31 Mar, Thu-Mon	10am-4pm
Closed	24-26 Dec and 1 Jan

HOW TO FIND US

Direction: Located at Middleham; 2 miles S of Leyburn on A6108

Middleham Castle

Bus: Dales & District 159 Ripon-Richmond

Tel: 01969 623899

Local Tourist Information Leyburn: 01969 623069

OVP

Disabled access (except keep).

MAP Page 273 (2F)
OS Map 99 (ref SE 127876)

Monk Bretton Priory

S. Yorkshire

The substantial ruins of a Cluniac monastery, with an unusually well-marked ground plan, an almost complete west range and a 15th-century gatehouse.

OPENING TIMES

1 Apr-30 Sep, daily	10am-6pm
1-31 Oct, daily	10am-5pm
1 Nov-31 Mar, daily (managed by a key-keeper)	10am-4pm
Closed	24-26 Dec and 1 Jan

Charge may apply on event days

HOW TO FIND US

Direction: Located 1 mile E of Barnsley town centre, off A633

Train: Barnsley 2½ miles

Bus: From surrounding areas

MAP Page 273 (5G)
OS Map 111 (ref SE 373065)

Mount Grace Priory

N. Yorkshire – DL6 3JG

Set amid woodland below the escarpment of the North York Moors and the Cleveland Way National Trail, Mount Grace is a monastic ruin of an unusual kind. It is the best-preserved of the ten British 'charterhouses', whose Carthusian monks lived as hermits in cottage-like cells. A reconstructed and furnished monk's cell and a recently revamped herb plot offer a glimpse into the lives of the medieval residents. The site hosts art exhibitions throughout the year, and the gardens are a haven for wildlife, including the famous 'Priory Stoats'. There is a children's story box, and special children's trails during school holidays.

Owned by The National Trust, maintained and managed by EH.

NON-MEMBERS

Adult	£4.00
Concession	£3.00
Child	£2.00
Family ticket	£10.00

National Trust members admitted free, except on special event days

OPENING TIMES

1 Apr-30 Sep, Thu-Mon	10am-6pm
1 Oct-31 Mar, Thu-Sun	10am-4pm

Closed 24-26 Dec and 1 Jan

Direction: 12 miles N of Thirsk; 6 miles NE of Northallerton, on A19

Train: Northallerton 6 miles

Mount Grace Priory

Bus: Arriva North East 80, 89 from Northallerton – Stokesley, alight Priory Road End, then ½ mile

Tel: 01609 883494

Local Tourist Information Northallerton: 01609 776864

MAP Page 273 (2G)
OS Map 99 (ref SE 449985)

Pickering Castle

N. Yorkshire – YO18 7AX

Pickering Castle is set in an attractive moors-edge market town. It is a classic and well-preserved example of an early earthwork castle refortified in stone during the 13th and 14th centuries, centred upon a shell-keep crowning an impressive motte. There is an exhibition in the chapel, and family-friendly books and activities.

NON-MEMBERS	
Adult	£3.00
Concession	£2.30
Child	£1.50
Family ticket	£7.50

OPENING TIMES	
1 Apr-30 Sep, daily	10am-6pm
1-31 Oct, Thu-Mon	10am-5pm

HOW TO FIND US

Direction: In Pickering; 15 miles SW of Scarborough

Pickering Castle

Train: Malton 9 miles; Pickering (N York Moors Rly) ¼ mile

Bus: Yorkshire Coastliner 840/2 from Malton; Scarborough & District 128 from Scarborough

Tel: 01751 474989

Disabled access (except motte).

MAP Page 273 (2H)
OS Map 100 (ref SE 799845)

Piercebridge Roman Bridge

N. Yorkshire

Stonework foundations, now marooned in a field, of a bridge which once led to Piercebridge Roman Fort.

OPENING TIMES

Any reasonable time

HOW TO FIND US

Direction: At Piercebridge; 4 miles W of Darlington, on B6275

Train: Darlington 5 miles

Bus: Arriva 75/6 Darlington – Barnard Castle (passes close to Darlington)

MAP Page 273 (1F)
OS Map 93 (ref NZ 214155)

Richmond Castle

N. Yorkshire – DL10 4QW

Breathtakingly sited on a rocky promontory above the River Swale, the great castle of Richmond is among the oldest Norman stone fortresses in Britain, begun in the decades after the Conquest. The towering keep, over 30 metres (100 feet) high and remarkably complete within, was added by Henry II in the 1170s: its roof provides splendid views over the clustered houses of the pretty market town. Traditionally King Arthur lies sleeping in a cavern beneath the castle: more certainly, conscientious objectors were imprisoned in the keep during World War I. Their story is told in an interactive exhibition exploring Richmond's nine centuries of history. There is also a garden created to reflect the castle's story, with vistas over the River Swale, and family-friendly books and activities and plant sales.

NON-MEMBERS	
Adult	£3.60
Concession	£2.70
Child	£1.80
Family ticket	£9.00

OPENING TIMES	
1 Apr-30 Sep, daily	10am-6pm
1 Oct-31 Mar, Thu-Mon	10am-4pm
Closed	24-26 Dec and 1 Jan

HOW TO FIND US

Direction: In Richmond

Bus: Arriva X26/7, 27/8 Darlington – Richmond (passes close to Darlington)

Tel: 01748 822493

MAP Page 273 (2F)
OS Map 92 (ref NZ 172007)

Rievaulx Abbey

See feature – Page 198

Roche Abbey

S. Yorkshire – S66 8NW

Beautifully set in a valley landscaped by 'Capability' Brown in the 18th century, the most striking feature of this Cistercian abbey is the tall eastern end of its church, built in the new Gothic style in about 1170. It also displays one of the most complete ground plans of any English Cistercian monastery, laid out as excavated foundations and incorporating the original drainage ditch. The story of the pillaging of Roche, recorded by the son of an eye-witness, is among the most vivid documents of the Dissolution of the Monasteries.

NON-MEMBERS

Adult	£3.00
Concession	£2.30
Child	£1.50

OPENING TIMES

1 Apr-31 Jul, Thu-Mon	10am-5pm
1-31 Aug, daily	10am-5pm
1-30 Sep, Thu-Mon	10am-5pm

HOW TO FIND US

Direction: 1½ miles S of Maltby, off A634

Train: Conisbrough 7 miles

Bus: First 1, 2, 10, Powell 122 Rotherham-Maltby, then 1½ miles

Tel: 01709 812739

OVP

MAP Page 273 (6G)
OS Map 111 (ref SK 544898)

St Mary's Church, Studley Royal

N. Yorkshire

This magnificent High Victorian Anglican church was designed in the 1870s by the flamboyant architect William Burges, and has been called his 'ecclesiastical masterpiece'. Its extravagantly decorated interior displays coloured marble, stained glass, a splendid organ, and painted and gilded figures in all their original glory.

EH property managed by The National Trust as part of the Fountains Abbey and Studley Royal Estate (see p.204).

OPENING TIMES

1 Apr-30 Sep, daily	1pm-5pm

HOW TO FIND US

Direction: Located 2½ miles W of Ripon, off B6265; in the grounds of the Studley Royal Estate

Bus: Arriva 802 Wakefield-Leyburn, Sun, May-Sep only; otherwise 'Ripon Roweller' from Ripon (booked on 01423 526655) (with connections from Harrogate)

Tel: 01765 608888

Parking (at visitor centre).

MAP Page 273 (3F)
OS Map 99 (ref SE 275693)

St Peter's Church, Barton-upon-Humber

Lincolnshire – DN18 5EX

With a history spanning over a millennium, this famous church features a remarkably complete Anglo-Saxon tower and baptistry, dating mainly from c. 970, and a large medieval nave and chancel displaying a range of architectural styles. An exhibition within illustrates the results of excavations and

research at this most studied of English churches. This includes the analysis of some 2,800 burials, yielding important information about disease and early medical practice.

OPENING TIMES

Daily	1pm-3pm
Closed	24-26 Dec and 1 Jan

Charge may apply on event days

HOW TO FIND US

Direction: In Barton-upon-Humber

Train: Barton-upon-Humber ½ mile

Bus: Road Car/E Yorks 350 Hull-Cleethorpes Barton-upon-Humber

Tel: 01652 632516

MAP Page 273 (5J)
OS Map 112 (ref TA 035219)

Scarborough Castle

See feature opposite

Skipsea Castle

East Riding of Yorkshire

An impressive Norman motte and bailey castle, dating from before 1086 and among the first raised in Yorkshire, with the earthworks of an attendant fortified 'borough'.

OPENING TIMES

Any reasonable time

HOW TO FIND US

Direction: Located 8 miles S of Bridlington; W of Skipsea village

Train: Bridlington 9 miles

Dogs on leads (restricted areas only).

Waterproof footwear recommended.

MAP Page 273 (3J)
OS Map 107 (ref TA 162551)

Scarborough Castle

North Yorkshire – YO11 1HY

Scarborough Castle defends a prominent headland between two bays, with sheer drops to the sea and only a narrow landward approach. Long before the castle was built, this natural fortress was favoured by prehistoric settlers – a splendid Bronze Age sword, perhaps deposited here as a sacrifice to the gods, has newly returned for display – and later housed a defended Roman signal station.

Henry II's towering 12th-century keep, dominating the approach, is the centrepiece of fortifications developed over later centuries in response to repeated sieges – notably by rebel barons in 1312, and twice during the Civil War. Though again strengthened with barracks and gun-batteries against Jacobite threats in 1745, the castle failed to defend the harbour against the American sea-raider John Paul Jones in 1779, and was itself damaged by German naval bombardment in 1914. During World War II it played the more covert role of hosting a secret listening post.

Specially constructed viewing platforms now offer wonderful views of the coastline. The site's 3,000-year history is explored in new interactive displays in the restored Master Gunner's House, accompanied by the prehistoric sword and artefacts from each period of Scarborough's past. Less mobile visitors can enjoy a ground-floor touch-screen virtual tour of the displays.

Timelined graphic panels around the castle focus on characters from times gone by, and there are free activity sheets, an audio tour and an investigative story box to help younger visitors visualise and understand the history of the castle.

www.english-heritage.org.uk/scarboroughcastle

NON-MEMBERS

Adult	£3.50
Concession	£2.60
Child	£1.80
Family ticket	£8.80

OPENING TIMES

1 Apr-30 Sep, daily	10am-6pm
1-31 Oct, Thu-Mon	10am-5pm
1 Nov-31 Mar, Thu-Mon	10am-4pm
Closed	24-26 Dec and 1 Jan

HOW TO FIND US

Direction: Castle Road, E of the town centre

Train: Scarborough 1 mile

Bus: From surrounding areas

Tel: 01723 372451

OVP

Parking (pre-booked parking only for disabled visitors, otherwise located in town centre).

MAP Page 273 (2J)
OS Map 101 (ref TA 050892)

Rievaulx Abbey North Yorkshire – YO62 5LB

'Everywhere peace, everywhere serenity, and a marvellous freedom from the tumult of the world.' These words, written over eight centuries ago by the monastery's third abbot St Aelred, could describe Rievaulx today. Set in a beautiful and tranquil valley, it is among the most atmospheric and complete of all the ruined abbeys of the north.

Words are not the only link to Rievaulx's medieval monks. Over the past few years, the site has become something of an archaeological treasure, with unexpected discoveries shedding new light on the lives of the abbey's former residents, and the extensive renewal and rebuilding of the abbey church in the Early English Gothic style. Archaeologists continue to study the wider landscape around Rievaulx, revealing the remarkable extent of the abbey's influence and industry: their discoveries are showcased in the site's annual archaeology day in July, and within the on-site museum.

The abbey was founded by St Bernard of Clairvaux, as part of the missionary effort to reform Christianity in western Europe. Just 12 Clairvaux monks came to Rievaulx in 1132. From these modest beginnings grew one of the wealthiest monasteries of medieval England and the first northern Cistercian monastery. Rievaulx also enjoyed the protection of Walter Espec of nearby Helmsley Castle, who provided much of the abbey's land. The monks of nearby Byland Abbey disputed land ownership with Rievaulx, which led to engineering works to divert the course of the River Rye, the boundary between their properties. You can still see traces of the old river and the channels dug by the monks.

A steady stream of monks came to Rievaulx Abbey, attracted by the prestige of Abbot Aelred, author and preacher, who was regarded then and later as a wise and saintly man. Following his death in 1167, the monks of Rievaulx sought canonisation for their former leader, and in the 1220s they rebuilt the east part of their church in a much more elaborate style to house his tomb. Most of this 13th-century 'presbytery' still stands to virtually its full impressive height, a reminder of Rievaulx's original splendour.

Rievaulx was still a vibrant community when Henry VIII dissolved it in 1538. Its new owner, Thomas Manners, first Earl of Rutland, swiftly instigated the systematic destruction of the buildings. But the substantial remains left behind still constitute one of the most eloquent of all monastic sites, free 'from the tumult of the world'.

Don't miss the exciting indoor exhibition, 'The Works of God and Man', which explores the agricultural, industrial, spiritual and construction aspects of Rievaulx's history, employing a variety of lively and interactive displays. There are family-friendly books and activities, and special childrens' trails during school holidays.

Byland Abbey and Helmsley Castle are both within reasonable travelling distance: Helmsley Castle can be reached on foot via the Cleveland Way National Trail (approx. 2.5 miles/1.5 hours each way, strong footwear required).

www.english-heritage.org.uk/rievaulxabbey

NEW FOR 2006 **Visitors to the abbey can now enjoy the new tearoom. A holiday cottage, set in the spectacular grounds of the abbey, will be available to let from 2006. Please ask for details.**

NON-MEMBERS	
Adult	£4.20
Concession	£3.20
Child	£2.10

OPENING TIMES	
1 Apr-30 Sep, daily	10am-6pm
1-31 Oct, Thu-Mon	10am-5pm
1 Nov-31 Mar, Thu-Mon	10am-4pm
Closed	24-26 Dec and 1 Jan

HOW TO FIND US

Direction: In Rievaulx; 2¼ miles N of Helmsley, on minor road off B1257

Bus: Moorsbus 198, M8 from Helmsley (connections on Scarborough & District 128 from Scarborough) Mon-Sat Jun-Sep, Suns, Apr-Oct, Tue, Thu & Sat only Oct-May.

Tel: 01439 798228

Local Tourist Information Helmsley: 01439 770173

E P OVP

Audio tours (also available for the visually impaired, those with learning difficulties and in French and German).

MAP Page 273 (2G)
OS Map 100 (ref SE 577850)

Spofforth Castle

N. Yorkshire

The ruined hall and chamber of a fortified manor house of the powerful Percy family, dating mainly from the 14th and 15th centuries. Its undercroft is cut into a rocky outcrop.

Managed by Spofforth-with-Stockeld Parish Council.

OPENING TIMES

1 Apr-30 Sep, daily	10am-6pm
1 Oct-31 Mar, daily	10am-4pm
(managed by a key-keeper)	
Closed	24-26 Dec and 1 Jan

HOW TO FIND US

Direction: 3½ miles SE of Harrogate; off A661 at Spofforth

Train: Pannal 4 miles

Bus: Harrogate & District 770/1 Harrogate-Leeds

Dogs on leads (restricted areas only).

MAP Page 273 (4G)
OS Map 104 (ref SE 360511)

Stanwick Iron Age Fortifications

N. Yorkshire

An excavated section, part cut into rock, of the ramparts of the huge Iron Age trading and power-centre of the Brigantes, the most important tribe in pre-Roman northern Britain. Some 4 miles (6.5 kilometres) long, the defences enclosed an area of 766 acres (310 hectares). Following Roman conquest, the Brigantian centre moved to Aldborough Roman Site (see p189).

OPENING TIMES

Any reasonable time

HOW TO FIND US

Direction: Located on a minor road off A6274, at Forcett Village

Train: Darlington 10 miles

Dogs on leads (restricted areas only).

MAP Page 273 (1F)
OS Map 92 (ref NZ 179124)

Steeton Hall Gateway

N. Yorkshire

A fine example of a small, well-preserved manorial gatehouse dating from the 14th century.

OPENING TIMES

Daily (exterior only)	10am-5pm

HOW TO FIND US

Direction: Located 4 miles NE of Castleford, on a minor road off A162 at South Milford

Train: South Milford 1 mile

Dogs on leads (restricted areas only).

MAP Page 273 (4G)
OS Map 105 (ref SE 484314)

Thornton Abbey and Gatehouse

Lincolnshire

The enormous and ornate fortified gatehouse of Thornton Abbey, an early example of brick building, proclaimed the prosperity of one of the wealthiest English Augustinian monasteries. Built in the years following the Peasants' Revolt of 1381, it may also have served to protect the abbey's treasures, as well as providing lodgings for the abbot and his guests. Within the grounds stand the remains of the monastic buildings, notably the elegantly decorated octagonal chapter house of 1282-1308.

OPENING TIMES

Abbey grounds:	
Apr-Sep daily	10am-6pm
Oct-Mar daily	10am-4pm
Gatehouse:	
1 Apr-30 Sep, 1st and 3rd Sun of the month	12pm-6pm
1 Oct-31 Mar, 3rd Sun of the month	12pm-4pm
Charge may apply on event days	

HOW TO FIND US

Direction: 18 miles NE of Scunthorpe, on a road N of A160; 7 miles SE of the Humber Bridge, on a road E of A1077

Train: Thornton Abbey ¼ mile

Disabled access (except gatehouse interior and part of chapter ruins).

Dogs on leads (restricted areas only).

MAP Page 273 (5J)
OS Map 113 (ref TA 118189)

Wharram Percy Deserted Medieval Village

N. Yorkshire

The most famous and intensively studied of Britain's 3,000 or so deserted medieval villages, Wharram Percy occupies a remote but attractive site in a beautiful Wolds valley. Above the substantial ruins of the church and a recreated fishpond, the outlines of many lost houses are traceable on a grassy plateau. First settled in prehistoric times, Wharram flourished as a village between the 12th and 14th centuries, before final abandonment c. 1500.

NEW FOR 2006 **New graphic interpretation panels tell its story, and recreate the original appearance of the buildings.**

OPENING TIMES

Any reasonable time

HOW TO FIND US

Direction: 6 miles SE of Malton, on minor road from B1248; ½ mile S of Wharram-le-Street. Park in car park, then ¾ mile walk via uneven track, steep in places. Site also accessible on foot via Wolds Way ramblers' path. Sturdy and waterproof footwear required. Parts of site slope steeply, and farm livestock likely to be present on site and access path.

Train: Malton 8 miles

Guidebooks (available from Kirkham Priory or Pickering Castle).

MAP Page 273 (3H)
OS Map 100 (ref SE 859644)

Wheeldale Roman Road

N. Yorkshire

A mile-long stretch of enigmatic ancient road – probably Roman but possibly later or earlier – amid wild and beautiful moorland, still with its hard core and drainage ditches.

Managed by North York Moors National Park.

OPENING TIMES

Any reasonable time

HOW TO FIND US

Direction: S of Goathland; W of A169; 7 miles S of Whitby

Train: Goathland (N York Moors Rly) 4 miles

MAP Page 273 (2H)
OS Map 94 (ref SE 806977)

York Cold War Bunker

N. Yorkshire – YO24 4HT

NEW FOR 2006 'Royal Observer Corps 20 Group Headquarters' is the formal description of the semi-submerged nuclear bunker in Holgate, York, now owned by English Heritage. Nicknamed the 'Aztec Temple' from its Ziggurat-like appearance, it was in a constant state of readiness from the 1960s to the 1990s – ready to react to an atomic explosion. Five years ago the government listed it as a scheduled monument on our recommendation. It will be opened to the public in early 2006.

York Cold War Bunker

NON-MEMBERS

Adult	£5.00
Concession	£4.00
Child	£3.00

OPENING TIMES

Term time, daily	10am-4pm
May-Oct, selected weekends	10am-4pm

Please call for details. Admission is by prebooked, timed ticket only. On quiet days a same day telephone call may be sufficient. To make a booking please ring 01904 646940

HOW TO FIND US

Direction: Off Acomb Road, approx. 1 mile from York city centre

MAP Page 273 (3G)
OS Map 94 (ref SE 580515)

Visit the Byland Abbey Inn, now in the care of English Heritage. Opposite Byland Abbey – see page 189.

Photo: Tony Bartholomew

Whitby Abbey North Yorkshire – YO22 4JT

Perched high on a cliff, the gaunt remains of this once magnificent abbey stand high above the picturesque seaside town of Whitby.

Arcading

The first abbey was founded in 657 by the formidable St Hilda, a princess of the Northumbrian royal house, whose Saxon name Hild means 'battle'. Recent archaeological research undertaken by English Heritage suggests that it was once a bustling settlement, as well as the burial place of monarchs, the setting of an epoch-making international meeting between Celtic and Roman clerics, and the home of saints such as the poet Caedmon.

The Saxon abbey was destroyed during a Viking invasion in 867, but one of William the Conqueror's knights refounded it in the late 1070s. By 1220, his Norman church proved inadequate for the many pilgrims, and the building of the present church began. After its dissolution by Henry VIII in 1538, the abbey did not suffer as much destruction as many other monasteries, as it was (and still is) used by shipping as a navigation marker. The site then passed to the Cholmley family, who built a mansion largely out of materials plundered from the monastery.

An imaginative visitor centre now sits within the walls of the Cholmley family mansion, part of a major interpretation and access project encompassing the whole of the headland, hailed as one of the most important archaeological sites in England. One of the aims of the project has been to enhance and protect the natural beauty and historic character of the headland. English Heritage's research excavations have added to our understanding of Whitby's complex history, including the discovery of a rare 17th-century 'hard garden', inspired by Cholmley's visits to France and Spain and now restored. Continuing research may yield further insights into this multi-layered site.

The visitor centre houses archaeological material excavated at Whitby, as well as computer-generated images revealing how the headland has changed over time. Rich finds from the Anglo-Saxon and medieval abbeys are also exhibited, together with objects relating to the Cholmley family. Spectacular audio-visual displays recreate the medieval abbey and the 17th-century house, its interiors and gardens. Visitors can also gain an insight into the people who have lived in Whitby, from St Hilda to Bram Stoker, author of Dracula.

Please note: from the Whitby harbour area, the abbey can only be directly reached on foot via the 199 'abbey steps' (or Caedmon's Trod): alternatively a well-signposted road leads from the town outskirts to the clifftop abbey.

www.english-heritage.org.uk/whitbyabbey

NON-MEMBERS	
Adult	£4.20
Concession	£3.20
Child	£2.10
Family ticket	£10.50

OPENING TIMES	
1 Apr-30 Sep, daily	10am-6pm
1-31 Oct, daily	10am-5pm
1 Nov-31 Mar, Thu-Mon	10am-4pm
Closed	24-26 Dec and 1 Jan

HOW TO FIND US

Direction: On cliff top, E of Whitby

Train: Whitby ½ mile

Bus: From surrounding areas

Tel: 01947 603568

Local Tourist Information Whitby: 01947 602674

OVP

Disabled access (south entrance parking, charged).

Dogs on leads (restricted areas only).

Parking (charge payable).

Tearoom (managed by Youth Hostel Association).

MAP Page 273 (1J)
OS Map 94 (ref NZ 903112)

Visitor centre

Other Historic Attractions

Discounted entry to our members (discounts may not apply on event days)

Castle Howard

N. Yorkshire – YO60 7DA

Magnificent 18th-century house with extensive collections and breathtaking grounds. Outdoor tours, costumed guides, exhibitions, events, adventure playground and boat trips. Cafés, farm shop and plant centre.

Managed by The Castle Howard Estate.

ENTRY

Adult	£9.50
Concession	£8.50
Child	£6.50

Prices subject to change. Please check website

EH DISCOUNT

With house and garden ticket only

Adult/Child	£1.50 off
Others	£1.00 off

OPENING TIMES

1 Mar-5 Nov, daily, from 10am

Please call for times or visit www.castlehoward.co.uk

Tel: 01653 648333

MAP Page 273 (3H)
OS Map 100 (ref SE 716701)

DIG, York

N. Yorkshire – YO1 8NN

Experience the ultimate archaeological adventure – a simulated excavation. Find real artefacts and study what they tell us about Roman, Viking, medieval and Victorian history.

ENTRY

Adult	£4.50
Concession	£4.00
Child	£4.00

10% discount for EH members.

DIG, York

OPENING TIMES

Open every day except Christmas Day. 10am-3.30pm (last admission)

Tel : 01904 654324

www.digyork.co.uk

MAP Page 273 (3H)
OS Map 105 (ref SE 606520)

Duncombe Park, Helmsley

N. Yorkshire – YO62 5EB

The recently restored home of Lord and Lady Feversham is surrounded by over 300 acres of stunning grounds and parkland.

Managed by Duncombe Park Estate Ltd.

ENTRY

Adult	£6.50
Concession	£5.00

Entry to house and gardens for EH members £2.50. Discount not available during special events

OPENING TIMES

Sun-Thurs from 30 April to 29 October 2006

Please call for times or visit www.duncombepark.com

Tel: 01439 770213

MAP Page 273 (2G)
OS Map 100 (ref SE 604830)

Fountains Abbey

N. Yorkshire – HG4 3DY

Fountains Abbey

Fountains Abbey has been described as the 'crown and glory of all that monasticism has left us in England'. There are 800 years of history to be explored in the 320-hectare (790-acre) estate, a World Heritage Site combining architecture and landscape of outstanding historical and aesthetic importance. The ruins of the Cistercian abbey, which was founded in 1132, are the largest such remains in Europe: they provide a dramatic focal point for the landscape garden, which was laid out during the first half of the 18th century by William and John Aislabie.

Fountains Mill, one of Europe's oldest surviving mills, once supplied the monks of Fountains Abbey with flour for baking. It has now been in continuous use for more than 800 years. Today, visitors can see the magnificent water wheel turning as it has for centuries, and explore the life and times of the mill through displays and ancient artefacts.

Other features within the estate include St Mary's Church (owned by English Heritage), a masterpiece of Victorian Gothic design (see p.196), and the Elizabethan mansion, Fountains Hall, built partly with stone from the abbey. St Mary's Church also provides a focus for the medieval deer park.

Fountains Abbey & Studley Royal is owned and managed by The National Trust. English Heritage works in partnership with The National Trust to protect this World Heritage Site.

NON-MEMBERS FOUNTAINS ABBEY & WATER GARDEN

Adult	£6.50
Concession	£3.50
Family ticket	£17.50

EH members admitted free to this NT site. Reduction for groups if booked in advance. Guided tours available. Deer Park: free of charge. Parking £3.00, free to members

OPENING TIMES

Abbey and Water Garden:

Mar-Oct, daily	10am-5pm
Nov-Feb, daily	10am-4pm*

*Closed Fridays Nov-Jan

Deer Park:
Daily during daylight hours

Closed	24-25 Dec

HOW TO FIND US

Direction: 4 miles W of Ripon, off B6265

Bus: Hutchinson 812 from York, with connections from Harrogate on Harrogate & District 36, Suns, May-Sep only; Arriva 802 from Wakefield and Leeds, Suns, May-Sep only; otherwise 'Ripon Roweller' from Ripon (booked on 01423 526655) (with connections from Harrogate)

Tel: 01765 608888

Box office: 01765 643199

Disabled access (not suitable for three-wheel battery cars).

MAP Page 273 (3F)
OS Map 99 (ref SE 275683)

JORVIK, York

N. Yorkshire – YO1 9WT

Explore Viking history on the very site where archaeologists discovered remains of Viking-Age York. Discover what life

was like 1,000 years ago, and journey through a reconstruction of Viking-Age streets.

ENTRY

Adult	£7.45
Concession	£6.30
Child	£5.25
Family (x4)	£21.95
Family (x5)	£26.50

Prices subject to change, please check website. 15% reduction for EH members

OPENING TIMES

Apr-Oct, daily	10am-5pm
Nov-Mar, daily	10am-4pm

Open every day except Christmas Day.

Tel: 01904 543403

www.vikingjorvik.com

MAP Page 273 (4H)
OS Map 105 (ref SE 604516)

Merchant Adventurers' Hall, York

N. Yorkshire – YO1 9XD

The finest surviving medieval guild hall in Britain, built 1357-1361 and largely unaltered. A visit includes an audio tour. The Hall and its collections are fully accessible from Fossgate.

Managed by The Company of Merchant Adventurers of the City of York.

ENTRY

Adult	£2.50
Concession	£2.00
Child (7-17 years)	£1.00
Under 7s	Free
Families (2 adults and 2 or more children)	£6

Half price admission for EH members

OPENING TIMES

Oct-Mar, Mon-Sat	9am-3.30pm
Apr-Sep, Mon-Thu	9am-5pm
Apr-Sep, Fri & Sat	9am-3.30pm
Apr-Sep, Sun	12pm-4pm
Closed	Christmas and New Year

Tel: 01904 654818

www.theyorkcompany.co.uk

MAP Page 273 (3H)
OS Map 105 (ref SE 605517)

York Minster

York – YO1 7HH

Enjoy the peaceful atmosphere of the largest Gothic cathedral in Northern Europe, a place of worship for over 1,000 years, and a treasure house of stained glass.

ENTRY

Minster Only

Adult	£5.00
Concession	£4.00

Combined Minster and Undercroft

Adults	£7.00
Concessions	£5.00

Free access to Undercroft for EH members on purchase of a Minster ticket (not valid with any other offer)

OPENING TIMES

Mon-Sat	9.30am-6.30pm (last entry 5.00pm)
Sunday	12.30pm-6.00pm (last entry 3.45pm)

Tel: 01904 557216

www.yorkminster.org

MAP Page 273 (4H)
OS Map 105 (ref SE 603522)

i

Sign-up on-line for our email Members' Newsletter at **www.english-heritage.org.uk**

Detail of prisoners' carving, Carlisle Castle – see page 212

North West

'Well have yon Railway Labourers to this ground
Withdrawn for noontide rest. They sit, they walk
Among the Ruins, but no idle talk
Is heard; to grave demeanour all are bound;
And from one voice a Hymn with tuneful sound
Hallows once more the long-deserted Quire
And thrills the old sepulchral earth, around.
Others look up, and with fixed eyes admire
That wide-spanned arch, wondering how it was raised,
To keep, so high in air, its strength and grace:
All seem to feel the spirit of the place,
And by the general reverence God is praised:
Profane Despoilers, stand ye not reproved,
While thus these simple-hearted men are moved?'

From 'At Furness Abbey' by William Wordsworth, June 21, 1845

www.english-heritage.org.uk/northwest

Properties

See individual listings for details

Cheshire

Beeston Castle, Chester Castle: Agricola Tower and Castle Walls, Chester Roman Amphitheatre, Sandbach Crosses

Cumbria

Ambleside Roman Fort, Bow Bridge, Brough Castle, Brougham Castle, Castlerigg Stone Circle, Carlisle Castle, Clifton Hall, Countess Pillar, Furness Abbey, Hadrian's Wall (see p222), Hardknott Roman Fort, King Arthur's Round Table, Lanercost Priory, Mayburgh Henge, Penrith Castle, Piel Castle, Ravenglass Roman Bath House, Shap Abbey, Stott Park Bobbin Mill, Wetheral Priory Gatehouse

Lancashire

Goodshaw Chapel, Sawley Abbey, Warton Old Rectory, Whalley Abbey Gatehouse

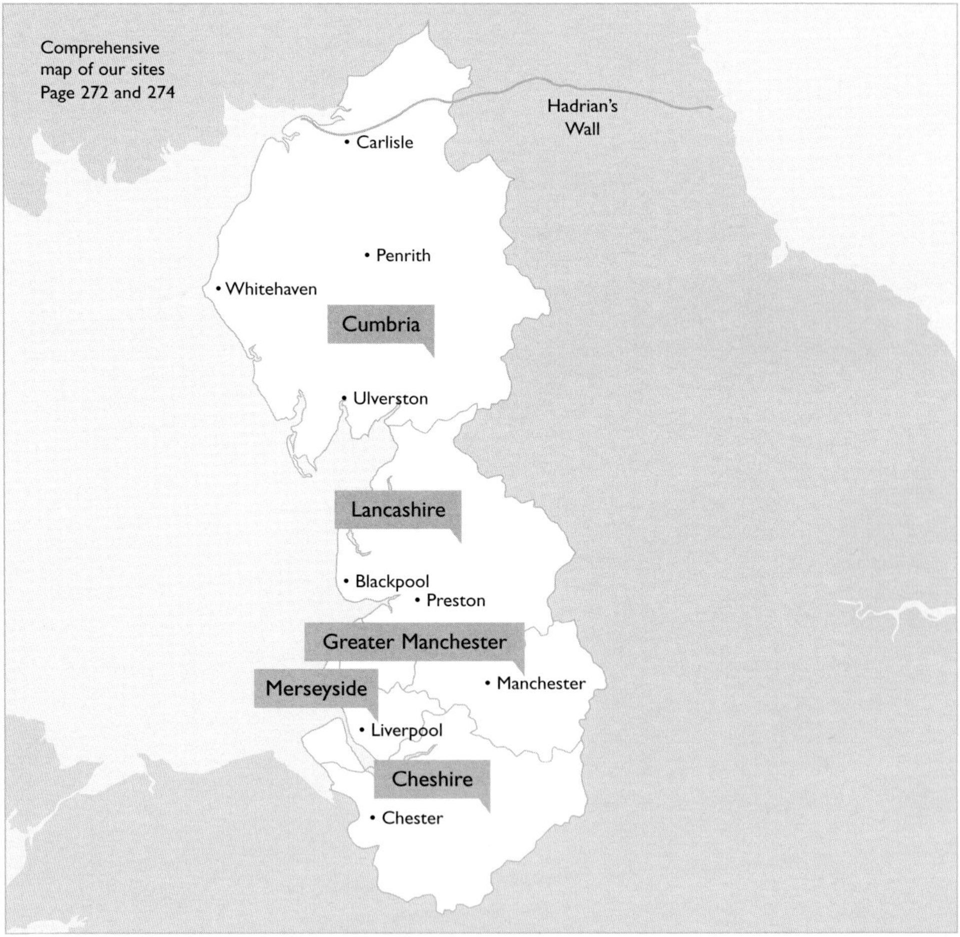

Monks, Marches and Mills

As the region's own laureate Wordsworth testifies in many of his poems, the historic monuments of the North West have long been appreciated by visitors, and many have survived 'Profane Despoilers' to be enjoyed by English Heritage members.

Furness Abbey, whose impressive remains recall its once-great prosperity, is only one of the region's many notable monastic ruins. These include remote **Shap Abbey**, the gatehouses of **Wetheral Priory** and **Whalley Abbey**, and **Sawley Abbey** – whose re-occupation after Henry VIII's dissolution is a reminder that this part of England was long a stronghold of 'the old religion.'

Perhaps the finest of them all, **Lanercost Priory** near Hadrian's Wall, still stands proudly despite frequent attacks by Scottish raiders: for the northern part of the region was for many centuries a much-disputed borderland. 'The West March towards Scotland', whose key was the great fortress of **Carlisle Castle**, was indeed the most turbulent end of the frontier from the days of the Romans, who built here the forts of **Ambleside**, dramatically-positioned **Hardknott**, and **Ravenglass** with its famous bath-house. Their medieval successors were castles like **Piel**, defending the Furness coast; **Penrith**; and **Brough** and **Brougham** – both re-occupying Roman sites – which guarded the strategic Stainmore pass. Invading armies from Scotland passed this way as late as 1745, when Bonnie Prince Charlie's Jacobites held Carlisle, and fought the last-ever battle on English soil near **Clifton Hall**.

Further south, another frontier – with Wales – was secured by Chester, a crucial fortress since Roman times, with spectacularly-sited **Beeston Castle** further east. But castles and abbeys are by no means the only English Heritage sites in this region of varied landscapes, which includes rugged **Cumbria** and the **Lake District**; the coastal plain, hills and towns of Lancashire; and the softer pastoral dairy-lands of Cheshire. The North West also boasts **Castlerigg Stone Circle**, one of the most atmospheric of all English prehistoric monuments; and the 'henges' of **Mayburgh** and adjacent **King Arthur's Round Table**. Elaborately carved **Sandbach Crosses** stand as testaments to Anglo-Saxon Christianity, while movingly simple **Goodshaw Chapel** – English Heritage's only Nonconformist chapel, still in use – exemplifies the straightforward religion which thrived alongside the Industrial Revolution here. A power-house of that Revolution is in fact still fully working: **Stott Park Bobbin Mill**, with its fascinating social history displays.

Ambleside Roman Fort

Cumbria

The well-marked remains of a 2nd-century fort with large granaries, probably built under Hadrian to guard the Roman road from Brougham to Ravenglass and act as a supply base.

Managed by The National Trust.

OPENING TIMES

Any reasonable time

HOW TO FIND US

Direction: 182 metres W of Waterhead car park, Ambleside

Train: Windermere 5 miles

Bus: Stagecoach in Cumbria 555/6, 599 from Windermere

MAP Page 274 (6D)
OS Map 90 (ref NY 372034)

Beeston Castle

Cheshire – CW6 9TX

Photo: Andrew Tryner

Standing majestically on a sheer rocky crag, Beeston has perhaps the most stunning views of any castle in England. Excavations indicate that a Bronze Age settlement and Iron Age hillfort occupied the site long before the castle was begun in 1225. For centuries an impregnable royal fortress, it finally fell to Parliamentarian forces in the Civil War.

The 'Castle of the Rock' exhibition outlines the 4,000 year history of this strategic site. There are family-friendly books and activities. Every summer the castle is brought to life by an action-packed programme of events.

NON-MEMBERS

Adult	£4.00
Concession	£3.00
Child	£2.00

OPENING TIMES

1 Apr-30 Sep, daily	10am-6pm
1 Oct-31 Mar, Thu-Mon	10am-4pm
Closed	24-26 Dec and 1 Jan

HOW TO FIND US

Direction: Located 11 miles SE of Chester, on minor road off A49

Train: Chester 10 miles

Tel: 01829 260464

Local Tourist Information Chester 01244 402111

E P OVP

Please note: Steep climb (no disabled access to the top of the hill).

MAP Page 272 (7D)
OS Map 117 (ref SJ 537593)

Bow Bridge

Cumbria

This narrow 15th-century stone bridge across Mill Beck carried an old pack-horse route to nearby Furness Abbey (see p.214).

OPENING TIMES

Any reasonable time

HOW TO FIND US

Direction: Located ½ mile N of Barrow-in-Furness, on minor road off A590; near Furness Abbey

Train: Barrow-in-Furness 1½ miles

Bus: Stagecoach in Cumbria 6/A Barrow-in Furness – Ulverston to within ¾ mile

MAP Page 274 (7D)
OS Map 96 (ref SD 224715)

Brough Castle

Cumbria

Commanding a magnificent view of the Pennines, medieval Brough Castle stands within the earth-works of a Roman fort guarding the strategic Stainmore routeway. The impressive tower-keep dates from c. 1200, replacing an earlier stronghold destroyed by William the Lion of Scotland in 1174. Like so many other castles hereabouts, Brough was restored in the 17th century by Lady Anne Clifford: traces of her interior fittings and kitchen gardens can still be seen.

OPENING TIMES

Any reasonable time

HOW TO FIND US

Direction: 8 miles SE of Appleby S of A66

Train: Kirkby Stephen 6 miles

Bus: Grand Prix 563 Penrith – Brough (passing Penrith)

P

MAP Page 275 (6F)
OS Map 91 (ref NY 791141)

Brougham Castle

Cumbria – CA10 2AA

Picturesque Brougham Castle was begun in the early 13th century by Robert de Vieuxpont, near the site of a Roman fort guarding the crossing of the River Eamont. His great keep largely survives, reinforced by an impressive double gatehouse and other 14th-century additions made by the powerful Clifford family, Wardens of the Marches. The castle thus became a formidable barrier to Scots invaders.

Though both James I and Charles I stayed here, Brougham was in poor condition by the time of the Civil War. It was thereafter restored as a residence by the indomitable Lady Anne Clifford (see also Brough Castle and the Countess Pillar): she often visited with her travelling 'court', and died here in 1676.

Today, the site features an introductory exhibition, including carved stones from the nearby Roman fort. The site has good wheelchair access to entry point, toilet, shop and small introductory exhibition. There is a wheelchair route to the castle ruins, which enables visitors to make a circuit of the site and read the interpretation panels. The keep is not accessible to wheelchairs.

Brougham Castle

NON-MEMBERS

Adult	£2.70
Concession	£2.00
Child	£1.40

OPENING TIMES

1 Apr-30 Sep, daily	10am-5pm
1-31 Oct, Thu-Mon	10am-4pm

HOW TO FIND US

Direction: 1½ miles SE of Penrith, off A66.

Train: Penrith 2 miles

Local Tourist information 01228 625600

Tel: 01768 862488

OVP

MAP Page 274 (5E)
OS Map 90 (ref NY 537290)

Carlisle Castle

See feature – Page 212

Castlerigg Stone Circle

Cumbria

Castlerigg is perhaps the most atmospheric and dramatically sited of all British stone circles, with panoramic views and the mountains of Helvellyn and High Seat as a backdrop. It is also among the earliest British circles, raised in about 3000 BC during the Neolithic period.

Managed by The National Trust.

Castlerigg Stone Circle

OPENING TIMES

Any reasonable time

HOW TO FIND US

Direction: 1½ miles E of Keswick

Train: Penrith 16 miles

Bus: Stagecoach in Cumbria X4/5 from Penrith to within 1 mile

MAP Page 274 (5D)
OS Map 90 (ref NY291236)

Chester Castle: Agricola Tower and Castle Walls

Cheshire

The original gateway to Chester Castle, this 12th-century tower houses a chapel with exceptionally fine wall paintings of c. 1220, rediscovered in the 1980s. An access stair to the castle's wall-walk is nearby.

Managed by Chester City Council.

OPENING TIMES

Walls open any reasonable time

Cell block open:

1 Apr-30 Sep, daily	10am-5pm
1 Oct-31 Mar, daily	10am-4pm
Closed	24-26 Dec and 1 Jan

HOW TO FIND US

Direction: Access via Assizes Court car park on Grosvenor St

Train: Chester 1 mile

Bus: From surrounding areas

Disabled access (parts only).

MAP Page 272 (7C)
OS Map 117 (ref SJ 405657)

i

Sign-up on-line for our email Members' Newsletter at **www.english-heritage.org.uk/newsletter**

Carlisle Castle Cumbria – CA3 8UR

Impressive and forbidding, Carlisle Castle is a formidable fortress, amply repaying exploration of its absorbing 900-year history.

Solar in de Ireby's Tower

Long commanding the especially turbulent western end of the Anglo-Scottish border, Carlisle has witnessed many conflicts and sieges. The earliest castle (on the site of a sequence of Roman forts dating from the 1st to 4th centuries AD) was of earth and timber, raised by King William Rufus in c. 1092. During the following century it was refortified in stone, possibly by Henry I. The 12th-century stone keep is the oldest surviving structure in the castle, which was frequently updated as befitted a stronghold always in the front line of Anglo-Scottish warfare. In 1315 it triumphantly saw off a determined Scots attack. The rounded 'shot-deflecting' battlements of the keep were added when Henry VIII adapted the castle for artillery in c. 1540.

Elaborate carvings in a small cell, by captives held here by the future Richard III in 1480, vividly demonstrate that Carlisle Castle was also a prison. Mary Queen of Scots was confined here after her flight from Scotland in 1568: but in 1596 the Border reiver Kinmont Willie Armstrong managed a daring night escape, to the fury of his captors.

Carlisle played its part in the English Civil War. Besieged for eight months by Parliament's Scots allies, its Royalist garrison surrendered in 1645 only after eating rats and even their dogs. A century later in 1746, the castle became the last English fortress ever to suffer a siege, when Bonnie Prince Charlie's Jacobite garrison vainly attempted to hold off the Duke of Cumberland's Hanoverian army. The fortress became their prison: many died here, and others left only for hanging or transportation.

Housed in the keep is a model of the city in 1745, and an exhibition on Bonnie Prince Charlie and the Jacobite rising of that year; visitors can also see the legendary 'licking stones', which parched Jacobite prisoners desperately licked for moisture in order to stay alive. Admission also includes entry to the King's Own Royal Border Regiment Museum. Another feature of the site is the Carlisle Roman Dig, a fully accessible exhibition displaying the finds from recent excavations.

www.english-heritage.org.uk/carlislecastle

NON-MEMBERS	
Adult	£4.10
Concession	£3.10
Child	£2.10

OPENING TIMES	
1 Apr-30 Sep, daily	9.30am-5pm
1 Oct-31 Mar, daily	10am-4pm
Closed	24-26 Dec & 1 Jan

HOW TO FIND US

Direction: In Carlisle city centre

Train: Carlisle ½ mile

Bus: From surrounding areas

Tel: 01228 591922

Local tourist information 01228 625600

OVP

Disabled access (except interiors).

Dogs on leads (restricted areas only).

Guided tours (available at peak times at a small extra charge; groups please pre-book).

Parking (disabled only, but sign-posted city centre car parks nearby).

MAP Page 274 (4D)
OS Map 85 (ref NY 396562)

Chester Roman Amphitheatre

Cheshire

The largest Roman amphitheatre in Britain, used for entertainment and military training by the 20th Legion, based at the fortress of 'Deva' (Chester). Excavations by English Heritage and Chester City Council in 2004-5 revealed two successive stone-built amphitheatres with wooden seating. The first included access to the upper tiers of seats via stairs on the rear wall, as at Pompeii, and had a small shrine next to its north entrance. The second provided seat access via vaulted stairways. The two buildings differed both from each other and from all other British amphitheatres, underlining the importance of Roman Chester.

Managed by Chester City Council.

OPENING TIMES

Any reasonable time

HOW TO FIND US

Direction: On Vicars Lane, beyond Newgate, Chester

Train: Chester ¾ mile

Bus: From surrounding areas

Disabled access (no access to amphitheatre floor).

MAP Page 272 (7C)
OS Map 117 (ref SJ 408662)

Clifton Hall

Cumbria

This 15th-century tower, sole survivor of the manor house of the Wybergh family, was plundered by Jacobites in 1745 before the Battle of Clifton Moor, the last battle fought on English soil.

Clifton Hall

OPENING TIMES

Any reasonable time

Closed 24-26 Dec and 1 Jan

HOW TO FIND US

Direction: Next to Clifton Hall Farm; 2 miles S of Penrith, on A6

Train: Penrith 2½ miles

MAP Page 274 (5E)
OS Map 90 (ref NY 530271)

Countess Pillar, Brougham

Cumbria

A monument erected in 1656 by Lady Anne Clifford of nearby Brougham Castle, to commemorate her final parting here from her mother. On the low stone beside it, money was given to the poor each anniversary of their parting.

OPENING TIMES

Any reasonable time

HOW TO FIND US

Direction: ¼ mile E of Brougham

Train: Penrith 2½ miles

Warning (site on a very busy main road).

MAP Page 274 (5E)
OS Map 90 (ref NY 546289)

Furness Abbey

Cumbria – LA13 0PS

The impressive remains of an abbey founded by Stephen, later King of England, including much of the east end and west tower of the church, the ornately decorated chapter house and the cloister buildings. Originally of the Savigniac order, it passed to the Cistercians in 1147, and despite damage by Scottish raiders became (after Fountains Abbey) the second most prosperous Cistercian abbey in all England. Set in the 'vale of nightshade', the romantic ruins were celebrated by Wordsworth in his *Prelude* of 1805.

An exhibition on the history of the abbey, with a display of elaborately carved stones, can be seen in the visitor centre. (See also Bow Bridge, p.210)

NON-MEMBERS	
Adult	£3.40
Concession	£2.60
Child	£1.70

OPENING TIMES	
1 Apr-30 Sep, daily	10am-5pm
1 Oct-31 Mar, Thu-Mon	10am-4pm
Closed	24-26 Dec & Jan 1

Furness Abbey

HOW TO FIND US

Direction: Located 1½ miles N of Barrow-in-Furness, off A590

Train: Barrow-in-Furness 2 miles

Bus: Stagecoach in Cumbria 6/A Barrow-in-Furness – Ulverston, to within ¾ mile

Tel: 01229 823420

OVP

Audio tours (also available for the visually impaired and those with learning difficulties).

Dogs on leads (restricted areas only).

MAP Page 274 (7D)
OS Map 96 (ref SD 218717)

Goodshaw Chapel

Lancashire

English Heritage's only Nonconformist place of worship, this atmospheric Baptist chapel displays a complete set of box-pews, galleries and pulpit dating from c. 1742 to 1809. A festival of hymns and sermons is held every first Sunday in July.

OPENING TIMES

Please call the keykeeper for details. Tel: 01706 227333

HOW TO FIND US

Direction: In Crawshawbooth, 2 miles N of Rawtenstall via A682 (in Goodshaw Ave – turning off A682 opp. Jester public house). Chapel approx. 1½ miles from main road

Train: Burnley Manchester Road 4½ miles

Bus: Burnley & Pendle X43/4 Nelson – Manchester. All pass Burnley Manchester Road

MAP Page 272 (4E)
OS Map 103 (ref SD 814261)

Hadrian's Wall

See page 222

Hardknott Roman Fort

Cumbria

This remote and dramatically-sited fort was founded under Hadrian in the 2nd century. Well-marked remains include the headquarters building, commandant's house and bath-house. The site of the parade-ground survives beside the fort, and the road which Hardknott guarded can be traced for some distance as an earthwork.

Managed by The National Trust.

OPENING TIMES

Any reasonable time

HOW TO FIND US

Direction: 9 miles NE of Ravenglass; at W end of Hardknott Pass

Train: Eskdale (Dalegarth) (Ravenglass & Eskdale Rly) 3 miles

Warning (access may be hazardous during the winter months).

MAP Page 274 (6C)
OS Map 90 (ref NY 218015)

King Arthur's Round Table

Cumbria

A Neolithic earthwork 'henge', dating from c. 2000 BC, but much later believed to be King Arthur's jousting arena. Mayburgh Henge is adjacent.

OPENING TIMES

Any reasonable time

HOW TO FIND US

Direction: Located at Eamont Bridge, 1 mile S of Penrith. Mayburgh Henge is nearby.

Train: Penrith 1½ miles

King Arthur's Round Table

MAP Page 274 (5E)
OS Map 90 (ref NY 523284)

Lanercost Priory

Cumbria – CA8 2HQ

Standing close to Hadrian's Wall, the Augustinian priory of Lanercost was much involved in the Anglo-Scottish wars. During his last campaign in 1306-7 the mortally sick Edward I rested here for six months, before dying as he prepared to enter Scotland. The abbey suffered terribly from Scottish raids, being sacked at least four times. It was finally dissolved by Henry VIII in 1537, but today its beautiful 13th-century church remains remarkably well-preserved, standing to its full height: part is now in use as the parish church. New interpretation for 2006.

Parish church not managed by English Heritage.

NON-MEMBERS

Adult	£2.70
Concession	£2.00
Child	£1.40

Lanercost Priory

OPENING TIMES

1 Apr-30 Sep, daily	10am-5pm
1-31 Oct, Thu-Mon	10am-4pm

HOW TO FIND US

Direction: Off a minor road S of Lanercost; 2 miles NE of Brampton

Train: Brampton 3 miles

Bus: Stagecoach in Cumbria 685 Carlisle-Newcastle-upon-Tyne to within 1½ miles

Tel: 01697 73030

OVP

MAP Page 274 (4E)
OS Map 86 (ref NY 556637)

Mayburgh Henge

Cumbria

A large and impressive Neolithic henge, much better preserved than neighbouring King Arthur's Round Table. Its banks stand up to 3 metres (10 feet) high, and unusually are constructed of pebbles collected from the nearby river. Near the centre is a single standing stone: old drawings suggest that it was one of a group of four here, four more having been removed from the entranceway.

OPENING TIMES

Any reasonable time

HOW TO FIND US

Direction: 1 mile S of Penrith off A6

Train: Penrith 1½ miles

MAP Page 274 (5E)
OS Map 90 (ref NY 519284)

Penrith Castle

Cumbria

The mainly 15th-century remains of a castle begun by Bishop Strickland of Carlisle and developed by the Nevilles and Richard III. Set in a municipal park opposite the railway station.

OPENING TIMES

Summer	7.30am-9pm
Winter	7.30am-4.30pm

HOW TO FIND US

Direction: Opposite Penrith railway station

Train: Penrith (adjacent)

MAP Page 274 (5E)
OS Map 90 (ref NY 513299)

Piel Castle

Cumbria

Piel Castle

The impressive ruins of a 14th-century castle with a massive keep, inner and outer baileys, and towered curtain walls still standing. It was built by the Abbot of Furness on the south-eastern point of Piel Island, to guard the deep-water harbour of Barrow-in-Furness against pirates and Scots raiders.

OPENING TIMES

Any reasonable time

HOW TO FIND US

Direction: By small boat: from 11am, from Roa Island, summer only; subject to tides and weather. There is a small charge for this service; for details, call Alan Cleasby on 01229 835809 or 07798 794550, or John Cleasby on 07799 761306

Direction: Piel Island, 3¼ miles SE of Barrow-in-Furness

Train: Barrow-in-Furness 4 miles

Bus: Stagecoach in Cumbria 11 Barrow-in Furness – Ulverston

MAP Page 274 (7D)
OS Map 96 (ref SD 233636)

Ravenglass Roman Bath House

Cumbria

The remains of the bath house of Ravenglass Roman fort, established in AD 130, are among the tallest Roman structures surviving in northern Britain: the walls stand almost 4 metres (13 feet) high. The fort at Ravenglass (whose earthworks can be seen near the bath house) guarded what was probably a useful harbour, and there is evidence that soldiers stationed here served in Hadrian's fleet.

Ravenglass Roman Bath House

OPENING TIMES

Any reasonable time

HOW TO FIND US

Direction: ¼ mile E of Ravenglass, off minor road leading to A595

Train: Ravenglass (adjacent)

MAP Page 274 (6C)
OS Map 96 (ref SD 088959)

Sandbach Crosses

Cheshire

The two massive Saxon stone crosses, elaborately carved with animals and Biblical scenes including the Nativity of Christ and the Crucifixion, dominate the cobbled market square of Sandbach. Probably dating from the 9th century, and originally painted as well as carved, they are among the finest surviving examples of Anglo-Saxon high crosses.

OPENING TIMES

Any reasonable time

HOW TO FIND US

Direction: Market Sq, Sandbach

Train: Sandbach 1½ miles

Bus: From surrounding areas

MAP Page 272 (7D)
OS Map 118 (ref SJ 759608)

Sawley Abbey

Lancashire

The remains of a Cistercian abbey founded in 1148, set on the banks of the Ribble against a backdrop of dramatic hills. After its dissolution in 1536, the monks were briefly returned to the abbey during the Pilgrimage of Grace. They remained in possession until the insurrection's collapse and the execution of their abbot.

Managed by the Heritage Trust for the North West.

OPENING TIMES

1 Apr-30 Sep, daily	10am-6pm
1 Oct-31 Mar, daily	10am-4pm
Closed	24-26 Dec and 1 Jan

HOW TO FIND US

Direction: Located at Sawley; 3½ miles N of Clitheroe, off A59

Train: Clitheroe 4 miles

MAP Page 272 (4D)
OS Map 103 (ref SD 777464)

i

You can find out more about the work of English Heritage at **www.english-heritage.org.uk/aboutus**

Shap Abbey

Cumbria

The impressive full-height 15th-century tower and other remains of a remote abbey of Premonstratensian 'white canons'.

OPENING TIMES

Any reasonable time

HOW TO FIND US

Direction: 1½ miles W of Shap, on the bank of the River Lowther

Train: Penrith 10 miles

Bus: Stagecoach in Cumbria/K&B 106/7 Penrith-Kendal to within 1½ miles

Disabled access (limited views from outside the site).

MAP Page 274 (6E)
OS Map 90 (ref NY 548152)

i

Don't forget your membership card when you visit any of the properties listed in this handbook.

Stott Park Bobbin Mill

Cumbria – LA12 8AX

This extensive working mill was begun in 1835 to produce the wooden bobbins vital to the Lancashire spinning and weaving industries. Although small compared to other mills, some 250 men and boys (some drafted in from workhouses) worked here in often arduous conditions to produce a quarter of a million bobbins a week. Guided tours lasting 45 minutes are included in the admission charge: the last tour begins one hour before closing.

NON-MEMBERS

Adult	£4.10
Concession	£3.10
Child	£2.10
Family ticket	£10.30

OPENING TIMES

1 Apr-30 Sep daily	10am-5pm
Steam days Mon-Thu	
1-31 Oct, Tue-Sat	10am-5pm
Steam days Tue-Thu	

HOW TO FIND US

Direction: Located 1½ miles N of Newby Bridge, off A590

Train: Grange-over-Sands 8 miles

Ferry: Windermere ferry from Ambleside or Bowness to Lakeside, then 1 mile

Tel: 01539 531087

Local Tourist Information Hawkshead: 01539 436525

OVP

Disabled access (ground floor only. Specific interpretation for visually impaired visitors).

Parking (lower car park).

MAP Page 274 (6D)
OS Map 97 (ref SD 372881)

Warton Old Rectory

Lancashire

A rare survival of a large 14th-century stone house with great hall and chambers. It served as a residence and courthouse for the wealthy and powerful rectors of Warton.

Managed by Heritage Trust for the North West.

OPENING TIMES

1 Apr-30 Sep, daily	10am-6pm
1 Oct-31 Mar, daily	10am-4pm
Closed	24-26 Dec and 1 Jan

HOW TO FIND US

Direction: At Warton; 1 mile N of Carnforth, on minor road off A6

Train: Carnforth 1 mile

Bus: Stagecoach in Lancashire 55/A from Lancaster (passing close Carnforth)

MAP Page 272 (3D)
OS Map 97 (ref SD 499723)

Wetheral Priory Gatehouse

Cumbria

The 15th-century gatehouse of a Benedictine priory, where wrongdoers could claim pardon if they enlisted to fight the Scots. It survived because it later served as the vicarage for the parish church.

OPENING TIMES

1 Apr-30 Sep, daily	10am-6pm
1 Oct-31 Mar, daily	10am-4pm
Closed	24-26 Dec and 1 Jan

HOW TO FIND US

Direction: In Wetheral village; 6 miles E of Carlisle, on B6263

Train: Wetheral ½ mile

Bus: Stagecoach in Cumbria 74/5 Carlisle-Wetheral

MAP Page 274 (4E)
OS Map 86 (ref NY 468541)

Whalley Abbey Gatehouse

Lancashire

The 14th-century gatehouse of the nearby Cistercian abbey, the second wealthiest monastery in Lancashire, beside the River Calder. The first floor was probably a chapel.

OPENING TIMES

Any reasonable time

HOW TO FIND US

Direction: In Whalley; 6 miles NE of Blackburn, on minor road off A59

Train: Whalley ¼ mile

Bus: Lancashire United 225 Bolton-Clitheroe (passes Blackburn)

MAP Page 272 (4D)
OS Map 103 (ref SD 729362)

Other Historic Attractions

Discounted entry to our members (discounts may not apply on event days)

Holker Hall

Cark-in-Cartnel, Cumbria – LA11 7PL

Holker Hall is a superb Victorian house built on a grand scale, with rich and varied gardens that offer 24 acres of woodland and magnificent formal garden areas.

ENTRY

25% off regular adult and senior citizen entry to the Hall & Gardens. Offer valid 26 Mar-29 Oct 2006. Not valid during special events.

OPENING TIMES

Hall & Gardens open daily except Saturday

Gardens	10.30am-5.30pm
Hall	11am-4.00pm

HOW TO FIND US

Direction: Exit junction 36 from M6. Signposted from A590

Tel: 015395 58328

www.holker-hall.co.uk

MAP Page 274 (7D)
OS Map 97 (ref SD 359774)

Muncaster Castle

Ravenglass, Cumbria – CA18 1RQ

An amazing castle with beautiful gardens, which has been home to the same family – the Penningtons – since 1208.

Managed by Peter and Iona Frost-Pennington.

OPENING TIMES

Please call 01229 717614

HOW TO FIND US

Direction: Signposted from A595

www.muncaster.co.uk

Discount for EH members. Discount does not extend to EH Corporate Partners.

MAP Page 274 (6C)
OS Map 96 (ref SD 103963)

Norton Priory Museum and Gardens

Runcorn, Cheshire – WA7 1SX

Discover the ruins of the 12th-century Augustinian Priory, set in 38 acres of beautiful gardens. Giant St Christopher statue, museum galleries and Georgian Walled Garden. Events all year round.

Norton Priory Museum and Gardens

ENTRY

Adult	£4.75
Concession	£3.45
Family tickets	£12.50
Group (10+)	£3.00 each

EH members: 2 adults for the price of 1 full paying adult (not Bank Holidays or with any other offer)

OPENING TIMES

Apr-Oct, Mon-Fri	12pm-5pm
Sat-Sun & Bank Hols	12pm-6pm
Nov-Mar, daily	12pm-4pm
Closed	24-26 Dec and 1 Jan

HOW TO FIND US

Direction: Take junction 11 off M56. Well signposted

Tel: 01928 569895

www.nortonpriory.org

MAP Page 272 (6D)
OS Map 108 (ref SJ 548830)

Pendle Heritage Centre

Barrowford, Lancashire – BB9 6JQ

The centre features an 18th-century walled garden and exhibitions about the area.

Managed by Heritage Trust for the North West.

ENTRY

50% discount for EH members. Discount does not extend to EH Corporate Partners.

OPENING TIMES

Open all year, daily	10am-5pm
Closed	25 Dec

HOW TO FIND US

Direction: Junction 13 from M65

Tel: 01282 661702

MAP Page 272 (4E)
OS Map 103 (ref SD 862398)

St George's Hall, Liverpool

Merseyside – L1 1JJ

A superb neo-Classical building, designed by Harvey Lonsdale Elmes as law courts and a venue for concerts. Completed in 1855. The small Concert Hall is an excellent example of early Victorian design, and the highly decorative Great Hall boasts one of the finest concert organs in the UK. Entry by guided tour only.

Owned and managed by Liverpool City Council.

NON-MEMBERS

Guided Tours (no concessions):	£4.50

EH members and up to 6 children within their family group get free entry. Discount does not extend to EH Corporate Partners or members of Cadw and Historic Scotland.

English Heritage membership makes a lovely gift. Call 0870 333 1181 or visit www.english-heritage.org.uk/gift for more details.

St George's Hall, Liverpool

OPENING TIMES

Please call 0151 233 2008

HOW TO FIND US

Direction: City Centre, adjacent to Lime Street railway station and Queen Street bus station

Train: Liverpool Lime Street, adjacent

Bus: From surrounding areas

Tel: 0151 233 2008

P ♿

Disabled access (for tours; limited). Parking (street).

MAP Page 272 (6C)
OS Map 108 (ref SJ 349907)

Salt Museum

Northwich, Cheshire – CW9 8AB

Discover the people whose lives were shaped by salt and glimpse some of the 14,000 uses of salt.

ENTRY

Adult	£2.50
Concession	£2.00
Child	£1.20
Family (2+2)	£6.00

EH members: 1 free entry for every full paying adult (not applicable for group visits)

OPENING TIMES

Tue-Fri	10am-5pm
Sat-Sun	2pm-5pm
Bank holidays and every Monday in August	10am-5pm

Tel: 01606 41331

www.saltmuseum.org.uk

MAP Page 272 (6D)
OS Map 118 (ref SJ 658731)

Smithills Hall

Bolton, Lancashire – BL1 7NP

Grade I-listed manor house, one of the oldest in the north west region.

ENTRY

Adult	£1.50

Reduction for EH members

OPENING TIMES

Please call 01204 332377

HOW TO FIND US

Direction: Signposted from A58

www.smithills.org

MAP Page 272 (5D)
OS Map 109 (ref SD 699119)

Stretton Watermill

Nr Farndon, Cheshire – SY14 7RS

Step back in time and visit a working mill in beautiful rural Cheshire. See one of the country's best-preserved demonstration water-powered corn mills.

ENTRY

Adult	£2.00
Child	£0.75
Family (2+2)	£4.75

EH members: 1 free entry for every full paying adult

OPENING TIMES

Apr-Sep, Sat & Sun	1pm-5pm
May-Aug, Tue-Sun & Bank Hols	1pm-5pm

HOW TO FIND US

Direction: 10 miles from Chester. Well signposted

Tel: 01606 41331

www.strettonwatermill.org.uk

MAP Page 272 (7C)
OS Map 117 (ref SJ 455531)

Hadrian's Wall

'…one long, low, rising and falling, and hiding and showing line of towers. And that is the Wall!'

From 'On the Great Wall' in Puck of Pook's Hill, by Rudyard Kipling, 1906

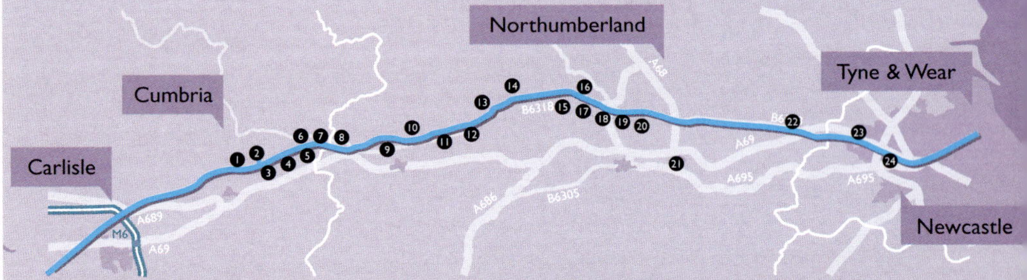

1 Hare Hill
2 Banks East Turret
3 Pike Hill Signal Tower
4 Leahill Turret and Piper Sike Turret
5 Birdoswald Roman Fort
6 Harrow's Scar Milecastle and Wall
7 Willowford Wall, Turrets & Bridge
8 Poltross Burn Milecastle
9 Walltown Crags
10 Cawfields Roman Wall
11 Winshields Wall
12 Vindolanda Fort
13 Housesteads Roman Fort
14 Sewingshields Wall
15 Temple of Mithras
16 Black Carts Turret
17 Chesters Roman Fort
18 Chesters Bridge
19 Brunton Turret
20 Planetrees Roman Wall
21 Corbridge Roman Town
22 Heddon-on-the-Wall
23 Denton Hall Turret
24 Benwell Roman Temple and Vallum Crossing

www.english-heritage.org.uk/hadrianswall

Hadrian's Wall winding its way over the Northumbrian landscape

Photo: britainonview / Rod Edwards

A Spectacular World Heritage Site

Incomparably the most impressive Roman monument in Britain, Hadrian's Wall was the 'north-west frontier' of the whole Roman Empire. It stretched for some 73 miles from sea to sea, from Wallsend near Newcastle in the east to Bowness-on-Solway in Cumbria in the west. Considerable portions of it still remain to be seen, often amid wild and dramatic countryside.

Begun at the command of the Emperor Hadrian in AD 122, the Wall defined the boundary between the Romanised province of 'Britannia' to the south and the unconquered lands to the north. It remained in service for some two and a half centuries, up until the collapse of Roman rule in Britain in the early 400s.

During this time the Wall underwent several changes, most still traceable in the 24 English Heritage sites along its length. A complex system of defence in depth, its core was the Wall itself, particularly impressive where it traverses rugged country at the **Walltown Crags**, **Sewingshields** and **Winshields** sites.

The eastern half was built in stone, completed to a narrower width than that first conceived, as seen at **Planetrees**. The Turf Wall in the west was wholly replaced in stone some 40 years later.

To the north of the Wall was a defensive ditch, and to the south (as at **Benwell**) ran the vallum earthwork and the military way. At each Roman mile along the Wall stood a milecastle (like **Poltross**), and between each milecastle were two turrets (as at **Willowford**). But the main garrisons of the system – 'Auxiliary' cavalry and infantry units originating from all over the Empire – were stationed at the 16 major Wall forts, including **Birdoswald**, **Chesters** and **Housesteads**.

Behind the Wall, serving as a supply-base and 'rest and recreation' centre for these troops, was **Corbridge Roman Town**.

i

Help conserve Hadrian's Wall for future generations: please do not walk on the Wall or climb on the Forts. This monument is very vulnerable to damage.

Birdoswald Roman Fort Cumbria – CA8 7DD

Birdoswald stands high above a bend in the River Irthing, in one of the most picturesque settings on Hadrian's Wall. A Roman fort, turret and milecastle can all be seen on this excellent stretch of the Wall.

Photo: Skyscan Balloon Photography

With probably the best-preserved defences of any Wall fort, this was an important base for some 1,000 Roman soldiers, succeeding an earlier fort of turf and timber. The section of wall to the east, also of stone replacing turf, is the longest continuous stretch visible today.

Archaeological discoveries over the past 150 years have revealed a great deal about Roman military life at Birdoswald. Three of the four main gateways of the fort have been unearthed, as have the outside walls, two granary buildings, workshops and a drill hall.

People continued to live at Birdoswald after the Roman withdrawal. In the 5th century a large timber hall was built over the collapsed Roman granaries, perhaps for a local British chieftain. Later, a medieval tower house was raised here, replaced in the 16th century by a fortified 'bastle' farmhouse designed to protect its inhabitants from the notorious 'Border Reivers'. Later still a more peaceful farmhouse stood here.

The Birdoswald Visitor Centre provides a good introduction to Hadrian's Wall, and tells the intriguing story of Birdoswald and the people who have lived there over the past 2,000 years. There is a cosy tearoom at the site if you need refreshments, and a well-stocked shop for souvenirs.

Accommodation

If you would like to stay within the walls of the fort, there is a 39 bed residential centre, which can be booked for groups. It provides a great base for exploring this and other sites on the Wall, and is an excellent educational resource.

If you would like to find out more about staying at Birdoswald, please contact us for a residential pack by calling 016977 47602.

NON-MEMBERS	
Adult	£3.80
Concession	£2.90
Child	£1.90
Family ticket	£9.50

Education charge applies – ring site for details

OPENING TIMES	
1-31 Mar, daily	10am-4pm
1 Apr-30 Sep, daily	10am-5.30pm (last entry 5pm)
1-31 Oct, daily	10am-4pm

HOW TO FIND US

Direction: 2¾ miles west of Greenhead off B6318. Signposted from A69

Tel: 016977 47602

OVP

Disabled access (to visitor centre, toilets, shop, tearoom and part of site. Disabled parking on site).

MAP Page 274 (4E)
OS Map 86 (ref NY 615663)

Photo: www.britainonview.com

Chesters Roman Fort

Northumberland – NE46 3EU

Chesters Fort was built to guard the Roman bridge which carried Hadrian's Wall and the military road over the River North Tyne. It was one of a series of permanent troop bases added soon after the Wall was built.

Occupied for nearly three centuries, its six-acre area housed a cavalry regiment of around 500 men: in the 3rd century its garrison was a unit from Asturias in northern Spain. There is much to see on the ground: all four principal gateways are well preserved, with the short lengths of Wall adjoining them. The entire foundations of the headquarters building are visible, with a courtyard, hall, regimental temple and strongroom clearly laid out: so is the commandant's house, the largest and most luxurious building in the fort.

Down by the river, the changing rooms, steam rooms and bathing areas of the garrison's bath house are extremely well preserved, as is the Roman bridge abutment on the opposite bank of the river.

The on-site museum, housed in a fine Victorian building, displays a collection of Roman finds retrieved by the local antiquarian John Clayton, including important early archaeological discoveries relating to the central section of the Wall.

NON-MEMBERS

Adult	£3.80
Concession	£2.90
Child	£1.90

OPENING TIMES

1 Apr-30 Sep, daily	9.30am-6pm
1 Oct-31 Mar, daily	10am-4pm
Closed	24-26 Dec and 1 Jan

HOW TO FIND US

Direction: ¼ mile W of Chollerford, on B6318

Train: Hexham 5½ miles

Bus: Stagecoach in Cumbria AD122 (Jun-Sep plus Suns Apr, May & Oct); also Tyne Valley 880/2 from Hexham, to within ½ mile

Tel: 01434 681379

Local Tourist Information Hexham: 01434 652220

P OVP

Disabled access (companion recommended. Disabled parking and toilets).

Dogs on leads (restricted areas only).

Tearoom (summer only; not managed by EH).

MAP Page 275 (4F)
OS Map 87 (ref NY 912702)

View towards Housesteads

Housesteads Roman Fort

Northumberland – NE47 6NN

Housesteads is the most complete example of a Roman fort in Britain, and now the most popular site on the Wall. It stands high on the exposed Whin Sill escarpment, commanding breathtaking views. Like Chesters, it was one of 12 permanent forts added to his new frontier by Hadrian in about AD 124. Known as 'Vercovicium' ('the place of effective fighters'), it was garrisoned by a cohort of around 800 infantry (for most of its history Tungrians from Belgium), later reinforced by Germanic cavalry.

Entry is through a small museum, displaying a complete model of how Housesteads once appeared. Excavations at the fort have revealed four double-portal gateways, the turreted curtain wall, three barrack blocks and of course the famous and well-preserved latrines. At the centre are the most important buildings: the commandant's house, head-quarters building and hospital.

The fort lies uphill from the car park (a ten minute walk).

Owned by The National Trust, in the care of English Heritage.

NON-MEMBERS

Adult	£3.80
Concession	£2.90
Child	£1.90
Family ticket	£9.50

Free entry to NT members

OPENING TIMES

1 Apr-30 Sep, daily	10am-6pm
1 Oct-31 Mar, daily	10am-4pm
Closed	24-26 Dec and 1 Jan

HOW TO FIND US

Direction: Bardon Mill 4 miles

Bus: Stagecoach in Cumbria AD122 (Jun-Sep plus Suns Apr, May & Oct); also Tyne Valley 880/2 from ⇌ Hexham, to within ½ mile

Tel: 01434 344363

Local Tourist Information Hexham: 01434 652220

OVP

Disabled access (companion recommended. Limited access to site. 50 metre walk on steep gradient. Car park at site; enquire at information centre on main road).

Parking (charge payable to National Park).

MAP Page 275 (4F)
OS Map 87 (ref NY 790688)

Banks East Turret

Cumbria

Imposing and well-preserved turret with adjoining stretches of Hadrian's Wall.

HOW TO FIND US

Direction: On minor road E of Banks village; 3½ miles NE of Brampton

MAP OS Map 86 (ref NY 575647)

Benwell Roman Temple

Tyne and Wear

The remains of a small temple to the native god 'Antenociticus', in the 'vicus' (civilian settlement) which stood outside Benwell fort.

HOW TO FIND US

Direction: Temple located immediately S of A69, at Benwell in Broomridge Ave; Vallum Crossing in Denhill Park

Train: Newcastle 2 miles

Bus: Frequent from centre of Newcastle

MAP OS Map 88 (ref NZ 217647)

Benwell Vallum Crossing

Tyne and Wear

A stone-built causeway, where the road from the south crossed the Vallum earthwork on its way to Benwell fort.

HOW TO FIND US

Direction: Temple located immediately S of A69, at Benwell in Broomridge Ave; Vallum Crossing in Denhill Park

Train: Newcastle 2 miles

Bus: Frequent from centre of Newcastle

MAP OS Map 87 (ref NY 884713)

Birdoswald Roman Fort

See feature – Page 224

Black Carts Turret

Northumberland

A 460-metre (1,509 feet) length of Hadrian's Wall including one turret.

Please note

It is not possible for visitors to park here.

HOW TO FIND US

Direction: 2 miles W of Chollerford on B6318

MAP OS Map 87 (ref NY 884713)

Brunton Turret

Northumberland

Wall section and a 2.5-metre (8.2 feet) high turret, built by men of the Twentieth Legion.

HOW TO FIND US

Direction: ¼ mile S of Low Brunton, off A6079

Train: Hexham 4 miles

Bus: Stagecoach in Cumbria AD122 (Jun-Sep plus Suns Apr, May & Oct); also Tyne Valley 880/2 from Hexham

MAP OS Map 87 (ref NY 922698)

Cawfields Roman Wall

Northumberland

Cawfields Roman Wall

A fine, consolidated stretch of the Wall on a steep slope, with turrets and an impressive mile-castle, built by the Second Legion.

HOW TO FIND US

Direction: 1¼ miles N of Haltwhistle, off B6318

MAP OS Map 87 (ref NY 716667)

Chesters Bridge Abutment

Northumberland

The remains of the bridge which carried Hadrian's Wall across the North Tyne are visible on both banks, but most impressively on the eastern side.

HOW TO FIND US

Direction: ½ mile S of Low Brunton, on A6079

Train: Hexham 4½ miles

Bus: Stagecoach in Cumbria AD122 (Jun-Sep plus Suns Apr, May & Oct); also Tyne Valley 880/2 from Hexham, to within ½ mile

MAP OS Map 87 (ref NY 914701)

Chesters Roman Fort

See feature – Page 226

Corbridge Roman Town

Northumberland – NE45 5NT

On the pivotal intersection of Roman Dere Street and Stanegate near the Tyne crossing, Corbridge played a vital role in every Roman campaign in northern Britain. The first forts here were founded c. AD 79-85 during the campaigns into Scotland under Agricola; the third in association with Hadrian's Wall; the last used during the campaigns of Antoninus Pius in the mid-2nd century. Corbridge then became a busy garrison town.

The extensively excavated remains include a fountain house with an aqueduct, a pair of granaries, and walled military compounds containing barracks, temples, houses and a headquarters building with a below-ground strongroom. You can even walk on the original Stanegate Roman road, which predated Hadrian's Wall and passes through the centre of the site.

The museum displays a rich selection of Roman finds, and has extensive schools handling collections of real and replica Roman objects, including armour. An audio tour is provided to guide you around the site.

NON-MEMBERS

Adult	£3.80
Concession	£2.90
Child	£1.90

OPENING TIMES

1 Apr-30 Sep, daily	10am-5.30 pm (last entry 5pm)
1-31 Oct, daily	10am-4pm
1 Nov-31 Mar, Sat-Sun	10am-4pm
Closed	24-26 Dec & 1 Jan

HOW TO FIND US

Direction: ½ mile NW of Corbridge, on minor road, then signposted

Train: Corbridge 1¼ miles

Bus: Arriva Northumbria/ Stagecoach in Cumbria 602, 685 Newcastle-upon-Tyne – Hexham, to within ½ mile

Tel: 01434 632349

Local Tourist Information 01434 652220

P OVP

Dogs on leads (restricted areas only).

Disabled access (parking, toilet, audio tour, access to the museum and perimeter of site).

MAP Page 275 (4F)
OS Map 87 (ref NY 982648)

Denton Hall Turret

Tyne and Wear

The foundations of a turret and a 65-metre (213 feet) length of Wall.

HOW TO FIND US

Direction: 4 miles W of Newcastle upon Tyne city centre, on A69

Train: Blaydon 2 miles

Bus: Frequent from centre of Newcastle

MAP OS Map 88 (ref NZ 198655)

Hare Hill

Cumbria

A short length of Wall, still standing 2.7 metres (8.8 feet) high.

HOW TO FIND US

Direction: ¾ mile NE of Lanercost

MAP OS Map 86 (ref NY 564646)

Harrow's Scar Milecastle and Wall

Cumbria

A mile-long section of the Wall, rebuilt in stone late in Hadrian's reign. It is linked to Birdoswald Fort.

HOW TO FIND US

Direction: ¼ mile E of Birdoswald, on minor road off B6318

P ♿
Parking at Birdsowald Roman Fort

MAP OS Map 86 (ref NY 620664)

Heddon-On-The-Wall

Northumberland

A consolidated stretch of Wall, up to 2 metres (6.5 feet) thick in places.

HOW TO FIND US

Direction: Immediately E of Heddon village; S of A69

Train: Wylam 3 miles

Bus: Go-Northern 684, Arriva Northumbria 685 from Newcastle upon Tyne

MAP OS Map 88 (ref NZ 137669)

Housesteads Roman Fort

See feature – Page 227

Leahill Turret and Piper Sike Turret

Cumbria

Turrets west of Birdoswald: Piper Sike has a cooking-hearth.

HOW TO FIND US

Direction: On minor road 2 miles W of Birdoswald Fort

MAP OS Map 86 (ref NY 586652)

Pike Hill Signal Tower

Cumbria

The remains of one of a network of signal towers predating Hadrian's Wall, Pike Hill was later joined to the Wall at an angle of 45 degrees.

HOW TO FIND US

Direction: On minor road E of Banks village

P

MAP OS Map 86 (ref NY 577648)

Planetrees Roman Wall

Northumberland

A 15-metre (49 feet) length of later narrow Wall on earlier broad foundations, marking the junction between the two wall types.

HOW TO FIND US

Direction: 1 mile SE of Chollerford on B6318

Train: Hexham 5½ miles

Bus: Stagecoach in Cumbria AD122 (Jun-Sep plus Suns Apr, May & Oct); also Tyne Valley 880/2 from ⇌ Hexham, to within ¾ mile

MAP OS Map 87 (ref NY 929696)

Poltross Burn Milecastle

Cumbria

One of the best preserved milecastles on Hadrian's Wall, Poltross includes an oven, a stair to the rampart walk, and the remains of its north gateway.

HOW TO FIND US

Direction: Immediately SW of Gilsland village, by old railway station

P
Parking (near the Station Hotel).

MAP OS Map 86 (ref NY 634662)

Sewingshields Wall

Northumberland

A length of Wall with milecastle remains, impressively sited along the Whin Sill, commanding fine views of many prehistoric and later earthworks to the north.

HOW TO FIND US

Direction: N of B6318; 1½ miles E of Housesteads Fort

MAP OS Map 87 (ref NY 805702)

Temple of Mithras, Carrawburgh

Northumberland

A fascinating temple near Carrawburgh fort to the god beloved by Roman soldiers, with facsimiles of altars found during excavation. Sited like many Mithraic temples near a military base, it was founded in the 3rd century, and eventually desecrated, probably by Christians. Nearby was the still more popular well shrine of the water-nymph Coventina.

HOW TO FIND US

Direction: 3¾ miles W of Chollerford, on B6318

P

MAP OS Map 87 (ref NY 859711)

Vindolanda Fort

Northumberland

An extensively excavated fort and much-studied civil settlement.

Owned and managed by Vindolanda Charitable Trust.

ENTRY

Adult	£4.50
Concession	£3.80
Child	£2.90

10% discount for EH members

OPENING TIMES

12 Feb-31Mar, daily	10am-5pm
1 Apr-30 Sep, daily	10am-6pm
1 Oct-13 Nov, daily	10am-5pm

For winter opening, see website

HOW TO FIND US

Direction: 1¼ miles SE of Twice Brewed; on minor road off B6318

Tel: 01434 344277

www.vindolanda.com

MAP OS Map 87 (ref NY 771664)

Walltown Crags

Northumberland

One of the best places of all to see the Wall, dramatically snaking and diving along the crags of the Whin Sill.

HOW TO FIND US

Direction: 1 mile NE of Greenhead, off B6318

MAP OS Map 132 (ref NY 674663)

Willowford Wall, Turrets and Bridge

Cumbria

A fine 914 metre (2,999 feet) stretch of Wall, including two turrets and impressive bridge remains beside the River Irthing.

HOW TO FIND US

Direction: W of minor road, ¾ mile W of Gilsland

MAP OS Map 132 (ref NY 627664)

Winshields Wall

Northumberland

The highest point on the Wall, in rugged country with spectacular views.

HOW TO FIND US

Direction: W of Steel Rigg car park; on minor road off B6318

MAP OS Map 87 (ref NY 742676)

i

Looking for a unique present?

Why not browse our online shop at **www.english-heritage.org.uk/shopping**

The Pillar Hall, Belsay Hall – see page 238

North East

'Now Liddesdale has ridden a raid,
But I wat they had better stayed at hame,
For Michael of Winfield he is dead
And Jock o'the Side is prisoner ta'en'

From 'Jock o'the Side': 16th century Border Ballad

www.english-heritage.org.uk/northeast

Properties

See individual listings for details

Durham
Auckland Castle Deer House, Barnard Castle, Bowes Castle, Derwentcote Steel Furnace, Egglestone Abbey, Finchale Priory

Northumberland
Aydon Castle, Belsay Hall, Castle and Gardens, Berwick-upon-Tweed Barracks, Berwick-upon-Tweed Castle, Berwick-upon-Tweed Main Guard, Berwick-upon-Tweed Ramparts, Black Middens Bastle House, Brinkburn Priory, Dunstanburgh Castle, Edlingham Castle, Etal Castle, Lindisfarne Priory, Norham Castle, Prudhoe Castle, Warkworth Castle and Hermitage

Redcar and Cleveland
Gisborough Priory

Tyne and Wear
Bessie Surtees House, Hylton Castle, St Paul's Monastery, Tynemouth Priory and Castle

Hadrian's Wall
See page 222

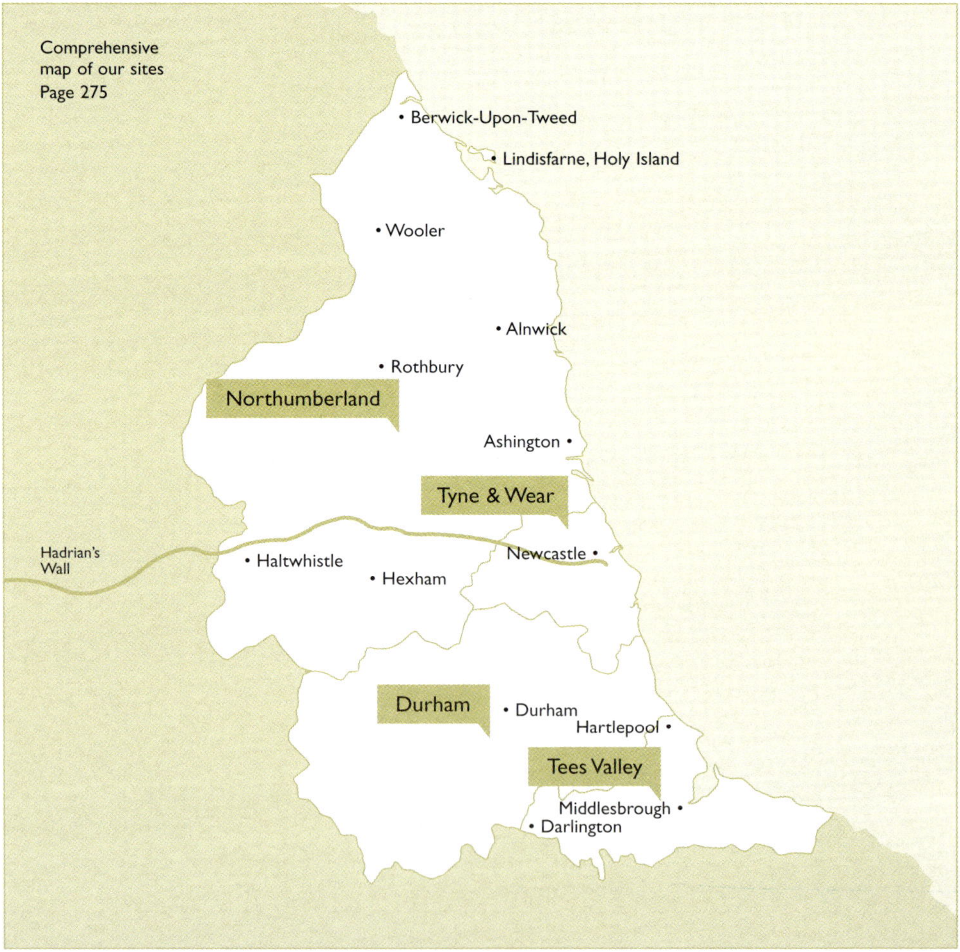

Tynemouth Priory and Castle – see page 247

Bastions of the Borders

Stretching from the Scottish Border to the Tees Valley, English Heritage's North East region includes some of the wildest countryside in England. It was also the most fought-over part of the kingdom, especially in the three centuries between 1300 and 1600. This period saw a dozen full-scale Anglo-Scottish wars, and countless raids: while in the intervals of nominal peace, the depredations of 'border reivers' like Jock o' the Side ('a greater thief did never ride') made it vital for even farmhouses like **Black Middens Bastle House** and manor houses like **Aydon Castle** to be fortified.

Most English Heritage sites in the region are therefore castles. On the border itself stands **Norham Castle**, 'the most dangerous and adventurous place in England'; **Etal Castle**; and the great fortress of **Berwick-upon-Tweed**, spectacularly updated in the 16th century with the most complete surviving set of bastioned defences in Britain. Further south are scenically-sited **Dunstanburgh Castle**, and mighty **Warkworth Castle**, seat of the locally all-powerful Percy family. Much-besieged **Prudhoe Castle** guarded the Tyne crossing; **Bowes Castle** watched over the Stainmore pass; and **Barnard Castle** defended the passage of the Tees – for even here, so far from the border, Scottish raiders penetrated during the dark years after Bannockburn.

Only after peace between England and Scotland came with the accession of James I in 1603 did the north east cease to be a border bastion. Within a few years, the fortified tower of **Belsay Castle** had been added to with a Jacobean mansion – followed much later by the building of the beautiful Greek Revival hall with its wonderful gardens, among the region's greatest glories.

Glories of another kind are the north east's religious sites, recalling that this area was a stronghold of early Christianity. Most famous of all is **Lindisfarne Priory** on Holy Island, original shrine of the region's patron Saint Cuthbert; while the great Anglo-Saxon church chronicler, the Venerable Bede, worked at **St Paul's Monastery**, Jarrow. **Tynemouth Priory** on its impregnable headland served as a fortress against Vikings and Scots, remaining the site of active coastal defences until World War II. **Brinkburn Priory**, **Finchale Priory** and **Egglestone Abbey**, each in a lovely riverside setting, are by contrast oases of deep tranquillity in this once warlike region.

Auckland Castle Deer House

Durham

A charming Gothic Revival 'eyecatcher' built in 1760 in the park of the Bishops of Durham. It provided deer with shelter and food, and had rooms for picnics and enjoying the view.

Managed by the Church Commissioners for England. There is a separate charge for members.

OPENING TIMES

Park:

1 Apr-30 Sep, daily	10am-6pm
1 Oct-28 Mar, daily	10am-4pm
Closed	24-26 Dec and 1 Jan

HOW TO FIND US

Direction: Located in Auckland Park, Bishop Auckland; N of town centre on A68

Train: Bishop Auckland 1 mile

MAP Page 275 (5G)
OS Map 93 (ref NZ 216304)

Aydon Castle

Northumberland – NE45 5PJ

One of the finest and most unaltered examples of a 13th-century English manor house, Aydon Castle stands in a secluded woodland setting. It was originally built as an undefended residence, but almost immediately fortified on the outbreak of Anglo-Scottish warfare. Nevertheless it was

pillaged and burnt by the Scots in 1315, seized by English rebels two years later, and again occupied by Scots in 1346. In the 18th century Aydon became a farmhouse, remaining so until 1966.

NON-MEMBERS

Adult	£3.40
Concession	£2.60
Child	£1.70

OPENING TIMES

1 Apr-30 Sep, Thu-Mon 10am-5pm

HOW TO FIND US

Direction: 1 mile NE of Corbridge, on minor road off B6321 or A68

Train: Corbridge 4 miles – approach via bridle path from W side of Aydon Rd, immediately N of Corbridge bypass

Tel: 01434 632450

P OVP

Disabled access (ground floor only).

Dogs on leads (restricted areas only).

MAP Page 275 (4F)
OS Map 87 (ref NZ 001663)

Barnard Castle

Durham

Set on a high rock above the River Tees, imposing Barnard Castle was the stronghold of the Balliol family. Taking its name from Bernard de Balliol, who rebuilt it in the 12th century, it includes a fine great

hall and a dominating round-towered keep. Unsuccessfully besieged by the Scots in 1216, it was confiscated when John de Balliol, briefly King of Scotland, was deposed by Edward I. It last saw action during the Northern Rising against Queen Elizabeth in 1569, surrendering to 5000 rebels, and was partly dismantled in 1630 to furnish materials for Sir Henry Vane's new Raby Castle.

NON-MEMBERS

Adult	£3.40
Concession	£2.60
Child	£1.70

OPENING TIMES

1 Apr-30 Sep, daily	10am-6pm
1-31 Oct, daily	10am-4pm
1 Nov-31 Mar, Thu-Mon	10am-4pm
Closed	24-26 Dec and 1 Jan

HOW TO FIND US

Direction: In Barnard Castle town

Bus: Arriva 75/6 Darlington – Barnard Castle (passes close to Darlington)

Tel: 01833 638212

OVP

MAP Page 275 (6G)
OS Map 92 (ref NZ 049165)

Belsay Hall, Castle and Gardens

See feature – Page 238

Berwick-Upon-Tweed Barracks & Main Guard

Northumberland

Berwick Barracks, among the first in England to be purpose-built, were begun in 1717 to the design of the distinguished architect Nicholas Hawksmoor. Today the Barracks hosts a number of attractions, including 'By Beat of Drum' – an exhibition on the life of the British infantryman. While there, visit the King's Own Scottish Borderers Museum, the Contemporary Art Gallery and the Berwick Borough Museum.

The Main Guard is a Georgian Guard House near the quay: it displays 'The Story of a Border Garrison Town' exhibition.

The Main Guard is managed by Berwick Civic Society.

NON-MEMBERS (BARRACKS)	
Adult	£3.30
Concession	£2.50
Child	£1.70

OPENING TIMES

Barracks

1 Apr-30 Sep, daily	10am-5pm
1-31 Oct, daily	10am-4pm
1 Nov-31 Mar	Call site for details

Closed 24-26 Dec and 1 Jan

Main Guard
Tel 01289 304493 for details

Berwick-Upon-Tweed Barracks & Main Guard

HOW TO FIND US

Direction: On the Parade, off Church St in town centre

Train: Berwick-upon-Tweed ¼ mile

Bus: From surrounding areas

Tel: 01289 304493

OVP

Disabled access (Main Guard).
Dogs on leads (restricted areas only).
Parking (in town).

MAP Page 275 (1F)
OS Map 75 (Barracks ref NU 001531, Main Guard ref NU 000525)

Berwick-Upon-Tweed Castle & Ramparts

Northumberland – TD15 1DF

The remains of a medieval castle crucial to Anglo-Scottish warfare, superseded by the most complete and breathtakingly impressive bastioned town defences in England, mainly Elizabethan but updated in the 17th and 18th centuries. Surrounding the whole historic town, their entire circuit can be walked.

OPENING TIMES

Any reasonable time

HOW TO FIND US

Direction: The castle is adjacent to Berwick-upon-Tweed railway station. The ramparts surround the town (accessed at various points)

Train: Berwick-upon-Tweed, adjacent

Bus: From surrounding areas

Disabled access (Ramparts).
Parking (Ramparts).

Note: Steep hidden drops.
Dangerous after dark.

MAP Page 275 (1F)
OS Map 75 (ref NT 993534)

Bessie Surtees House

Tyne and Wear – NE1 3JF

These two 16th and 17th-century merchants' houses are examples of Jacobean domestic architecture. The house is best known as the scene of the elopement of Bessie Surtees and John Scott, who later became Lord Chancellor of England. An exhibition illustrating the history of the two buildings is on the first floor.

OPENING TIMES

Year round, Mon-Fri	10am-4pm

Closed Bank Hols and 24 Dec-3 Jan

HOW TO FIND US

Direction: 41-44 Sandhill, Newcastle upon Tyne

Train: Newcastle ½ mile

Metro: Central ½ mile

Bus: From surrounding areas

Tel: 0191 269 1200

MAP Page 275 (4G)
OS Map 88 (ref NZ 252638))

Bishop Aucklands Deer House

See Auckland Castle Deer House

i

Sign-up on-line for our email Members' Newsletter at **www.english-heritage.org.uk/newsletter**

Belsay Hall, Castle and Gardens Northumberland – NE20 0DX

Belsay has something for everyone. A fine medieval castle, enlarged into a mansion in the 17th century; the imposing Greek Revival villa which was built later; and the outstanding, plant-rich gardens linking the two buildings.

The whole ensemble is the creation of the Middleton family, over more than seven centuries. First came the castle, still dominated by its massive 14th century 'peel tower', one of the best surviving examples in England. Though built as a refuge at a time of endemic Anglo-Scottish warfare, it was also designed to impress: its first-floor great chamber still displays rare traces of elaborate medieval wall paintings.

Following the coming of peace under James I, a column-entranced mansion wing was added to the castle in 1614: here the family lived until Christmas Day 1817, when they moved into Belsay Hall.

Belsay Hall, now displayed without furnishings, revealing the fine craftsmanship of its construction, is an austerely Classical Greek Revival villa. Begun in 1807, it was designed by Sir Charles Monck (formerly Middleton), a man inspired by Ancient Greece, and the buildings he had seen on his honeymoon in Athens, particularly the Temple of Theseus. It had nevertheless a comfortable and up-to-date interior, arranged round its amazing central two-storey 'Pillar Hall.'

The vast gardens which provide a magnificent setting for castle and hall are also largely the work of Sir Charles Monck. His rugged and romantic Quarry Garden, created where stone was cut for his hall, has ravines, pinnacles and sheer rock faces inspired by the quarries of Sicily. His grandson Sir Arthur Middleton, likewise a pioneering plantsman, further embellished the Quarry with a wider range of exotic species, as well as adding the Winter Garden, Yew Garden, and Magnolia Terrace.

Level paths and short grass make the gardens suitable for wheelchairs, and there are plenty of seats. There is a tearoom in summer, and food can be brought out into the picnic area.

www.english-heritage.org.uk/belsayhall

Belsay Castle

NON-MEMBERS

Adult	£5.50
Concession	£4.10
Child	£2.80
Family ticket	£13.80

OPENING TIMES

1 Apr-30 Sep, daily	10am-5pm
1-31 Oct, daily	10am-4pm
1 Nov-31 Mar, Thu-Mon	10am-4pm
Closed	24-26 Dec & 1 Jan

HOW TO FIND US

Direction: In Belsay; 14 miles NW of Newcastle, on A696

Train: Morpeth 10 miles

Bus: Snaith's 808 from Newcastle; Arriva 508 from Newcastle (Sun only, Jun-Oct)

Tel: 01661 881636

Local Tourist Information Morpeth: 01670 500700

OVP

Disabled access (grounds, tea room and ground floor only; toilets).

Dogs on leads (restricted areas only).

Tearooms open daily Apr-Oct, Sat-Sun in Mar).

New guidebook.

MAP Page 275 (3G)
OS Map 88 (ref NZ 086785)

Black Middens Bastle House

Northumberland

A fortified farmhouse with thick stone walls, of a type distinctive to the troubled 16th-century Anglo-Scottish borders. The living quarters were only accessible at first floor level. Set in splendid walking country, on the Reivers Route cycle trail.

OPENING TIMES

Any reasonable time

HOW TO FIND US

Direction: 180 metres N of minor road, 7 miles NW of Bellingham; or along a minor road from A68

MAP Page 275 (3F)
OS Map 80 (ref NY 773900)

Bowes Castle

Durham

The massive ruins of Henry II's 12th-century tower keep, set within the earthworks of a Roman fort guarding the strategic Stainmore pass over the Pennines.

OPENING TIMES

Any reasonable time

HOW TO FIND US

Direction: In Bowes Village off A66; 4 miles W of Barnard Castle town

Bus: Hodgson's 72, 574 from Barnard Castle

MAP Page 275 (6F)
OS Map 92 (ref NY 992135)

Brinkburn Priory

Northumberland – NE65 8AR

The beautiful 12th-century church of the Augustinian priory of Brinkburn survives completely roofed and restored. Picturesquely set by a bend in the River Coquet, it is reached by a scenic 10 minute walk from the car park. Parts of the monastic buildings are incorporated into the elegant adjacent manor house.

NON-MEMBERS

Adult	£2.70
Concession	£2.00
Child	£1.40

OPENING TIMES

1 Apr-30 Sep, Thu-Mon 10am-5pm

HOW TO FIND US

Direction: 4½ miles SE of Rothbury, off B6344

Train: Acklington 10 miles

Bus: Arriva/Northumbria Coaches 516 Morpeth – Thropton (passes Morpeth), with connections from Newcastle (passes Tyne & Wear Metro Haymarket) to within ½ mile.

Tel: 01665 570628

OVP

Picnic area (1/3 mile).

MAP Page 275 (3G)
OS Map 81 (ref NZ 116983)

Derwentcote Steel Furnace

Durham

Built in the 1720s, Derwentcote is the earliest and most complete steel-making furnace in Britain. It produced high-grade steel for springs and cutting tools. Small exhibition within.

OPENING TIMES

Please call for details

HOW TO FIND US

Direction: 10 miles SW of Newcastle, on A694; between Rowland's Gill and Hamsterley

Train: Metro Centre, Gateshead, 7 miles

Bus: Go North East 45/6 Newcastle – Consett

Tel: 0191 269 1200 (Mon-Fri)

P

Dogs on leads (restricted areas only).

MAP Page 275 (4G)
OS Map 88 (ref NZ 130566)

Dunstanburgh Castle

Northumberland – NE66 3TT

Dramatic Dunstanburgh Castle was built at a time when relations between King Edward II and his most powerful baron, Earl Thomas of Lancaster, had become openly hostile. Lancaster began the fortress

in 1313, and the latest archaeological research carried out by English Heritage indicates that he built it on a far grander scale than was hitherto recognised, perhaps more as a symbol of his opposition to the king than as a military stronghold. The innovative gatehouse, for instance, competed with the new royal castles in Wales.

The earl failed to reach Dunstanburgh when his rebellion was defeated, being taken and executed in 1322. Thereafter the castle passed eventually to John of Gaunt, who strengthened it against the Scots by converting the great twin-towered gatehouse into a keep. The focus of fierce fighting during the Wars of the Roses, it was twice besieged and captured by Yorkist forces, but subsequently fell into decay. Its impressive ruins now watch over a headland famous for seabirds.

Owned by The National Trust, maintained and managed by EH. Free to NT members.

NON-MEMBERS

Adult	£2.70
Concession	£2.00
Child	£1.40

OPENING TIMES

1 Apr-30 Sep, daily	10am-5pm
1-31 Oct, daily	10am-4pm
1 Nov-31 Mar, Thu-Mon	10am-4pm

Dunstanburgh Castle

HOW TO FIND US

Direction: 8 miles NE of Alnwick; on footpaths from Craster or Embleton – 1½ miles flat coastal walk

Train: Chathill (U), not Sun, 5 miles from Embleton, 7 miles from Castle; Alnmouth, 7 miles from Craster, 8¼ miles from Castle

Bus: Arriva 401, 501 Alnwick – Belford with connections from Berwick-upon-Tweed and Newcastle (passing Metro Haymarket); alight Craster, 1½ miles

Tel: 01665 576231

OVP

Parking (in Craster village; approx 1½ miles walk. A charge is payable).

MAP Page 275 (2G)
OS Map 75 (ref NU 257219)

Edlingham Castle

Northumberland

The riverside ruins, principally the solar tower, of a manor house progressively fortified against the Scots during the 14th century.

Managed by the Parochial Church Council of St John the Baptist, Edlingham, with Bolton Chapel.

OPENING TIMES

Any reasonable time

HOW TO FIND US

Direction: At E end of Edlingham village, on minor road off B6341; 6 miles SW of Alnwick

Train: Alnmouth 9 miles

Note: waterproof footwear is recommended.

MAP Page 275 (2G)
OS Map 81 (ref NU 116092)

Egglestone Abbey

Durham

The charming ruins of a small monastery of Premonstratensian 'white canons', picturesquely set above a bend in the River Tees near Barnard Castle. Remains include much of the 13th-century church and a range of living quarters, with traces of their ingenious toilet drainage system.

OPENING TIMES

Daily	10am-6pm

HOW TO FIND US

Direction: 1 mile S of Barnard Castle, on a minor road off B6277

Bus: Arriva 79 Richmond – Barnard Castle; 75/6 Darlington – Barnard Castle (passes close to Darlington), then 1½ miles

MAP Page 275 (6G)
OS Map 92 (ref NZ 062151)

Etal Castle

Northumberland – TD12 4TN

Etal was built in the mid-14th century by Robert Manners as a defence against Scots raiders, in a strategic position by a ford over the River Till. It fell to James IV's invading Scots army in 1513, immediately before their catastrophic defeat at nearby Flodden. An award-winning exhibition tells the story of Flodden, and the Anglo-Scottish border warfare which ended with the accession of James I in 1603.

NON-MEMBERS

Adult	£3.40
Concession	£2.60
Child	£1.70
Family ticket	£8.50

OPENING TIMES

1 Apr-31 Oct, daily	11am-4pm

HOW TO FIND US

Direction: In Etal village, 10 miles SW of Berwick

Train: Berwick-upon-Tweed 10½ miles

Bus: Border Villager 267 Berwick-upon-Tweed – Wooler

Tel: 01890 820332

OVP

Audio (the audio tour guides visitors around the castle and the exhibition). Dogs on leads (restricted areas only). Toilets (in village).

MAP Page 275 (1F)
OS Map 74 (ref NT 925393)

Finchale Priory

Durham – DH9 5SH

The very extensive remains of a 13th-century priory, founded on the site of a retired pirate's hermitage. Part of it later served as a holiday retreat for the monks of Durham Cathedral. Beautifully sited by the River Wear, it can be reached from Durham via a delightful riverside and woodland walk.

OPENING TIMES

Please call keykeeper on 0191 386 3828.

HOW TO FIND US

Direction: 3 miles NE of Durham; on minor road off A167

Train: Durham 5 miles

Parking (on south side of river; charge applicable).

Tearoom (not managed by EH).

MAP Page 275 (4G)
OS Map 88 (ref NZ 296471)

Gisborough Priory

Redcar and Cleveland

The ruins of an Augustinian priory founded by the Bruce family, afterwards Kings of Scotland. They are dominated by the dramatic skeleton of the 14th-century church's east end.

Managed by Redcar and Cleveland Borough Council.

NON-MEMBERS

Adult	£1.10
Concession	£0.75
Child	£0.55

OPENING TIMES

1 Apr-30 Sep, Tue-Sun	9am-5pm
1 Oct-28 Mar, Wed-Sun	9am-5pm
Closed	24 Dec-1 Jan

HOW TO FIND US

Direction: In Guisborough town, next to the parish church

Train: Marske 4½ miles

Bus: Arriva X56, 65, 93, 765 from Middlesbrough (passes close to Middlesbrough)

Tel: 01287 633801

Toilets (in town).

MAP Page 275 (6H)
OS Map 94 (ref NZ 617160)

Hadrian's Wall

See page 222

Hylton Castle

Tyne and Wear

The distinctive and highly decorative gatehouse-tower of a castle built by the wealthy Sir William Hylton, shortly before 1400. Originally containing four floors of self-contained family accommodation, its entrance front displays royal and family heraldry, including Richard II's white hart badge.

Managed by Sunderland City Council.

OPENING TIMES

Any reasonable time (grounds only)

HOW TO FIND US

Direction: 3¾ miles W of Sunderland

Train: Seaburn 2½ miles

Bus: From surrounding areas

Disabled access (grounds only).

Parking (in town centre).

MAP Page 275 (4H)
OS Map 88 (ref NZ 358588)

Lindisfarne Priory

See feature – Page 244

Norham Castle

Northumberland – TD15 2JY

Commanding a vital ford over the River Tweed, Norham was one of the strongest of the border castles, and the most often attacked by the Scots. Besieged at least thirteen times – once for nearly a year by Robert Bruce – it was called 'the most dangerous and adventurous place in the country'. But even its powerful 12th-century keep and massive towered bailey walls could not resist James IV's heavy cannon, and it fell to him in 1513, shortly before his defeat at Flodden. The extensive 16th century rebuilding which followed, adapting the fortress for its own artillery, is still clearly traceable.

OPENING TIMES

Admission limited. Please call 01289 304493.

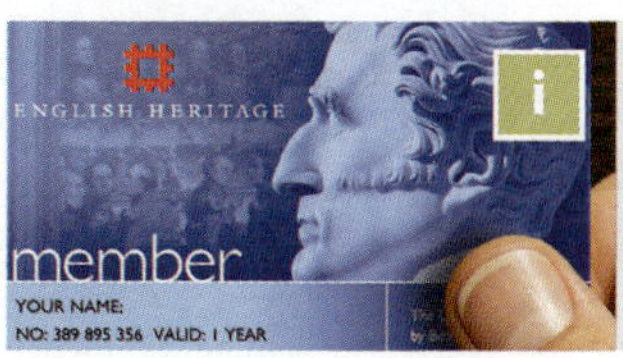

Norham Castle

HOW TO FIND US

Direction: In Norham village; 6 miles SW of Berwick-upon-Tweed, on minor road off B6470 (from A698)

Train: Berwick-upon-Tweed 7½ miles

Bus: Swan/Munro 23 Berwick-upon-Tweed – Kelso

Disabled access (excluding keep).

MAP Page 275 (1F)
OS Map 74 (ref NT 906476)

Many sites have plant sales and shops. Check property listings for details.

English Heritage membership makes a lovely gift.

Call 0870 333 1181 or visit **www.english-heritage.org.uk/gift** for more details.

Lindisfarne Priory Northumberland – TD15 2RX

Lindisfarne Priory on Holy Island was one of the most important centres of early Christianity in Anglo-Saxon England. It is still a place of pilgrimage today, the dramatic approach across the causeway adding to the fascination of the site.

Sculpture depicting St Cuthbert

St Aidan founded the monastery in AD 635, but St Cuthbert, Prior of Lindisfarne, is the most celebrated of the priory's holy men. After many missionary journeys, and 10 years as a hermit on lonely Farne Island, he reluctantly became Bishop before retiring to die on Farne in 687. Buried in the priory, his remains were transferred to a pilgrim shrine there after 11 years, and found still undecayed – a sure sign of sanctity.

From the end of the 8th century, the isolated island with its rich monastery was easy prey for Viking raiders. In 875 the monks left, carrying Cuthbert's remains, which after long wanderings were enshrined in Durham Cathedral in 1104, where they still rest. Only after that time did Durham monks re-establish a priory on Lindisfarne: the evocative ruins of the richly decorated priory church they built in c.1150 still stand, with their famous 'rainbow arch' – a vault-rib of the now-vanished crossing tower. The small community lived quietly on Holy Island until the suppression of the monastery in 1537.

The museum has been refurbished, offering a clear and lively interpretation of the story of St Cuthbert and the development of Lindisfarne Priory.

The causeway floods at high tide, so it is very important to check the tide times before crossing.

www.english-heritage.org.uk/lindisfarnepriory

NON-MEMBERS	
Adult	£3.70
Concession	£2.80
Child	£1.90

OPENING TIMES	
1 Apr-30 Sep, daily	9.30am-5pm
1-31 Oct, daily	9.30am-4pm
1 Nov-31 Jan, Sat-Mon	10am-2pm
1 Feb-31 Mar, daily	10am-4pm
Closed	24-26 Dec and 1 Jan

HOW TO FIND US

Direction: On Holy Island, only reached at low tide across causeway; tide tables at each end, or details from tourist info

Train: Berwick-upon-Tweed 14 miles, via causeway

Bus: Travelsure 477 from Berwick-upon-Tweed (passes close to ⇌ Berwick-upon-Tweed); times vary with tides

Tel: 01289 389200

Tourist Information Centre 01289 330733

OVP

Dogs on leads (restricted areas only). New guidebook.

MAP Page 275 (1G)
OS Map 75 (ref NU 126417)

Prudhoe Castle

Northumberland – NE42 6NA

Begun between 1100 and 1120 to defend a strategic crossing of the River Tyne against Scottish invaders, Prudhoe Castle has been continuously occupied for over nine centuries. After two sieges during the 1170s – the Scots attackers reportedly declaring 'as long as Prudhoe stands, we shall never have peace' – the mighty stone keep and a great hall were added, followed in about 1300 by two strong towers. Passing from its original Umfraville owners to the powerful Percies in 1398, it was again updated with a fashionable new great hall.

Even after its last military action against the Scots in 1640, Prudhoe's importance as the centre of a great landed estate continued. Early in the 19th century the Percies restored it, building a fine new manor house within its walls. All these developments are now vividly interpreted in a new family-friendly exhibition including site finds, helping visitors to explore and understand the extensive remains of this formidable and long-lived fortress.

Prudhoe Castle

NON-MEMBERS

Adult	£3.40
Concession	£2.60
Child	£1.70

OPENING TIMES

1 Apr-30 Sep, Thu-Mon 10am-5pm

HOW TO FIND US

Direction: In Prudhoe, on minor road off A695

Train: Prudhoe ¼ mile

Bus: From surrounding areas

Tel: 01661 833459

OVP

Dogs on leads (restricted areas only).

New guidebook.

MAP Page 275 (4G)
OS Map 88 (ref NZ 091634)

St Paul's Monastery, Jarrow

Tyne and Wear

The home of the Venerable Bede, chronicler of the beginnings of English Christianity, Jarrow has become one of the best-understood Anglo-Saxon monastic sites. The Anglo-Saxon church – with the oldest dedication stone in the country, dated AD 685 – partly survives as the chancel of the parish church. English Heritage members also receive a discount on the entry fee to the nearby Bede's World Museum.

Managed by Bede's World.

St Paul's Monastery, Jarrow

OPENING TIMES

Monastery ruins any reasonable time

HOW TO FIND US

Direction: In Jarrow, on minor road N of A185; follow signs for Bede's World

Metro: Bede ¾ miles

Bus: Go North East 527 Newcastle – South Shields

Tel: 01914 897052

MAP Page 275 (4H)
OS Map 88 (ref NZ 339652)

Check *Heritage Today* for news and information on forthcoming events and exclusive members' offers.

English Heritage members can take up to 6 children, as part of a family group, into our properties at no extra cost (see page 7).

Photo: John Critchley

Tynemouth Priory and Castle

Tyne and Wear – NE30 4BZ

Set in an almost impregnable position on a steep headland between the river and the North Sea, Tynemouth has always been as much a fortress as a religious site.

Here stood a 7th-century Anglian monastery, burial place of Oswin, sainted king of Northumbria. After its destruction by Danish raiders, the present Benedictine priory was refounded on its site in c. 1090.

The towering east end of the priory church, built in c. 1200 with slender lancet windows and soaring arches, still survives almost to its full height, dominating the headland. Beyond it stands a small but complete and exceptionally well-preserved chapel, with a rose window and an ornately-sculpted roof vault, built in the mid-15th century as a chantry for the souls of the powerful Percy family, Earls of Northumberland.

Enclosing both headland and monastery, and still surviving in part, were the strong walls which once made Tynemouth among the largest fortified areas in England, and an important bastion against the Scots. Probably begun by Edward I in 1296, they were strengthened and updated in the 15th century. Thus when the priory's 19 monks surrendered Tynemouth to Henry VIII in 1539, it was immediately adopted as a royal castle. Thereafter the fortress-headland continued to play its centuries-old part in coastal defence, both against Napoleon and during the two World Wars. The restored magazine of its gun battery can be seen at weekends.

www.english-heritage.org.uk/tynemouthcastle

NON-MEMBERS	
Adult	£3.40
Concession	£2.60
Child	£1.70
Family ticket	£8.50

OPENING TIMES

1 Apr-30 Sep, daily	10am-5pm
1-31 Oct, daily	10am-4pm
1 Nov-31 Mar, Thu-Mon	10am-4pm
Closed	24-26 Dec & 1 Jan

Gun Battery: Access limited, please ask site staff for details.

HOW TO FIND US

Direction: In Tynemouth, near North Pier

Metro: Tynemouth ½ mile

Bus: From surrounding areas

Tel: 0191 257 1090

OVP

Disabled access (priory only).

MAP Page 275 (4H)
OS Map 88 (ref NZ 373694)

Warkworth Castle and Hermitage

Northumberland – NE65 0UJ

The magnificent cross-shaped keep of Warkworth, crowning a hilltop rising steeply above the River Coquet, dominates one of the largest, strongest and most impressive fortresses in northern England. The castle's most famous owners were the Percy family, whose lion badge can be seen carved on many parts of their stronghold. Wielding almost kingly power in the north, their influence reached its apogee under the first Earl of Northumberland and his son 'Harry Hotspur', hero of many Border ballads as the bane of Scots raiders and a dominant character in Shakespeare's *'Henry IV'*. Having helped to depose Richard II, these turbulent 'kingmakers' both fell victim to Henry IV: the next three Percy earls likewise died violent deaths.

Still roofed and almost complete, the uniquely-planned keep dates mainly from the end of the 14th century. It presides over the extensive remains of a great hall, chapel, fine gatehouse and a virtually intact circuit of towered walls.

Half a mile from the castle, tucked away by the Coquet and accessible only by boat, stands a much more peaceful building: the late medieval cave Hermitage and chapel of a solitary holy man.

There are free tours of the Duke's Rooms in the castle keep on Wed, Sun and Bank Hols, 1 April-30 Sept.

www.english-heritage.org.uk/warkworthcastle

NON-MEMBERS (CASTLE)	
Adult	£3.40
Concession	£2.60
Child	£1.70
Family ticket	£8.50

NON-MEMBERS (HERMITAGE)	
Adult	£2.40
Concession	£1.80
Child	£1.20

OPENING TIMES

Castle:

1 Apr-30 Sept, daily	10am-5pm
1-31 Oct, daily	10am-4pm
1 Nov-31 Mar, Sat-Mon	10am-4pm
Closed	24-26 Dec and 1 Jan

Hermitage:

1 Apr-30 Sep, Wed, Sun & Bank Hols	11am-5pm

HOW TO FIND US

Direction: In Warkworth; 7½ miles S of Alnwick, on A1068

Train: Alnmouth 3½ miles

Bus: Arriva 518 Newcastle – Alnwick

Tel: 01665 711423

P OVP

Audio tours (also available for the visually impaired and those with learning difficulties).

Disabled access (limited access only).

Dogs on leads (restricted areas only).

MAP Page 275 (2G)
OS Map 81 (ref NU 247058)

Other Historic Attractions

Discounted entry to our members (discounts may not apply on event days)

Bede's World Museum

Tyne and Wear – NE32 3DY

A significant site which celebrates the extraordinary life of the Venerable Bede. Interactive museum and recreated Anglo-Saxon farm buildings with rare breed animals.

Managed by Bede's World.

ENTRY

Half-price for EH members. Discount does not extend to EH Corporate Partners

OPENING TIMES

1 Apr-31 Oct

Mon-Sat	10am-5.30pm
Sun	12pm-5.30pm

1 Nov-31 Mar

Mon-Sat	10am-4.30pm
Sun	12pm-4.30pm

HOW TO FIND US

Direction: 2 miles from A19 Tyne Tunnel

Tel: 0191 489 2106

MAP Page 275 (4H)
OS Map 88 (ref NZ 388654)

Bowes Museum

Co Durham – DL12 8NP

One of the country's most fascinating museum experiences. Go on a wonderful journey of discovery in this magical house of treasures. A great day out for all the family.

ENTRY

10% off normal admission charge to English Heritage members throughout 2006

OPENING TIMES

Open daily	11am-5pm
Closed	25-26 Dec & 1 Jan

HOW TO FIND US

Direction: In Barnard Castle, off A66

Tel 01833 690606

www.bowesmuseum.org.uk

MAP Page 275 (5G)
OS Map 92 (ref NZ 056163)

Chesters Walled Garden

Northumberland – NE46 4BQ

Historic two acre walled garden famous for herbs and flower filled borders, organically grown. A haven of peace, scent and colour.

ENTRY

Concessionary rate for English Heritage members. Cannot be used with any other offers. Please call for details.

OPENING TIMES

24 Mar-31 Oct	10am-5pm

HOW TO FIND US

Direction: ¼ mile W of Chollerford, off B6318

Tel: 01434 681483

MAP Page 275 (4F)
OS Map 87 (ref NY 906703)

Segedunum Roman Fort, Baths and Museum

Tyne and Wear – NE28 6HR

The reconstruction of a Roman bathhouse and a section of Hadrian's Wall, including an Interactive Museum.

Managed by Tyne and Wear Museums.

ENTRY

10% reduction for English Heritage members, please call site for details

Discount does not extend to EH Corporate Partners

OPENING TIMES

1 Apr-31 Oct, daily	10am-5pm
1 Nov-31 Mar, daily	10am-3.30pm

HOW TO FIND US

Direction: In Wallsend

Tel: 0191 236 9347

MAP Page 275 (4H)
OS Map 88 (ref NZ 300660)

Other Historic Attractions

Scotland, Wales and the Isle of Man

In addition to free admission to English Heritage properties featured in this handbook, members of English Heritage are also entitled to free or reduced-price entry to a host of other historic attractions in Scotland, Wales and on the Isle of Man. Entry is discounted in the first year of membership and free in subsequent years.

Manx National Heritage

English Heritage members can gain half-price admission to Manx National Heritage attractions during the first year of membership and free entry in subsequent years.

For more details please write to:
Manx National Heritage, Douglas, Isle of Man IM1 3LY

Please call **01624 648000** or you can visit the Manx National Heritage website at **www.storyofmann.com**

Laxey Wheel

Castle Rushen
Castletown

Cregneash Folk Village
Cregneash

The Grove Rural Life Museum
Ramsey

House of Manannan
Peel

Laxey Wheel and Mines Trail
Laxey

Manx Museum
Douglas

Nautical Museum
Castletown

Niarbyl Café & Visitor Centre, Dalby

Old Grammar School
Castletown

Old House of Keys
Castletown

Peel Castle
Peel

Rushen Abbey
Ballasalla

Sound Visitor Centre
Port St Mary

Photo: Manx National Heritage

Cadw: Welsh Historic Monuments

English Heritage members can gain half-price admission to Cadw attractions during the first year of membership and free entry in subsequent years.

For more details on Cadw, write to:
Plas Carew, Unit 5/7 Cefn Coed, Parc Nantgarw, Cardiff, CF15 7QQ

Please call **01443 336000** or you can visit the Cadw website at **www.cadw.wales.gov.uk**

Photo: Cadw Welsh Historic Monuments

Tintern Abbey

Beaumaris Castle,
Anglesey
Tel: 01248 810361

Blaenavon Ironworks,
Nr Pontypool,
Torfaen
Tel: 01495 792615

Caerleon Roman Fortress, Caerleon, Newport
Tel: 01633 422518

Caernarfon Castle,
Caernarfon,
Gwynedd
Tel: 01286 677617

Caerphilly Castle,
Caerphilly
Tel: 02920 883143

Carreg Cennen Castle,
Nr Trapp,
Carmarthenshire
Tel: 01558 822291

Castell Coch, Cardiff
Tel: 02920 810101

Chepstow Castle,
Chepstow,
Monmouthshire
Tel: 01291 624065

Cilgerran Castle,
Nr Cardigan,
Ceredigion
Tel: 01239 621339

Conwy Castle, Conwy
Tel: 01492 592358

Criccieth Castle,
Nr Criccieth, Gwynedd
Tel: 01766 522227

Dolwyddelan Castle,
Dolwyddelan,
Gwynedd
Tel: 01690 750366

Harlech Castle,
Harlech, Gwynedd
Tel: 01766 780552

Kidwelly Castle,
Kidwelly,
Carmarthenshire
Tel: 01554 890104

Laugharne Castle,
Laugharne,
Carmarthenshire
Tel: 01994 427906

Oxwich Castle,
Oxwich, Swansea
Tel: 01792 390359

Plas Mawr, Conwy,
Tel: 01492 580167

Raglan Castle,
Nr Raglan,
Monmouthshire
Tel: 01291 690228

Rhuddlan Castle,
Rhuddlan, Denbighshire
Tel: 01745 590777

Rug Chapel and
Llangar Church,
Corwen, Denbighshire
Tel: 01490 412025

St Davids Bishop's
Palace, St Davids,
Pembrokeshire
Tel: 01437 720517

Strata Florida Abbey,
Pontrhydfendigaid,
Ceredigion
Tel: 01974 831261

Tintern Abbey,
Tintern,
Monmouthshire
Tel: 01291 689251

Tretower Court
and Castle,
Tretower,
Powys
Tel: 01874 730279

Valle Crucis Abbey,
Nr Llangollen,
Denbighshire
Tel: 01978 860326

Weobley Castle,
Nr Llanrhidian, Swansea
Tel: 01792 390012

White Castle,
Nr Abergavenny,
Monmouthshire
Tel: 01600 780380

Historic Scotland

English Heritage members can gain half-price admission to Historic Scotland attractions during the first year of membership and free entry in subsequent years.

For more details on Historic Scotland, write to: Longmore House, Salisbury Place, Edinburgh EH9 1SH

Please call **0131 668 8999** or you can visit the Historic Scotland website at **www.historic-scotland.gov.uk**

Edinburgh Castle

Photo: Historic Scotland

Aberdour Castle and Garden, Aberdour, Fife
Tel: 01383 860519

Arbroath Abbey, Angus
Tel: 01241 878756

Argyll's Lodging, Stirling, Central
Tel: 01786 431319

Balvenie Castle, Dufftown, Grampian
Tel: 01340 820121

Bishop's and Earl's Palaces, Kirkwall, Orkney
Tel: 01856 871918

The Black House, Arnol, Lewis, Western Isles
Tel: 01851 710395

Blackness Castle, Firth of Forth, Edinburgh and Lothians
Tel: 01506 834807

Bonawe Historic Iron Furnace, Taynuilt, Argyll
Tel: 01866 822432

Bothwell Castle, Bothwell, Greater Glasgow
Tel: 01698 816894

Broch of Gurness, Aikerness, Orkney
Tel: 01856 751414

Caerlaverock Castle, Nr Dumfries, Dumfries and Galloway
Tel: 01387 770244

Cairnpapple Hill, Torphichen, Edinburgh and Lothians
Tel: 01506 634622

Calanais Standing Stones, Isle of Lewis, Western Isles
Tel: 01851 621422

Cardoness Castle, Nr Gatehouse of Fleet, Dumfries and Galloway
Tel: 01557 814427

Castle Campbell, Dollar Glen, Central
Tel: 01259 742408

Corgarff Castle, Nr Strathdon, Grampian
Tel: 01975 651460

Craigmillar Castle, Edinburgh and Lothians
Tel: 0131 6614445

Craignethan Castle, Lanark, Greater Glasgow
Tel: 01555 860364

Crichton Castle, Nr Pathhead, Edinburgh and Lothians
Tel: 01875 320017

Crossraguel Abbey, Nr Maybole, Greater Glasgow
Tel: 01655 883113

Dallas Dhu Historic Distillery, Nr Forres, Grampian
Tel: 01309 676548

Dirleton Castle and Gardens, Dirleton, Edinburgh and Lothians
Tel: 01620 850330

Doune Castle, Doune, Central
Tel: 01786 841742

Dryburgh Abbey, Nr Melrose, Borders
Tel: 01835 822381

Dumbarton Castle, Dumbarton, Greater Glasgow
Tel: 01389 732167

Dundonald Castle, Dundonald, Greater Glasgow
Tel: 01563 851489

Dundrennan Abbey, Nr Kirkcudbright, Dumfries and Galloway
Tel: 01557 500262

Dunfermline Palace and Abbey, Dunfermline, Fife
Tel: 01383 739026

Dunstaffnage Castle, Nr Oban, Argyll
Tel: 01631 562465

Edinburgh Castle, Edinburgh and Lothians
Tel: 0131 225 9846

Edzell Castle and Garden, Edzell, Angus
Tel: 01356 648631

Elcho Castle, Nr Bridge of Earn, Perthshire
Tel: 01738 639998

Elgin Cathedral, Elgin, Grampian
Tel: 01343 547171

Fort George, Nr Ardersier village, Highlands
Tel: 01667 460232

Glasgow Cathedral, Glasgow
Tel: 0141 552 6891

Glenluce Abbey, Nr Glenluce, Dumfries and Galloway
Tel: 01581 300541

Hackness Martello Tower and Battery, Hoy, Orkney
Tel: 01856 811397

Hermitage Castle, Nr Newcastleton, Borders
Tel: 01387 376222

Huntingtower Castle, Nr Perth, Perthshire
Tel: 01738 627231

Huntly Castle, Huntly, Grampian
Tel: 01466 793191

Inchcolm Abbey,
Firth of Forth,
Fife
Tel: 01383 823332

Inchmahome Priory,
Lake of Menteith,
Central
Tel: 01877 385294

Iona Abbey and Nunnery,
Island of Iona, Central
Tel: 01681 700512

Jarlshof Prehistoric and Norse Settlement,
Sumburgh Head,
Shetland
Tel: 01950 460112

Jedburgh Abbey and Visitor Centre,
Jedburgh, Borders
Tel: 01835 863925

Kildrummy Castle
Nr Alford,
Grampian
Tel: 01975 571331

Kinnaird Head Castle,
Lighthouse and Museum,
Fraserburgh,
Grampian
Tel: 01346 511022

Kisimul Castle,
Isle of Barra,
Western Isles
Tel: 01871 810313

Linlithgow Palace,
Linlithgow, Edinburgh and Lothians
Tel: 01506 842896

Lochleven Castle,
Lochleven, Perthshire
Tel: 07778 040483

MacLellan's Castle,
Kirkcudbright, Dumfries and Galloway
Tel: 01557 331856

Maeshowe Chambered Cairn, Nr Kirkwall,
Orkney
Tel: 01856 761606

Meigle Sculptured Stone Museum,
Meigle, Angus
Tel: 01828 640612

Melrose Abbey,
Melrose, Borders
Tel: 01896 822562

New Abbey Corn Mill,
New Abbey, Dumfries and Galloway
Tel: 01387 850260

Newark Castle,
Port Glasgow,
Greater Glasgow
Tel: 01475 741858

Rothesay Castle,
Rothesay, Isle of Bute
Tel: 01700 502691

St Andrews Castle,
St Andrews, Fife
Tel: 01334 477196

St Andrews Cathedral,
St Andrews, Fife
Tel: 01334 472563

St Serf's Church and Dupplin Cross,
Dunning, Perthshire
Tel: 01764 684497

Seton Collegiate Church, Nr Cockenzie,
Edinburgh and Lothians
Tel: 01875 813334

Skara Brae and Skaill House,
Nr Kirkwall,
Orkney
Tel: 01856 841815

Smailholm Tower,
Near Smailholm,
Borders
Tel: 01573 460365

Spynie Palace,
Nr Elgin, Grampian
Tel: 01343 546358

Stirling Castle,
Stirling, Central
Tel: 01786 450000

Sweetheart Abbey,
New Abbey,
Dumfries and Galloway
Tel: 01387 850397

Tantallon Castle,
Nr North Berwick,
Edinburgh and Lothians
Tel: 01620 892727

Threave Castle,
Nr Castle Douglas,
Dumfries and Galloway
Tel: 07711 223101

Tolquhon Castle,
Nr Aberdeen,
Grampian
Tel: 01651 851286

Urquhart Castle,
Drumnadrochit,
Highlands
Tel: 01456 450551

Skara Brae

Photo: Historic Scotland

Ayshford Chapel, Devon

The Friends of Friendless Churches

The Friends own redundant but beautiful places of worship that would otherwise have been demolished or left to ruin. We now have 38 Grade II* and Grade I buildings in England and Wales. We have recently finished work on the tower to our church at Boveney on the banks of the Thames near Eton, with the help of an enormous English Heritage grant of £150,000. Without this grant the tower might well have collapsed.

We are a small, voluntary organisation which welcomes visitors. Our churches are places for quiet study and contemplation. We do not claim sophistication in terms of parking, toilets, attendants or shops, and access may require approach to a key-holder. You can support our work by becoming a member.

Left: Hardmead, Buckinghamshire
Middle: Llanfair Kilgeddin, Monmouthshire
Right: Tal-y-Llyn, Anglesey

THE FRIENDS OF FRIENDLESS CHURCHES
St. Ann's Vestry Hall, 2 Church Entry, London EC4V 5HB

Tel: 020 7236 3934
Email: **office@friendsoffriendlesschurches.org.uk**

www.friendsoffriendlesschurches.org.uk

St Lawrence, Snarford – see page 258

The Churches Conservation Trust

The Churches Conservation Trust is the leading charity that cares for and preserves English churches of historic, architectural or archaeological importance that are no longer needed for regular worship. It promotes public enjoyment of them and their use as an educational and community resource.

Whatever the condition of the church when the Trust takes it over its aims are, first and foremost, to put the building and its contents into a sound and secure condition as speedily as possible. Then the church is repaired so that it is welcoming to visitors and those who attend the public events or occasional services that may be held there (Trust churches are still consecrated). Our objective is to keep it intact for the benefit of present and future generations, using traditional and sustainable materials and methods.

There are now over 335 Trust churches scattered widely throughout the length and breadth of England, in town and country, ranging from charmingly simple buildings in lovely settings to others of great richness and splendour. Twenty are featured in the following pages to whet your appetite.

To discover more for yourself about this great heritage go to the website where you will find descriptions, directions, photos and much else of interest about Trust churches.

THE CHURCHES
CONSERVATION TRUST

1 West Smithfield
London EC1A 9EE

Tel: 020 7213 0660
Fax: 020 7213 0678
Email: **central@tcct.org.uk**
www.visitchurches.org.uk

Buckinghamshire

St Lawrence, Broughton

In a quiet cul-de-sac on the edge of Milton Keynes, St Lawrence's contains some of the most stunning medieval wall paintings to be found in England. They portray a Doom scene, SS Helena and Eligius, and St George slaying a particularly ferocious dragon. Pevsner considered the most interesting to be a pietà surrounded by young men carrying Christ's heart, feet and bones, beneath which two men quarrelling over a backgammon board represent a sermon against swearing by God's wounds.

OPENING TIMES

Keyholder nearby

HOW TO FIND US

Direction: 1 mile S of M1 at Junction 14. Turn off M1 at Junction 14. Take A409 towards Milton Keynes. At 1st roundabout (Northfield) turn left to Broughton. After ¼ mile take 1st right to Broughton. At the corner with Broughton Hotel turn right up no-through road to reach the church and village.

Train: Milton Keynes Central 5 miles, Woburn Sands 3 miles

MAP OS Map 152 (ref SP 894 401)

Cambridgeshire

All Saints, Cambridge

The spire of this fine church, opposite the gates of Jesus College, is a prominent Cambridge landmark, while the interior represents a milestone of the Gothic Revival. Designed and built by G F Bodley in the 1860s, All Saints' contains richly painted stencil wall decoration and stained glass by some of the most famous names from the Pre-Raphaelite movement, including William Morris, Edward Burne-Jones and Ford Maddox Brown. The exquisite Christ in Majesty above the chancel arch is another treasure.

OPENING TIMES

Keyholder nearby. It is hoped to be opening regularly soon.

HOW TO FIND US

Direction: In Jesus Lane, opposite Jesus College. 250 yards from roundabout on A1303 at S end of Victoria Avenue.

Train: Cambridge 1 mile

MAP OS Map 154 (ref TL 452 587)

Cornwall

St Anthony, St Anthony-in-Roseland

Delightfully situated behind Place, home of the Spry family, looking across the creek to St Mawes, St Anthony's unusually retains its original medieval cruciform plan. Despite extensive 19th-century restoration, it was described by Pevsner as 'the best example in the county of what a parish church was like in the 12th and 13th centuries'. The Victorian wooden roofs, floor tiles and stained glass are notable, and in the north transept are impressive monuments to members of the Spry family spanning three centuries.

OPENING TIMES

Open daily

HOW TO FIND US

Direction: 20 miles SW of St Austell off A3078, opposite St Mawes and 4 miles S of Gerrans. Take unclassified road from Gerrans to St Anthony Head. Proceed past turning to St Anthony Head and along single track road for ¼ mile. Pedestrian access only to churchyard via stile on left side of road.

Train: Truro 13 miles

MAP OS Map 204 (ref SW 855 320)

Devon

Holy Trinity, Torbryan

The approach to Holy Trinity through narrow Devon lanes to an isolated wooded valley does not prepare visitors for a building of such size and grandeur. The fine Perpendicular tower rising in three stages, with an octagonal stair turret on the south wall, is a dramatic feature. Inside, a magnificent rood screen spans the width of the church. The delicacy of the wood carving is echoed by the elegant tracery of the windows, many of which contain medieval stained glass.

OPENING TIMES

Open daily

HOW TO FIND US

Direction: 4 miles SW of Newton Abbot, off A381. From Newton Abbot turn right off A381 to Ipplepen. Follow main street passing church on right. Holy Trinity is 1¼ miles opposite Church House Inn.

Train: Newton Abbot or Totnes 5 miles (each)

MAP OS Map 202 (ref SX 820 669)

Herefordshire

St Bartholomew, Richard's Castle

St Bartholomew's enjoys a spectacular location, high above the village, next to one of the earliest 'marcher castles' with views to the Black Mountains, Malvern and Shropshire Hills. The unrestored interior has a timeless quality, with a chantry chapel for the Knight Templars of St John, a superb 17th-century canopied pew for the lords of the manor and silvery-grey Georgian box pews. To the east is a detached bell tower of 1400. This is one of the most atmospheric of Trust churches.

OPENING TIMES

Open daily

HOW TO FIND US

Direction: 3½ miles SW of Ludlow off B4361. From Ludlow follow signs to Richard's Castle. In village take unmarked lane NW alongside Castle Inn. Church is ¾ mile up steep hill. (The 'new' church of 1892 is on the B4361 nearer Ludlow.)

Train: Ludlow 3½ miles

MAP OS Map 137 (ref SO 484 703)

Kent

St James, Cooling

St James' in its desolate position, with marshes stretching north to the Thames estuary, is strongly associated with the opening pages of Charles Dickens' *Great Expectations*. The churchyard is believed to be the setting for the first encounter of his hero Pip with the convict Magwitch, and the pathetic tombs of 13 babies are now known as 'Pip's graves'. The interior of the church is impressively spacious and the tiny vestry is lined with thousands of cockle shells, emblem of the patron saint.

OPENING TIMES

Open daily

HOW TO FIND US

Direction: In centre of Cooling village 2 miles E of Cliffe and 6 miles N of Rochester, signposted from B2000.

Train: Higham 3 miles

MAP OS Map 178 (ref TQ 756 759)

Leicestershire

St Mary Magdalene, Stapleford

Built in the 18th century by the 4th Earl of Harborough, the church is an elegant example of Gothic Revival architecture, with a tall gracious tower. The cool spacious interior has attractive plasterwork on walls and ceiling, and oak pews facing each other on either side of the nave. An oak gallery across the west end served as the Earl's family pew. The finest monument, by Rysbrack, shows the 1st Earl reclining in a Roman toga and gesturing to his wife who holds their son on her knee.

OPENING TIMES

Keyholder nearby

HOW TO FIND US

Direction: 3 miles E of Melton Mowbray. From A606 Oakham to Melton Mowbray turn right after Langham and travel through Whissendine, or turn off B676 between Melton Mowbray and Colsterworth just west of Saxby.

Train: Melton Mowbray 3 miles

MAP OS Map 130 (ref SK 812 183)

Lincolnshire

St Lawrence, Snarford

The treasure of this small medieval church lies in three wonderful 16th and 17th-century monuments to members of the St Paul family. The lavish and highly-coloured tomb to Sir Thomas is almost like a six-poster bed, and the alabaster monument to Sir George and his wife Frances dominates the north chapel. Frances appears again with her second husband the Earl of Warwick, on the third and most unusual monument, depicting their heads and shoulders in profile carved in relief.

OPENING TIMES

Open daily

HOW TO FIND US

Direction: 8 miles NE of Lincoln. From Lincoln take A46 past Dunholme and turn left. Snarford is signposted.

Train: Lincoln 8 miles

MAP OS Map 121 (ref TF 051 825)

Norfolk

St Michael the Archangel, Booton

This extraordinary building is the product of one man's eccentric imagination. The Revd Whitwell Elwin built the church at the end of the 19th century, without the help of an architect, borrowing details from other churches throughout the country. But the slender twin towers which soar over the East Anglian landscape seem to have sprung solely from his imagination. Inside, dramatic wooden angels hold up the roof and there are delicately coloured stained glass windows.

OPENING TIMES

Open daily

HOW TO FIND US

Direction: 12 miles NW of Norwich, 1m S of Cawston and 1½ miles E of Reepham, both on B1145.

Train: Norwich 12 miles

MAP OS Map 133 (ref TG 123 224)

Norfolk

St Margaret, Hales

This little church in the middle of open countryside gives visitors a strong sensation that time has stood still. The round tower, semicircular apse and thatched roof have changed little since it was built. It is an almost perfect Norman building – the north and south doorways and the columns at their sides are magnificently carved. Inside there is fine Norman stonework and a beautiful 15th-century octagonal font, carved with angels and Tudor roses.

OPENING TIMES

Open daily

HOW TO FIND US

Direction: 12 miles SE of Norwich and W of A146. Travelling from Norwich on A146 towards Beccles, take next left after junction with B1136 up narrow lane.

Train: Norwich 12 miles

MAP OS Map 134 (ref TM 384 962)

North Yorkshire

Christ the Consoler, Skelton-cum-Newby

Christ the Consoler was built by the flamboyant architect William Burges in the grounds of Newby Hall in the 1870s, as an extravagant memorial to a young man murdered by brigands while travelling in Greece. The exuberance of style makes an immediate impact on the visitor. The design is a unique interpretation of medieval French architecture, and the interior is wonderfully rich and colourful. The best craftsmen of the day were employed and every detail of their work repays close attention.

OPENING TIMES

Open daily

HOW TO FIND US

Direction: 4 miles SE of Ripon off B6265 between Boroughbridge and Ripon, in the grounds of Newby Hall.

Train: Harrogate 9 miles

MAP OS Map 99 (ref SE 360 679)

North Yorkshire

Holy Trinity, Goodramgate, York

Set in a secluded churchyard in the shadow of York Minster, the appeal of this unpretentious medieval church lies in the warmth and charm created by the uneven floors, the arcades slightly askew, the colour of the of the stone and the light from the stained glass. The east window, donated by the rector in the 1470s, has marvellous glass in a series of five panels with the figures of the Holy Trinity in the central light. The furnishings and memorials are also of great interest.

OPENING TIMES

Summer, Mon-Sat	10am-5pm
Sun	12pm-5pm
Winter Tue-Sat	10am-4pm

HOW TO FIND US

Direction: Off Goodramgate in city centre. A 3 minute walk from York Minster.

Train: York ½ mile

MAP OS Map 105 (ref SE 605 522)

Shropshire

St Andrew, Wroxeter

Set amid the Roman city of Viroconium, St Andrew's features much reused Roman material, including the columns at the gateway, massive stones in the nave walls and a huge font made from a column capital. The church reflects a long history of building over many centuries. The interior has excellent woodwork in the box pews, pulpit and altar rails, and a splendid series of 16th-century monuments. The finest, carved in alabaster, commemorates Lord Chief Justice Sir Thomas Bromley and his wife Mabel.

OPENING TIMES

Open daily

HOW TO FIND US

Direction: 5 miles E of Shrewsbury. From Shrewsbury ring road take B4350, signposted Wroxeter, Ironbridge. Follow signs to Wroxeter Roman City (EH). The church is in Wroxeter village 150yd S of the EH site.

Train: Shrewsbury 5½ miles, Wellington Telford West 6 miles

MAP OS Map 126 (ref SJ 564 083)

Somerset

St James, Cameley

Set in a fold of the Mendip hills, St James' is a delightful unspoilt church. The noble 15th-century tower, built of warm red Mendip stone, has a handsome parapet. The interior has fixtures and fittings from a variety of periods, with medieval benches, an early 17th-century pulpit, Georgian pews and 18th-century pegs along the nave walls for gentlemen to hang their hats. A fine wall painting of the Ten Commandments over the chancel arch is framed in twining leaves with cherubs' faces peering out.

OPENING TIMES

Open daily

HOW TO FIND US

Direction: 10 miles NE of Wells off A37. From Bristol take right turn, on S side of Temple Cloud, to Hinton Blewett, also signposted St James' Church Cameley. The church is 1 mile on right.

Train: Oldfield Park (Bath) 11 miles

MAP OS Map 172 (ref ST 610 576)

Suffolk

All Saints, Icklingham

All Saints' is of Norman origin but was largely rebuilt in the 14th century. The great prosperity in the region at the time is reflected in the high quality of workmanship. The roofs are thatched and the walls of local flint. The atmospheric interior has a fine arcade with exquisitely carved cornices above. There is elegant window tracery and excellent medieval stained glass in the south windows, while the 14th-century floor tiles form a brilliant mosaic of pattern.

OPENING TIMES

Apr-Oct, Sun	10am to dusk
Other times keyholder nearby	

HOW TO FIND US

Direction: 8 miles NW of Bury St Edmunds on A1101. There are two churches in Icklingham; approaching from Bury St Edmunds, All Saints' is the first, standing on the right.

Train: Bury St Edmunds 8 miles

MAP OS Map 144 (ref TL 776 726)

Surrey

St Peter and St Paul, Albury

Standing peacefully among trees in the middle of Albury Park, this charming, ancient church enjoys a delightful setting. The building dates from Saxon and Norman times with later additions, including an attractive 18th-century cupola over the tower. The lavishly decorated south chapel was remodelled by Augustus Welby Pugin in the 19th century as a mortuary chapel for the Drummond family of Albury Park, and is a wonderful example of Victorian taste for richness and colour.

OPENING TIMES

Open daily

HOW TO FIND US

Direction: 5 miles SE of Guildford in private grounds of Albury Park. Access via lodge gate at junction of Albury Street (A248) and New Road, to the E of Albury village.

Train: Chilworth 2½ miles

MAP OS Map 187 (ref TQ 063 479)

West Sussex

North Stoke Church, North Stoke

In an idyllic rural setting on the South Downs, North Stoke Church combines rustic charm, fine architecture and an evocative atmosphere. The church is in the shape of a cross and is virtually unaltered since medieval times. Its simplicity and elegant proportions give an impression of height and space. There is very early and rare stained glass, and intriguing stone-carving, including a sheep's head above a recessed stone seat on the west wall – an appropriate symbol in sheep-rearing country.

OPENING TIMES

Open daily

HOW TO FIND US

Direction: 5 miles N of Arundel at end of no-through road signposted from Amberley Station off B2139.

Train: Amberley 1½ miles

MAP OS Map 197 (ref TQ 019 108)

West Yorkshire

All Saints, Harewood

All Saints' lies within the park of Harewood House. The 15th-century church was much restored by Sir George Gilbert Scott in the 1860s. The interior contains a spectacular and fascinating series of six alabaster tombs, dating from 1419 to 1510, commemorating the owners of Harewood. Intricately carved and virtually without rival in England, they provide a unique history of medieval armour and costume, and of the development of alabaster carving for which England was justly famed throughout Europe.

OPENING TIMES

Apr-Oct	10am-6pm

Other times call Harewood House Trust on 0113 2181010

HOW TO FIND US

Direction: 6 miles N of Leeds off A61, in the grounds of Harewood House.

Train: Leeds 6 miles

MAP OS Map 104 (ref SE 314 451)

Wiltshire

St John the Baptist, Inglesham

This beautiful and fascinating church stands on a slight mound above the Thames water meadows. Of Saxon origin, most of the building dates from the 13th century. The unusual and powerful carving of the Mother and Child in the south wall is certainly Saxon. An extensive series of wall paintings from seven centuries cover most of the walls. The woodwork of the roofs, screens and box pews is all original, and their arrangement is much as it would have been in the time of Oliver Cromwell.

OPENING TIMES

Open daily

HOW TO FIND US

Direction: 1 mile S of Lechlade off A361. From Lechlade turn right signposted 'Inglesham 11th Century Church'. Church is ¼ mile on the right at end of single track road.

Train: Swindon 9 miles

MAP OS Map 163 (ref SU 205 984)

Worcestershire

St Mary Magdalene, Croome D'Abitot

Built in the 18th century as an eye-catcher for the 6th Earl of Coventry, the church is set on a low hill in Croome Park clearly visible from Croome Court. Designed by Robert Adam and Capability Brown, the elegant windows, plasterwork and fittings were commended by Betjeman as 'a good and complete example' of the fantastic Gothick style. The chancel is a mausoleum to the Coventry family with magnificent 17th to 19th-century monuments to the Earls.

OPENING TIMES

Same as Croome Landscape Park (NT). Please call 01905 371006 for details and arrangements at other times

HOW TO FIND US

Direction: 4 miles W of Pershore off A38 and A44. Follow NT signs to Croome Landscape Park. Croome Landscape Park (NT) surrounds the church.

Train: Pershore 6 miles

MAP OS Map 150 (ref SO 886 450)

Visitor Information

Opening Arrangements

Many churches are open daily. Otherwise a notice giving the location of keyholders will normally be found near the church door. Details are also on our website **www.visitchurches.org.uk**

Travel Information

Road: Each entry includes the Ordnance Survey grid reference for the church and detailed information on how to reach the church by road.

Rail: For information about national rail services telephone 08457 48 49 50 or go to **www.nationalrail.co.uk**

Bus: For countrywide bus information telephone 0870 608 2608. For a directory of printed bus timetables and local enquiry offices, go to **www.barrydoe.co.uk**

Cycle: For information on the nearest National Cycle Network route, telephone Sustrans 0117 929 0888 or go to **www.sustrans.org.uk**

Disabled Access

Please telephone the Trust's London office on 020 7213 0660 during office hours Mon–Fri for information. In due course details will be incorporated in our website.

SOUTH WEST

BRISTOL
CORNWALL
DEVON
DORSET
GLOUCESTER
ISLES OF SCILLY
SOMERSET
WILTSHIRE

F
G
H
J
K
2
3
4
5
6
7
HEREFORDSHIRE
GLOUCESTERSHIRE
OXFORDSHIRE
S.GLOUCESTERSHIRE
BRISTOL
N.SOMERSET
BATH & N.E. SOMERSET
WILTSHIRE
HAMPSHIRE
SOMERSET
DORSET
ISLE OF WIGHT
Bristol Channel
Bill of Portland
Llanwrtyd Wells
Queenswood
Hay-on-Wye
Arthur's Stone
Hereford
Great Malvern
Pershore
Evesham
Rotherwas Chapel
Ledbury
Upton-upon-Severn
Broadway
Banbury
Longtown Castle
St Mary's Church Kempley
Tewkesbury
Belas Knap Long Barrow
Moreton-in-Marsh
Rollright Stones
Brecon
Hailes Abbey
Chipping Norton
Newent
Odda's Chapel
Winchcombe
Deddington Castle
Tretower Court & Castle
Tretower
Ross-on-Wye
Goodrich Castle
CHELTENHAM
Notgrove Long Barrow
Stow-on-the-Wold
Crickhowell
White Castle
Over Bridge
Woodstock
Pen-y-Cae
GLOUCESTER
Minster Lovell Hall & Dovecote
Abergavenny
Monmouth
Blackfriars & Greyfriars
Great Witcombe Roman Villa
Northleach
North Leigh Roman Villa
Pont Nedd Fechan
Merthyr Tydfil
Raglan Castle
Coleford
St Briavel's Castle
Burford
Witney
Blaenavon Ironworks
Blaenafon
Tintern Abbey
Stroud
Cirencester
Aberdare
Offa's Dyke
Nympsfield Long Barrow
Woodchester Mansion
Cirencester Amphitheatre
Lechlade
North Hinksey Conduit House
Chepstow
Kingswood Abbey Gatehouse
Uley Long Barrow
Windmill Tump Long Barrow
Faringdon
Abingdon
Abingdon County Hall
Caerphilly Castle
Caerleon
Pontypridd
Caerphilly
Chepstow Castle
Tetbury
Wayland's Smithy
Wantage
Caerleon Roman Fortress
Magor
Malmesbury
SWINDON
NMR
Uffington Castle, White Horse & Dragon Hill
Castell Coch
Chipping Sodbury
Avebury Stone Circles & Alexander Keiller Museum
Bridgend
Porthcawl
Avonmouth
Sir Bevil Grenville's Monument
Donnington Castle
Windmill Hill
Silbury Hill
Temple Church
Chippenham
Penarth
Avebury
Hungerford
Barry Island
West Kennet Avenue & Long Barrow
Marlborough
Newbury
WESTON-SUPER-MARE
BATH
Melksham
The Sanctuary
Chisbury Chapel
Stanton Drew Circles & Cove
Bradford-on-Avon Tithe Barn
Devizes
Stoney Littleton Long Barrow
Trowbridge
Hatfield Earthworks
Cheddar
Farleigh Hungerford Castle
Ludgershall Castle & Cross
Burnham-on-Sea
Westbury
Bratton Camp & White Horse
Netheravon Dovecote
Yarn Market & Butter Cross
Wells
Nunney Castle
Frome
Andover
Minehead
Meare Fish House
Glastonbury Tribunal
Warminster
Stonehenge
Woodhenge
Amesbury
Glastonbury
Flowerdown Barrows
Gallox Bridge
Cleeve Abbey
Bridgwater
Stockbridge
Old Wardour Castle
Mere
Old Sarum
Winchester Wolvesey Castle
Salisbury
Taunton
Muchelney Abbey
Podimore
EASTLEIGH
Bampton
Wellington
Ilchester
Sherborne Old Castle
Shaftesbury
Romsey
Sherborne
Yeovil
Fordingbridge
SOUTHAMPTON
Medieval Merchant's House
Coldharbour Mill Museum
Ilminster
Sherborne Castle
Fiddleford Manor
Tiverton
Chard
Knowlton Church & Earthworks
Netley Abbey
Lyndhurst
Blandford Forum
Ringwood
Crediton
Honiton
Wimborne Minster
Calshot Castle
Christchurch Castle & Norman House
Ottery St Mary
The Nine Stones
Maiden Castle
Lymington
Cowes
Axminster
Winterbourne Poor Lot Barrows
Yarmouth Castle
Blackbury Camp
Bridport
Christchurch
Hurst Castle
EXETER
Kingston Russell Stone Circle
Dorchester
Jordan Hill Roman Temple
POOLE
Seaton
Lyme Regis
Wareham
BOURNEMOUTH
Yarmouth
Sidmouth
Abbotsbury
Carisbrooke Castle
Lulworth Castle
Exmouth
Budleigh Salterton
St Catherine's Chapel
Weymouth
Swanage
St Catherine's Oratory
Dawlish
Newton Abbot
Teignmouth
Abbotsbury Abbey Remains
Portland Castle
Berry Pomeroy Castle
TORQUAY
Paignton
Kirkham House
Brixham
Bayard's Cove Fort
Dartmouth
Dartmouth Castle
M4
M5
M50
M40
M27

Royal Leamington Spa
Warwick
Daventry
Althorp
NORTHAMPTON
78, Derngate
St. Neots
Bushmead Priory
WARWICKSHIRE
Stratford-upon-Avon
BEDFORD-SHIRE
Sandy
BEDFORD
Biggleswade
Towcester
Newport Pagnell
MILTON KEYNES
Houghton House
Pershore
Evesham
Banbury
Brackley
De Grey Mausoleum
Wrest Park Gardens
Broadway
Moreton-in-Marsh
Rollright Stones
Buckingham
Bletchley
Letchworth
Belas Knap Long Barrow
Hailes Abbey
Winchcombe
Chipping Norton
Deddington Castle
BUCKINGHAMSHIRE
Dunstable
Stevenage
LUTON
CHELTENHAM
Notgrove Long Barrow
Stow-on-the-Wold
Bicester
HERTS
Woodstock
Old Gorhambury House
Northleach
Minster Lovell Hall & Dovecote
North Leigh Roman Villa
Aylesbury
Wendover
Great Witcombe Roman Villa
Burford
Rycote Chapel
Berkhamsted Castle
Tring
Roman Wall
GLOUCESTERSHIRE
Witney
Berkhamsted
St. Albans
Cirencester
North Hinksey Conduit House
OXFORD
Thame
HEMEL HEMPSTEAD
Cirencester Amphitheatre
Lechlade
Faringdon
Abingdon County Hall
Abingdon
Amersham
Windmill Tump Long Barrow
HIGH WYCOMBE
OXFORDSHIRE
Apsley House
Wayland's Smithy
Kenwood
Malmesbury
SWINDON
Wantage
Didcot
Wallingford
Marlow
Kensal Green Cemetery
NMR
Uffington Castle, White Horse & Dragon Hill
Maidenhead
SLOUGH
Wellington Arch
Henley-on-Thames
Albert Memorial
Windmill Hill
Avebury Stone Circles & Alexander Keiller Museum
Donnington Castle
Chiswick House
READING
Windsor
Chippenham
Silbury Hill
Marble Hill House
Avebury
Bracknell
West Kennet Avenue & Long Barrow
Marlborough
Hungerford
Newbury
BERKSHIRE
Coombe Conduit
The Sanctuary
Chisbury Chapel
Silchester Roman City Walls & Amphitheatre
Devizes
Aldermaston
Hatfield Earthworks
CAMBERLEY
WOKING
Leatherhead
WILTSHIRE
Ludgershall Castle & Cross
BASINGSTOKE
Fleet
Aldershot
Reigate
Bratton Camp & White Horse
Netheravon Dovecote
GUILDFORD
Dorking
Farnham Castle Keep
Farnham
Waverley Abbey
Stonehenge
Woodhenge
Andover
SURREY
Amesbury
HAMPSHIRE
Alton
Stockbridge
Flowerdown Barrows
Northington Grange
CRAWLEY
Old Sarum
Haslemere
Horsham
Salisbury
Winchester
Itchen Abbas Roman Villa
Old Wardour Castle
Wolvesey Castle
Bishop's Waltham Palace
Petersfield
Midhurst
Petworth
EASTLEIGH
Romsey
Weald & Downland Open Air Museum
WEST SUSSEX
SOUTHAMPTON
Fordingbridge
Medieval Merchant's House
Southwick Priory
Fishbourne Roman Palace
Boxgrove Priory
Bramber Castle
Knowlton Church & Earthworks
Netley Abbey
Titchfield Abbey
Fontwell
Lyndhurst
FAREHAM
Portchester Castle
CHICHESTER
Arundel
Hove
Ringwood
WORTHING
Wimborne Minster
Christchurch Castle & Norman House
Calshot Castle
PORTSMOUTH
Royal Garrison Church
Marlipins Museum
Lymington
Fort Cumberland
Bognor Regis
Cowes
Hayling Island
POOLE
Christchurch
Hurst Castle
Selsey
Ryde
King James's & Landport Gates
BOURNEMOUTH
Yarmouth
Yarmouth Castle
Newport
Fort Brockhurst
Wareham
Carisbrooke Castle
Sandown
Osborne House
ISLE OF WIGHT
Shanklin
Swanage
St Catherine's Oratory
Ventnor
Appuldurcombe House

LONDON AND SOUTH EAST

BERKSHIRE
BUCKINGHAMSHIRE
EAST SUSSEX
HAMPSHIRE
ISLE OF WIGHT
KENT
OXFORDSHIRE
SURREY
WEST SUSSEX

English Heritage Sites
Other Historic Attractions

EAST OF ENGLAND

BEDFORDSHIRE
CAMBRIDGESHIRE
ESSEX
HERTFORDSHIRE
NORFOLK
SUFFOLK

English Heritage Sites
Other Historic Attractions

F
G
H
J
K
1
2
3
4
5
6
7
Sibsey Trader Windmill
Boston
Blakeney Guildhall
Wells-next-the-Sea
Hunstanton
Creake Abbey
Sheringham
Cromer
Holt
Baconsthorpe Castle
The Wash
Binham Priory
Binham Market Cross
Mundesley
Castle Rising Castle
Fakenham
North Walsham
Aylsham
Holbeach
Long Sutton
King's Lynn
Castle Acre Bailey Gate
Castle Acre Castle
North Elmham Chapel
Hoveton
Hemsby
Castle Acre Priory
Great Yarmouth Row Houses & Greyfriars' Cloisters
Caister Roman Site
Wisbech
East Dereham
Cow Tower
NORWICH
Great Yarmouth
Downham Market
Swaffham
Time & Tide Museum
Berney Arms Windmill
NORFOLK
Wymondham
Loddon
Burgh Castle
March
Grimes Graves
Attleborough
St Olave's Priory
LOWESTOFT
Thetford Warren Lodge
CAMBRIDGESHIRE
Weeting Castle
Bungay
Thetford Priory
Beccles
Chatteris
Brandon
Thetford
Kessingland
Isleham Priory Church
Church of the Holy Sepulchre
Diss
Ely
Halesworth
Southwold
SUFFOLK
Denny Abbey & the Farmland Museum
Bury St Edmunds Abbey
Framlingham Castle
Saxtead Green Post Mill
Newmarket
Bury St Edmunds
Leiston Abbey
Moulton Packhorse Bridge
Stowmarket
CAMBRIDGE
Aldeburgh
Woodbridge
Duxford Chapel
Lavenham
Lindsey/ St James's Chapel
Orford Castle
Orford
Haverhill
IPSWICH
Sudbury
Saffron Walden
Audley End House & Gardens
Mistley Towers
Felixstowe
Felixstowe Museum
St Botolph's Priory
Landguard Fort
Halstead
Prior's Hall Barn
ESSEX
Flatford
Harwich
Lexden Earthworks & Bluebottle Grove
St John's Abbey Gate
Bishop's Stortford
Braintree
COLCHESTER
Walton-on-the-Naze
HERTS.
Frinton-on-Sea
Birchanger Green
Tiptree
Hertford
Witham
Clacton-on-Sea
HARLOW
West Mersea
Waltham Abbey Gatehouse & Bridge
CHELMSFORD
Maldon
Waltham Abbey
Epping
Hill Hall
Southminster
GREATER LONDON
Brentwood
Chapter House
Islington
BASILDON
Hadleigh Castle
London Wall
Canvey Island
SOUTHEND-ON-SEA
Winchester Palace
Tilbury Fort
Greenwich
Bexley
Rochester Castle
Sheerness
Eltham Palace
Milton Chantry
Upnor Castle
Faversham Stone Chapel
Reculver Towers & Roman Fort
Jewel Tower
The Wernher Collection
Temple Manor
Chatham Historic Dockyard
Herne Bay
MARGATE
Broadstairs
Ramsgate
Eynsford Castle
GILLINGHAM
Whitstable
St Augustine's Cross

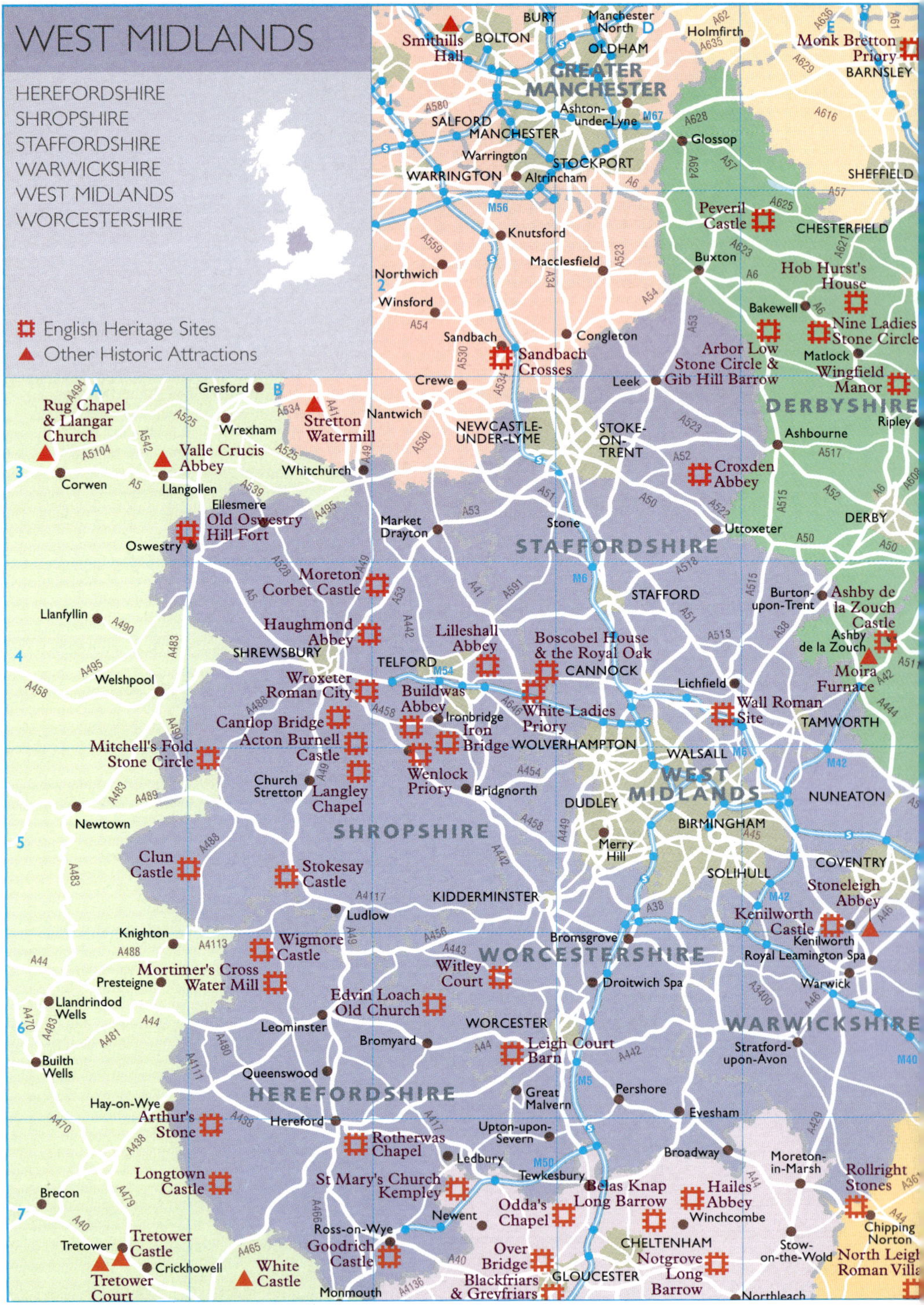
WEST MIDLANDS
HEREFORDSHIRE
SHROPSHIRE
STAFFORDSHIRE
WARWICKSHIRE
WEST MIDLANDS
WORCESTERSHIRE
English Heritage Sites
Other Historic Attractions
GREATER MANCHESTER
Smithills Hall
BOLTON
BURY
Manchester North
OLDHAM
Holmfirth
Monk Bretton Priory
BARNSLEY
SALFORD
MANCHESTER
Ashton-under-Lyne
Glossop
Warrington
WARRINGTON
STOCKPORT
Altrincham
SHEFFIELD
Peveril Castle
CHESTERFIELD
Knutsford
Macclesfield
Buxton
Hob Hurst's House
Northwich
Winsford
Bakewell
Nine Ladies Stone Circle
Sandbach
Congleton
Sandbach Crosses
Arbor Low Stone Circle & Gib Hill Barrow
Matlock
Wingfield Manor
Crewe
Leek
DERBYSHIRE
Ripley
Gresford
Rug Chapel & Llangar Church
Wrexham
Stretton Watermill
Nantwich
NEWCASTLE-UNDER-LYME
STOKE-ON-TRENT
Ashbourne
Valle Crucis Abbey
Corwen
Llangollen
Whitchurch
Croxden Abbey
Ellesmere
Old Oswestry Hill Fort
Oswestry
Market Drayton
Stone
Uttoxeter
DERBY
STAFFORDSHIRE
Moreton Corbet Castle
STAFFORD
Burton-upon-Trent
Ashby de la Zouch Castle
Llanfyllin
Haughmond Abbey
Lilleshall Abbey
Boscobel House & the Royal Oak
Ashby de la Zouch
SHREWSBURY
TELFORD
CANNOCK
Moira Furnace
Welshpool
Wroxeter Roman City
Buildwas Abbey
Lichfield
Wall Roman Site
White Ladies Priory
TAMWORTH
Cantlop Bridge
Ironbridge
Iron Bridge
Acton Burnell Castle
WOLVERHAMPTON
Mitchell's Fold Stone Circle
WALSALL
Wenlock Priory
WEST MIDLANDS
Church Stretton
Langley Chapel
Bridgnorth
NUNEATON
Newtown
DUDLEY
BIRMINGHAM
SHROPSHIRE
Merry Hill
Clun Castle
Stokesay Castle
COVENTRY
SOLIHULL
Stoneleigh Abbey
KIDDERMINSTER
Ludlow
Kenilworth Castle
Kenilworth
Knighton
Wigmore Castle
Bromsgrove
WORCESTERSHIRE
Royal Leamington Spa
Mortimer's Cross Water Mill
Presteigne
Witley Court
Droitwich Spa
Warwick
Llandrindod Wells
Edvin Loach Old Church
WARWICKSHIRE
WORCESTER
Leominster
Bromyard
Leigh Court Barn
Stratford-upon-Avon
Builth Wells
Queenswood
HEREFORDSHIRE
Great Malvern
Pershore
Hay-on-Wye
Arthur's Stone
Hereford
Evesham
Rotherwas Chapel
Upton-upon-Severn
Ledbury
Broadway
Moreton-in-Marsh
Rollright Stones
Longtown Castle
Tewkesbury
Belas Knap Long Barrow
Hailes Abbey
Brecon
St Mary's Church Kempley
Odda's Chapel
Newent
Winchcombe
Chipping Norton
Tretower
Tretower Castle
Ross-on-Wye
CHELTENHAM
Goodrich Castle
Over Bridge
Notgrove Long Barrow
Stow-on-the-Wold
North Leigh Roman Villa
Crickhowell
White Castle
Tretower Court
Blackfriars & Greyfriars
GLOUCESTER
Monmouth
Northleach

EAST MIDLANDS
DERBYSHIRE
LEICESTERSHIRE
LINCOLNSHIRE
NORTHAMPTONSHIRE
NOTTINGHAMSHIRE
RUTLAND
English Heritage Sites
Other Historic Attractions
SOUTH YORKS.
NORTH EAST LINCOLNSHIRE
LINCOLNSHIRE
NOTTINGHAMSHIRE
LEICESTERSHIRE
RUTLAND
NORTHAMPTONSHIRE
CAMBRIDGESHIRE
BEDFORDSHIRE
BUCKINGHAMSHIRE
Brodsworth Hall
DONCASTER
SCUNTHORPE
GRIMSBY
Cleethorpes
Brigg
Caistor
Conisbrough Castle
Gainsthorpe Medieval Village
ROTHERHAM
Roche Abbey
Gainsborough Old Hall
Gainsborough
Market Rasen
Louth
Mablethorpe
Sutton-on-Sea
Mattersey Priory
Retford
Worksop
Sutton Scarsdale Hall
Bolsover Cundy House
Bolsover Castle
Wragby
Alford
Lincoln Medieval Bishops' Palace
LINCOLN
Horncastle
Bolingbroke Castle
Ingoldmells
Skegness
Woodhall Spa
Ollerton
Rufford Abbey
Hardwick Old Hall
Mansfield
Tattershall College
Coningsby
Newark-on-Trent
Sibsey Trader Windmill
Papplewick Pumping Station
Sleaford
Boston
NOTTINGHAM
West Bridgford
Grantham
Hunstanton
The Wash
Castle Rising Castle
Castle Acre Bailey Gate
Castle Acre Priory
Melton Mowbray
Loughborough
Spalding
Holbeach
Long Sutton
King's Lynn
Coalville
Kirby Muxloe Castle
LEICESTER
Jewry Wall
Oakham
Rutland Water
Stamford
Wisbech
Downham Market
Longthorpe Tower
PETERBOROUGH
Flag Fen Excavations
March
Lyddington Bede House
Kirby Hall
Hinckley
Market Harborough
Corby
Oundle
Lutterworth
Rushton Triangular Lodge
Eleanor Cross
Chatteris
Weeting Castle
Brandon
Isleham Priory Church
Ely
RUGBY
Kettering
Kelmarsh Hall
Huntingdon
Chichele College
Wellingborough
Althorp
Daventry
St. Neots
78, Derngate
NORTHAMPTON
Bushmead Priory
Towcester
Sandy
BEDFORD
Newport Pagnell
Biggleswade
MILTON KEYNES
Houghton House
Banbury
Brackley
Buckingham
Bletchley
De Grey Mausoleum
Wrest Park Gardens
Deddington Castle
Bicester
Dunstable
LUTON
Woodstock
Aylesbury
Created by Arka Cartographics Ltd. for English Heritage. © 10/05

NORTH WEST (BOTTOM)
CHESHIRE
GREATER MANCHESTER
LANCASHIRE
MERSEYSIDE
English Heritage Sites
Other Historic Attractions
CUMBRIA
LANCASHIRE
MERSEYSIDE
GREATER MANCHESTER
CHESHIRE
Maryport
Cockermouth
Workington
WHITEHAVEN
Egremont
Keswick
Castlerigg Stone Circle
Ullswater
Seatoller Barn
Penrith Castle
PENRITH
Mayburgh Henge
Brougham Castle
Countess Pillar
Clifton Hall
King Arthur's Round Table
Appleby-in-Westmorland
Shap Abbey
Brough Castle
Brough
Barnard Castle
Bowes Castle
Grasmere
Ambleside
Waterhead
Hardknott Roman Fort
Ambleside Roman Fort
Hawkshead
Sellafield
Ravenglass
Ravenglass Roman Bath House
Muncaster Castle
Coniston
Windermere
Tebay
Kirkby Stephen
Reeth
Kendal
Sedbergh
Hawes
Aysgarth Falls
Broughton-in-Furness
Stott Park Bobbin Mill
Bootle
Millom
Ulverston
Grange-over-Sands
Kirkby Longsdale
Horton-in-Ribblesdale
Holker Hall
Furness Abbey
Bow Bridge
BARROW-IN-FURNESS
Piel Castle
Piel Island
Warton Old Rectory
Carnforth
Ingleton
Clapham
High Bentham
Morecambe Bay
Morecambe
Lancaster
Settle
Grassington
Malham
Skipton
Fleetwood
Garstang
Sawley Abbey
Barnoldswick
Cleveleys
Clitheroe
Pendle Heritage Centre
Whalley Abbey Gatehouse
BLACKPOOL
BURNLEY
Accrington
Hebden Bridge
Lytham St. Anne's
PRESTON
BLACKBURN
Goodshaw Chapel
Oswaldtwistle
Todmorden
Rawtenstall
SOUTHPORT
Chorley
Smithills Hall
ROCHDALE
Ormskirk
BURY
Manchester North
BOLTON
OLDHAM
Formby
BOOTLE
KIRKBY
ST. HELENS
St Helens
SALFORD
Ashton-under-Lyne
MANCHESTER
LIVERPOOL
Glossop
St George's Hall
Warrington
STOCKPORT
BIRKENHEAD
Runcorn
WIDNES
WARRINGTON
Altrincham
Llandudno
Rhos-on-Sea
Rhyl
Prestatyn
Conwy
Colwyn Bay
Conwy Castle
Plas Mawr
Rhuddlan Castle
RUNCORN
Norton Priory Museum & Gardens
Neston
ELLESMERE PORT
Knutsford
Flint
Salt Museum
Northwich
Macclesfield
Denbigh
CHESTER
Winsford
Mold
Chester Castle
Chester Roman Amphitheatre
Sandbach
Congleton
Beeston Castle
Sandbach Crosses
Ruthin
Crewe
Leek
Betws-y-Coed
Gresford
Wrexham
Stretton Watermill
Nantwich
Dolwyddelan Castle
Rug Chapel & Llangar Church
Valle Crucis Abbey
NEWCASTLE-UNDER-LYME
STOKE-ON-TRENT
Blaenau Ffestiniog
Corwen
Whitchurch
Llangollen
Created by Arka Cartographics Ltd. for English Heritage. © 10/05

YORKSHIRE
EAST RIDING OF YORKSHIRE
NORTH EAST LINCOLNSHIRE
NORTH LINCOLNSHIRE
NORTH YORKSHIRE
SOUTH YORKSHIRE
WEST YORKSHIRE
English Heritage Sites
Other Historic Attractions
DURHAM
TEES VALLEY
NORTH YORKSHIRE
EAST RIDING OF YORKSHIRE
WEST YORKSHIRE
SOUTH YORKSHIRE
NORTH LINCOLNSHIRE
NORTH EAST LINCOLNSHIRE
DERBYSHIRE
NOTTINGHAMSHIRE
Spennymoor
Auckland Castle Deer House
Bishop Auckland
HARTLEPOOL
Billingham
Redcar
STOCKTON-ON-TEES
MIDDLESBROUGH
Brotton
Gisborough Priory
Guisborough
Barnard Castle
Piercebridge Roman Bridge
DARLINGTON
Stanwick Iron Age Fortifications
Egglestone Abbey
Great Ayton
Whitby
Whitby Abbey
Danby
Scotch Corner
Richmond
Easby Abbey
Richmond Castle
Catterick
Mount Grace Priory
Wheeldale Roman Road
Northallerton
Leyburn
Bedale
Leeming Bar
Middleham Castle
Rievaulx Abbey
Helmsley Castle
Helmsley
Pickering Castle
Pickering
Scarborough Castle
SCARBOROUGH
Filey
Thirsk
Byland Abbey
Duncombe Park
Marmion Tower
St Mary's Church, Studley Royal
Fountains Abbey
Ripon
Aldborough Roman Site
Easingwold
Castle Howard
Malton
Norton
Bridlington
Pateley Bridge
Boroughbridge
Kirkham Priory
Wharram Percy Deserted Medieval Village
Burton Agnes Manor House
York Cold War Bunker
Knaresborough
Merchant Adventurers' Hall
Driffield
Skipsea Castle
HARROGATE
Clifford's Tower
DIG
YORK
JORVIK
York Minster
Pocklington
Ilkley
Otley
Wetherby
Spofforth Castle
Hornsea
Keighley
Tadcaster
Market Weighton
Beverley
BRADFORD
Haworth
LEEDS
Steeton Hall Gateway
Selby
Howden Minster
KINGSTON UPON HULL
Withernsea
HALIFAX
Humber Bridge
Goole
St Peter's Church
Barton-upon-Humber
WAKEFIELD
Thornton Abbey & Gatehouse
HUDDERSFIELD
Hemsworth
Immingham
Monk Bretton Priory
Brodsworth Hall & Gardens
SCUNTHORPE
Holmfirth
GRIMSBY
BARNSLEY
DONCASTER
Brigg
Cleethorpes
Gainsthorpe Medieval Village
Caistor
Conisbrough Castle
ROTHERHAM
Gainsborough Old Hall
Roche Abbey
Gainsborough
Mattersey Priory
Peveril Castle
SHEFFIELD
CHESTERFIELD
Worksop
Retford
Buxton
Hob Hurst's House
Sutton Scarsdale Hall
Bolsover Cundy House
Bolsover Castle
Bakewell
Ollerton
Nine Ladies Stone Circle
Arbor Low Stone Circle & Gib Hill Barrow
Matlock
Hardwick Old Hall
Rufford Abbey
Mansfield
Wingfield Manor
Newark-on-Trent
Ripley
Ashbourne
Papplewick Pumping Station
Croxden Abbey
NOTTINGHAM

Created by Arka Cartographics Ltd. for English Heritage. © 10/05

NORTH EAST

COUNTY DURHAM
NORTHUMBERLAND
TYNE AND WEAR
TEES VALLEY

A
B
C
D
E
Created by Arka Cartographics Ltd. for English Heritage. © 10/05
SCOTLAND
1
2
3
4
5
6
7
The Black House, Arnol
Calanais Standing Stones
Elgin Cathedral
Spynie Palace
Kinnaird Head Castle Lighthouse & Museum
Fort George
Dallas Dhu Historic Distillery
Huntly Castle
Balvenie Castle
Tolquhon Castle
Urquhart Castle
Corgarff Castle
Kildrummy Castle
imul Castle
SCOTLAND
Meigle Sculptured Stone Museum
Edzell Castle & Garden
Elcho Castle
Bonawe Historic Iron Furnace
Huntingtower Castle
Dunstaffnage Castle
Arbroath Abbey
Dunfermline Abbey & Palace
Lochleven Castle
Iona Abbey & Nunnery
St Serf's Church & Dupplin Cross
St Andrews Castle
Castle Campbell
St Andrews Cathedral
Doune Castle
Aberdour Castle & Garden
Inchmahome Priory
Inchcolm Abbey
Argyll's Lodging
Dirleton Castle & Gardens
Tantallon Castle
Newark Castle
Stirling Castle
Seton Collegiate Church
Rothesay Castle
Edinburgh Castle
Dumbarton Castle
Glasgow Cathedral
Crichton Castle
Bothwell Castle
Smailholm Tower
Dundonald Castle
Melrose Abbey
Dryburgh Abbey
Craignethan Castle
Cairnpapple Hill
Jedburgh Abbey & Visitor Centre
Linlithgow Palace
Crossraguel Abbey
Blackness Castle
Craigmillar Castle
Hermitage Castle
Threave Castle
Sweetheart Abbey
Cardoness Castle
Caerlaverock Castle
Glenluce Abbey
New Abbey Corn Mill
Dundrennan Abbey
MacLellan's Castle
Shetland Islands
Jarlshof Prehistoric & Norse Settlement
Orkney Islands
Broch of Gurness
Skara Brae & Skaill House
Bishop's & Earl's Palaces
Maeshowe Chambered Cairn
Hackness Martello Tower & Battery
WALES
Conwy Castle
Beaumaris Castle
Rhuddlan Castle
Plas Mawr
Caernarfon Castle
Rug Chapel & Llangar Church
Dolwyddelan Castle
Valle Crucis Abbey
Criccieth Castle
Harlech Castle
WALES
Strata Florida Abbey
White Castle
Cilgerran Castle
Tretower Court & Castle
Raglan Castle
St Davids Bishop's Palace
Carreg Cennen Castle
Tintern Abbey
Laugharne Castle
Kidwelly Castle
Blaenavon Ironworks
Weobley Castle
Caerphilly Castle
Chepstow Castle
Oxwich Castle
Castell Coch
Caerleon Roman Fortress
ISLE OF MAN
Peel Castle
The Grove Museum
House of Manannan
Laxey Wheel & Mines Trail
Niarbyl Café & Visitor Centre
Manx Museum
Rushen Abbey
Old House of Keys
Cregneash Folk Village
Castle Rushen
Sound Visitor Centre
Nautical Museum & Old Grammar School

PROPERTY ENTRY	PAGE REF	MAP ENTRY
A		
Abbotsbury Abbey Remains	85	265 5H
Abingdon County Hall	42	266 3C
Acton Burnell Castle	164	270 4B
Albert Memorial, The	37	266 4E
Aldborough Roman Site	189	273 3G
Alexander Keiller Museum, Avebury	84	265 3J
Althorp	158	271 6F
Ambleside Roman Fort	210	274 6D
Anne of Cleves House	76	267 6F
Apsley House	24	266 4E
Appuldurcombe House	42	266 7C
Arthurian Centre, The	117	264 5C
Arbor Low Stone Circle and Gib Hill Barrow	146	270 2E
Arthur's Stone	164	270 7B
Ashby De La Zouch Castle	147	270 4E
Auckland Castle Deer House	236	275 5G
Audley End House and Gardens	122	269 5F
Avebury	84	265 3J
Avebury Stone Circles	84	265 3J
Aydon Castle	236	275 4F
B		
Baconsthorpe Castle	124	269 1H
Ballowall Barrow	85	264 7A
Banks East Turret	228	–
Bant's Carn Burial Chamber and Halangy Down Ancient Village	116	264 5B
1066 Battle of Hastings, Abbey and Battlefield	44	267 6G
Barnard Castle	236	275 6G
Bayard's Cove Fort	85	265 6F
Bayham Old Abbey	42	267 5G
Bede's World Museum	249	275 4H
Beeston Castle	210	272 7D
Belas Knap Long Barrow	85	265 1J
Belsay Hall, Castle and Gardens	238	275 3G
Benwell Roman Temple and Vallum Crossing	228	–
Berry Pomeroy Castle	85	265 6F
Berkhamsted Castle	124	268 6D
Berney Arms Windmill	124	269 3K
Berwick-upon-Tweed Barracks & Main Guard	237	275 1F
Berwick-upon-Tweed Castle & Ramparts	237	275 1F
Bessie Surtees House	237	275 4G
Binham Priory	124	269 1H
Binham Market Cross	125	269 1H
Birdoswald Roman Fort	224	274 4E
Bishop Aucklands Deer House	237	275 5G
Bishop's Waltham Palace	43	266 6C
Blackbury Camp	86	265 5G
Black Carts Turret	228	–
Blackfriars, Gloucester	86	265 2J
Blakeney Guildhall	125	269 1H
Black Middens Bastle House	240	275 3F
Bolingbroke Castle	146	271 2J
Bolsover Castle	148	271 2F
Bolsover Cundy House	146	271 2F
Boscobel House and the Royal Oak	165	270 4C
Bow Bridge	210	274 7D
Bowes Castle	240	275 6F
Bowes Museum	249	275 5G
Boxgrove Priory	43	266 6D
Bradford-on-Avon Tithe Barn	86	265 3H
Bramber Castle	43	266 6E
Bratton Camp and White Horse	86	265 3J
Brinkburn Priory	240	275 3G
Brodsworth Hall and Gardens	186	273 5G
Brough Castle	210	275 6F
Brougham Castle	211	274 5E
Brunton Turret	228	–
Buildwas Abbey	164	270 4C
Burgh Castle	125	269 3K
Burton Agnes Manor House	189	273 3J
Bury St Edmunds Abbey	125	269 4G
Bushmead Priory	125	268 4E
Butter Cross	86	265 4F
Byland Abbey	189	273 2G
C		
Caister Roman Site	125	269 2K
Calshot Castle	46	266 6C
Camber Castle	46	267 6H
Cantlop Bridge	164	270 4B
Carisbrooke Castle	48	266 7C
Carlisle Castle	212	274 4D
Carn Euny Ancient Village	87	264 7A
Castle Acre Bailey Gate	126	269 2G
Castle Acre Castle	126	269 2G
Castle Acre Priory	127	269 2G
Castle Howard	204	273 3H
Castlerigg Stone Circle	211	274 5D
Castle Rising Castle	126	269 2G
Cawfields Roman Wall	228	–
Chapter House and Pyx Chamber	26	267 4F
Chester Castle: Agricola Tower and Castle Walls	211	272 7C
Chester Roman Amphitheatre	214	272 7C
Chesters Bridge Abutment	228	–

PROPERTY ENTRY	PAGE REF	MAP ENTRY
Chesters Roman Fort	226	275 4F
Chesters Walled Garden	249	275 4F
Chichele College	146	271 6G
Chisbury Chapel	87	265 3K
Chiswick House	27	266 4E
Christchurch Castle and Norman House	87	265 5K
Church of the Holy Sepulchre, Thetford	129	269 3H
Chysauster Ancient Village	87	264 7B
Cirencester Amphitheatre	87	265 2J
Cleeve Abbey	89	265 4F
Clifford's Tower	190	273 3G
Clifton Hall	214	274 5E
Clun Castle	166	270 5B
Coldharbour Mill Museum	117	265 5F
Conisbrough Castle	190	273 5G
Coombe Conduit	26	266 4E
Corbridge Roman Town	229	275 4F
Countess Pillar	214	274 5E
Cow Tower, Norwich	129	269 2J
Creake Abbey	129	269 1H
Cromwell's Castle	116	264 4A
Croxden Abbey	166	270 3D
D		
Danson House	37	267 4F
Dartmouth Castle	88	265 6F
Deal Castle	46	267 4J
Deddington Castle	47	266 2C
De Grey Mausoleum, Flitton	129	268 5E
Denny Abbey and the Farmland Museum	129	269 4F
Denton Hall Turret	229	–
78 Derngate	158	271 6G
Derwentcote Steel Furnace	240	275 4G

PROPERTY ENTRY	PAGE REF	MAP ENTRY
DIG, York	204	273 3H
Donnington Castle	47	266 4C
Dover Castle and the Secret Wartime Tunnels	50	267 5J
Dover Museum and Bronze Age Boat Gallery	76	267 5J
Down House, The Home of Charles Darwin	54	267 4F
Duncombe Park, Helmsley	204	273 2G
Dunstanburgh Castle	240	275 2G
Dupath Well	89	264 6D
Duxford Chapel	130	269 4F
Dymchurch Martello Tower	47	267 5H
E		
Easby Abbey	190	273 2F
Edlingham Castle	241	275 2G
Edvin Loach Old Church	166	270 6C
Egglestone Abbey	241	275 6G
Eleanor Cross, Geddington	150	271 5G
Eltham Palace	28	267 4F
Etal Castle	242	275 1F
Eynsford Castle	47	267 4F
F		
Farleigh Hungerford Castle	89	265 3H
Farnham Castle Keep	55	266 5D
Faversham Stone Chapel	55	267 4H
Felixstowe Museum	141	269 5J
Fiddleford Manor	90	265 4H
Finchale Priory	242	275 4G
Fishbourne Roman Palace	76	266 6D
Flag Fen Excavations	141	268 3E

PROPERTY ENTRY	PAGE REF	MAP ENTRY
Flowerdown Barrows	55	266 5C
Fort Brockhurst	55	266 6C
Fort Cumberland	56	266 6C
Fountains Abbey	204	273 3F
Framlingham Castle	128	269 4J
Furness Abbey	214	274 7D
G		
Gainsborough Old Hall	150	271 1G
Gainsthorpe Medieval Village	191	273 5J
Gallox Bridge	90	265 4F
Garrison Walls	116	264 5A
Gisborough Priory	242	275 6H
Glastonbury Tribunal	90	265 4H
Great Witcombe Roman Villa	91	265 2J
Great Yarmouth Row Houses and Greyfriars' Cloisters	130	269 2K
Greyfriars, Gloucester	91	265 2J
Grime's Graves	132	269 3G
Grimspound	91	264 5E
Goodrich Castle	168	270 7C
Goodshaw Chapel	215	272 4E
H		
Hadleigh Castle	131	269 7G
Hadrian's Wall	222	–
Hailes Abbey	91	265 1J
Halesowen Abbey	166	–
Halliggye Fogou	92	264 7B
Hardknott Roman Fort	215	274 6C
Hardwick Old Hall	150	271 2F
Hare Hill	229	–
Harrow's Scar Milecastle and Wall	230	–
Harry's Walls	116	264 5B
Hatfield Earthworks	92	265 3J
Haughmond Abbey	166	270 4B
Heddon-on-the-Wall	230	–

PROPERTY ENTRY	PAGE REF	MAP ENTRY
Helmsley Castle	192	273 2G
Hill Hall	131	269 6F
Historic Dockyard, Chatham	76	267 4G
Hob Hurst's House	151	270 2E
Holker Hall	219	274 7D
Home of Charles Darwin, Down House	54	267 4F
Horne's Place Chapel	56	267 5H
Houghton House	133	268 5E
Hound Tor Deserted Medieval Village	92	264 5E
Housesteads Roman Fort	227	275 4F
Howden Minster	191	273 4H
Hurlers Stone Circles	92	264 6D
Hurst Castle	56	266 7B
Hylton Castle	243	275 4H
I		
Innisidgen Lower and Upper Burial Chambers	116	264 5B
Iron Bridge	169	270 4C
Isleham Priory Church	133	269 4G
Isles of Scilly	116	–
Itchen Abbas Roman Villa	56	266 5C
J		
Jewel Tower	32	267 4F
Jewry Wall	151	271 4F
Jordan Hill Roman Temple	92	265 5H
Jorvik, York	205	273 4H
K		
Kelmarsh Hall	158	271 5G
Kenilworth Castle	170	270 5E
Kensal Green Cemetery	37	266 3E
Kenwood	30	266 3E
King Arthur's Round Table	215	274 5E

PROPERTY ENTRY	PAGE REF	MAP ENTRY
King Charles's Castle	116	264 4A
King Doniert's Stone	92	264 6D
King James's and Landport Gates	56	266 6C
Kingston Russell Stone Circle	93	265 5H
Kingswood Abbey Gatehouse	93	265 2H
Kirby Hall	153	271 5G
Kirby Muxloe Castle	151	271 4F
Kirkham Priory	191	273 3H
Kirkham House	93	265 6F
Kit's Coty House and Little Kit's Coty House	57	267 4G
Knights Templar Church, Dover	57	267 5J
Knowlton Church and Earthworks	93	265 4J
L		
Landguard Fort	133	269 5J
Lanercost Priory	215	274 4E
Langley Chapel	167	270 5B
Launceston Castle	93	264 5D
Leahill Turret and Piper Sike Turret	230	–
Leeds Castle	76	267 5G
Leigh Court Barn	167	270 6C
Leiston Abbey	133	269 4K
Lewes Castle and Barbican House Museum	77	267 6F
Lexden Earthworks and Bluebottle Grove	134	269 5H
Lilleshall Abbey	167	270 4C
Lincoln Medieval Bishops' Palace	154	271 2H
Lindisfarne Priory	244	275 1G
Lindsey/St James's Chapel	134	269 5H
London Statues	36	–
London Wall	32	267 3F

PROPERTY ENTRY	PAGE REF	MAP ENTRY
Longthorpe Tower	134	268 3E
Longtown Castle	172	270 7B
Ludgershall Castle and Cross	94	265 3K
Lullingstone Roman Villa	57	267 4F
Lulworth Castle	94	265 5J
Lyddington Bede House	152	271 5G
Lydford Castle and Saxon Town	94	264 5E
M		
Maiden Castle	94	265 5H
Maison Dieu	57	267 4H
Marble Hill House	34	266 4E
Marlipins Museum	77	266 6E
Marmion Tower	191	273 3F
Mattersey Priory	152	271 1G
Mayburgh Henge	216	274 5E
Meare Fish House	95	265 4G
Medieval Merchant's House	58	266 6B
Merchant Adventurers' Hall, York	205	273 3H
Merrivale Prehistoric Settlement	95	264 6E
Michelham Priory	77	267 6F
Middleham Castle	194	273 2F
Milton Chantry	58	267 4G
Minster Lovell Hall and Dovecote	58	266 2B
Mistley Towers	134	269 5H
Mitchell's Fold Stone Circle	172	270 5B
Moira Furnace	159	270 4E
Monk Bretton Priory	194	273 5G
Moreton Corbet Castle	172	270 4C
Mortimer's Cross Water Mill	173	270 6B
Moulton Packhorse Bridge	135	269 4G
Mount Grace Priory	194	273 2G

PROPERTY ENTRY	PAGE REF	MAP ENTRY
Muchelney Abbey	95	265 4G
Muncaster Castle	219	274 6C
N		
Netheravon Dovecote	96	265 3J
Netley Abbey	58	266 6C
Nine Ladies Stone Circle	152	270 2E
Nine Stones, The	96	265 5H
Norham Castle	243	275 1F
North Elmham Chapel	135	269 2H
North Hinksey Conduit House	59	266 3C
Northington Grange	59	266 5C
North Leigh Roman Villa	59	266 2B
Norton Priory Museum and Gardens	219	272 6D
Notgrove Long Barrow	96	265 1J
Nunney Castle	96	265 3H
Nympsfield Long Barrow	96	265 2H
O		
Odda's Chapel	97	265 1J
Offa's Dyke	97	265 2H
Okehampton Castle	97	264 5E
Old Blockhouse	116	264 4A
Old Gorhambury House	135	268 6E
Old Oswestry Hill Fort	173	270 3B
Old Sarum	98	265 4J
Old Soar Manor	60	267 5G
Old Wardour Castle	99	265 4J
Orford Castle	135	269 4J
Osborne House	62	266 7C
Over Bridge	100	265 1H
P		
Papplewick Pumping Station	159	271 3F
Pendennis Castle	102	264 7C
Pendle Heritage Centre	219	272 4E
Penhallam	100	264 5D
Penrith Castle	216	274 5E
Penshurst Place	77	267 5F
Pevensey Castle	60	267 6G
Peveril Castle	155	270 2E
Pickering Castle	195	273 2H
Piel Castle	216	274 7D
Piercebridge Roman Bridge	195	273 1F
Pike Hill Signal Tower	230	–
Planetrees Roman Wall	230	–
Poltross Burn Milecastle	230	–
Portchester Castle	66	266 6C
Porth Hellick Down Burial Chamber	116	264 5B
Portland Castle	104	265 6H
Priest House, The	77	267 5F
Prior's Hall Barn, Widdington	136	269 5F
Prudhoe Castle	246	275 4G
R		
Ranger's House – The Wernher Collection	33	267 4F
Ravenglass Roman Bath House	216	274 6C
Reculver Towers and Roman Fort	60	267 4J
Restormel Castle	100	264 6C
Richborough Roman Fort and Amphitheatre	60	267 4J
Richmond Castle	195	273 2F
Rievaulx Abbey	198	273 2G
Roche Abbey	196	273 6G
Rochester Castle	61	267 4G
Rollright Stones	68	266 2B
Roman Wall, St Albans	136	268 6E
Rotherwas Chapel	173	270 7B
Royal Citadel, Plymouth	100	264 6E
Royal Garrison Church	68	266 6C
Royal Pavilion, Brighton	78	267 6F
Rufford Abbey	152	271 2F
Rushton Triangular Lodge	156	271 5G
Rycote Chapel	78	266 3C
S		
St Augustine's Abbey	68	267 4J
St Augustine's Abbey Conduit House	68	267 4J
St Augustine's Cross	69	267 4J
St Botolph's Priory	136	269 5H
St Breock Downs Monolith	101	264 6C
St Briavels Castle	101	265 2H
St Catherine's Castle	101	264 6C
St Catherine's Chapel	101	265 5H
St Catherine's Oratory	69	266 7C
St George's Hall, Liverpool	220	272 6C
St John's Abbey Gate	137	269 5H
St John's Commandery	69	267 5J
St Leonard's Tower	69	267 4G
St Mary's Church, Kempley	101	265 1H
St Mary's Church, Studley Royal	196	273 3F
St Mawes Castle	105	264 7C
St Olave's Priory	137	269 3K
St Paul's Monastery, Jarrow	246	275 4H
St Peter's Church, Barton-upon-Humber	196	273 5J
Salt Musuem	220	272 6D
Sanctuary, The	105	265 3J
Sandbach Crosses	217	272 7D
Sawley Abbey	217	272 4D
Saxtead Green Post Mill	136	269 4J
Scarborough Castle	197	273 2J
Segedunum Roman Fort, Baths and Museum	249	275 4H

PROPERTY ENTRY	PAGE REF	MAP ENTRY
Sewingshields Wall	231	–
Shap Abbey	217	274 6E
Sherborne Castle	117	265 4H
Sherborne Old Castle	105	265 4H
Sibsey Trader Windmill	156	271 3J
Silbury Hill	109	265 3J
Silchester Roman City Walls and Amphitheatre	70	266 4C
Sir Bevil Grenville's Monument	109	265 3H
Skipsea Castle	196	273 3J
Smithills Hall	220	272 5D
Southwick Priory	70	266 6C
Spofforth Castle	200	273 4G
Stanton Drew Circles and Cove	109	265 3H
Stanwick Iron Age Fortifications	200	273 1F
Steeton Hall Gateway	200	273 4G
Stokesay Castle	174	270 5B
Stonehenge	106	265 4J
Stoneleigh Abbey	181	270 5E
Stoney Littleton Long Barrow	109	265 3H
Stott Park Bobbin Mill	218	274 6D
Stretton Watermill	220	272 7C
Sutton Scarsdale Hall	156	271 2F
Sutton Valence Castle	70	267 5G
T		
Tattershall College	157	271 2H
Temple Church	110	265 3H
Temple Manor	70	267 4G
Temple of Mithras, Carrawburgh	231	–
Thetford Priory	137	269 3G
Thetford Warren Lodge	137	269 3G
Thornton Abbey and Gatehouse	200	273 5J
Tilbury Fort	140	269 7G
Time and Tide Museum	141	269 2K
Tintagel Castle	112	264 5C
Titchfield Abbey	70	266 6C
Totnes Castle	110	264 6E
Tregiffian Burial Chamber	110	264 7B
Trethevy Quoit	110	264 6D
Tynemouth Priory and Castle	247	275 4H
U		
Uffington Castle, White Horse and Dragon Hill	70	266 3B
Uley Long Barrow (Hetty Pegler's Tump)	110	265 2H
Upnor Castle	71	267 4G
Upper Plym Valley	111	264 6E
V		
Vindolanda Fort	231	–
W		
Wall Roman Site (Letocetum)	176	270 4D
Walltown Crags	231	–
Walmer Castle and Gardens	72	267 5J
Waltham Abbey Gatehouse and Bridge	140	269 6F
Warkworth Castle and Hermitage	248	275 2G
Warton Old Rectory	218	272 3D
Waverley Abbey	71	266 5D
Wayland's Smithy	71	266 3B
Weald and Downland Open Air Museum	78	266 6D
Weeting Castle	140	269 3G
Wellington Arch	35	266 4E
Wenlock Priory	176	270 5C
West Kennet Avenue	111	265 3J
West Kennet Long Barrow	111	265 3J
Western Heights	71	267 5J
Wetheral Priory Gatehouse	218	274 4E
Whalley Abbey Gatehouse	218	272 4D
Wharram Percy Deserted Medieval Village	201	273 3H
Wheeldale Roman Road	201	273 2H
Whitby Abbey	202	273 1J
White Ladies Priory	176	270 4C
Wigmore Castle	177	270 6B
Willowford Wall, Turrets and Bridge	231	–
Winchester Palace	34	267 4F
Windmill Hill	111	265 3J
Windmill Tump Long Barrow, Rodmarton	114	265 2J
Wingfield Manor	157	270 3E
Winshields Wall	231	–
Winterbourne Poor Lot Barrows	114	265 5H
Witley Court and Gardens	178	270 6C
Wolvesey Castle (Old Bishop's Palace)	75	266 5C
Woodchester Mansion	117	265 2H
Woodhenge	114	265 4J
Wroxeter Roman City	180	270 4B
Wrest Park	138	268 5E
Y		
Yarmouth Castle	75	266 7B
Yarn Market	114	265 4F
York Cold War Bunker	201	273 3G
York Minster	205	273 4H

English Heritage
Members' & Visitors' Handbook 2006/7

For English Heritage: Dan Wolfe, Kate Linnell, Kathryn Steele-Childe, Tersia Mountford, Charles Kightly.

Design and Publishing: Turnbull Ripley

For Turnbull Ripley: David Creedy, Tania Wood, Bede Blake, John-Paul Shaw, Owain Gosling

Print: St Ives.

Transport Information: Barry Doe.